LAW AND AUTHORITY
IN A
NIGERIAN TRIBE

LAW AND AUTHORITY
IN A
NIGERIAN TRIBE

A STUDY IN INDIRECT RULE

BY

C. K. MEEK, M.A., D.Sc. Oxon.

*Lately Anthropological Officer, Nigerian
Administrative Service.*

*Author of
"The Northern Tribes of Nigeria"
"A Sudanese Kingdom"
"Tribal Studies in Northern Nigeria"*

WITH A FOREWORD BY

The Right Hon. LORD LUGARD
G.C.M.G., &c.

Formerly Governor-General of Nigeria

BARNES & NOBLE, Inc.
NEW YORK
PUBLISHERS & BOOKSELLERS SINCE 1873

'If we set out to found a new Rome it is wise to do what Aeneas did, and take our fathers on our shoulders.'

Lord Tweedsmuir.

First published in 1937
by Oxford University Press

This edition reprinted, 1970
by Barnes & Noble, Inc.
through special arrangement with
Oxford University Press

SBN 389 04031 2

Printed in the United States of America

FOREWORD

By LORD LUGARD

DR. C. K. MEEK belongs to that modern school of Anthropology —better described as 'Sociology'—which is concerned with research into the social constitution, the beliefs, and the methods of maintaining internal discipline in the tribes of Africa. The result has been to place at the disposal of administrators in the Tropics invaluable information and suggestions which the meagre cadre of officials in the earlier years had neither the training nor the time to acquire.

As Anthropologist to the Government of Nigeria, Dr. Meek had already rendered invaluable service to the cause of African research in the Northern Provinces, and established a high reputation. The problems presented by the Ibo Inquiry in the South were of a more difficult and indeed exceptional nature, and the Government were fortunate in having so competent a specialist at hand to guide and assist the officers on the spot in their investigations. This book contains ample evidence of the complexity of the problem, and of the thorough and successful way it was dealt with by Dr. Meek, though handicapped by the rapidity which the exigencies of the Administration made necessary, and finally by a complete breakdown in health, the result of overwork and climate.

But Dr. Meek's study of the Ibo—a tribe estimated to number about 4,000,000, and therefore one of the largest in Africa, with an exceptionally difficult language—is much more than a mere investigation of tribal characteristics and customs, amazingly exhaustive though it is. The necessity of the Government was to determine how the principles of 'Indirect Rule' should be applied to Iboland—principles which, as Dr. Meek testifies, were popular elsewhere in Nigeria, where 'there were few areas which could not boast their own Native Administrations including Chiefs, Councillors, Judges, Police, Treasuries, Hospitals, and Schools'.

On the amalgamation of the Governments of Northern and Southern Nigeria in January 1914, it had been recognized that the system of so-called 'Native Courts' under 'Warrant Chiefs' had proved a disastrous failure in both their Administrative and Judicial functions. They had been created, says Dr. Meek, on the model of the Consular Courts of Equity at a time when these territories were under Foreign Office control. The Warrant Chiefs had become oppressive tyrants, detested by the people, and the right of appeal to the Supreme Court, especially in land cases, had encouraged ruinous and futile litigation. The small British Staff who were supposed to preside in these Courts were unable properly to supervise and control them. During the Great War the majority of the administrative staff were withdrawn, and though some attempt was made to modify this system of Direct Rule nothing really effective could at that time be done.

Misconceptions regarding the incidence of the direct tax introduced in 1927, added to the fall in the prices of native produce, served to set fire to the highly inflammable material and produced the strange phenomenon of the women's riots in 1929. The Government could not afford to delay the introduction of the necessary reforms.

Such was the situation which confronted Dr. Meek and his colleagues. The result of their labour under the wise direction of the Governor, Sir Donald Cameron, has already vindicated the principles of co-operation and adaptation in local self-government, and the section which led the revolt is now the most zealous in support of the new system.

This book has thus a double interest—first as an exhaustive account of the social institutions of the various clans differing widely from each other, and secondly as an account of how this knowledge was successfully applied to the solution of a problem of first-class administrative importance.

LUGARD.

CONTENTS

MAPS

NOTE ON ORTHOGRAPHY

THE old spellings of native proper names have usually been retained, and it has not been considered necessary to distinguish the half-open vowel o from the open vowel $ɔ$, except in a few words where the latter sound is indicated by $ǫ$. Nor have the vowel sounds represented by $ε$ and $ө$ in the new orthography been indicated.

INTRODUCTION

TOWARDS the close of 1929 riots of an unprecedented kind broke out with startling suddenness in two of the South-Eastern Provinces of Nigeria. The rioters were women—not a few enthusiasts, but women *en masse*—who formed themselves into mobs, armed themselves with cudgels, and marched up and down the country, holding up the roads, howling down the Government, setting fire to the Native Court buildings, assaulting their chiefs, and working themselves generally into such a state of frenzy that on several occasions they did not hesitate to challenge the troops sent to restore order. The rioting continued vigorously for several weeks, and then faded gradually away, as the frenzy subsided and reason began to resume its place. But in the meantime many of the rioters had lost their lives and heavy damage had been done to the property of the Native Administrations and of numerous European trading firms.

Nigeria had always been noted and quoted for the success of its methods of administration and the contentment and friendliness of its twenty million people. This violent and widespread rebellion, therefore, fell upon the Government like a bolt from the blue. A Commission was appointed to inquire into the causes of the disturbances and, after hearing hundreds of witnesses, produced a report which is one of the most interesting commentaries on colonial administration that have been published in recent times. The riots, it appeared, were primarily due to an unfounded fear that direct taxation, which had recently been applied to the male members of the community, was now to be extended to the female. And this fear was intensified by the scarcity of money caused by a heavy fall in the price of palm-produce, the principal source of the people's income, without any corresponding fall in the price of imported goods. But the manner in which the riots had been conducted had made it evident that there were other predisposing causes of discontent, and chief among these was the widespread hatred of the system of Native Administration conducted through the artificial channel of Native Courts, the members of which, under the name of 'Warrant Chiefs', had come to be regarded as corrupt henchmen of the Government, rather than as spokesmen and protectors of the people. Had there been a genuine system of Native Administrations based on the institutions of the people and giving full freedom of expression, the riots, if they had occurred at all, could not have attained the dimensions they did, and would not have taken the form of vicious attacks on 'Warrant Chiefs' and the wholesale destruction of Native Administration property. Nor were the opinions expressed by the women confined to them. They were shared also by the men. But the women had believed that they could show their resentment with an impunity which would not be accorded to their menfolk.

Elsewhere in Nigeria the form of government known as 'Indirect Rule' had been applied with marked success for many years, pre-existing native institutions being fully utilized for the establishment of local self-government on progressive lines. From the large emirates or states such as Sokoto, Bornu, or Kano in the north, and Oyo, Abeokuta, or Benin in the south, to the numerous petty chiefdoms scattered all over the country, there were few areas that could not boast their own Native Administration, including chiefs, counsellors, judges, police, treasuries, hospitals, and schools.

But in South-Eastern Nigeria indirect rule on these lines had not been considered possible, as no framework had been discovered on which Native Administrations could be erected. There were no chiefs with substantial territorial jurisdiction. Indeed, in most areas there were no chiefs at all, and there was no higher unit of government than the commune or small group of contiguous villages. The British system of administration had therefore been direct. For judicial purposes central Native Courts, each with jurisdiction over a large area, had been established to dispose of all but the most serious crimes and torts. No objection had been taken to these courts as such, but the judges of the courts soon became unpopular when they began to assume, as they were often compelled by the British District Officer to assume, executive authority within their own villages. They became, in fact, 'chiefs' armed with an authority far in excess of that possessed by the village-councils in former times. This and their venality as judicial officials had made them feared and disliked, though many individuals among them were men of the highest character. With the introduction of direct taxation in 1927 the dislike of the Native Court members became intensified, as they had been used by the Government to persuade the people to accept taxation, and indeed had become the principal agents for collecting the tax. Thus, when in 1929 the price of palm-produce fell to an uneconomic figure, it merely needed the spark of a rumour that women, the preparers and marketers of palm-produce, were to be taxed to set the whole country ablaze.

It might be inferred that the Government of Nigeria had not
devoted sufficient attention to the administration of these South-
Eastern Provinces, and it must be admitted that there is some ground
for this opinion. Yet it had been no mean achievement on the part
of the British Administrative Staff that in a single generation the
most lawless part of Nigeria had been converted to a state of comparative peace and contentment. Moreover, the administrative difficulties
had been largely inherent in the situation, owing to the absence of
any form of central authority. The Government had made numerous
attempts to bring to light the indigenous leaders of the people, but
little progress had been made prior to the riots, as investigations had
not been carried out in the intensive, scientific manner which would
alone reveal the framework on which stable Native Administrations
could be built. The Secretary of State for the Colonies was not therefore unjustified when he endorsed the opinion of the Lieutenant-
Governor and of the Commission of Inquiry that direct taxation
should not have been introduced into the South-Eastern Provinces of
Nigeria until fuller knowledge had been obtained of the social institutions of the people. The cart had been put before the horse.

As soon as the riots had subsided, the Government proceeded to
retrieve the position by embarking on an intensive campaign of
inquiry into the indigenous social and political organization of the
peoples of South-Eastern Nigeria, with a view to setting up Native
Administrations which would be more in accordance with the institutions and wishes of the people than the bureaucratic system which
had so signally failed. Residents (or Commissioners) of Provinces and
their administrative assistants were directed to prepare proposals for
reconstruction, accompanied by Intelligence reports on each unit.
As Government Anthropologist and a senior Administrative Officer
I was instructed to assist in these investigations, having been transferred from the Northern Provinces where I had worked for the
previous eighteen years. I was to deal with the Intelligence reports
from the point of view of applied anthropology, and at the same time
conduct inquiries of my own among the Ibo of Onitsha and Owerri
Provinces. I was handicapped by having had no previous experience
of any of the peoples of the Southern Provinces, who differ considerably
from those of the north both in culture and psychology. Moreover,
in view of the urgency of reorganization, there was no opportunity of
learning the Ibo language and I was compelled therefore to work
through interpreters.

During the years that followed, a prodigious amount of local investigation was accomplished by the Administrative Staff, and reorganization has proceeded apace on lines which appear to meet the needs and wishes of the people. My own contribution towards this work of reconstruction ceased in May 1932, when my health broke down and, after a protracted illness, I was obliged to retire from the Service. Nevertheless I had been able, during the two preceding years (1930–1), nine months of which had been spent in field work, to acquire a considerable knowledge of the indigenous system of Ibo government and law, and to submit numerous reports and recommendations to the Government. After my retirement it appeared to me that the material I had myself collected in the field might be of value to students of anthropology and sociology, as well as to Administrative, Judicial, and Education Officers of the Colonial Service, and I decided therefore to prepare it for publication as a final contribution to my studies of the peoples of Nigeria, more especially as my previous works had dealt very lightly with the subject of native law. Moreover, apart from Dr. Rattray's volume on *Ashanti Law and Constitution,* there are few English works which deal adequately with the subject of African government and law, a surprising omission considering that in practical administration the British have been foremost in stressing the necessity of studying and utilizing as instruments of government the political and legal institutions of the peoples committed to their charge.

Having explained the genesis of the present work, it should hardly be necessary to add that it does not pretend to be a complete corpus of Ibo jurisprudence. My studies among the Ibo were not directed towards this end, but rather towards ascertaining the general principles by which the Ibo communities governed themselves. Moreover, a complete compendium of Ibo law would involve an almost complete account of the culture of the Ibo, as law in the widest sense of the term enters into most phases of Ibo life. But even if I had the knowledge to attempt a comprehensive account of Ibo culture, the European reader, seeking to understand the principles of Ibo government and law, might be unable to see the wood for the trees. I have, therefore, selected my data in such a way that general principles can be discerned, but at the same time I have endeavoured to present them not as isolated facts but in their proper setting as part and parcel of the social life of the people.

It will be observed, however, that a good deal of my material is

concerned with conditions which are passing away or have already
ceased to exist. Where this is so my excuse must be that no culture,
more especially one which is rapidly changing, can be comprehended
apart from its immediate past. And even if in the near future much
of the law and authority described in these pages shall have become
little more than a memory, the account given should still continue to
serve a useful purpose by providing an historical and psychological
background.

As regards the title of this book, a word of explanation is required
on the use of the word 'law'. The mentality of primitive[1] peoples
does not differ essentially from our own, as any European knows who
has lived at close quarters with 'natives'. It is not to be expected,
therefore, that their norms of conduct should diverge very profoundly
from ours. And so what are crimes or torts to us are for the most
part crimes or torts to them. We may go even further and say that
their 'gentlemen' are ours and ours are theirs. But as their social,
political, and economic organization, and also their religious conceptions, are different from ours, and they have not yet formed the habit
of 'departmentalizing' their thoughts and activities, it is not an easy
matter to define, in terms of what we understand by 'law', all those
authoritative forces which regulate the conduct of members of primitive communities. For our word 'law' carries with it very definite
implications of state authority, judges and magistrates, codes and
courts,[2] police and prisons, which have no counterpart in primitive
society where the regulation of conduct is not 'departmentalized' or
standardized into a rigid institution.

Professor Malinowski has in recent writings[3] done a great deal
towards introducing a newer and truer conception of the nature
of primitive law, and removing a multitude of misconceptions, such
as the assumption that the primitive individual is completely dominated by the group,[4] or that 'communism is in general existence in
the domain of law'.[5] He insists that social order rests on a complex

---

[1] Throughout this work the term 'primitive' is used in a purely relative sense.

[2] Judge Cardozo defines law as 'court-enforced rules of conduct'.

[3] See, e.g., his paper 'The Forces of Law and Order in a Primitive Community'
(read before the Royal Institution of Great Britain, Feb. 13, 1925), *Crime and Custom
in Savage Society*, and the Introduction to Dr. Hogbin's *Law and Order in Polynesia*.

[4] e.g. Dr. Rivers says 'Among such peoples as the Melanesians there is a group
sentiment which makes unnecessary any definite social machinery for the exertion of
authority'. *Soc. Organ.*, p. 169.

[5] Durkheim in *The Division of Social Work*.

interaction of stimuli, that the criminal side of primitive law has been
over-emphasized, that the forces of moral conviction are infinitely
more powerful than the fear of punishment, and that the principle
of mutuality is one of the basic elements of legal validity. In looking
for law and legal forces we should, he insists, try to discover and
analyse all the rules conceived and acted upon as binding obligations.

While all must agree with Professor Malinowski that primitive law
cannot be adequately described in terms of modern jurisprudence or
by the mere enumeration of lists of crimes and torts, yet it would
appear to be going rather too far to include as law every item of
culture that makes for order, uniformity, and cohesion. In all societies
there are many forces which make for order and yet are not 'law', in
any recognized sense of that term. Law is hardly synonymous with
socially sanctioned behaviour, as Professor Radcliffe-Brown has aptly
observed.

But if we refuse to include within the term 'law' all processes of
social control, and restrict it to processes of control exercised authorita-
tively by the body politic, we are confronted with other difficulties.
Roscoe Pound, for example, defines 'law' as 'social control through
the systematic application of the forces of politically organized
society', and Professor Radcliffe-Brown, one of the greatest authorities
on primitive law, adopts this limited application of the term,[1] treating
obligations imposed on individuals, where there are no legal sanctions,
as mere matters of social convention. But this definition drives Professor Radcliffe-Brown into the somewhat equivocal position of having
to say that 'Some simple societies have no law, although all have
customs supported by sanctions'. Yet customs supported by sanctions
may be tantamount to 'law'. Moreover, as Professor Malinowski has
pointed out, Pound's definition would appear to exclude from the
domain of law the regulation of conduct in such well-ordered forms
of society as an extended-family and kindred, which are social rather
than political bodies. It would also exclude one of the most prominent
features of primitive law, viz. private boards of arbitration, which,
though obviously a legal institution, do not systematically apply
force, as there is frequently no compulsion, moral or other, to accept
the recommendation of the board. Even a broad definition of law,
such as 'the authoritative regulation of social relations',[2] would seem

[1] See his admirable article on 'Primitive Law' in *The Encyclopedia of the Social Sciences.*
[2] This is the working definition used by Dr. Marett.

to be open to the same objection that some means of regulating social relations, though clearly entitled to the epithet of 'legal', are not always fully entitled to that of 'authoritative'. It will meet our difficulty if it is understood that the word 'law' is used loosely to include modes of regulating conduct which, at most, have only a quasi-legal character.

It will have been gathered that, in instituting anthropological inquiries in Iboland, the Government of Nigeria was not actuated by any academic or antiquarian interest, but by the purely practical motive of bettering the administration. This indeed has always been the Government's attitude towards anthropological research, namely, that it should serve as a handmaiden of administration, by throwing light on the history, relationships, organization, and thoughts of the people, and so providing data which would help the Government to make the fullest use of native institutions as instruments of local administration. There is a popular misapprehension that anthropology is the natural ally of reaction, and that its interest in the past obscures its vision of the present and makes it totally blind to the needs of the immediate future. Educated Africans are sometimes inclined to share this view, and mistrust anthropological research as a kind of henchman of 'Indirect Rule', which they mistakenly regard as a means of 'keeping Africans in their place' or of denying to them the full benefits of the civilization which we ourselves enjoy, or are supposed to enjoy. There is no ground for this attitude, in so far as Nigeria is concerned, and it will be seen in these pages that stress is constantly laid on the importance not merely of avoiding the alienation of the educated Ibo, however few they may be at the moment, but of securing their active co-operation and indeed leadership in the various spheres of local administration.

In the Southern Provinces of Nigeria there is almost a mass movement towards Christianity and Western education, and it is true to say that in the most populous tribes the majority of the younger generation are already professing Christians and have some knowledge of reading and writing. The result has been a cultural clash between the old and the young. It would be a fatal mistake, therefore, to concentrate local authority exclusively in the hands of the elders, most of whom are still pagans, and to fail to give to the younger generation, who no longer respect the ancient sanctions, a reasonable share in the administration of local affairs. This would merely alienate or create active hostility among the educated members of the community, and give them just ground for believing that the policy of 'Indirect Rule' is indeed an anachronism and a means of keeping them in a state of subjection to institutions which have outlasted their usefulness. 'Indirect Rule', after all, is merely another name for local self-government, and self-government implies a form of government acceptable to the people as a whole. The pursuit of a static policy would defeat the main purpose of 'Indirect Rule', which is to enlist the activities of all the social elements in a common loyalty and solidarity. The old and young will have to work out the synthesis by tact and forbearance, but the Government can assist in the adjustment by adhering to a broad dynamic policy. Such a policy has been well and truly laid down in Sir Donald Cameron's recent memorandum on 'The Principles of Indirect Administration', and this memorandum should be sufficient to allay, once for all, the fears that have been expressed in recent years regarding the wisdom and purpose of the policy of 'Indirect Rule'.

In conclusion I would express my most cordial thanks to Sir Walter Buchanan Smith, C.M.G., M.C., the late Lieutenant-Governor of the Southern Provinces of Nigeria, under whose direction and encouragement it was my privilege to work; to the officers in charge of the Ibo Divisions, namely, Major Stevenson, O.B.E., Capt. O'Connor, M.C., and Mr. M. H. W. Swabey, who provided facilities for the investigations; to the numerous members of the Ibo tribe, particularly Mr. F. Ejiogu of Owerri, and Mr. M. O. Ibeziako of Onitsha, who gave ready, patient, and courteous assistance; to Mr. W. E. Hunt, C.M.G., C.B.E. (Chief Commissioner of the Southern Provinces), Capt. E. G. Hawkesworth, M.C., Miss Margery Perham, and Miss Margaret Green, for a number of helpful criticisms; to Dr. R. R. Marett, the Rector of Exeter College, Oxford, both for his kindly interest and many valuable suggestions; and to the Principal and Fellows of Brasenose College, Oxford, for their great generosity in providing a financial grant.

C. K. MEEK.

1 *February* 1937.

I

THE IBO. THEIR HISTORY AND ENVIRONMENT

THE Ibo-speaking[1] peoples are located in South-Eastern Nigeria, between latitude 5°–7° North of the Equator and longitude 6°–8° East of Greenwich. They occupy the whole of the Provinces of Owerri and Onitsha, and about half of the Province of Ogoja; and there are also extensive groups in the Provinces of Benin and Warri. Numerically they are one of the principal peoples of Africa. In the 1931 decennial census their numbers were given provisionally at 3,184,585, but it is certain that this was an under-estimate and that the 1921 figures of 3,930,085, or approximately four million people, represent more accurately the strength of the Ibo-speaking communities.[2] If this is so, they would outnumber all other Nigerian tribes, not excluding the Hausa, who are generally regarded as the most numerous and most important tribe in West Africa, if not in the whole of Africa.[3]

The Ibo are not strictly homogeneous. They may be described as a 'tribe' because they speak a common language, occupy a common territory, and on the whole share a common culture and common outlook on life. But there are marked dialectal[4] and cultural variations between the subdivisions and there is no central tribal authority. Dr. Talbot[5] divides the Ibo into some thirty 'sub-tribes' and twice that number of 'clans', but these terms must not be construed too literally as most of the sub-tribal titles are little more than territorial descriptions,[6] and the clan titles also are more geographical than

---

[1] It may be suggested that the term Ibo means, like so many tribal titles in Nigeria, 'The Men' or 'The People'. The root in this sense is found among the Ijo as *oyibo*; among the Jarawa as *bo*; and among the Ababua as *ngbo*. But the word is sometimes used contemptuously by some Ibo groups towards others with the connotation of 'slaves'. Among the Igala, neighbours of the Ibo, the word for slave is *onigbo* (*oni* = person).

[2] Owing to the recent political trouble it was not considered advisable to attempt an accurate count of the Ibo during the 1931 census. For the inference that the 1921 figures are to be preferred to those of 1931 see *Census of Nigeria*, vol. i, pp. 5–7.

[3] In Nigeria alone the Hausa numbered 3,629,562 at the 1931 census. But there are numerous Hausa communities outside Nigeria.

[4] The linguistic situation in Iboland is well described by Miss Margaret Green in the October issue of *Africa*, 1936.

[5] *The Peoples of Southern Nigeria*, vol. iv, pp. 39–41.

[6] Awhawzara, for example, means '(The people of) the scrub lands' and Awhawfia = '(The people of) the forest lands'.

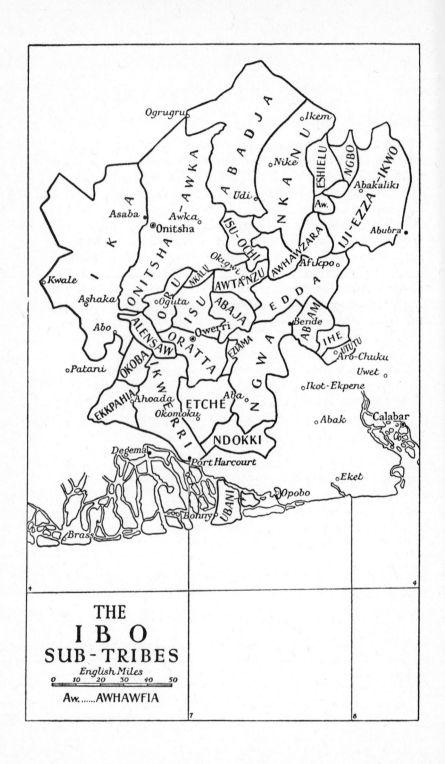

THE
I B O
SUB - TRIBES
English Miles
0   10   20   30   40   50

Aw........AWHAWFIA

sociological. It may be said generally that the most characteristic feature of Ibo society is the almost complete absence of any higher political or social unit than the commune or small group of contiguous villages, whose customs and cults are identical, who in former times took common action against an external enemy (though they frequently also fought amongst themselves), and whose sense of solidarity is so strong that they regard themselves as descendants of a common ancestor. These communes may be regarded as clans, and if so there must be at least 2,000 Ibo clans. Concrete examples of these will be given later. In the meantime it will be convenient to include here Dr. Talbot's list of Ibo sub-tribes and clans, together with a map.

Sub-tribe	Clan	Persons
Abadja	Abadja	640,326
Abaja	Abaja	72,896
,,	Abaja-Ozu	27,213
,,	Obowo	34,299
,,	Osu	51,070
,,	Ekwarazu	33,681
,,	Ugiri	14,889
Abam	Awhawfia	40,000
,,	Abam	20,094
,,	Abiriba	11,064
Alensaw	Ozuzu-Uzuama	26,966
,,	Alensaw	7,048
Aro	..	56,024
Awhawfia	..	3,834
Awhawzara	Awhawzara	54,318
,,	Okpossi	14,107
,,	Onitsha	12,602
,,	Isu	10,420
,,	Uburu	7,515
,,	Oshiri	5,727
Awtanzu	Awtanzu	22,930
,,	Awtanchara	17,311
Edda	Elei	40,005
,,	Edda	29,078
,,	Isu-Kweataw	22,929
,,	Afikpo	17,859
,,	Amasiri	8,986
,,	Ake-Eze	5,391
,,	Unwana	2,918
Ekkpahia	..	22,784
Eshielu	..	9,174
Etche	Etche	33,807
,,	Ozuzu	5,988

Sub-tribe	Clan	Persons
Eziama	Eziama-Abaja	44,241
,,	Eziama	22,662
Ihe	..	6,641
Iji-Ezza-Ikwo	Ezza	68,845
,,	Iji	60,191
,,	Ikwo	72,087
,,	Okauo	10,031
Ika	Asaba	109,774
,,	Abaw-Kwale	66,394
,,	Agbor	49,467
,,	Abaw	12,772
,,	Abaw-Afaw	3,848
Ikwerri	..	145,736
Isu	..	246,581
Isu-Ochi	Isu-Ochi	39,277
,,	Lome	6,208
Ndokki	Ndokki	23,392
,,	Asia	21,614
Ngbo	..	8,130
Ngwa	Ngwa	210,669
,,	Ohonhaw	63,581
,,	Oboro	70,407
Nkalu	..	59,389
Nkanu	..	150,991
Okogba	Okogba	23,425
Onitsha-Awka	Onitsha	397,511
,,	Awka	212,591
Oratta	Oratta	155,357
Oru	Ossun	65,750
,,	Olu (or Olo)	39,197
,,	Mboaha	20,477
,,	Oru	12,000
,,	Umuoma	4,731
Ubani	Opobo	12,440
,,	Bonny	10,958
Ututu	Ututu	3,368
Unclassified	..	13,433
Total	. . . .	3,927,419

History.

It follows from what has been said of their social and political organization that the Ibo have no tribal history. Their only form of history is the purely local traditions of the various communes or village-groups. Linguistically the Ibo belong to the Sudanic family, whose members speak languages of an isolating, monosyllabic, and

THE IBO. THEIR HISTORY AND ENVIRONMENT 5

highly tonal type. But it cannot be argued from this that the Ibo
have been settled in South-Eastern Nigeria for a longer or shorter
time than those of their neighbours who speak a Bantoid tongue.
And no purpose would be served by engaging in speculations
about ancient cultural contacts, such as that the prevalence of sun-
worship, of forms of mummification, and of a dual organization
points to some distant connexion with Ancient Egypt. As far back
as we can see within historic times the bulk of the Ibo peoples
appear to have lived an isolated existence. But it is probable that in
the fifteenth century the power of the kingdom of Benin, which had
been founded from the ancient Yoruba state of Ife, had already made
itself felt directly or indirectly in Iboland.[1] Many traits of European
culture also must, in the sixteenth century, have begun to filter
through to the Ibo communities, which had by now already become
a fruitful source of supplies for the slave-markets of the coast. During
this century the Portuguese appear to have penetrated as far as Aro-
Chuku which, in later times at least, contained a large Ibo element,
and, as the centre of a famous oracle, exerted an enormous influence
throughout the length and breadth of Iboland. Agents of the oracle,
backed by fighting clans which were kept supplied with European
arms, established themselves in every Ibo community, and used the
oracle as an easy means of obtaining continuous supplies of slaves.
Bonny, one of the principal slave-markets of the coast, was largely
peopled by Ibo, and was in 1688 described by Dr. Dapper in the
following terms:[2]

'South of Moko, towards the sea, lies a third district called Bani, in which
there is a fairly big market centre, called Kuleba' (Bonny), 'where a certain
captain or governor lives, who has about eight or ten villages under his surveil-
lance, and rules a stretch of about three miles from west of the river Kalbaria
to the village Sangma. In the district of Moko a certain kind of money is
used, made of flat iron in the form of a fish, in circumference as large as the
palm of a hand, with a tail almost three sixteenths of a yard long.

'Along the river of Kalbaria the white races, especially the Hollanders,
trade with the inhabitants, and in exchange for slaves offer rough grey copper
armlets, which must be oblong with a rounded curve and very well made,
since the natives are very particular on these points and frequently will
reject two or three hundred out of one barrel. In exchange for slaves we
often give them red and smooth copper rods (for the rods that are the smooth-
est are considered the best out there), each weighing a pound and a quarter,

---

[1] There is direct evidence of Bini influence at Onitsha. See pp. 11 ff.
[2] See Talbot, op. cit., vol. i, pp. 240–1.

and being a yard and a quarter long; fourteen or fifteen of these are given for a good slave. The natives beat these rods out as long and thin as possible, until they look as smooth as if they had been pulled out. They divide them into three pieces, two of which they twine together, interlacing the third as if it were a cable formed by twisting together three strands; and from this they proceed to make armlets, large and small, and also necklets. But the armlets brought there by white men, which they call Bochie, are used solely for money.

'The natives sail the river of Kalbaria in enormous canoes in which as many as twenty rowers or paddlers propel the boat on each side, and fully sixty, nay, as many as eighty men, can be carried in one.

'The slaves, which the natives bring down the river Kalbaria for sale, are mostly those which they have taken captive alive in war, for they eat those they kill. Then these natives also buy from, and trade in slaves with those who have brought them from yet higher up the river; indeed the very natives who bring these slaves to sell to the Kalbarians buy them from other natives who come from further up the river. The natives who bring these slaves down the river Kalbaria in their canoes to be sold on board our ships, also bring with them suitable food for the slaves, which they sell, such as injames, bananas, palm-oil, pigs, antelope, and fowls.'

Under the name of 'Hackbous' the Ibo are described by Barbot about this time as 'a people much addicted to war and preying on their neighbours to the northward, and are themselves lusty tall men. In their territories are two market days every week, for slaves and provisions.'[1]

'The king of Bonny' [he continues] 'had on an old-fashioned scarlet coat, laced with gold and silver, very rusty, and a fine hat on his head, but bare-footed; all his attendants showing great respect for him. . . . Pepprel, his brother, being a sharp blade, and a mighty talking black, perpetually teasing us for this or that Dassy, or present, as well as for drams, etc.'

At this time (i.e. 1699) Bonny was said to consist of about three hundred houses.

'It is well peopled with Blacks, who employ themselves in trade, and some at fishing, like those of New Calabar town . . . by means of long and large canoes, some sixty feet long and seven broad, rowed by sixteen, eighteen or twenty paddlers, carrying European goods and fish to the upland Blacks; and bring down to their respective towns, in exchange, a vast number of slaves, of all sexes and ages, and some large elephants' teeth, to supply the Europeans trading in that river. Several of those Blacks act as factors, or brokers, either for their own countrymen, or for the Europeans; . . . for all that vast number

---

[1] Barbot, quoted by Talbot, op. cit., p. 245.

of slaves which the Calabar Blacks sell to all European nations, but more especially to the Hollanders, who have there the greatest trade, are not their prisoners at war, the greatest part being bought by those people of their inland neighbours, and they also buy them of other nations, yet more remote from them.'

Writing in 1790 Adams says that not fewer than 20,000 slaves were sold annually at Bonny, of whom 16,000 were Ibo.

'Fairs are held every five or six weeks at several villages in the interior, to which the traders of Bonny resort to purchase them. Large canoes capable of carrying 120 persons are launched and stored for the voyage. At the expiration of the sixth day they generally return bringing with them 1500 or 2000 slaves. . . . The Heebos' (Ibo) 'in their persons are tall and well-formed. . . . A class of Heebos, called Breeché, and whom many have very erroneously considered to be a distinct nation, masters of slave ships have always a strong aversion to purchase: because the impression made on their minds, by their degraded situation, was rendered more galling and permanent from the exalted rank which they occupied in their own country. . . . Breeché,[1] in the Heebo language, signifies gentleman or the eldest son of one, and who is not allowed to perform in his own country any menial office. He inherits, at his father's death . . .

'The power of the King of Bonny is absolute; and the surrounding country, for a considerable distance, is subject to his dominion. His war canoes are capable of carrying one hundred and forty persons each, and have often a gun of large calibre mounted on the bow. He has destroyed the town of New Calabar twice and boasts of having eaten part of the heart of its King. . . .'[2]

These episodes are described by Robertson and Smith as follows:

'An army commanded by Pepple in person surprised the town' (New Calabar) 'in the night, took many of the inhabitants prisoners and secured all their canoes. Most of the unfortunate people who fell into their hands were put to death. Pepple has paved the floor of his jew-jew house, place of worship, with their skulls. Their bones have been cleaned and placed on a scaffold, erected near the centre of the town for the purpose: and are shown to Europeans as a trophy of his power and consequence.'

At a feast given to celebrate the victory 'was the bloody heart of the king of Calabar just as it had been torn from the body. He took it in his hand and devoured it with gusto, remarking "This is the way I serve my enemies" '.[3] At the beginning of the nineteenth century it

---

[1] Adams possibly refers to the titled class known as Ndichie. (See p. 189.)
[2] Talbot, op. cit., p. 249.
[3] Quoted by Talbot, op. cit., p. 251.

was estimated that 16,000 slaves were exported annually from Bonny, of whom three-quarters were Ibo. In 1808 the last British slaver sailed, but the trade in slaves continued until 1841, when a treaty was made between King Pepple and the commander of H.M.S. *Iris* by which the chiefs of Bonny agreed to the total abolition of the trade, in return for an annual subsidy of 2,000 dollars for a period of five years. It is noteworthy that this treaty was signed not merely by the king but by all the chiefs of Bonny. By 1846 the Rev. Hope Waddell was able to report that Bonny had become the centre of the palm-oil trade, as it had formerly been that of the slave-trade. Fifteen thousand tons were being shipped annually. But the people of Bonny were represented to be cannibals, and King Pepple regarded them 'all as his slaves, himself alone as really free. To provide for the feast on the death of his father, of which he was said to have been a partaker, an attack was made on a distant unsuspecting village, where boys and girls were captured, to form the delicacies of the occasion.'[1] In 1847 an episode occurred which illustrates the power of priests in an Ibo community. Two British seamen had been murdered while proceeding from New Calabar to Bonny. The instigator of the murders was found to be one of the principal priests of Bonny, who was accordingly arrested by Commander Birch. While the priest was under arrest Birch was asked by the chiefs of Bonny to put him to death. They 'regretted that the sacred character of his person removed him from the pale of human laws and enabled him to execute crimes of great atrocity with impunity. Their only stipulation was that his body should be interred in the country, otherwise their good fortune would assuredly forsake them.'[2] In the same year (1847) Lord Palmerston authorized the British Commodore to compel King Pepple and the chiefs of Bonny, by force if necessary, to respect the lives and property of British subjects, and to carry out their financial engagements with British merchants. In the following year Koehler estimated that the population of Bonny was about 5,000, of whom only a small proportion were free-born. He added the interesting observation that 'the language of the Ibo, through their great industry and war-like temper, had gained a certain supremacy'. In 1854 there is a further sidelight on the local system of government. The chiefs of Bonny stated to the British Consul (Beecroft) that owing to the oppression and tyranny of King Pepple they wished to replace him by his elder

---

[1] Talbot, op. cit., p. 254.
[2] Sir Charles Hotham, quoted by Talbot, op. cit., p. 255.

brother's son. Beecroft agreed, and Pepple, in fear of his life, asked the consul to take him to Fernando Po. Pepple's successor, Dappo, died in the following year, and, when an oracle in Iboland was consulted to ascertain the cause of Dappo's death, it declared that he had been poisoned by two men named Ishacco (Fred Pepple) and Yanibo. These two fled to a British ship for protection, but their wives, children, and slaves were immediately massacred, and an attack was also made on the adherents of the deposed King Pepple. 'The last remnants of the ex-king's people, who had defended themselves in his mud house until the means of sustenance were totally exhausted, ignited some gunpowder and thus ended their miserable existence.'[1] Four regents were appointed to succeed King Dappo, and it is of interest to note (for future purposes) that one of these was so youthful that two elderly men were appointed as his advisers and spokesmen. In 1858 Consul Hutchinson wrote that, at the request of the European traders at Bonny and New Calabar, he had remonstrated with King Amakiri

'touching his attempt to renew the old custom which was prejudicial to trade and had been stopped by Beecroft, by which the supercargoes' (agents) 'were compelled to receive a visit from the Kalabar juju king before Amakiri visited their vessels. He sometimes demanded red cloth to be spread on the deck for him to walk over. He is the priest of the town and deputed articles to be paid for comey' (dues), 'and the delay consequent on these tomfooleries very much retarded the expedition of business.'[2]

In 1859 a state of anarchy prevailed at Bonny owing to jealousy between the houses of the regents. The British Consul reported that some of the people wished to have King Pepple back 'because they are more willing to endure a despotic rule than to suffer under a condition of insubordination, which must ever exist during the present regency—constituted, as it is, of men who, being of the slave class, can have no authority'. In the following year the Consul reported that the regents had no authority except in their own houses and that the consent of the mob was necessary for any measure of importance. In 1863 Burton tells us that the chiefs of Bonny

'openly beg that the rules' (against slavery) 'may be relaxed, in order that they may get rid of their criminals. . . . When the slave has once surmounted his dread of being shipped by the white men, nothing under the sun would, I believe, induce him willingly to return to what he should call his home. And

[1] Lynslager, quoted by Talbot, op. cit., p. 261.   [2] Talbot, op. cit., p. 263.

as they were, our West Indian colonies were lands of happiness compared with the Oil Rivers; and as for the Southern States the slave's lot is paradise when succeeding what he endures on the West Coast of Africa.'[1]

We shall see later that one of the commonest objections to the British system of justice at the present time is that prisons are too comfortable to be corrective and that communities have no means of ridding themselves permanently of habitual criminals.

The first Christian mission was started in Bonny by Bishop Crowther in 1864, but this did not prevent the continuance of civil strife, and in 1879 Ellis compared Bonny very unfavourably with other West African towns. It was, he said, indescribably filthy. 'George Pepple is king—but Oko Jumbo is the real power; he has some seven or eight thousand men, all armed with breech-loading rifles—and Jaja about the same. One war between Oko Jumbo and Jaja has just come to an end in which several of Jaja's wives were captured and eaten by the enemy.'

The last King Pepple abdicated in 1882, and Oko Jumbo, the chief power in Bonny, was degraded by the British Consul four years later. In 1877 Jaja, the notorious Ibo Chief of Opobo, was also degraded and deported by Consul (afterwards Sir H. H.) Johnston. This was an event of first-class importance in the history of the Ibo, as it led to the establishment of free trade with the teeming markets of the hinterland. In 1889 the Oil Rivers Protectorate was constituted, and Consular Courts, primarily for British subjects, were established. 'Up to this time each river had been governed by a Court of Equity, composed of the local leading merchants, who decided cases not only in their own community, but also among the natives, backed by a threat of appeal to the Consul and the presence of a gunboat.'[2]

In 1893 the Oil Rivers Protectorate was extended indefinitely into the interior under the name of the Niger Coast Protectorate, which in 1900 became the Protectorate of Southern Nigeria, and in 1914 the Southern Provinces of Nigeria. In 1897 Major Leonard and Mr. F. S. James penetrated as far as Bende, a centre of the slave-trade. They had a hostile reception, and it was not until 1901–2 that Bende, Owerri, Aba, and other important centres of the Ibo peoples were brought under control by the Aro expeditionary force. In 1904 a punitive force of 200 troops had to be sent against the Ibo of Ekkpahia who had murdered a number of traders and attacked the British

[1] Quoted by Talbot, op. cit., p. 269.   [2] Talbot, op. cit., vol. i, p. 68.

Commissioner. The troops met with a stout resistance. In 1905 and 1906 also there was sharp fighting in the district of Ahiara, where Dr. Stewart had been murdered in mistake for the District Commissioner, and near Eziama, where 18,000 fire-arms were surrendered by or captured from the natives. Civil authority was not established in the Umuduru area until 1907, and patrols were necessary in 1914, when serious disturbances occurred in the districts of Aba, Okigwi, Bende, and Owerri. Since then such unrest as has shown itself has been purely local, with the exception of the women's riots of 1929, which were widespread throughout the south-eastern section of Iboland.

Turning now to that part of Iboland which borders the Niger River, it may be of interest to record some notes on the history of Onitsha, which for the last eighty years has been one of the most important centres of European trade and missionary effort. Onitsha at the present time consists of two divisions: (a) the Inland Town with a population of about 1,300 people, and (b) the Waterside Town with a population of upwards of 14,000. Three-quarters of these inhabitants are Ibo-speaking, the remainder being composed of members of the Hausa, Nupe, Yoruba, and Kakanda tribes. But the Ibo-speaking section contains an Edo or Bini element. For not only is there a traditional connexion between Onitsha and Benin, but the Onitsha system of government, with its kingship and hierarchy of officials, is non-Ibo and bears a close resemblance to that of Benin.

The story of the Bini immigration is given as follows. In ancient days there lived at Benin a personage called Chima who was compelled to leave the capital on account of a quarrel over the kingship.[1] He and his followers travelled east to the Niger. Here the party split into two groups, one of which proceeded down river to Aboh, while the other, after spending some time on the western bank, crossed over to the present site of Onitsha. Chima had died on the western bank, and a successor had not been appointed at the time of the crossing of the Niger. It is related that, prior to the crossing, Oreze, one of the sons of Chima, advised the people to destroy their

---

[1] According to a variant account Chima lived not at Benin itself but to the east of Benin and was driven across the Niger by the Bini Commander-in-Chief Gbunmara in consequence of an insult to the mother of the king of Benin—the insult being, perhaps, a refusal to pay tribute to the king's mother who controlled a large number of villages (see Talbot, op. cit., vol. iii, p. 587). Still another account is that Onitsha is an offshoot of Obbior.

gongs lest some indiscreet person should, by beating his gong, fore-
warn the Ibo inhabitants of their presence. They could fashion new
ones on the other side, and whoever made the one which most closely
resembled the old royal gong in tone could have the kingship. So all
the people destroyed their gongs, but Oreze kept Chima's, covered it
with a mat and sat on it while crossing the Niger. On reaching the
other side new gongs were made. But as none resembled the old
gong of Chima so much as that of Oreze (who had redecorated it to
give it the appearance of being new), Oreze was elected king. After
his election he conferred on the kindred known as Asele the right of
bestowing on all successive kings the royal *Ọfọ* or sacred symbol of
office. This was done with a view to preventing any one from
assuming the kingship by force.[1] The kingship itself became confined
to two groups known as Umu Dei and Umu Eze-Arole. These two
groups are included in the clan known as 'Eze Chima'. The invaders
drove out the Ibo of Oze and settled in the present Inland Town,
where in due course they fused with Ibo-speaking groups and were
joined later by small groups of Igala. They adopted the language and
much of the culture of the Ibo.

It is not possible to assign with certainty a date to this influx of
Bini. Some say that Agboala and others that Asije was king of Benin
at the time. Agboala is no doubt to be equated with Ogwola or
Ogwo-ala, a famous king of Benin who reigned *c.* 1400–30,[2] while
Asije is probably the Esigie of Benin tradition who, on his father's
death in 1520, destroyed Udo, the city occupied by his elder brother
Aruonya. Various Bini rebels are said to have been driven eastwards
towards the Niger at this time[3] and it is possible that Chima was one
of these. In favour of this view it may be remarked that the kings of
Onitsha are consecrated at a shrine which is known as Udo. The
events may, however, refer to a later date, for Dr. Talbot in his
record of the history of Benin states that *c.* 1702 'Two families appear
to have left Benin at this time one of which settled at Agbor, while
the other went on to Obbior, whence some continued to Onitsha
Ugbo and others at a later date to Onitsha Olona. Of the same
Obbior family came also the ancestors of Ezi, Abongpa and Onitsha

---

[1] The kindred or group known as Ọbiọ was given the privilege of consecrating the
king by a special rite which included the ceremonial shaving of the king, leaving a
hair-lock which is, in many parts of Nigeria, as it was in ancient Egypt, a symbol
of royalty.

[2] See Talbot, op. cit., vol. i, p. 153.   [3] See ibid., p. 158.

Mili.'[1] Whatever date is assigned to these migrations it is noteworthy that two of the subdivisions of the present town of Onitsha are known as Ọbiọ (Obbior) and Obangkpa.

The authority of the kings of Onitsha does not appear to have extended much beyond the confines of their own town. At any rate no claim is put forward at the present time that the surrounding Ibo communities were ever in any real sense subject to them. It is said, however, that the king of Onitsha was frequently appealed to as arbiter in disputes in or between the communes of Obosi, Ogidi, Nkpo, Nsube, Nkwelle, Oze, Umunya, and Ogbunike. The leading men of these communes used to give occasional gifts to the king of Onitsha and in some cases received titles from him. It was also stated by the present Onowu of Onitsha that all leopards, bush-cow, wart-hogs, manatees, and hippopotami killed by members of these communes had to be delivered to the king of Onitsha. No confirmation was obtained of this claim, and it may be said generally that the kings of Onitsha never exercised any form of suzerainty beyond the limits of their own town, and that any influence they possessed over the neighbouring Ibo communities was of an informal character and varied with the personality of the reigning king.

On the other hand, there is some evidence that the kings of Onitsha at one time occupied a position of subservience to those of Aboh. This is strenuously denied by the people of Onitsha at the present time, but it is clear from the records of British travellers that Aboh claimed Onitsha as part of its domains during the first half of the nineteenth century, Aboh itself having been a domain of Benin for two centuries at least. Thus in 1841 the Trotter-Allen expedition reported that the Obi of Aboh claimed Onitsha as part of his dominions, though he admitted that the people of Onitsha were constantly rebellious. In 1854 Hutchinson remarked that at Onitsha the territory of Aboh ended and that of Igala began. In 1861 it was reported that the power of the king of Onitsha was small, the people being 'very independent and lawless'.

A few years previously (in 1856) the Church Missionary Society obtained a site at Onitsha and began the work which has resulted in a widespread adoption of Christianity.[2] In the same year also a trading station was opened by Macgregor Laird, and other companies

---

[1] See Talbot, op. cit., vol. i, p. 168.

[2] The Roman Catholic Mission, which has had marked success, was started in 1885.

(including Hall & Jack, Miller Brothers, the West African Company, and James Pinnock) followed suit. A number of these companies were amalgamated in 1879 to form the United African Company, but this company, in its very first year, closed down its premises at Onitsha in consequence of outrages committed there. As a punishment for these outrages the town was attacked and partially burnt by a naval force acting in conjunction with Hausa constabulary. The United African Company, which in 1881 had become the National African Company, was in 1886 renamed the Royal Niger Company, having been given a charter and authorized to administer those areas in which it had acquired rights by treaties or cession. The Company, with its head-quarters at Asaba, established at Onitsha a British Court with jurisdiction from the Waterside as far as the compound of the Church Missionary Society, with a view to protecting the interests of traders, particularly native-foreigners. The king of Onitsha, however, continued to exercise authority over his own people, and he and his principal officials received an annual subsidy from the Company in the form of numerous gifts. In 1900 the Company's territories were transferred to the Crown, and Onitsha continued to be administered from Asaba. A Native Court was established at Onitsha. The judges of this court were at first selected by the Government, but the principle of selection by the people was substituted later, as complaints had been made that the judges were in many cases foreigners. It may be remarked that prior to 1860 there were no communities resident at the Waterside. Onitsha consisted solely of the Inland Town, whose population was estimated at 16,000. But when the trading firms arrived, groups of people from the Inland Town and from Aboh began to take up residence at the Waterside. The early Waterside population also included a considerable number of Africans from Sierra Leone and Lagos, who had been introduced by the trading firms and also by the Church Missionary Society. Soon after the assumption of control by the Government the population of the Waterside became further increased by groups of Hausa, Yoruba, Nupe, and Kakanda. The Waterside population is now about 14,000,[1] while that of the Inland Town has sunk from 16,000 to 1,300—an interesting example of the immense effect which contact with European civilization can produce on an African community.

In 1904 severe fighting occurred between Government troops and

[1] The 1931 Census figures for Onitsha Township were 17,969.

the inhabitants of a number of towns in the Asaba district, which, under the influence of an age-grade organization known as Ekumeku, had formed a confederacy for certain purposes such as taking common action against any community which harboured runaway criminals. The Ekumeku of the towns concerned assumed an overbearing attitude, burnt a number of Mission Stations, and defied the authority of the Government. Since then patrols have been necessary among the northern Ibo at various times to settle local disturbances, but the general attitude of the people has been very friendly. The Ibo of Onitsha Province took no part in the riots of 1929.

In 1906 Government schools were opened at Onitsha and Owerri, and by 1931 there were in the Onitsha and Owerri Provinces 11 Government schools, 74 schools assisted by the Government, and 1,092 non-assisted schools. The total number of scholars was returned as 61,526 and there were 2,935 African teachers. In these two provinces, also, there were in 1931 298,081 'adherents' of Christian churches, so that the total number of professing Christians in Iboland may be estimated at not less than 600,000. It is evident from these figures that the Ibo are strong in their demand for Western education, and that there is a powerful movement towards Christianity.

Economics.

As regards the economic life of the people a few remarks only are required for the purpose of this chapter. The rainfall in Iboland varies from 105 inches in the extreme south to 60 in the extreme north. There are two well-defined seasons, a wet and a dry. The wet season lasts from March to November, June, July, and September being the wettest months. The comparative dry spell in August is of considerable importance to the farmer, as it enables him to harvest his early crops of maize and ground-nuts, and at the same time dries and stimulates the soil for fresh production. And the absence of the drought conditions which occur so frequently in Northern Nigeria, coupled with the general fertility of the soil, are no doubt mainly responsible for the marked density of population. For whereas in Northern Nigeria there are only 40 persons to the square mile, there are in Iboland 287.[1] In the area round Owerri (viz. the country occupied by the Oratta and Isu groups) the density is no less than 500 to the square mile, and there is therefore a relative shortage of

---

[1] Using the 1921 Census figures for the Provinces of Owerri and Onitsha.

farming land, a fact which is likely to raise economic and political difficulties at no distant date.[1]

It is almost true to say that there are no landless families in Iboland and that there are few families which do not provide from their own farms the major part of their food-supplies. Even the traders and artisans are generally farmers as well. This places the Ibo household in a strong economic position. For it is not dependent for its existence on external trade. It can live a prosperous, though not a luxurious, life on its own resources. A slump in world trade may cause discontent, forcing the people to give up many luxuries which they had come to regard as necessaries, but it cannot lead to general starvation or any serious degree of unemployment. The only danger is that the population may increase beyond the limits of the productivity of the land, thereby giving rise to a non-agricultural floating population with nothing to give in exchange for the food it requires.

The staple food-crop of the Ibo is the yam, and all other crops are merely subsidiary. Much of the social and religious life of the people, therefore, centres round the cultivation of the yam. There are yam festivals, yam deities, and yam titles. And there are innumerable varieties of yams. Yams are usually planted in March (or April) or in November in mounds 1 or 2 feet high[2] and 3 or 4 feet apart. The preparation of these mounds entails immense labour, and the Ibo farmer knows that the bigger the mound the better is the yield.[3] The clearing of the land is itself heavy work. Any part of the tuber may be used as 'seed', but usually a piece of the head of a large yam or an entire small yam is planted. When the tendrils or vines are long enough they are trained on stakes. At harvest the tubers are removed without disturbing the vines, and this results in a secondary growth of the small tubers which are commonly used for seed purposes. In some districts yams are left in the ground until required for food purposes. Otherwise they are stored on wooden racks,

---

[1] In Europe the maximum population which can be supported by agriculture is 250 per sq. mile. The density can be considerably greater in certain parts of Africa, not merely on account of the greater fertility of the soil but also because the necessities of life are fewer in a less rigorous climate. Nevertheless, a steady increase in the population of certain crowded areas of Iboland can only be viewed with alarm.

[2] In some areas (e.g. the Abakaliki Division) the mounds may be as much as 5 feet high and 8 or 9 feet in diameter at the base.

[3] The average yield is about 3 tons per acre. I am indebted for these and other agricultural details to the excellent monograph entitled *West African Agriculture*, by O. T. Faulkner and J. R. Mackie (Cambridge University Press, 1933).

shaded from the sun. A man's social prestige depends to a great extent on the number of yams he is able to display in this way. Yams are eaten roasted whole, or boiled and pounded into balls, after the fibres have been removed. A vegetable soup, which sometimes contains fish, may be used as a condiment.

Subsidiary crops are maize, beans, cotton, okra, and gourds, all of which may be interplanted with yams, and coco-yams, cassava, and rice. In the plots surrounding the homesteads minor crops such as coco-yams, red peppers, and okra are commonly grown. In most areas the men do all the heavy work, i.e. fell the small trees, burn down the large ones, clear the ground, make the yam mounds, collect the props for the vines, and prepare the ground for the women's crops. The women do the planting and weeding. But custom varies. In the Owerri Division, for instance, women take a very active part in farming, assisting the men in making the mounds and in planting, and being entirely responsible for weeding. But among the Ika-Ibo women contribute little if anything to the work of the men. In other areas again (e.g. at Nkpologu) it is an offence for women to plant yams, and if a woman is detected breaking this rule the yams she has planted are forfeit to the principal officials of the town.

Next to yams the most important product of Iboland is the oil-palm. If yams are the staple food of the people, oil-palms are their principal source of income. For palm-kernels and palm-oil, being the sole commodities produced for export, are the sole means the people have of purchasing the European goods which they have come to regard as essential to their comfort and happiness. The oil-palms occur in house-lands, deserted house-lands, farm-lands, and forest-lands. In the first three cases the palms are owned individually or collectively by the family, in the last case they are usually owned collectively by the village community. Those which grow or have been planted on house-lands or within the confines of the village are the most important economically, as they attain a better development and produce a higher yield than the farm or forest variety, which seldom fruits until it has reached a height of at least 30 feet. The harvesting of the produce of neglected palms is slow, toilsome, and dangerous work, as it entails climbing slender trees sometimes of prodigious height. The climbers not infrequently fall and lose their lives or suffer serious injuries.

When the fruit has been gathered it is softened by being allowed to ferment and is then mashed, the oil being squeezed out. This process produces a 'hard' or strongly acid oil, and entails a loss of 35–45 per cent. of the oil in the fruit.[1] Efforts are being made by the Agricultural Department to introduce small hand-presses by which 80 per cent. of the oil can be extracted. The use of treadle machines for extracting the kernels is also being encouraged, and a definite programme of palm-grove improvement is being steadily carried out. For, unless the natives of Nigeria learn to improve their palms and methods of production, they may find it increasingly difficult to compete with the planters of Sumatra and Malaya.[2] The latter have the advantage of capital and large-scale methods, but the Nigerian peasants have that of independent ownership. From this point of view the communal ownership of palms, where it occurs in Iboland, would seem to be a hindrance to progress. But actually palms which are held communally are of little value for export purposes, and indeed many are communal merely because nobody wants them.

The Ibo are not great hunters, and fishing is confined for the most part to the Niger River communities. In the 1921 Census only 8,553 Ibo were shown as engaged in fishing. In many villages it is taboo to fish in the local rivers, as the fish are believed to embody the souls of the people's ancestors. Keen resentment is frequently expressed against itinerant Hausa fishermen who disregard the feelings of the local inhabitants in this matter. As regards metal-work the Ibo have never been noted for their brass-work, like their neighbours of Benin. But the blacksmiths of Awka have long been notorious, not merely for their skill as workers in iron, but for the enormous influence, religious, social, political, and legal, which they have exerted throughout the northern half of Iboland, an influence comparable with, but on the whole more salutary than, that of the traders of Aro-Chuku in the south. They formed a close guild and travelled extensively, as smiths, doctors, purveyors of cults and cultus-symbols, circumcisers, teeth-filers, missionaries of the priest-chiefs of Nri and of the system of title-taking associated with Nri, and above all as agents of the oracle of Agbala, which was a final court of appeal in all disputes.

The Ibo are noted also for their great skill in carving wood, particularly wooden stools and images representing gods and ancestors.

---

[1] A softer oil is produced in some areas by boiling and pounding the fruit. The pulp is then worked in water, and the oil as it rises is skimmed off the surface.

[2] Nigeria has also to face strong competition from the Congo.

Many have become carpenters on European lines. But perhaps the most striking feature of Ibo life is the keenness displayed by the women in petty trade. Many women, indeed, seem to do little else but attend markets, and from the small profits made it would appear that markets are attended almost as much for social as for commercial purposes. The markets are the news centres of the district. Among men the propensity towards trade varies considerably in different groups. Thus, in Owerri Division, the large group of people known as Isu are noted traders, and on any of the main roads leading to Port-Harcourt hundreds of Isu can be seen making their way on foot or on bicycles to and from this centre of trade. But their immediate neighbours, the Oratta, take very much less interest in trade and affect, indeed, to despise the Isu for their trading propensities. The reason for the distinction between the two groups of people appears to be that the Oratta are possessed of better farming land than the Isu, and have not the same necessity for seeking a livelihood by other means than agriculture.

We may conclude this short summary of environmental and economic conditions by noting that early in this century a large coal-field was discovered in the neighbourhood of Enugu, the present capital of the Southern Provinces of Nigeria. The mines began to yield coal in 1915, and at the present time the output is about 260,000 tons annually. In 1913 Port-Harcourt was founded, and the construction of a railway from this seaport to Northern Nigeria was begun. This railway passes through the heart of Iboland and has been a main factor in opening the country to outside influence. Iboland is also covered by a network of magnificent roads, and an immense amount of trade is now carried on by motor vehicles, many of which are owned by members of the Ibo tribe.

II

THE SACRED SANCTION

A. Gods and Godlings

AMONG most peoples of the world religion is, in varying degrees, the handmaiden of the law, even when the Church and State are no longer one. Indeed, one of the primary functions of religion would seem to be the formulation of rules and standards of social behaviour. Among the Ibo religion and law are so closely interwoven that many of the most powerful legal sanctions are derived directly from the gods. As a preliminary, therefore, to the study of the legal system of the Ibo it will be necessary to give some description of their theology.

Firstly, there is a pantheon of high gods, headed by Chuku or Chineke the Supreme Spirit, Anyaṅu (the Sun), Igwe (the Sky), Amadi-Ọha (Lightning), and Ala (the Earth deity). Then there are innumerable minor deities: water and agricultural godlings; spirits which are the personification of fortune, destiny, wealth, strength, divination, and evil; spirits which are the counterparts of living human beings; and finally the ancestors, who control the fortunes of their living descendants.

The Supreme Being, or it might be more correct to say the Supreme Spirit or World-Oversoul, is known as Chuku, a word which is a contraction of *Chi* = Spirit and *uku* = great. In some areas Chuku is known alternatively as Obasi (or Obasi-Idinenu or Idi n'elu). In his creative aspect he is known as Chineke, or Chukwoke, or Chi-Okike. He is the author of heaven and earth, he sends the rain, makes the crops grow, and is the source from which men derive their *chi* or accompanying soul. He is the father of the gods, for some at least of the gods are said to be his 'sons'. But he is a distant deity of vague personality, and sacrifice is seldom offered to him directly. Yet he is regarded as the ultimate recipient of all sacrifices. Thus, if sacrifice is offered to Anyaṅu, the officiant asks Anyaṅu to accept the sacrifice and bear it to Chuku. And in former times, before the destruction of the oracle of Chuku at Aro-Chuku (known in pidgin English as 'The Long Juju'), the members of a village-group might unite to present a slave to Chuku, through the mediumship of the oracle and of Anyaṅu. The slave was handed to an agent of the oracle, with a prayer addressed to Anyaṅu that he (Anyaṅu) would receive the slave and hand him to Chuku, that he would avert sickness from the community, and cause their wives to be fruitful. Moreover, prayers or petitions are commonly addressed directly to Chuku, accompanied sometimes by gifts or libations of water. Thus, when the head of a family wakes up in the morning he may, after washing his hands, lay a kola or some snuff on the ground, saying, 'Obasi-Idinenu (Chuku), watch over me and my children this day.' And any one setting forth on a journey may ask Chuku to make the object of the journey successful and bring him home again in safety.

Although Chuku is sometimes spoken of as the father of Anyaṅu,[1] the sun, he is also sometimes identified with Anyaṅu, and the phrase 'Anyaṅu Eze Chuku Okike' (The Sun, the Lord God, the Creator) is applied apparently to a single personality. This identification is paralleled among numerous other Nigerian tribes.[2] But it is not complete, and in modern phraseology Anyaṅu might be described as a manifestation or emanation of Chuku. Moreover, while there are no shrines or cultus-symbols of Chuku, there are few non-Christian households which are without some symbol of Anyaṅu. A libation of water may be offered to Chuku, but Anyaṅu, like all the other gods and spirits, must be served with wine.

In the Nsukka Division most households have a shrine of Anyaṅu. The shrine may be set up by a man as soon as he establishes a home of his own, but some married men postpone erecting a shrine until they are directed to do so by a diviner. The symbol of Anyaṅu is a branch or cutting of an *obo*, *apo*, *ogirisi*, or *ọha* tree, planted outside the hut which serves as the entrance to the compound and also as the common meeting-place. Beside it there may be a stripped branch of an *oterre* or *ururu* tree, and at the base of the tree an earthenware bowl which receives the sacrificial blood. A species of grass known as *otonile* is sometimes placed in the bowl. In some groups (e.g. Uzaba)[3] a pot with four holes bored in it is placed on the roof of the hut and is connected with the tree by a creeper. The pot may contain the

---

[1] The word Anyaṅu appears to mean 'the eyes above'. Phonetically it should be written *anjaŋu* (according to the script of the International Phonetic Association).

[2] See my *A Sudanese Kingdom*, p. 183.

[3] At Uzaba the *ogirisi* tree is called 'Anyaṅu', the *ọha* tree is called 'the face of Anyaṅu', and the *ururu* tree 'the creation of Anyaṅu'. The pot is known as Oshimare Anyaṅu. At Obibi young palm-leaves and a strip of white cloth are attached to one or other of the tree symbols.

feathers of a certain bird[1] and a pad such as is used for carrying produce to market. Occasionally, at the base of the tree-symbol, a round
pottery dish is sunk into the ground bottom upwards, and this was
said to represent the sun's disk. Beside the symbol there is usually
(in the Nsukka Division) a double hand-gong of iron, which is beaten
with an antelope's horn immediately before sacrifice is offered. The
offerings, which are always made at sunrise or sunset, consist of the
blood of a white chicken (poured over the pottery symbol and the
branches of the *obo* tree), kola-nuts, and palm-wine. The ritual observed at Nkpologu was as follows. The head of the family took up
his stand before the symbol of the cult, which in this case consisted
of an *obo* tree, with a mound of sand built round the base of the tree.
A number of stones were laid on the mound of sand, the centre
being occupied by one large flat stone which served as an altar. Some
of the branches of the *obo* tree had been pruned, the cuttings being
used as props for yam tendrils, in the belief that they would have a
magical effect on the crop. The officiant produced a kola-nut which
he split into pieces. He laid two of the pieces on the stone altar
saying, 'Anyaṅu, Eze Chukwoke, protect me and my people.' He
then handed other fragments of the kola to all present in order of
seniority, and all ate. After a minute or two a small boy handed a
platter of palm-oil to the officiant, who poured the oil over the kolas,
saying, 'I do not offer sacrifice to you with an evil heart. Protect me,
therefore, and protect my family.' His senior wife, standing in the
background, added, 'Protect us all.'

This concluded the sacrifice on this occasion, but usually food is
cooked and eaten at the shrine after the rites described above, scraps
of food being first placed on the altar. It may be noted that when
rites are due there must be no quarrelling in the compound, and at
Nkpologu, during my visit, a man was fined (one goat) by the head
of his compound for quarrelling with his brother on the evening preceding rites to Anyaṅu.

In the Awgu Division very much less attention is paid to Anyaṅu
than in the Nsukka Division. Indeed, the only rites observed were
those already referred to, namely the sacrifice to Chuku through
Anyaṅu. Any one may perform this sacrifice when he feels inclined,
or when directed to do so by a diviner. He takes a white chicken and
hangs it by the feet in a cleft piece of bamboo which is stuck into the
ground. This may be done at sunrise or sunset with some such

[1] e.g. parrots and other species known as *ugu*, *abubu-ogazi*, and *ọdanuru*.

prayer as, 'You, Anyañu, who are coming forth (or going home), receive this chicken and bear it to Obasi. Protect my life and that of my family, and avert all forms of evil. May sickness be kept at a distance and grant that I may obtain children, male and female.' In offering this petition he assumes a squatting position, facing the sun, and when he has finished he leaves the chicken to die and ultimately to rot.

In the Owerri Division there is a special form of sacrifice to Anyañu which is known as *Ndayo*. This word means 'bringing down', and the sacrifice is performed when the owner of an Anyañu cult is ill, with a view to 'bringing down' to the world the spirit of the sick man which had begun to rise to Anyañu. The sick man's brother (or son), by the direction of a diviner, plants four sticks near the symbol of Anyañu and sacrifices a fowl or goat there, with some such words as, 'My brother is ill, and I perform these rites to bring him back to life. May you, Anyañu, Chineke, and all the ancestors, grant that he may be restored to health.' It is said that if the diviner has formed the opinion that there is no hope of the sick man's recovery he prescribes a sacrifice far beyond the means of the relative who had consulted him!

Anyañu appears to be regarded in a special way as the god of good fortune or as a wealth-giving deity. Thus, before a man goes to market, he may pour a little palm-wine into the bowl of Anyañu, dip his fingers in the bowl, touch his tongue with his fingers, and say, 'I am going to market: may Anyañu grant that my words may sound sweet to those with whom I trade.' If a man fails to recover money owed to him, and consults a diviner, he is generally advised to offer sacrifice to Anyañu. Every morning the head of a household may go before the symbols of Anyañu, wash his hands, and say, 'Anyañu, Chineke, I pray to you for life for myself and those that belong to me. May I have children and wealth in plenty, and may my crops excel those of other men. Protect me from my enemies, and grant that those who think evil of me shall be met by evil, and that those who think good of me shall be met by good.'

The art and practice of dancing are closely associated with Anyañu. When a new dance is invented, or an old one resuscitated, it is practised in the dark, and before it is publicly performed in the day-time the emblem of Anyañu is set up in the open space used for dancing, and a white cock is sacrificed by a senior member of the dancing party or some elder indicated by a diviner. This is done to secure the

success of the dance and protect the dancers from the jealousy of
evil spirits.

There is no moon-cult parallel with that of the sun, but when
any one sees the new moon he holds up both his hands and says,
'New moon, protect me as the last moon protected me.' Or, if he
had been unlucky the previous month, he may ask the new moon to
bring him better luck than had been brought by the last. Nor is
Igwe, the sky, a general object of religious rites, even though he is
regarded as a son of Chuku and husband of Ala, the Earth deity.
Just as a husband fertilizes his wife, so Igwe, in the form of rain,
fertilizes Ala (the soil). And yet Igwe has no place in Ibo life comparable with that of the Mother-goddess. Nevertheless, he is not
altogether neglected. Installed in his shrine at Umunǫha (Owerri
Division), Igwe was one of the highest courts of appeal in Iboland.
The manner in which this oracle was used as an integral part of the
legal machinery will be demonstrated at a later stage.[1]

Another cult of general public importance is that of Amadi-Ǫha,
the god of lightning. Most villages of each village-group possess a
shrine of this deity, but there is not as a rule any central or senior
shrine (as in the case of Ala). The cultus-symbols are an *apo*, *mbom*,
ǫha, *ogirisi*, *obo*, and (or) *ururu* tree, with a stripped branch of *oterre*
wood stuck in the ground close by. At the base of the tree (or trees)
there may be two pots (one large and one small) sunk into the ground.
Rites are performed annually before the digging-up of yams. Each
householder is expected to take an offering of four lumps of pounded
yam to the shrine, wave them round his head, and deposit them before
the cultus-emblem. The priest then sacrifices a chicken (brought by
the householder) and makes a petition for the welfare of the householder. The body of the chicken is taken home by the householder,
cooked and eaten on the following morning, one leg being sent to the
priest. This is the ritual followed at the village-groups of Okolochi
and Obibi, but yam-rites there and elsewhere are carried out in
connexion with many other cults besides that of Amadi-Ǫha.

The most important deity in the public and private life of the Ibo
is not Chuku or Anyańu or Amadi-Ǫha, but Ala, or Ale or Ana or
Ane or Ani,[2] the Earth-deity, who, like Ma among the Jukun, ap-

---

[1] See pp. 45–7 and 238 ff.

[2] Among a number of tribes of the Northern Territories of the Gold Coast the
Earth-deity is known as Tingani. As this word seems to embody the same name
(Ani) as the Ibo Earth-deity, Dr. Rattray's suggestion that Tingani is derived from

pears to be a modern representative of the ancient cultus of the Great Mother, the symbol of life.[1]

Ala is regarded as the owner of men, whether alive or dead. The cult of ancestors is, therefore, closely associated with that of the Earth-deity, who is Queen of the Underworld. Ala is the fount of human morality, and is, in consequence, a principal legal sanction. Homicide, kidnapping, poisoning, stealing, adultery, giving birth to twins or cripples or abnormal children, are all offences against Ala which must be purged by rites to her.[2] Ala deprives evil men of their lives, and her priests are the guardians of public morality. Laws are made in her name[3] and by her oaths are sworn. She is the mainspring of the social life, and, in many localities, if any one wishes to better his social position by taking a title, he must first secure the good offices of Ala. Ala is, in fact, the unseen president of the community, and no group is complete without a shrine of Ala. The common possession of a shrine of Ala is, indeed, one of the strongest integrating forces in Ibo society.

Each of the hamlets or villages composing a village-group has a shrine and priest of Ala, but there is always a senior shrine, namely, that of the particular hamlet or village which originally occupied the locality. Here it is that the component units of a village-group or commune meet periodically to offer common sacrifice. The symbols of the deity are usually a tree,[4] with a pottery dish which serves as a receptacle for offerings. But in some localities stones, cairns,[5] iron spears, flat iron rods, and wooden gongs known as *ikoro* are also associated with Ala. These gongs have at one end a carved head of a female. They are beaten to summon a general meeting and in former times were used as a war-signal. It is said that it was customary in olden days to consecrate the gongs by sacrificing a slave, this being done before the work of hollowing out the tree-trunk had been begun,

---

ti = trees and *gane* = surpass and refers to the sacred groves of the Earth-deity seems hardly probable.

[1] The Jukun Ma or Ama appears to be the same name as was borne by the Great Mother in Asia Minor (Ma or Ammas). The name Ala is possibly related to the Babylonian Allatu, who like Ala was both a personification of the Earth and ruler of the lower world.

[2] See Chapter X, *passim.*

[3] See pp. 247 ff.

[4] *Ogirisi, obo, ọha, apo,* or *obossi* trees are the commonest species used.

[5] A cairn observed at Owele was 3 feet high and 5 feet in diameter. It was flat-topped and surmounted by a monolith.

with a view to pacifying the *obi* or heart-soul of the tree. Nowadays an *ikoro* is consecrated with the blood of a ram.

Public sacrifice to Ala may be offered periodically at the beginning of the agricultural season, before clearing new land, or after clearing old, before planting yams, or at the end of the yam harvest. Thus, at Awgu, the beginning of the wet season is an occasion for sacrifice to Ala by the young men of the village. Each goes to the senior shrine with a pot of palm-wine. The senior priest pours some of the wine into a gourd and then addresses Ala, saying: 'Your children have brought palm-wine to you. Protect them and their farms. Grant that none may meet with any untoward event, such as falling from a palm tree.' Having said this he pours the wine into the hollow of the monolith (Awgu). All the wine is then divided out equally among the kindreds represented, and after it has been consumed the young men betake themselves to the market and engage in dancing and wrestling.

In the Nsukka Division the conclusion of the yam harvest is an occasion for rites to Ala.[1] All the people of the village attend, each bringing with him a yam, and saluting the symbols of Ala by cracking his fingers and saying, 'Ala, we have come.' The priest, standing before the symbols, declares that he is there to perform the rites performed by his forefathers, that he harbours no evil in his heart, and is at one with all the people of the village. With offerings of palm-wine, yams, and food, he asks Ala to protect them all, to increase their numbers, and to give them a successful new agricultural year, so that they may be able to bring similar offerings in the following year. He then takes a chicken and walks round the people, waving it over their heads and calling for Ala's blessing. The chicken is killed and the blood sprinkled on the pots and branches of the tree-symbol. The chicken is cooked, and parts are deposited before the symbol. Each person present then cuts off the head of his yam and lays it aside to be planted as an amulet in the middle of his farm. The rest of the yam is cooked and eaten *in situ*.

At Owele common sacrifice to Ala is only offered every third year. All the Ala priests of the various villages, together with the senior elders, meet at the senior shrine where the senior priest (of Enugu) kneels before the symbol and asks Ala to protect him and all the people of Owele, to prevent any one from seeking to poison his fellow

[1] The Owerri spelling of Ala is used throughout for the sake of uniformity. But in the Nsukka and Awgu Divisions the word is usually pronounced Ale or Ane.

man, to give fertility to their women,[1] and to allow strangers, who had come to attend the feast, to return home in safety. He then pours a libation, and, after a short interval, repeats the prayer and slays a goat, pouring the blood over the stone symbol. The conclusion of the rites is marked by the firing of a gun. Each householder then offers sacrifice to his own Ala-obi or protecting genius, and a general feast is held, accompanied by dancing, wrestling, and the firing of guns. Fighting is supposed to be taboo on such occasions, but the rule is not always observed. Those who infringe it are obliged, subsequently, to offer a special sacrifice to Ala. It is also a rule that no one who had been guilty of homicide is allowed to take part in public rites to Ala. If he does not leave the town during the festival he is obliged to sit on a platform, so as to avoid contact with the Earth. The festival is concluded by a final sacrifice, the priest on this occasion being unaccompanied by others.

On special occasions, also, public sacrifice may be offered to Ala if it has been ascertained by divination that Ala requires propitiation. In this connexion it may be of interest (both generally and from the particular point of view of method in tax collection) to note the procedure adopted by a village-group for providing the sacrificial animal. The elders, feeling that things were amiss, would call a general meeting to discuss the question whether a public sacrifice was necessary, and if so to whom it should be offered and what should be the nature of the offering. If it were decided that a cow should be offered to Ala, and that a suitable cow could be obtained for £5, the meeting would agree that the two main divisions of the town should contribute to the cost equally, irrespective of numbers, i.e. each should find a sum of £2 10s. The elders of each division would then direct that their two subdivisions should each contribute £1 5s. The next stage would be that the elders of each subdivision would call on the various householders to contribute equally; or they might say that all grown-up men should contribute so much; or they might call on the women to contribute half, and exempt young men on the ground that they were accustomed to render other public services such as building bridges, clearing paths, or (in the olden days) fighting enemies. Very poor or sick people would not be called on to contribute. It would be agreed that the money should be handed to the official head of the group or, if he were unreliable, to its most trusted elder. When all the groups had obtained their money

[1] Childless people are often debarred from taking part in these rites.

the total amount would be handed to the senior elders of the village-group, who would appoint one or two of their number to buy the cow; or if the cow had to be obtained from a distance would authorize some young men to go and purchase it. When the cow had been obtained the priest of the cult would, in consultation with the elders, make all the necessary arrangements for the sacrifice, the day chosen being a day sacred to the deity.

Many priests of Ala are chosen by divination (from particular families). It may thus happen that the official priest is a mere lad. In such cases he receives instruction from an uncle or elder brother or cousin. The latter may even act as the lad's deputy, and, before offering sacrifice, would explain to Ala that he was acting on his young relative's behalf. During the sacrifice the lad places his hand on his relative's arms as a sign that he is conferring the necessary authority.

In some cases, where it is considered that the deity has been polluted, sacrifice may be performed not by the local priest but by some stranger hired for the purpose. Thus, in cases of death from dropsy, which is regarded as an 'abominable' disease, a stranger would be invited to offer sacrifice to Ala.[1] The family of the dead man would provide a tortoise, fowl (of special breed), and sheep. The stranger, a medicine-man, would call on Ala to prevent the recurrence of the extraordinary thing (death by dropsy), and then would consign the tortoise to the 'evil bush'. The sheep and fowl would be appropriated by himself. He would now proceed to make a 'medicine' by cutting a fowl into pieces, adding oil, eggs, and certain secret materials. As he mixed them together he would keep repeating, 'Ala, I seek to appease your wrath. Do not punish many for the sin of one. One man committed abomination and is dead. The others (his relatives) have done no sin.' He would then sprinkle some of the mixture here and there in the compound, and some also on the bodies of the various members of the deceased's family.

Priests of Ala were always important members of the community. But the degree of their importance varied with their own personal characters, and also with local circumstances. In some communities they were unimportant compared with the members of the titled societies, but in others again they were regarded as the ceremonial presidents of the group. Indeed, in a few groups the priest of Ala was

[1] If the deceased had died in his own home. If he had been previously segregated in the 'bush' no sacrifice would be necessary.

said to be the 'owner' of the group. In these communities, therefore, the priest had a principal say in all matters of importance. At the hearing of any dispute he frequently opened the proceedings with a libation to Ala, and, if the elders arrived at a decision which he considered unfair, he did not hesitate to express disapproval and to call for a reconsideration of the verdict on the ground that unfair judgements led to a 'spoiling of the land'. If any member of the group wished to take a title he had first to obtain the blessing of the Ala priest, to whom he took a pot of palm-wine. The priest tied a palm-leaf round the neck of the pot as a sign that the wine was consecrated to Ala, and then conducted the candidate to the shrine, where he poured some of the wine into a buffalo-horn and spoke as follows: 'Ala, this man is about to take a title; but before doing so he has brought this offering of palm-wine to you. Do you protect his life and that of all the members of his family. Avert from him the envy and hatred of others.' He then poured a libation four times over the symbol of the cult, emptying the horn at the fourth libation. Both drank the remainder of the wine together.

Similarly, before any one proceeded to perform the final funeral rites for his dead father, he might go to the local priest of Ala with a yam and a pot of wine. The priest escorted the man to the shrine of Ala, placed the yam on the ground, poured some of the wine into a gourd or horn, and spoke as follows: 'This man is about to perform the final funeral rites for his father. Many people will come from many towns to join in the rites; may they not fall in with thieves by the way. Grant that those who collect palm-wine for the rites may not fall from the palm-trees in doing so. May all who attend the rites behave with decorum. Let none kill another by striking him, and let no accident occur with the guns that are fired. Accept this man's offering and protect his life.' After pouring a libation on the cultus-symbol, the priest took the yam, touched the ground with it, placed it against the man's chest, and said: 'May your heart be strong.' Then he drank some of the palm-wine and gave some to the man. There was no fee for these services, but the man would, after killing the cow which is sacrificed at the final funeral rites, send a gift of beef to the priest of Ala.

In some communities the priest of Ala avoided taking any direct part in disputes, lest he should cause offence to Ala by mixing himself up in disreputable affairs. But in other communities he took a prominent part in trials, with a view to preserving good order in the community. Thus, if a man in one hamlet owed a debt to one in another, the creditor would approach the Ala priest of the debtor's hamlet, who, if the debtor refused to pay, would summon the elders of his own and the creditor's hamlet to a conference. The litigants would each be required to produce a pot of palm-wine as a fee to the elders. If the two parties of elders disagreed, each side would call elders from other hamlets of the village-group and they, together with the priests of Ala, would proceed to the defendant's compound. If the further inquiry showed that the debtor did in fact owe the debt, he would be called upon to pay a fine of one hundred currency rods for the unnecessary trouble he had given. If either party had shown disrespect to the elders, more particularly to the priests of Ala, during the hearing of the case, he would be required to apologize and bring a pot of oil. The senior priest of Ala would pour some of the oil into a wooden dish, dip his fingers in the oil, and apply it to his lips with the intention of assuaging the anger of Ala. He would then pour some of the oil on the ground, saying, 'There is now an end to this man's quarrel with the priests of Ala and the elders.' Then, pouring a libation on the ground, he would ask the deity to refrain from pursuing the offender. The proceedings would be concluded by all drinking palm-wine together.

Priests of Ala are subject to a number of taboos. Thus they are forbidden, as a rule, to eat food in another's house, or food cooked by a menstruous woman, or to sit or have sexual intercourse on the ground. In some communities widows and tattooed persons are forbidden to enter the houses of priests of Ala, and any one breaking this rule is required to hand a chicken to the priest, who waves it round the offender's head and then round the compound, and finally throws it away into the 'bush'.

It may be of interest to observe that just as men become taboo when they are involved in abnormal or 'unnatural' occurrences, so also do animals. Thus, if a goat climbs on to the roof of a house it is regarded as having committed an offence against Ala and is, or was in the olden days, handed over to an Aro trader to kill. For, if this were not done, one of the owner's kindred would die or be shot by an enemy in war. A cock that crows, or a hen that lays, at night in an open space is killed. The flesh is taboo to all save very old men, who are considered to be possessed of a dynamism which renders them immune from the consequences of eating a polluted thing. Just as human twins must be put to death, so it is ordained that a hen which hatches out a single chicken shall be deprived of its life. A fowl which pecks at an *aka* snake—a species sacred to Ala—must be handed over to the priest of Ala. A cow which bears two calves must be taken out of the community.

Individuals may, when directed by a diviner, make offerings to Ala through the priest of the public cult. On these occasions the priest, before offering sacrifice, takes a piece of chalk and marks the petitioner on the brow, chest, and shoulders. He also puts marks on himself and on the sacrificial animal. At some common shrines of Ala, however, sacrifice may be offered directly by any grown-up male at the instance of a diviner. Or the diviner himself may offer sacrifice on the man's behalf. The intervention of the priest is not required. But there is a rule in some localities[1] that sacrifice must never be offered by one whose teeth had not been chipped and filed, for Ala would refuse to accept the sacrifice of such a person. In former times it was also considered an 'abomination' for a man whose teeth had not been chipped to beget a child. If he did so the child was at birth handed over to Aro slavers. With this we may compare the rule which enforced banishment on a man who had begotten a child without having been circumcised.

Again, sacrifice may be performed on behalf of individuals or the whole community by an *osu*, i.e. by a slave who had been dedicated to a cult. As regards these *osu* it may be noted that any rich man might in former times purchase a slave and dedicate him to one of his household deities. Such slaves were despised, but they did not lose all civil rights. Their property remained their own and was heritable by their descendants. Incidentally, no free-born person would use for seed purposes yams grown on the farm of an *osu*, as it is believed that such yams would infect his crop. The underlying conception appears to be that the yams and other property of an *osu* are dynamized or infected by the deity served by the *osu*.

Many families have their own private cults of Ala, and sacrifice is offered by the head of the family on all important occasions if the divining-apparatus indicates that this is necessary. If the family migrates to some other locality, the head of the family takes away with him the symbols of the deity, including the stones which had marked the former shrine, and the pot which is so often buried in the ground beneath the stones. In his new compound he digs a hole in which he places the pot and an egg, symbols of fertility. Covering

[1] e.g. at Ugbo (Awgu Division).

up the pot and egg he replaces the soil and plants the stones (three usually) on the surface. He then speaks as follows: 'I have left the former site of my home and come to reside here. I have brought you with me, that you may abide with me. You protected me well in my former abode and I beseech you to protect me equally well here.' If he had been unfortunate in his old home he would say: 'Aforetime you permitted me to suffer misfortune, but I pray that in my new home you will protect me better.' He then splits a kola and places the fragments, together with a libation of palm-wine, on the stones.

Under the control of Ala are numerous godlings or spirits, of whom the most prominent is Ajọku or Ajọkuji,[1] the guardian-spirit of yams. The cult of this spirit may be public or private, and he is symbolized in a variety of ways. Branches of ọha, ururu, and ogirisi trees may be planted together with a certain species of lily, a pot or bowl being sunk in the ground at the base of the trees. One or two monoliths, or a circle of stones, may also be associated with the cult, and at Ama-Imo the cultus-emblems included a wooden carving something like the following sketch:

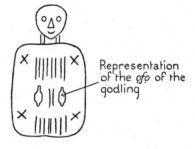

Representation of the ọfọ of the godling

Annual rites are performed before the planting of yams, and it is an offence in many communities for any one to plant yams until the completion of these rites. Thus, at Eha-Amufu, any one breaking this rule is required to give a gift to the Atama Aji or priest of the yams, and at Ache in former times the holders of titles seized a goat belonging to the offender, cooked it and shared the meat with the principal elders of the group. It is also essential that peace should reign in the community for some days prior to the rites, and any one breaking

---

[1] The word Ajọkuji seems to mean 'Spirit' (ajộ) 'great' (uku) 'yams' (ji), i.e. the great yam spirit. The term ajộ or jộ = spirit is found among the Jukun and among many African peoples. (See my A Sudanese Kingdom, p. 289.) Among the Ibo other variants of Ajọku are Njọku, Ojọku, Ifijiọku, &c.

this rule is liable to a fine. There may even be a rule that if a death occurs the relatives must refrain from announcing it in the usual noisy manner, by wailing and the firing of guns.

In the Awgu Division the rites followed before planting yams are usually as follows: On the appointed day each family-head brings a yam to the shrine of Njǫku. The yams are piled before the symbols of the cult, and the elders then squat behind the priest, who takes a pullet, and, holding it up in his right hand, speaks as follows: 'Njǫku, I have come to give you food and to tell you that we are preparing to plant our yams. May these yams grow up well, and may we remain alive to eat them. Grant that no one may meet with an injury during this farming year. Protect the lives of our men, women, and children.' The elders then hold out their hands, palms upwards, to the priest, who touches each with the pullet. The pullet is killed and as it gives its last kick the priest says: 'Njǫku has received the sacrifice.' He allows the blood to drip into the pottery dish, or between the stone symbols, saying, 'Njǫku, you have heard what we have said.' Next he plucks out a few of the wing feathers and fixes them in the congealed blood. The body of the fowl is thrown on the ground. The priest now cuts a yam into four pieces and deposits these on the symbol of the deity. Lastly he pours out slowly a libation of palm-wine, saying, 'Njǫku, come and drink palm-wine; Ala, come and drink palm-wine; Ndichie (ancestors), come and drink palm-wine. Njǫku, you have heard what we have said, protect our lives and our yams.' The remaining yams and the flesh of the fowl are cooked and eaten by the elders present, after small offerings have been deposited on the symbols. No women or young persons are allowed to be present at these rites.

Among the Ibo known as Oratta, before planting yams, the farmer (if not a Christian) takes a hen to his yam store, knocks its head against some yams, kills it, and pours some of the blood on the symbol of Ajǫkuji. (If he has no shrine or symbols he pours the blood on the ground.) As he does so he says, 'We are now about to plant our yams. May no accident befall us during the farming season, and may we live to eat the new yams.' This rite is known as *Epû ji opû*, i.e. removing badness from the yams. It is said that in former times some of the blood of the fowl was poured over the seed-yams and feathers were stuck in the congealed blood. But this practice was given up because of the opinion that the blood injured the yams.

Similar rites are performed at the yam harvest (in July), and in many communities the priest goes into seclusion for a period prior to the rites. Thus at Mpu and Okpanko (Awgu Division) the priest of Njọku goes into seclusion for a complete lunar month before the new-yam rites. During this period he may not look on a new calabash or on a man who has dug up a new yam or has visited another town and seen new yams being eaten. Not only is it an offence to eat new yams before the performance of the rites, but it is also an offence to introduce new yams from another town. Any one doing so, even if he were a stranger,[1] was in former times subjected to a fine of one ram, one cock, eight yams, and a pot of palm-oil which had to be at least one year old (Lokpanta). The priest, accompanied by the elders, then proceeded to the shrine of Njọku and spoke as follows: 'Njọku, a yam has been brought into our town before the time appointed. It was not our desire that this mischance should occur, and we bring to you these things in order that your wrath may be appeased. Do not, therefore, trouble us or prevent our yams from reaching maturity. May we derive a bountiful harvest of yams, possessing the full measure of nourishing qualities.' The ram and cock were then killed and, after small offerings had been placed on the symbols, the head and liver were appropriated by the priest, the rest being divided out equally among the kindreds represented. The head of each kindred subdivided his share among the other elders of his kindred. Some of the oil was used for cooking the portions offered to the deity, and the rest was appropriated by the priest. The yams were divided out without any offering being made to Njọku.

At Eha-Amufu (Nsukka Division) the yam-harvest rites are as follows. On a day appointed every householder proceeds to the compound of the Atama or priest, taking with him a wisp of grass. The Atama begins the rites by putting chalk marks on his forehead and shoulders. He then lays the piece of chalk on the ground and all the householders present mark themselves in similar fashion. The Atama now collects all the wisps of grass and ties them up into a bundle, which, together with a chicken and lizard, he waves round the heads of those present. After pouring a libation of palm-wine on the bundle of grass he lays some new cooked yams on the bundle and some on the ground. A rite of sympathetic magic follows. The Atama takes a snake's head, a thorn, and a dead bee, and encloses them in a pod, saying, 'Snake and bee, I close your eyes with this thorn.' Each

[1] If the stranger refused to pay the fine he would be roughly treated, and his host would be required to pay instead.

householder then comes up and places a thorn on the pod, saying as he does so, 'Snake and bee, I close your eyes.' When all have performed this rite, the Atama digs a hole in the ground and buries the pod, saying, 'Snake, bee, and thorn, I bury you so that you may hurt no one.' A heavy stone is then placed over the buried pod. A feast follows, and in this the new yams dug up on the priest's farm form part of the fare. That night the priest rings his gong as a signal that no one must leave his house. He then proceeds to a particular spot in the 'bush' which is taboo, and there throws away the bundle of grass, and with it all the evil and sickness of the previous year.

Among the Oratta, when the yams are ready for digging, each householder ties a palm-leaf round the symbol of each of his cults, kills a cock, sprinkles the blood on the symbols, cuts up a yam, and places pieces beside the symbols, saying, 'I and the members of my household are now ready to eat the new yams. May they give us health and cause us no injury. Accept, we beseech you, our gifts of yams, and may you not be defiled thereby.' The cock and some of the new yams are cooked, and morsels are placed on (or beside) the cultus-emblems. The members of the household then eat some of the new yams and the remainder of the chicken. This rite is known as *Era Nsi*, a phrase which seems to mean 'drinking poison'.[1]

In many communities (e.g. Mboo) coco-yam rites are also performed in honour of Njọku-Ede (the coco-yam spirit). These rites are commonly confined to females, and the cult is served by a priestess. No woman may plant her coco-yams until the priestess has first planted hers. For the rites the women of each section contribute a quota of coco-yams and a sum of money with which a goat and chicken are purchased. The priestess, accompanied by the senior women of the community, then proceeds to the shrine (men and young women being excluded). There the old women kneel, while the priestess walks round them with the goat and chicken, saying, 'Njọku-Ede, grant that the coco-yams which we are about to plant may grow up well. Grant also that our women may bear children, male and female. May males exceed females in numbers, for men-are producers, while women are consumers.' The goat and chicken are then killed and eaten, offerings being first deposited on the cult symbols. On the following day the priestess plants the first coco-yams. There are similar rites at harvest, the priestess being the first to dig her yams.

[1] Some of the younger generation who are Christians deride the elders for 'drinking poison' before eating new yams.

In some communities (e.g. Amowere, Ngbwidi, &c.) the year, i.e. the agricultural year, is personified under the name of Aho, in whose honour an annual sacrifice is made after the planting of the yam crop. If the year has been unfortunate, rites known as *Ichu Aho* or 'The driving out of the year' may be performed. In the evening, after sundown, every householder lights a fire of old palm-leaves outside his compound, and keeps beating a gourd, or some other resonant object, with a stick. The young men discharge guns on the paths leading to the town. In this way all the evil of the year is driven out of the community. At Ngbwidi the rites are initiated without warning by the priest of Ohara, for it is believed that, if preliminary arrangements were first made, the evil spirits, being forewarned, would succeed in concealing themselves.

One of the commonest public cults is that of the water-spirit known as Iyafo or Iyi Afo (*iyi* = river, and *afo* is either 'year', i.e. annual, or the name of the second day of the week sacred to the deity).[1] The Iyafo cult may also be known by the name of the local river. Thus at Owerri the cult is known either as Iyafo or Nworie, while at Ihiagwa and Okolochi it is known as Otamiri. In the Umu Oyima group at Owerri the cult is also known as Otamiri, and the ritual is as follows. During July a day is fixed for the rites, which must be carried out on the day of the week known as *Nkwo*. On the afternoon of the day, women of the group who are married in other groups return to their parents' homes, and each places packets of raw yams in a calabash, together with broken eggs, leaves (cut up), a few cowries, and some chalk. Before setting out for the shrine of Otamiri they shout out, 'Otamiri, olo! olo!' and as they go along the road they mark with chalk the face of every man, woman, or child they meet, saying, 'May Otamiri give you life so that you may be present at his feast next year also.' Those marked then enter their houses and maintain strict silence, while the women proceed to the shrine. Arrived there, they wave the calabash round their heads and deposit it on the ground beside the cultus-symbol, with a prayer for health for themselves, their husbands and children, and for the peace of their fathers'

[1] Compare the name of the Owerri River and the river-cult known as Nworie, which is a compound of *Nwa* = child and *Orie* = the first day of the week, i.e. Nworie = the child of Orie day. The Ibo week consists of four days named *Orie, Afo, Nkwo,* and *Eke*. But the four-day week is sometimes doubled and called a 'big week', and in this case the first day is known as *Orie uku* (big Orie), the fourth as *Eke uku* (big Eke), the fifth as *Orie nta* (little Orie), and so on. The day begins at sunset, so that if anything is taboo on a certain day the taboo lasts from sunset to sunset.

and husbands' towns. The women then take water-lilies from the river, place them in a calabash of water, and return home singing, 'We are returning home in peace, bringing with us children, health, and riches.' When they reach home they hand the calabashes to young men, saying, 'Here are the children we have brought. Drink of this water—it is life-giving water.' Some of the water may be given also to wives of the men of Okolochi in order to induce conception. The young men run about with the lilies, and then start throwing them at each other, the lilies being swept up on the following morning and thrown away.

At Nekede, Ihiagwa, and Okolochi the offering of the women at the shrine is followed by an offering by the elders. Four elders of each family-group split a yam in two, lay the pieces before the cultus-symbol, touch their foreheads, and say: 'May we be given health to perform this rite next year also.' On returning home the elders (or some of them) utter prophecies in the name of Otamiri, such as that the yam crop would be good or money scarce, many children would die, and many would be injured playing with their bows and arrows. The use of bows and arrows should, therefore, be discontinued by the children for a year. The prophecies are generally concluded by the elders saying, 'Otamiri declared to us that he had seen young women passing by, that he had seen many in childbed, and that he had seen many babies arriving in the town.'

At Owerri there is an annual feast (known as Oru Owerri) in honour of Iyafo or Nworie, but owing to the spread of Christianity the feast is now kept by a few elders only. At Ubomiri the cultus-symbols of Iyafo are four carved wooden figures resting against some small trees. Close by is a large tree at the base of which there is an 'altar' of stones. At the entrance to the grove (which is also the grove of Eze-Ala, the Earth-deity, represented by two wooden images) there is an interesting adaptation of the cult to meet modern requirements in the form of a miniature shelter with a roof of corrugated iron. If any one contemplates building a house with a roof of corrugated iron, he will (unless he is a scrupulous Christian) ask the priest of Iyafo and Eze-Ala to perform sacrifice on his behalf at this miniature shelter. The fish in the rivers tenanted by Iyafo are regarded as the children of Iyafo and are therefore sacred. It is a cause of offence to the non-Christian elders that Hausa settlers and young Christians disregard the ancient taboo by catching fish in these rivers.

At Ache in the Awgu Division there is a cult of a river-spirit known as Achihi who is regarded as the mother of the people of Ache. Every year in December the heads of households bring a yam, and (or) some palm-wine to the priest.[1] The yams are piled outside the shrine. The priest selects eight yams and four pots of wine and places them in front of the symbol, which consists of a stone taken from the river-bed. As he does so he says, 'Achihi, behold your children! We have come to offer sacrifice to you. Protect our lives and help our yams to grow, in order that we may be able to make a suitable offering to you each year.' Then taking the eight yams he walks round the people, saying, 'Achihi, protect those assembled here and their wives and children. Increase the number of children and let no one sustain injury by falling from a palm-tree.' The priest cuts the yams in pieces, lays the pieces before the symbol, and pours a libation of wine over them. Finally he salutes the people four times by saying, 'Do you agree?' They reply, 'We agree.' The rites are concluded by the firing of guns.

It is customary also to offer a goat or cow to Achihi in March, and cows may also be dedicated to the spirit by any individual who feels so inclined. It was stated that in former times the members of the priest's local group claimed the right to appropriate goats from members of all other groups at Ache for a period of a fortnight before the Achihi rites were due. But as this custom led to inter-village fighting it was prohibited by the Government.

At Eha-Amufu (Nsukka Division) there is a river-cult, the priest of which is known as the Atama Ebe. Ebe is the spirit of the river and controls the fish, who are regarded as the spiritual counterparts of the inhabitants of Eha-Amufu. The big fish are the counterparts of the principal men of the village-group, while the fry are the counterparts of persons of no consequence. When a villager dies a fish dies, and when a fish dies a villager dies. It is taboo, therefore, to catch fish in the river, and much annoyance has been caused by visits of foreign fishermen who disregard the local scruples. Ebe, the spirit of the river, being the guardian of the fish, which are his children and messengers, is regarded as the giver of children to men, and is thus the object of public and private worship. Every year at the beginning of the rainy season a chicken is sacrificed to him. It is held in the water until a large fish comes and bites off its head. The chicken is then cooked, and parts of the offal are thrown into the river. Private sacri-

[1] The priest is known as *Ofọkanshi*, i.e. '*Ofọ* exceeds poison (black magic)'.

fice may be offered through the priest at any time by individuals who are directed to do so by a diviner.

Ikenga is the personification of a man's strength of arm, and consequently of his good fortune. At Owerri the symbol occurs only (so far as I could ascertain) in the form of a forked piece of wood some 6 to 8 inches long, with a flat bottom so that it can stand upright, and is part of the paraphernalia of a diviner, who carries it in his bag together with his *ọfọ* and his 'Ndum Agu' (symbol representing the spirit of divination). At Ubomiri (and no doubt in other groups also) rich men may have carved symbols of Ikenga with one or two horns. They are bought from a carpenter and are formally handed to the owner by some relative indicated by a diviner. The relative spits on the symbol and says, 'Ikenga, be pleased to endow this man with wealth and children, and do not burn him.' The owner offers sacrifice when he feels inclined, and on his death the symbol is thrown into the 'bush of evil'.

But Ikenga is not a cult of much importance at the present time, as it was formerly associated with the practice of head-hunting. In the Awgu Division every head-getter used to have a shrine of Ikenga, the symbol of which was an *ọha* tree. When a young man first obtained the head of an enemy in war he asked a lucky old head-getter to establish for him an Ikenga. An *ọha* tree was planted, and the old man laid a fowl at the base of the tree with some such prayer as follows: 'Ikenga, I have come to-day to "cut open" the Ikenga of this man. From you I have derived profit, whether I went to the right or to the left. Grant that things may go equally well for this man. May his sheep and goats bear numerous offspring, may he be successful in his hunting, and may his wives bear many children.' He then cut off the fowl's head and left the body *in situ* to rot.

The principal head-hunting cult, however, was that known as Ekweesu (or Ekwêsu). Ekweesu is an evil spirit, akin to some extent to the Satan or Devil of Christian, Jewish, and Muslim peoples. Crimes such as murder are due to his instigation. Owing to his evil nature it is usually taboo for any one to eat the meat of any animal which had been sacrificed to Ekweesu. When a man had obtained an enemy's head in war he took it immediately to the priest of Ekweesu, together with a chicken. The head was laid in front of the carved image of the deity. The priest then poured a concoction of *akọro* leaves over the head-getter's hands, saying, 'You are washing off the evil.' He also poured a libation over the skull, saying, 'Let not your

ghost worry this man who killed you. He is not the first man to begin
the thing he did.' Then addressing Ekweesu he said, 'This man went
out somewhere and returned with a head. He is not the first or second
to do so. He followed the ancient practice permitted by Chuku and
Ala. Do not kill him, therefore, and do not permit the ghost (*nkporobia* or *obi*) of the man to pursue him.' The chicken was then killed
and left in the cleft bamboo to rot.[1] The priest finally shaved the
head-getter's hair. A public dance by all head-getters followed, and
in this the new head-getter joined, holding the head in his left hand
and his matchet in his right. He sported an eagle feather on one side
of his head and a parrot feather on the other. The enemy's head was
subsequently cleaned (by being buried in the ground)[2] and handed
over to the senior member of the household who hung it up in the
roof of his house. Those who had taken heads were said 'to have
placed their hands on Ekweesu' and joined the warriors' age-grades
which acted as the policemen of the community.

There are numerous other minor deities. Thus at Ikem there is
Ora whose shrine consists of a large mound of earth surmounted by
cactus, each stem of which is laden with pottery dishes, gifts to the
spirit. Inside the compound of the Atama or priest there is a collection of over fifty pots which had been given by devotees of the cult.
These pots are of all shapes and sizes, and some are embossed with
human figures. The Atama has also a private shrine in his own house
at which he offers daily sacrifice. The shrine consists of a rectangular
mud wall $1\frac{1}{2}$ feet high enclosing a well containing a matchet, pot, and
some stones. Suspended above the shrine is a bundle of feathers with
a handle infixed. Before performing sacrifice the Atama lays this
bundle on the right-hand side of the shrine and places his whisk (a
buffalo tail) on the left-hand side. After ringing a double iron-gong
he proceeds to make his prayer and offerings of kola. It may be noted
that no one is allowed to sit on the Atama's seat and that no menstruous woman may enter his house or cook his food. When any of
his wives is in this condition she must confine herself to her own hut,
and on the conclusion of her period she is not permitted to cook
again until another of the Atama's wives has tapped all the cooking

[1] In some groups the priest pressed the chicken against the head-getter's arm and
then killed and ate it, the head-getter receiving a share. The priest might also rub
the head-getter's arm with white chalk.
[2] But according to a variant account the head was boiled by the priest of Ekweesu
and the flesh was buried.

utensils with the bone of a buffalo—a signal to the spirit that the woman is 'clean'.

One of the most important cults at Eha-Amufu is that known as Obum, who is regarded as a fertility spirit, the giver of rain, of crops, and of children. Public sacrifice is offered annually in the month of March, and if this were not done girls circumcised during the previous year would be unable to take up formal residence with their husbands. On the day appointed a goat is taken to the shrine and slain, the blood being poured over the symbol of the cult. The corpse is then carried to the priest's house, where it is cut up by one of the priest's assistants, who has to perform special purificatory rites before carrying out the duty. Yams are roasted and pounded into puddings by young men who are also required to make a seasoning for the puddings. The prepared foods, after being tasted by the priest's assistant, are covered with the goat's skin and carried to the shrine, where they are taken down from the shoulders of the young men by the priest's assistant, who has previously washed his hands in the holy water kept at the shrine. The priest then makes offerings to the spirit with the usual prayer, and his assistant distributes the viands in wooden platters brought by the heads of each kindred. Any deviation from the customary ritual vitiates the whole proceedings, and a case recently occurred in which the foods prepared could not be offered, as the priest's assistant, owing to a quarrel with the priest, had refused to wash his hands in the holy water. As no offerings could be made to the spirit all the foods prepared had to be thrown away, since it would have been deadly for any to eat of sacrificial foods of which the spirit had not first partaken. Grave scandal was caused by the inconsiderate and impious conduct of the priest's assistant, who was summoned before the Native Court and heavily fined.

The Atama of this cult, who is regarded as the senior member of the village-group council, is subject to a number of taboos. He must avoid eating the flesh of leopard or any reptile, and if the word for dog is mentioned while he is eating a meal he must leave the meal unfinished. He must always sleep on a bedstead of mud and may not cross the boundary of his own town. If he is about to cross a river every one must make way for him and remain on shore until he has crossed. He is always chosen from a particular kindred (the Umoshibo of Umufu) and is saluted as Edoga—a form of salutation which is also found among the Okpoto tribe.

A private cult which has a wide distribution at Owerri is that known as Mbatako, a wealth-giving spirit. The shrine of this spirit is located at the threshold of the porch of the compound, and takes the form of a small platform of indurated clay containing rows of shells or cowries. A jaw of a goat or pig may be fixed into the clay, and a bowl is sunk so that the mouth of the bowl is level with the platform. A piece of twine, with nuts or pods of the *okpo ede* tree attached to it, is suspended from the roof to the bowl. It appeared that the twine was regarded as a conductor of wealth, Anyañu receiving wealth from Chineke, and passing it down to Mbatako by means of the twine. Every morning the householder sprinkles some water over the shrine, washes his hands, and asks Mbatako to bring him prosperity.

Among fertility cults there is one known as Ajọ-Omumu, the spirit of child-bearing. The symbol of this spirit is usually a circular collection of stones surrounding a mud pillar or tree (e.g. the *osismera* tree). Some of these cairns are as much as 15 feet in height, owing to the custom by which the father of a male child of three years presents to the priest a stone taken from the bed of a river which does not dry up. The priest adds this stone to the cairn, at the same time waving a chicken round the child's head and saying, 'May Ajọ-Omumu make you strong and enable your mother to obtain another male child.' He then kills the fowl, pours the blood on the stone, and sticks a feather on it. Sacrifice may be offered annually by the priest on behalf of each household, of which each grown-up male member[1] must provide a chicken (cock) and a piece of palm midrib, which is stuck into the ground before the shrine. The priest takes one of the chickens and speaks as follows: 'Ajọ-Omumu protect this man and all the members of his family. May their wives who are pregnant be delivered safely. But may they miscarry if their unborn children have the nature of thieves. May Ajọ-Omumu also bless the crops of this family.' The chickens are then killed by the priest and cooked by his wife or by the owners. Morsels of the cooked meat are placed on the cultus-symbol and the rest is eaten by the priest and members of the family.

Other spirits are Ihi, Agu, and Ngelisi. Ihi is said to be the personification of pity and the advocate of peace. If peace had been proclaimed between two towns, and Ihi had been invoked as a witness, he would take vengeance on any one who broke the peace. Agu is the spirit of divination, and all diviners periodically resort to the shrine

---

[1] Or a single chicken may be provided for the whole household.

of Agu, with a petition that their vision may be cleared, coming events may be foreseen, sickness cured, and their own pockets filled with money. Ngelisi is a protector of property, and if a person loses anything by theft he calls on Ngelisi to pursue and kill the thief. A case occurred recently of a woman helping herself to a few branches of a dead palm-tree. The owner, discovering the loss, called on Ngelisi to punish the thief. The woman, hearing of the curse, went to the owner and, explaining that she had taken the wood without any felonious intent, asked him to withdraw the curse. The latter refused. The woman then took the matter to the Native Court, as she had been assailed with an infection of the eyes, which she ascribed to Ngelisi. The court directed the palm-owner to withdraw the curse, the woman being ordered to meet the necessary costs. Oaths are commonly sworn by Ngelisi, and, if a person is believed to have died in consequence of swearing a false oath, his relatives are required to pacify the spirit by the sacrifice of a kid and the payment of two hundred and eighty currency rods to the priest of the cult.

Another example of the use of cults for the purpose of swearing oaths is the sacred stone at Ichi known as Nkum-Ichi. This stone is said to have been brought originally from Ida. The priest in charge offers private sacrifice to the indwelling spirit on every day of the week except *Eke*,[1] and twice a year public sacrifice on behalf of the whole town. When oaths are sworn on Nkum-Ichi the priest deposits a kola in the hole beneath which the sacred stone is buried. The accused kneels down and asks Nkum-Ichi to kill him if he is guilty, but if guiltless to let him go free. If the man dies within a year the priest goes to his compound and confiscates half his property, leaving the other half to his children. He also empties a dish containing oil, water, and split-kolas at the door of the dead man's hut, saying, 'You, Nkum-Ichi, killed this man. Let your anger now be assuaged, and allow the members of your victim's family to continue in life.' The body of the victim is buried in ground sacred to the cult, and in a manner dictated by a diviner, who may declare that the body must be buried naked or thrown away in the forest. But the relatives of the deceased may bribe the diviner and priest to allow the customary form of burial.

If the magico-religious system is to be an effective instrument of law, the supernatural powers to whom appeal is made must be champions of truth and justice. But there are bad spirits as well as

[1] See p. 36, footnote.

good, and the badness of certain spirits is sometimes only revealed
by bitter experience. In other words, supernatural sanctions do not
always work. A case of this kind occurred in the Awgu Division. At
Ache there is a water-spirit known as Nnemmiri-Ọha, symbolized by
an ọha tree and a number of material objects on which oaths may be
sworn. At one time these objects were constantly being requisitioned
by other communities as a medium for swearing oaths in cases which
could not be decided by direct evidence. But to-day many of these
communities would refuse to refer any dispute to the decision of
Nnemmiri-Ọha, as litigants who had sworn by him and had died had
been proved by subsequent evidence to have been guiltless. Nnemmiri-
Ọha, therefore, could be nothing but a lying-spirit—an assertion
which has given great offence to the people of Ache, who still seek
the spirit's aid on occasions of misfortune, particularly in cases of
children's illnesses.

Perhaps the most powerful of all legal instruments in Iboland were
certain well-known oracles which functioned as the highest courts of
appeal. Among these the most famous were Ubinokpabe or the oracle
of Chuku at Aro-Chuku, the oracle of Igwe-Ke-Ala at Umunọha, and
of Agbala at Awka. Before the destruction of the oracle of Ubinokpabe[1]
(or of the 'Long Juju' as it is called in pidgin English) pilgrimages were
made to Aro-Chuku from all parts of Iboland by disputants or persons
seeking divine assistance, either on their own account or on that of
the community they represented. Thus, if one man had accused
another of having practised witchcraft, the two men, accompanied
by their friends, might agree to refer the matter to the decision of
Ubinokpabe. Or, if sickness had carried off a number of a man's family,
he might set out for Aro-Chuku in order to ascertain the cause of his
misfortune and prevent any further loss. If he had suffered a serious
loss by theft he might go to Aro-Chuku in order to call down vengeance on the thief and if possible ascertain his name. If a name were
indicated he would, on returning home, arraign the person named,
have his house searched, and if the stolen goods were found would
seize the thief and hand him over to the local agent of the oracle. But
if the goods were not discovered the accused might merely be requested by the local elders to swear an oath of innocence.

Before setting out for Aro-Chuku the pilgrim first consulted the
local agent of the oracle as to ways and means. For if the journey was
not always long it was at least usually dangerous. The pilgrim had to

---

[1] By Government troops in 1901.

provide himself with introductions to the agents of the oracle in the various villages through which he would pass. Moreover, he had to be made acquainted with the numerous taboos which had to be observed on arrival. Thus it was taboo to utter the word *ede* (coco-yam), and a breach of this rule entailed a fine payable to the priests. It was taboo for any one's bag to come in contact with the water of the local river, and a breach of this rule entailed the confiscation of the bag and all its contents. And so on. In important cases the pilgrims or disputants were personally conducted by the local agent of the oracle, who on arrival privately primed the priests with full details of the points at issue. In due course the disputants were escorted to the mouth of a cave, and, after the priest had recounted to the god the story of each side, the god was heard to speak in a muffled voice. If the charge were one of witchcraft or poisoning, and the accused had been found guilty, he might be ordered to hand over one of his children to the family of his victim, or to pay heavy damages, or to go home and hang himself. But frequently the person adjudged to be guilty was seized by the ministers of the oracle, and was either put to death or secretly sold as a slave.

Those who had visited Aro-Chuku always brought back some water from the sacred stream and used it as a medicine for their sick relatives, who drank it and rubbed it on their faces and bodies. A pilgrim might also bring back from Aro-Chuku some sand taken from the river-bed, and with this he would set up at his own home the cult known as Nnemmiri-Chuku. The procedure was as follows. He planted first a branch of an *ọha* tree. Beside this he would also plant a palm-branch, the leaves of which he had knotted together. At the base of the *ọha* tree he would sink a pottery dish in which he would deposit the sand taken from the sacred river, together with some oil and water. He would then summon one of the local agents of the Aro, who, holding a fowl, would speak as follows: 'Nnemmiri-Chuku, this man is establishing you to-day in order that you may protect him and his children and his brothers and sisters, and that his wives and the wives of his relatives may bear children. When he goes to market may he obtain profit, may his crops grow well, and may he be brought home safely from any journey which he undertakes.' Then, waving the fowl round the heads of all present, he would kill it and allow the blood to drip into the pottery dish.

The influence of the oracle of Igwe-Ke-Ala at Umunọha was almost as great as that of Ubinokpabe. Thus if small-pox had been devastating a village-group, a number of men belonging to one of the hamlets or villages which had not yet been attacked by the disease might decide to seek assistance from Igwe-Ke-Ala. On arriving at Umunọha they would probably be told to return home and summon the principal elders of the village-group, as Igwe desired to see them and help them in their difficulties. (This was done with a view to extracting as much money as possible.) A general meeting of the elders of the whole village-group would then be called, and arrangements made for the collection of the fee required by the officials of the oracle. All the villages of the village-group would contribute equally, and all the kindreds of each village would also contribute equally (irrespective of their numbers). Each village would appoint a delegate, and when all the money had been collected the various delegates would set out for Umunọha. On their arrival there the deity (Igwe) would demand that a ram should be sacrificed to himself, and when this had been done he would instruct one of his ministers to accompany the delegates to their homes in order to carry out a local sacrifice on behalf of the stricken community. On returning home the delegates would introduce the minister of Igwe at a common meeting in the market, and arrangements would be made for a public religious ceremony and a further collection of money. On the day appointed for the ceremony the whole populace would assemble in the market-place, and there the minister of Igwe, holding a rattle in his right hand and a chicken and ram (led by a rope) in his left, would walk round the confines of the market, saying, 'May Igwe protect the people of this community; may he help their crops to grow well; and their women to bear children abundantly. May he drive away the sickness which oppresses the people.' He would then sprinkle the people with a medicine which he had brought from Umunọha, saying, 'I wipe away the evil of this community; and if this commune prospers in consequence of these rites then I direct that a share of the prosperity be paid to Igwe.' All present would then raise their hands in the air as a salutation to Igwe, and would take a leaf and smack it over the closed fist as a signal to Igwe that they had paid him honour and proffered a request. The leaves which had been smacked and broken would then be collected and placed in a pottery dish. To this collection the senior elder in each village would add a piece of *ọfọ*[1] stick as a guarantee of the good faith of all holders of *ọfọ*, and evidence of their participation in the rites. The dish would be handed to the minister

[1] See pp. 63 and 104.

of Igwe, who would take it back to Umuṇọha, together with the ram, chicken, and a sum of money. When the small-pox left the commune the people would be expected to present a further gift of one cow to Igwe.

If one commune had been waging an unsuccessful war against another, the elders might send a deputation to Umuṇọha in order to secure the good offices of the god. Similar rites to those described would then be performed. If a man's wife had proved unfruitful he would go to Umuṇọha with a substantial gift, and would be accompanied home by a minister of Igwe, who, on arrival, would take a chicken and say, 'Igwe, this man has come to you in search of children. It is not right that a man's wife should be childless. If there is an evil spirit that has followed this woman from her parents' home, may you, Igwe, cause it to depart.' The minister would then rub the woman's body with a medicine brought from Umuṇọha, and if in due course a child were born the father would take a cow to Umunoha as a gift to Igwe. (He would not usually fail to make this offering for fear that Igwe might kill the child.)

Disputes between two village-groups might also be referred to the decision of Igwe, each group contributing one-half of the expenses. Thus a few years ago the people of Ugueme accused those of Awgu of murdering one of their members, and the case was referred to Igwe. On arrival at Umuṇọha the suspected murderer was made to sit on a mat in front of the hut of the god. There he swore an oath as follows: 'Igwe-Ke-Ala, if I know how the dead man met his death may you take my life, that I may accompany him to the land of the dead. But if I am wholly ignorant of what befell him then do you pronounce my innocence.' Immediately, it is said, there was a sound like thunder, and the whole place was enveloped in smoke. The sonorous voice of Igwe was then heard to say, 'Hold up your right hand. I declare you to be innocent.'[1]

Local oracles of similar pattern were established at various places in the Awgu Division, and one or two have continued to carry on business secretly up to the present day. The site of the oracle consists usually of two huts, one of which is fenced off and is used by the personator of the god, his message being interpreted by a man outside —the god's minister. People resort to the oracles in cases of sickness or disputes. If a person suspects another of having committed theft

[1] For a further account of the part played in the judicial system by the oracle at Umuṇọha see pp. 238–42.

or adultery he will endeavour to obtain the sand or clay of the suspect's footprint and send it to the minister of the oracle. The latter will surround it with leg-irons as a magical means of effecting the suspect's arrest. Similarly, the soul of a suspect may be pinioned by driving a nail, representing the man, into the ground.

In the Nsukka Division there were also a number of oracles. Thus at Umujiofo (Eha-Amufu) the local cult of Ala was so organized that it had, like the Aro-Chuku oracle, agents scattered over a wide area, who induced disputants, or those who had met with misfortune, to seek the counsel or assistance of the deity at Umujiofo, and acted as their guides in return for a substantial fee. On the road to the shrine the agents elicited all the facts of the case and retailed them to the priest immediately on arrival. The priest's assistant, who acted the part of the deity, covered with a cloth in a recess of the shrine, was thus able to give an apposite answer to any question asked and might even forestall the question. In case of sickness the deity might prescribe a medicine to be taken by the patient on his return home. Or, if the inquirer suspected some one of having caused the death of a relative, the deity would direct him to take home a certain medicine, sacrifice a chicken in his compound and a pup which had not opened its eyes, chew or swallow the medicine, and then call for the death of the person who had caused the death of his relative. If the suspected person, whose name might be indicated by the deity, died within a year, his property was forfeit to the priest of the cult. In all cases in which the advice of the god and his medicines had proved to be efficacious additional fees were demanded by the priest.

It is obvious that oracles of the kind described were open to serious abuse and might be used as a means of committing murder, levying blackmail, dealing in slaves, and fomenting local enmities. Owing to their venality and the expense entailed in visiting them they favoured the rich against the poor. The most notorious oracles have therefore been suppressed by the Government. Nevertheless, it must be admitted that these oracles could hardly have attained and retained their enormous influence unless they had been administered with a considerable degree of impartiality and very considerable skill in the sifting of evidence. Their decisions can seldom have run counter to the weight of local opinion. At the present time many elders of the Awgu Division regard the destruction of the oracle at Aro in 1901 as an abominable outrage which has caused Chuku to withdraw his presence and protection from Iboland.

This chapter may be concluded by a reference to the custom found in the southern regions of Iboland (and possibly therefore imported from the Ibibio) of building at periodic intervals structures known as *mbari*, in honour of the gods or to avert their wrath. These buildings have the appearance of temples, but can hardly be described as such as they are not used for worship and serve a purely temporary purpose, being allowed to crumble into decay soon after their completion.

If the priest of a public cult has been sick for some time or has had mishaps in his family, or if leopards or epidemics have invaded his town, he may, on consulting a diviner, be informed that the deity he serves is demanding an *mbari*. The priest thereupon invites the principal elders of the village-group to a meeting at his house, and after providing them with palm-wine informs them of the wishes of the god. If the elders agree to the proposal, the general public are invited to plant a piece of ground (selected by the diviner) with yams for the subsistence of those selected to build the *mbari*; the married daughters of clansmen are summoned home to sing songs in honour of the god; and public subscriptions are raised to provide the priest with a wife, pay off any debts he may have, and add to his comfort generally.

When the yams are harvested the elders, assisted by a diviner, proceed to select the builders, each extended-family being required to provide one male and one female worker. Or in the case of small families one male may be chosen from one family and one female from another. Those chosen may be of any age, provided they are not grey-haired, and any one refusing to serve would become an object of public scorn, even in these days of Christian missions. In addition a number of persons who are considered specially adept at building may be selected by a diviner, one of whom is appointed as the principal architect. If the community has no highly skilled architect one may be hired from another village-group, sacrifice being offered to the god with a petition that he will accept the services of the stranger. Moreover, a doctor or medicine-man may be engaged to look after the health of the workers, as it would be a misfortune and pollution if any worker were to die during the construction of the building. On the appointed day a diviner ties a cord, with feathers attached, round the necks of all the chosen workers as a symbol of their bondage to the god; and their bodies and clothes are dyed with yellow pigment. The builders chosen give up their entire time to the work and must not engage in any private enterprise. They give their services free to

E

please the god, and to protect themselves and their families from his displeasure.

The first stage in the proceedings is the clearing of a space for the building on the confines of the village. This is done on a day sacred to the deity, and the builders are assisted by the townspeople. The cleared space is then enclosed by a fence so that the builders may be able to carry out their task in privacy. When the fence is completed the builders are formally escorted inside, together with the priest and doctor, and there they live a life of seclusion and abstinence for twenty-four days, singing songs in honour of the god and calling down his wrath on all who fail to carry out their duties. Such food as they eat is brought to them by selected messengers, but certain foods such as cassava, coco-nuts, and palm-nuts are forbidden during this period. Cassava, indeed, is taboo until the *mbari* has been completed.

After these preliminary rites the builders appear in public arrayed in their special *mbari* dress, with their clothes and bodies smeared with camwood oil. And then they begin the task of erecting the various buildings in which the clay statues of the gods and other representations of the life of the people are to be housed. The materials for the buildings are provided by the townspeople, each contributing a bamboo pole, a piece of matting, and some twine. The walls of the buildings are made of indurated clay, and the hut of the deity who had demanded the *mbari* is given the place of honour in the centre.

On the completion of the buildings there may be a further period of seclusion and then the immense task is begun of designing and executing the various representations of the local deities and of the various phases of local life. These are made from the hard soil of ant-hills, which is powdered down, mixed with water, and kneaded with soft clay. The ant-hill soil is obtained by the workers late at night, and as they go to the 'bush' in search of it they are escorted by a cult-slave who rings a bell to warn townspeople of their approach, for the workers must not be seen by the general public or any non-worker. Whoever breaks this rule or enters the enclosure during the period of construction is required to pay a fine of one or two goats. If any domestic animal wanders into the enclosure it is immediately put to death.

Work is continued daily and may last for a year or longer, the workers sleeping nightly in a special house built for them in the priest's compound. When all is completed the fencing is removed and the workers migrate for one night to a neighbouring village. They return next morning, inspect their own work, and give vent to expressions of surprise and wonder as though they had seen it for the first time. They then run to the waterside, rub themselves with a chicken (which they throw away), and wash themselves, using palm-fibre as a sponge or loofa. It was stated that one object of the washing was to purify the builders from the pollution of unavoidable sexual intercourse with relatives, the male and female builders being (for the most part) members of a single exogamous group. After this rite the building is thrown open to the general public, a festival (marked by considerable sexual licence) being held to celebrate the occasion.

It may be noted that during the building of an *mbari* the towns-people are expected to refrain from engaging in disputes, and are even requested to avoid taking out summonses in the Native Courts. The priest acts as adjudicator and, assisted by the elders, may fine any one for creating a disturbance or shedding blood, the fine being appropriated by the priest and builders. Christian members of the community do not now feel it incumbent on them to observe these regulations, and in due course, no doubt, one more taboo, which had served a useful purpose as a controlling force, will have disappeared altogether.

An *mbari* built recently at Owerri is still in good condition. One section of the building contains clay images of Olugba (the spirit of Nwa-Eberre pond), his wife, and children. There are also figures of an elephant, baboon, and a man shooting a leopard. Near by is an image of Amadi-Qha (the god of lightning) with his wife and children, and clay figures of a woman grinding corn, a number of Christian converts, a man shooting an elephant, and a baboon riding an elephant. (There is an Ibo folk-story which tells how a baboon made fun of an elephant by riding it.) Behind the shrine of Olugba there is a representation in clay of a woman giving birth, seated on the ground. A female attendant is shown standing behind her, holding her shoulders, while in front the midwife is receiving the baby. At the side is a medicine-man holding a bunch of leaves or some other charm to facilitate delivery. Behind Amadi-Qha's shrine there are representations (in clay) of a number of dancing-girls, and in a separate compartment a European District Officer is shown, accompanied by police. There is also a trial scene in a Native Court. At one corner of the main courtyard a team of British maxim-gunners is shown, with the gun pointed at a team of German gunners at the opposite corner of the courtyard. Another section of the building contains pottery images of a horseman, a man riding an ostrich, four policemen on guard-duty, and a number of young men and women talking together. Close by are representations of a motor-lorry, men and women engaged in making palm-oil, and children bringing firewood to the workers. In another direction a bandmaster and band are shown, and a hunter with a dog. In one corner a man and woman are shown in the act of copulating, and in another corner there is a representation of a woman copulating with a dog. It was stated that this was a woman of Ihiagwa whose name had become a by-word, and that the object of depicting her was to deter other women from following her example. What appear to us to be gross indecencies were excused on the ground that an *mbari* should reveal every phase of human existence, being as it were a concentration of the whole social life of the community. Hence the figures depicting the details of childbirth, which are ordinarily considered to be the secret of women and unmentionable in the presence of men.

The whole arrangement of an *mbari* displays a high measure of organizing ability, and the figures are skilfully designed and extremely realistic. There is a considerable variety of colour. Yellow pigments obtained from a yellow clay or species of decayed wood are employed, black pigments from charcoal, slate-coloured from clay, red from camwood, and white from chalk. Apart from its ostensibly religious object, the building of an *mbari* provides an outlet for the aesthetic feelings of the people. And the possession of such a building adds not a little to the prestige of the commune.

III

THE SACRED SANCTION (*continued*)

B. Ghosts and Secret Societies

THERE is a tradition among the Ibo that, when death first invaded the world, men sent a dog as a messenger to Chuku, asking that the dead might be restored to life and sent back to their old homes. The dog did not go straight to Chuku, but dallied on the road. A toad, which had overheard the message and wished to punish mankind, overtook the dog and, reaching Chuku first, said he had been sent by men to say that after death they had no desire at all to return to the world. Chuku declared that he would respect their wishes, and, when the dog arrived later with the true message, Chuku refused to alter his previous decision. And thus, though a human soul may be reincarnated, it does not return with the same body and personality as before.

This seems to be a garbled version of a tradition which is widely current in Africa. It occurs in a more coherent form among the Margi of Nigeria, who say that, when death first entered the world, men sent a chameleon to God to ascertain the cause. God told the chameleon to let men know that if they threw baked porridge over a corpse it would be restored to life. But as the chameleon was slow in returning, and death was rampant in their midst, men sent a second messenger—a lizard this time. The lizard reached the abode of God soon after the chameleon had left, and God, being angered at the second message, told the lizard that men must dig a hole in the ground and bury their corpses there.[1] The lizard reached home before the chameleon, and when the chameleon arrived the corpses had already been buried. And thus, owing to the impatience of men, or the deceit of the lizard, the ghosts of the dead are forced to hover round their graves until they are released by the final funeral rites to a realm from which they may be reborn.

Traditions of this kind, however inconsistent they may be, show a deep interest in things metaphysical, and this is illustrated further by the Ibo view of the human personality. A man's body is known as *aho*,[2] and the general word for life is *ndo*. But the word

---

[1] A variant says that God gave the lizard the same reply as he had given the chameleon; but the lizard falsified the reply.   [2] Or *aro* (*arɵ*).

for heart, namely *obi*, is also used in the sense of life or personality
or soul. The life-giving principle or vital essence may be more
particularly described as *nkporo obi* or 'heart-seed'. The most general
word, however, for 'soul' (whether of a living or a dead person)
is *mmuọ*.[1] In a living person the *mmuọ* is regarded as centred in the
heart, and so is synonymous with the *nkporo obi*. If a man is suddenly
frightened it is said that his *obi* or his *mmuọ* has taken temporary flight.
A man's shadow is known as *inyunyuro* and this appears to be a manifestation of the *mmuọ*. A worker of black magic can, it is thought,
kill a man by making a 'medicine' to stab his shadow. Since the *mmuọ*
leaves the body at death, a corpse is presumed to be incapable of casting
a shadow. (And care is therefore taken by knowledgeable people to lay
out a corpse in such a position that the light will not cause it to cast
a shadow.) The surviving part of a dead man is the *mmuọ* which is
propitiated by his descendants. But it is the *mmuọ* which becomes
reincarnated (or at any rate part of the *mmuọ*, for propitiatory
rites are still offered to the *mmuọ* of a dead man, even though he is
believed to have been reborn in a living descendant). Some of the
Owerri Ibo say that a rich, important man may be reborn into more
than one person: his hand may be reincarnated in one man, his foot
in another, his head in another, and the main part of his *mmuọ* in a
fourth. Persons who are reborn are usually reborn into the families
of their fathers. But some are reborn into the families of their
mothers. A case was cited of a new-born baby dying immediately
after a visit by its mother's relatives. It was stated that the child
was a reincarnation of one of the mother's relatives, and died because
it could not bear to be left in the father's group. In another case a
woman, who was known to be devoted to her sons but disliked her
daughters, died. When her favourite son became the father of a baby
girl it was declared by a diviner that the baby was the reincarnation
of the father's mother. The father's sisters were accordingly forbidden
for a considerable time to go near the child, but permission was
eventually given, after the sisters had offered sacrifice to the father's
ancestors through the *okpara* or senior elder of the extended-family.

It is said that a bad man may be reborn as an animal, and an animal
as a man. A man may also be reincarnated as a tree. In cursing
another, therefore, an Ibo may sometimes express the hope that the

---

1 This word (*mmɵɔ*) varies tonally and otherwise in different localities and is to be
distinguished from *mmọ* (*mmɔ*) = the maskers who personate the ghosts. The spelling
given in both cases is provisional.

other will be reborn not as a human being, but as a tree or a wild beast, or as an *okpango* or ape-like being!

One of the most striking doctrines of the Ibo is that every human being has, associated with his personality, a genius or spiritual double known as his *chi*. This conception of a transcendent self is not confined to the Ibo, for it has been found and described among the Jukun of the Northern Provinces.[1] And it seems to persist even among the Muslim Hausa, in the veneration commonly paid to the after-birth, which is regarded as the child's spiritual counterpart. It closely resembles the Egyptian conception of the *ka*, which was the double or genius of a man, an ancestral emanation, apparently, which guided and protected him during his lifetime and to which he returned after death.

The Ibo *chi* or personal genius is associated with a child from the moment of its conception, and if the child of a rich man dies at birth it is said that the child's *chi* had treated it badly (by preventing the child from enjoying the good fortune of having a rich father). When a dead person is reincarnated he is given (by Chineke) a different *chi* from that possessed by him in his former life. Hence the saying that a rich man in this life will be poor in the next. A man's abilities, faults, and good or bad fortune are ascribed to his *chi*, and this explains, to some extent, the fatalistic attitude of the Ibo. If a man's conduct gets him into trouble he excuses himself by saying (and believing) that his *chi* and not he himself is responsible. If he stumbles on the road or is bitten by a snake, his misfortune may be ascribed to his *chi* who is annoyed, perhaps because his associate had sacrificed to him a chicken when he could easily have afforded a goat! When a child whimpers in his sleep it is a sign that he is quarrelling with his *chi*, and when he derives no benefit from his food it is because his *chi* has devoured the essence or nourishing qualities of the food.

Animals have their *chi*, and if a hunter misses an animal he ascribes his failure to the animal's *chi*. An animal may become the *chi* of a man, and people who behave in a brutal manner are believed to have the *chi* of an animal It is said that the children of hunters are liable to have the *chi* of animals slain by their fathers. In this way animals revenge themselves on men.

[1] See my *A Sudanese Kingdom*, pp. 206–8. The Jukun commonly describe the companion spirit as their 'mother in Kindo' (Underworld). With this we may compare the Ewe doctrine of the *tasi* or spiritual aunt.

In speaking of the connexion between the *chi* and animals it may be observed that sometimes, where there is no *chi*-cult, the people believe that they have spiritual counterparts in fish or snakes. Thus at Okpanko the male members of the village have no *chi*-symbols, but they believe that their doubles reside in the fish of the River Ivo, each fish being part of a man's *obi*, i.e. heart or vital essence. Ivo is therefore regarded as the mother of the people, and as a creator of men on behalf of Chi-Okike. When a man dies his soul goes to Ivo, and Ivo gives it back to Chi-Okike. When he is to be reborn Chi-Okike gives back the soul to Ivo, who recreates simultaneously a man and a fish.

The Ibo, therefore, have some very definite totemic beliefs. But they are of religious rather than social significance. Nevertheless, it is of interest to observe that where two persons are deemed to share the same *chi* their children must not intermarry. If the children were to intermarry they would either fail to generate children themselves, or, if they obtained children, those children would soon die. Persons who share the same *chi* (a fact revealed by a diviner) regard themselves as one, and refrain, therefore, from injuring or even saying evil things of one another.

Although the *chi* comes into association with a person immediately on conception, the person associated with it does not usually establish a formal *chi*-cult until he (or she) marries or becomes a parent.[1] During the owner's youth his *chi* shares in the sacrifice which his father or uncle offers to his own *chi*. But after his marriage or the birth of his first child a separate *chi*-cult is established for himself and his wife and child. Thus, in many localities of the Awgu Division, a month or two after the birth of his first child the husband goes to a river-bed and obtains a round stone, the idea of the roundness being that the child's life shall be smooth. This is done at night with a view to avoiding any one infected with evil influences. He places the stone in his barn beside an *ọha* or *obo* tree previously planted there, and at the base of the tree digs a hole and inserts a pottery dish to serve as a receptacle for food-offerings.[2] The husband's elder brother, or the head of his family, then takes a fowl and, standing before the symbols, speaks as follows: '*Chi* of So-and-So, to-day we are establishing you here. May you protect So-and-So well, and enable him to beget

[1] But in some localities (e.g. at Abọ) boys and girls may be given their *chi*-symbols at the age of seven or eight, though their fathers and mothers perform the rites until the children set up homes for themselves.

[2] E.g. oil and pieces of fish or fowl.

children who will live to a good old age. Prosper his crops and give increase to his cows and sheep, and grant that no evil may overtake him.' He then kills the fowl and sprinkles the symbols with the blood, sticking a few of the feathers in the blood as it congeals.

Simultaneously a *chi*-cult is established for the wife, by the wife's brother, close to her kitchen. He, too, seeks a rounded stone from the bed of a river that does not dry up during the dry season (with the intention that the woman's life shall flow on uninterruptedly like the river). He then hands the stone to his sister's mother, who places it on the stone symbol of her own *chi*, saying, 'My *chi*, to-day I am giving my daughter her *chi*. Be pleased, my own *chi* and *chi* of my daughter, to look after me and her and our children well.' The husband may then take a chicken and speak as follows: '*Chi*, you have heard what has been said. Give ear to our petition and you shall be the recipient of many offerings.' He then kills the fowl and pours the blood on the stone. The flesh is cooked and eaten, after morsels have been deposited on the stone.

The woman now places the stone in a basket and goes back to her husband's home, where her brother or her husband's senior brother (or cousin) plants branches of *ogirisi*, *obo* and *ichichiri* trees, and lays the stone beside them with a prayer for her prosperity, and that '*one by one* her house may be filled with children'. This phrase is used as a preventive of twin-births. In the evening food is prepared by the wife, and pieces of food are again deposited at the respective shrines with the words: 'You have heard what we have said. If you protect this man and his wife and child, you shall have everything you want—whether it be a fowl, dog, or goat.' The woman herself places some morsels of food on the stone, saying, 'My *chi*, look after me well, and look after my husband and child. Keep me in health and help me to obtain profit in the market, and a good harvest of crops.'

Thereafter the man and his wife offer sacrifice to their respective *chi* as they feel inclined. New yams are seldom eaten without sacrifice to the *chi*. Thus, in the Owerri area, the rites known as *Erọ Chi* or 'The Purification of the *Chi*' are always performed at the yam-harvest. The wife takes an *oboba* leaf, folds it, fills it with water, and empties it over the symbols,[1] saying, '*Chi*, wash your hands and eat.' The husband

---

[1] The symbols at Owerri are three pieces of *oboba* branch each about 6 inches long. One is said to represent Chi, one Eke (Creation), and one Owa (Destiny). They are kept in a pot which is hung up in a corner of the wife's hut. If a man has more than one wife, each wife has a pot-symbol, and the husband's symbols are kept in the pot

THE SACRED SANCTION

58

follows suit. The wife then takes some pieces of a boiled egg and mashed yam, mixes them into four lumps, places them in a calabash spoon, waves the spoon round the heads of her husband and children, and throws the lumps on the symbols,[1] saying, 'May your lives be maintained by my *chi*.' The husband does likewise. The wife then takes chalk from the *chi* pot and marks her face and the faces of her husband and children. The husband follows suit. The husband and wife then go before the symbols of the husband's *chi* and the above rites are repeated, the husband acting first in this instance, and concluding the rites by saying, 'Our *chi*, having done what you require, may you do what we require.' He replaces the *chi*-symbols in the pot, and if he has a goat which has been dedicated to his *chi* he may place a few of the goat's hairs in the pot.

If a person is consistently unfortunate, he may give up sacrificing to his *chi* on the ground that it is not worthy of sacrifice. Some say that the reason why a person does not begin sacrificing to his *chi* until he has married and obtained children is that the *chi* of a person who is unable to found a family is unworthy of notice. It is for this reason that in some communities (e.g. Ugbo) it is unusual to establish a *chi*-cult until a large family has been obtained, i.e. until the *chi* of the parents has proved itself to be of substantial worth.

It would appear, then, that the *chi*-cult is to a great extent a fertility cult, and it may be for this reason that in many localities the husband's and wife's symbols (a stick and pot respectively) seem to be emblematic of the male and female genital organs. Moreover, husbands sacrifice to their *chi* when their wives are in labour, and in many localities when a man dies his wife's *chi*-symbols are thrown away with his own, as a woman cannot sacrifice to her *chi* without her husband's presence. Similarly, when a married woman dies, both her and her husband's *chi*-symbols are destroyed.[2] If the husband remarries, he sets up a

of the wife who was the last to bear a child. At Ama-Imo the symbols are four pieces of *ọha* wood representing (1) Chi, (2) Eke, (3) Owoma, and (4) Ezumeze. Owoma is the Ama-Imo equivalent of Owa, and Ezumeze is the personification of 'completeness'. Ezumeze seems only to be added when a man becomes a grandfather.

[1] The lumps of yam and egg are eaten by rats in the night, or are swept up and thrown away next morning.

[2] But the husband's symbols are retained if he has another wife. And in some localities (e.g. Ọgwa) a husband may retain his *chi*-symbols after the death of his wife. If he remarries he offers sacrifice to his *chi*, informing his *chi* that he has taken a new wife. If a wife leaves her husband she may take away her *chi*-symbols after her bride-price has been repaid.

fresh *chi*-symbol when his wife bears a child. He may, if directed by a diviner, set up a fresh symbol before his new wife bears a child, but when he offers sacrifice the wife must stand outside the hut. A widower or widow may, however, offer sacrifice to his or her *chi* even though the regular symbols have been destroyed, using as a symbol the prong of a palm-leaf broom which is stuck into the ground below the spot where the *chi*-pot formerly hung. In some localities men have no *chi*-cult at all, and women only establish the cult when they have become mothers. At Mboo women establish the cult after they have borne four children, but at other places in the Awgu Division a woman may establish the cult if she has conceived three times, even if she has never given birth to a live child. In other places again (e.g. at Nkwe) a woman is not allowed to establish a *chi*-cult during the life-time of her mother. Lastly, in some communities (e.g. at Ọgwa) the *chi*-symbols are not destroyed on the death of the husband or wife but are left for the use of their children. But nowhere are the *chi*-symbols of a dead man preserved after the death of his children, as it is said that a grandfather cannot injure his grandchildren, a belief which is almost universal in Negro Africa.

At Owele and a number of other localities men have no *chi*-cults, but their cult of Ala-Ubi seems to serve the same purpose; for the cult is established one month after the birth of their first child and the symbols are an *obo* tree surrounded by a pile of stones, with one flat stone in the centre. After setting these up the owner holds a goat by a rope in his right hand, and a chicken in his left, and speaks as follows: 'To-day I am establishing you, my Ala-Ubi. Protect me and my wife and child and everything I own. May my crops increase and help me to obtain wealth. Guard my home from all evil.' He then kills the goat and pours the blood over the central stone and then on the other stones. He smears some also on the *obo* branch, and sticks feathers in the congealed blood. After cooking the flesh he deposits morsels on the symbols. Later he cleans the skull of the goat and lays it on the flat stone, as evidence of his sacrifice.

Just as the constituent elements of a village-group are united by the common possession of a cult of Ala, so occasionally the various villages of a village-group or clan may claim to be one by the possession of a common *chi*. Thus the four villages of the Umu-Chi-Eze clan appear to be united by the belief that they have a common *chi* which is the mother of them all. Every year in January sacrifice is performed in honour of this *chi*, which is symbolized by a stone and an African oak-tree. On the morning of the appointed day the priest goes to the shrine, which is located in a grove, and, standing before the symbols, throws a pinch of snuff on the ground, saying, '*Chi-ǫha* of the Umu-Chi-Eze, take snuff and use it.' He then takes a kola, splits it, and throws a piece on the ground, saying, '*Chi-ǫha* of the Umu-Chi-Eze, accept this kola. I have come to clean your shrine, in order that sacrifice may be offered to you. Protect me and my family and every member of the Umu-Chi-Eze, excepting those who tamper with the lives of others.' He then sweeps the shrine and goes away. At midday he returns, accompanied by his relatives, male and female, who squat round in a circle. The priest, holding the sacrificial goat, then speaks as follows: '*Nnǫche* (grandmother), *Chi-ǫha* of the Umu-Chi-Eze, I have come to offer sacrifice to you on behalf of all the Umu-Chi-Eze. Avert evil, of whatever kind, from them. Protect the lives of all save poisoners and thieves, and grant that women who are childless may bear children.' He then cuts the throat of the goat and pours the blood on the stone. Taking a gourd of palm-wine he waves it over the heads of the people and pours a libation, saying, 'Protect the lives of great and small; let no one be lost.' Refilling the gourd he drinks some wine himself, and then gives a share to the others present. The flesh of the goat is now cooked (by young lads), and when it is ready some is placed in a special wooden dish which the priest lays on the stone, saying: '*Chi-ǫha*, you have heard our request. Be pleased to comply.' The rest of the meat is divided out and eaten by all present. On the conclusion of the repast one of the priest's sons rubs some chalk on the left hand and chest of all males present, the priest included. He rubs some also on the breasts and abdomen of the women. Finally the priest rings a bell and says: 'Our mother, you have done well by us—permit us to depart.' In the evening the whole populace assembles near the shrine and engages in dancing and the firing of guns.

The priest of this cult is subject to a number of taboos. He may not sleep away from his home, or have sexual relations with a widow, or allow a menstruous woman to enter his home, or sympathize with a mourner. The reason for the last prohibition is that, as Chi-Okike may have taken the dead man's life, an expression of sympathy would be an affront to the deity.

It did not appear that the belief in a common *chi* was so strongly held that it prevented the component villages of the group from fighting among themselves. Nor had it any effect on the marriage regulations, as intermarriage between the different villages and hamlets of the group is frequent.

The Cult of Ancestors.

All Ibo believe that their lives are profoundly influenced by their ancestors, and this belief has far-reaching sociological consequences. Any departure from custom, for example, is likely to incur the displeasure and vengeance of the ancestors. The ancestors, under the presidency of Ala, are the guardians of morality and the owners of the soil. The cult of ancestors is also one of the strongest forces for maintaining the unity of the social group. The head of the group owes his authority largely to the fact that he is the representative and mouthpiece of the ancestors. The belief in the power of the ancestors also influences the relations of parents and children, for many parents show an excessive indulgence towards their children on the ground that they will be dependent on their children for their nourishment and status[1] in the next world. Moreover, as they may be reborn into the world by their own children, they may expect harsh treatment if they had previously treated their children harshly. A son who ill-uses his father is often excused on the ground that his father had in a former life ill-treated him. On the other hand, many parents are not afraid of dealing roughly with their children when necessary; for if, after their (i.e. the parents') death, the children vindictively refuse to perform adequately the final funeral rites, the dead parents can retaliate by heaping misfortunes on their descendants. The ancestors are believed to be the cause of many illnesses. Sacrifice has, therefore, to be offered to them at regular intervals, or when a diviner indicates. And it is customary also at meal-times for the head of the family to throw small offerings of food on the ground as a gift to the family ancestors.

Sacrifice[2] to the ancestors can only be performed directly by the senior representative of the family-group concerned. Thus the senior member of a household sacrifices on behalf of himself or any member of his household, and the senior member of a kindred on behalf of the kindred. If the whole local group claims a common ancestor the sacrifice must be performed by the senior member of that group, i.e.

---

[1] Inadequate final funeral rites affect adversely a dead man's status in the Underworld.

[2] The word sacrifice is used with reservation. The Ibo 'sacrifice' to the ancestors is often more a communion of food than a gift or anything else.

by the oldest of the whole group or by the oldest of the senior branch
(as the case may be). It is not permissible, as a normal rule, for a man
to offer sacrifice to his dead father if his elder brother or cousin is
alive and physically able to perform the sacrifice.

The ancestors are known as 'Ndichie' or 'Ndi-Oke', and the symbols
used to represent them are frequently addressed by one or other of
these titles. The symbols may be a mud pillar, iron staff, stones, or
other object. At Owerri and neighbouring towns the symbol of the
ancestors is a wooden pillar about a foot thick and one and a half feet
high. It is fixed inside the householder's *obi* (entrance hut) facing
outwards, so that the ancestors can see what is going on. In the wall
immediately behind the pillar a wooden panel is fixed, with a number
of holes bored in it, so as 'to give eyes to the ancestors'. There are
variants of the design as, for example, in the following sketch.

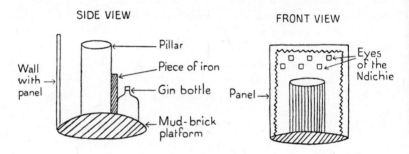

Female ancestors are not represented. The owner of the cult offers
sacrifice at the various agricultural festivals, or when a diviner advises
him to do so. Or, if he is about to drink some wine, he may first pour a
little over the pillar.

Sometimes four sticks known (at Owerri) as *Ndiuku* are planted
close to the Ndichie symbols. When they are first set up, the officiant,
accompanied by the householder and two male and two female elders
of the group, kills a chicken and pours the blood over the sticks,
saying, 'To-day we are planting *Ndiuku* that the owner of this house
may live long and defeat all his enemies.' Kola-nuts and palm-wine
are also offered, and a tortoise is fixed to the spot by a skewer passed
through its body. The tortoise is left there to rot (and some entrance
huts have, therefore, an offensive smell). It was not clear whether the
Ndiuku represented ancestors directly, or a protecting spirit emanat-
ing from the ancestors. In other groups, particularly among the Isu,

the ancestors are directly represented by four sticks (two of *oha* trees and two of *ururu*) planted in an open part of the compound.

Yet another symbol of the ancestors (in the Owerri Division) is that known as *umunne*. This word means 'children of one mother'.[1] An *umunne* symbol, therefore, represents the ancestors of an undivided extended-family, and in particular the founder of the family. One observed at Obokpo (Ubomiri group) consisted of a wooden pillar, with carved human features, mounted on a mud-brick platform in which six sticks were stuck. The pillar represented the founder of the extended-family, while the six sticks represented various deceased descendants. A knotted palm-leaf was lying among the six sticks, and it was said that this had been placed there before the various householders had offered sacrifice at the time of dividing out the family farm-land (i.e. at the beginning of the agricultural season). The intention was (it was said) to prevent the ancestors, the original occupiers of the land, from displaying jealousy towards the present occupiers. Beside the pillar were eight carved figures representing Agu-Nsi, the spirit of divination or god of medicine. When sacrifice is offered to the ancestors it is offered also to Agu-Nsi.

But the most important symbol of the ancestors is the sacred portable stick known as an *ofo*.[2] This is a section of a branchlet of the *ofo* or *Detarium senegalense* tree, which is believed to have been set aside by Chuku as a symbol and guarantee of truth. When freshly obtained and ritually treated it becomes a personal charm charged with magic, and when it is inherited it is additionally dynamized by the ancestors who held it. An inherited *ofo* becomes, therefore, a symbol of authority. Indeed, the principal sanction for the authority held by the heads of families is their *ofo*. *Ofo* are also used as representations or part of the regalia of the gods. And just as priests tend to become identified with the gods they serve, so the cult-*ofo* of priests, handed down from generation to generation, are regarded as charged with the spirit, not merely of the god, but of all the priests who had served him in bygone days. The *ofo*, in short, is the Ibo means of transmitting 'Holy Orders'.

A new *ofo* may be acquired in the following manner.[3] When a man

---

[1] The word for ancestral symbol and for children of one mother may be *tonally* differentiated, but they are *radically* the same.

[2] Both vowels in this word are open. The phonetic spelling is, therefore, *ɔfɔ*.

[3] This is the procedure followed in one of the Awgu villages. A parallel account of the procedure at Owerri will be found at p. 107.

marries and establishes a home of his own, i.e. becomes the potential
founder of a family, he generally proceeds to acquire an *ọfọ*. This is a
ritual affair, and the candidate must provide for the rites two goats
(m. and f.), two chickens (m. and f.) of ordinary breed, two chickens
of the special breed known as *avuke* and *aiagare*, a newly hatched
chicken, and the feathers of a parrot and eagle. He then goes out to
the forest and obtains an *ọfọ* branch which he cuts into three parts,
one long and two short. A general meeting of the local group or
kindred is then convened, including women and children. The senior
elder ties the three[1] *ọfọ* sticks together with a piece of palm midrib,
and may insert into the bundle three razors, with the intention that
the razors may cut or injure any one who does an injury to the owner
of the *ọfọ*. As he does so he says: 'This *ọfọ*, which we are about to
confer on our son, is not an *ọfọ* which will take the life of an innocent
man. He has collected and presented to us all the materials enjoined
by custom, and we therefore confer the *ọfọ* with open hearts. He is
not taking it by force. *Ọfọ*, lend a ready ear to whatever truth he
tells to you, but if he speaks lies turn away from him. *Ọfọ*, avert all
evil from this man and increase his family. *Ọfọ*, you are a witness
that we, both young and old, are assembled here in this man's house
for a good and not for an evil purpose.' The goats and fowls are
then slain by the senior elder, the blood being allowed to drip on
to the *ọfọ*. Later, a few feathers are stuck into the congealed blood.
The meat is then cooked and eaten. After the meal the candidate
stands up and holds out his hands, palms upwards. The senior
elder takes the *ọfọ*, and the senior matron present places her hands
on his as he recites these words: 'We are now giving to you this *ọfọ*,
an *ọfọ* that confers life and children, and not an *ọfọ* that takes away
life.' The two old people then both say simultaneously: 'One, two,
three, four.' At the fourth time the old man places the *ọfọ* in the
candidate's hands, and all present exclaim: 'May it bring you good
luck!'

The new *ọfọ*-holder uses his *ọfọ* in the first instance more as a charm
than an object of religious rites. For the formal propitiation of the
family ancestors is the concern of his senior relatives. Nevertheless
he pours periodic libations on his *ọfọ*, and on all occasions of common
sacrifice to the ancestors of his kindred he is entitled to bring his *ọfọ*
and lay it with the others, that it may receive a share of the libations.
In due course, if he himself becomes the head of the kindred, his *ọfọ*

---

[1] But most *ọfọ* consist of a single stick.

becomes the kindred *ọfọ*,[1] i.e. the symbol of all the ancestors of the kindred, and every morning he lays a kola on it, saying, 'Ọfọ and ancestors' (naming all the ancestors he knows) 'and Obasi-Idinenu, protect me and my children and wives and all the members of my kindred, even as you protected us yesterday. If any one prepares evil for us let it rebound on to his own head.' On all occasions when he performs religious rites (of whatever cult) he produces his *ọfọ* and pours over it a libation with the words, 'May *ọfọ* drink palm-wine. My father, &c. (naming all his ancestors), drink palm-wine and bless me and my family.' If he is the victim of a theft he produces his *ọfọ* and lays a kola nut on it, saying, 'If a man of my village has stolen this thing from me may you cause him to restore the stolen article. But if the thief is a member of another village then do you follow him and kill him.' It is an offence for any one to use his *ọfọ* for the purpose of destroying any of his fellow villagers, and any one so doing would be summoned before the elders and ordered to produce a goat, which would be sacrificed by the senior elder, who would pour a libation of blood on the offender's *ọfọ*, saying, 'Ọfọ, our son in a moment of anger uttered evil words. Let those words pass away without effect.'

It will be observed that an *ọfọ* is addressed as though it had a single personality of its own. Nevertheless, as it is handed down from generation to generation, it becomes the embodiment of all the spirits of the ancestors. In this connexion it may be noted that among some Ibo groups an *ọfọ* is placed against the body of a dying man, with the intention that his soul shall enter therein. In other groups pieces of the hair and nail-parings of the deceased, taken from him immediately after death, may be wrapped up and tied to his *ọfọ*.[2]

In the district of Onitsha the ancestors are believed to tenant the family stools or *okposi*, and when rites are offered the officiant places

---

[1] But in most communities the kindred *ọfọ* is not a personal *ọfọ* but a hereditary *ọfọ* passed on from each head of a kindred to his successor.

[2] According to Mr. Dewhurst it is the custom among the Obanliku of the Obudu Division that when a man or woman dies one of his children obtains a stick or stone which is placed on the breast of the dead person. In one group phallic-shaped sticks are used for men and egg-shaped for women. When the deceased is buried the objects are placed with the *Babutan* or sacred symbols, and when sacrifice is offered to the ancestors it is offered on these sticks or stones. Captain Hawkesworth has also reported that among the Okun of Calabar Province it is customary on the death of a head of a family to carve on a stick a representation of a human head (some Ibo *ọfọ* are so carved) and to place this stick in a cave containing the images of ancestors.

a cake of yam on this cultus-symbol, and then calls on members of the family to partake. They advance one by one, and as each arrives before the symbol he kneels on his right knee, and either takes a piece of the cake himself or else receives it from the priest in his crossed hands. He then rises, salutes the priest by his title, withdraws, and eats the piece of cake. If there is a supply of palm-wine, the priest pours a libation, and then calls on one or two senior persons present to come and drink. Each receives the calabash of wine from the hands of the priest, and then kneels on one knee and drinks a little. When all have been served, an assistant, known as 'the divider', hands one final cupful of wine to the priest and one also to the general crowd.

Further instances will be given in later chapters to illustrate the important part played in the legal system by the ancestors and their *ọfọ*, and we may now pass on to describe another phase of the cult of ancestors which had, and still has, a determining influence in regulating conduct. I refer to the secret societies, which are based on the belief that the dead continue to live and to take an active interest in the affairs of their living descendants.

Chief among these societies is that known as Mmọ, a word which is clearly associated with, though slightly differentiated from, that which means ghosts or spirits of the dead.[1] The Mmọ are in fact ancestral spirits personated by maskers who appear in public at seasonal periods, at festivals, and at celebrations of final funeral rites. The society, or part of it, also functions at night, for purposes which will be made clear presently.

At Onitsha the rough organization of small boys into the group known as Mbekwe serves as a kind of kindergarten for the Mmọ society. Boys join this group automatically without formal introduction, and they build for themselves a club-house which they call 'the house of Eze'.[2] Here they learn songs and dances of their own, and how to carve human figures on sticks or on the inner tissues of plantain stalks. They arm themselves with whips and short sticks and beat imaginary people, imitating the maskers of Mmọ, who chastise non-members of the society. Led by their most expert dancer they parade the town, calling at houses and receiving gifts from the womenfolk. Nowadays, as most of the boys at Onitsha are required by their parents to go to school, the Mbekwe society no longer flourishes as of old.

[1] See footnote on p. 54.
[2] Eze = king or lord. The term is applied to the holders of the highest titles (see p. 153) and also to the Supreme Being.

The first real step in initiation into the Mmọ society is taken when boys of from eight to ten years of age are given partial membership by the rite known as *Inye-ori* ('stepping over'). The candidates are required to pay a fee of two bottles of trade gin[1] and are then taken to the courtyard outside the hut of Mmọ and made to strip and prostrate themselves on the ground. As they do so the masker gives vent to terrifying shrieks, and then makes as though he would tear off the testicles of the boys, declaring that he must feed thereon. This is done to test the courage of the boys, who are considerably relieved when, at the instance of the adult members of the society, the masker consents to forgo the feast, and contents himself with beating the boys two or three times and walking across them, twice one way and twice another. They are then bidden to roll over and get up, and as they do so the masker breaks into song and orders the boys to join in the chorus. Then they all go out and parade round the village, and when any of the candidates comes to his own home he is allowed to enter it, having first washed himself in water into which *egbo* or plantain leaves have been introduced, in order to purge his body of the infection of the Mmọ.

These initial rites merely entitle the boys to follow in the train of the maskers on public occasions. The boys need no longer run away and hide themselves, as they were formerly bound to do. They become *umu-ukwu-Mmọ*. They may join in the songs of the Mmọ and they may use the solemn oath of the Mmọ, namely, 'If what I say is not the truth then may the Mmọ devour me, remove my testicles, and pour a cock's blood into my eyes.'[2] But they are not admitted into the full secrets of the Mmọ, having not yet reached the age of full discretion. They are not allowed to enter the club-house of the society, and if during the public appearance of the Mmọ one of the maskers has to adjust his costume or his voice-disguiser[3] the *umu-ukwu-Mmọ* must stoop and close their eyes.

The full and final rites of initiation are known as *Ikpu-Ane*, i.e. the entry into the earth, as the initiates are supposed to pay a visit to the underworld. Candidates are admitted to these rites when they are considered old enough to be entrusted with all the secrets of the

[1] The gin is consumed by the members in the hut of Mmọ or at the house of a senior member of the society.

[2] A cock's blood is sometimes poured into the eyes of a corpse. See p. 305.

[3] The voice-disguiser consists of a wooden tube or the bone of an animal covered with spider's egg capsule or the skin of a bat.

society. The fees are two large yams, two pots of palm-wine, fish, and various condiments,[1] and the initiation takes place on one of the nights of some important annual festival. The candidate is conducted into the official hut of the Mmọ, is stripped and forced into a corner by the fireplace. A member of the society brings a plantain stalk and begins beating it on the floor of the hut and shouting 'Egugu, oh!'[2] It is then announced that the ghosts, in answer to the summons (made by beating the ground), will come up from the underworld, through a hole made by ants. The candidate is told, therefore, to bend down and close his eyes. As he does so the masker slips on his mask, and immediately shrieks are heard. The summoner then hails the arrival of the leader of the ghosts, saying, 'Our father, our father.' The masker, speaking through his voice-disguiser, says in reply, 'Do you know the Mmọ?' The summoner replies, 'Nay, father, the Mmọ can never be known.' At this the masker begins to chant one of the songs of the Mmọ, and the members present join in the chorus. Then the masker turns to the novice, saying, 'You there! you must come with me to the spirit world.' And as he says so he makes a dive at the novice's testicles. But the members plead for mercy. The masker insists, however, that the novice shall come with him to the spirit world. And the road thereto, he says, is narrow, and only the just can follow it. By the wayside is a large cotton tree crowned with thorns. And an old woman sitting there will require the novice to scale the tree and fetch her some article from the top. If the novice is a person unfit to execute commissions assuredly he will fall from the tree. But if so a spider will mend his injuries, unless indeed he were a person who killed spiders.[3] Moreover, on this side of the spirit world is a broad river which can only be crossed by means of a spider's web. The web is strong enough to bear the weight of one who is wont to obey the elders, but will crumple under the feet of a disobedient youth. Later, the masker may stand with his legs apart and order the novice to crawl between them, beating him with a cane as he does so. And he may administer strokes with his cane at various intervals, saying, 'So-and-So, *Ndei* (a secret word).' The novice re-

[1] But during the initiation the members of the society keep sending messengers to the boys' parents with a view to extracting further gifts in return for guaranteeing the safe return of their sons.

[2] Egugu is the Yoruba word for Mmọ and the spirits of the dead. The Ibo cult at Onitsha has clearly been influenced by the Yoruba-speaking Igala.

[3] It is taboo, apparently, for members of the Mmọ society to kill spiders, as the capsules of the eggs of spiders are used to disguise the voices of the maskers.

plies, 'Our father, our father.' The masker may then ask, 'Do you know Egugu?' And the novice will reply 'Our father, Egugu can never be known.' If the novice gives way to tears he is given an additional thrashing. Throughout the night the members of the society drink wine, cook and eat yams, and sing the songs of the Mmọ.[1] The novice is given charcoal to eat and is told that this is the 'chalk' on which the Mmọ feed. Some one may throw him a bone to eat, the 'meat' of the Mmọ, and the novice will have to keep biting it. If he were known to have a truculent character he would be subjected to special forms of torture, the masker declaring that he would now proceed to feast on the ears and feet of his victim!

All these ordeals, occurring as they do in pitch darkness, are said to make many initiates believe next morning that during the night they had indeed visited the lower world, and this impression is enhanced by members of the society, who inform the novice that, but for their own good offices, he would never have returned. The appearance of his own body, covered with dirt from lying prostrate on the ground for several hours, confirms him and his uninitiated friends in the belief that he had just emerged from the grimy regions of the underworld. Nevertheless, before the initiate leaves in the morning, he is told that the maskers are not themselves spirits, but personators of spirits, and that their natural voices are disguised by speaking through tubes covered with the capsules of spiders' eggs.[2] The initiate is then sworn to secrecy and enrolled as a full member of the society. While the oath is being administered the members of the society say: 'If you go about gossiping, or in any way divulge our secrets, even to your own mother, may this oath bring about your death. And may this oath bind you to obey the instructions of the society, under all circumstances. Otherwise may your life become forfeit to the Mmọ.' At daybreak the initiate is escorted home, the masker giving him the *egbo* or plantain leaves to bathe his body before entering his home.

The maskers of Mmọ, when they appear in public, are saluted by a variety of expressions. They may be addressed as 'Our father', 'Owner of the village', 'Owner of the soil', 'Our Owner', or 'Killer of sons of

---

[1] One of the songs is 'Ogbodi ma ma ma ma, ogbodi ma go Ngegu', which seems to mean, 'A non-initiate may know some things, but he does not know Ngegu.' (Ngegu being a fancy word for the Mmọ).

[2] But boys who appear to be untrustworthy may be told little, though they would otherwise be treated as members of the society.

men without paying'. And there are various grades of Mmọ, each with its own function. Thus the excessively tall genius known as 'Mmọ afia', representing some titled person of bygone days, appears at burial rites and performs the duty of pouring cock's blood into the eyes of the dead man (provided he was a man of rank).[1] And it is this Mmọ also which expels an adulteress from her husband's kindred, or in former times ordered persons charged with witchcraft to undergo the trial by ordeal, or persons convicted of witchcraft to be put to death or banished from the town. Then there is Mmọ Ulaga which parades the town at all the feasts and is responsible for the punishment of those who commit a nuisance in a forbidden area (e.g. a public playing-ground or highway). He would whip the offender. Agbogo Mmọ is the patron of maidens and of dancing, and Nne Māu is her mother who sings for Agbogo during the dance. Mmọ Otuiche or 'The Thrower' appears once a week between January and March, and also at the death of any distinguished man. Young men invite Otuiche to chase them in order to draw attention to themselves and display their agility. There are numerous Mmọ which serve the double purpose of controlling and amusing the community.

The oath 'May Mmọ eat me' is regarded as a guarantee of truth-speaking by the members of the society, and the oath 'May Mmọ eat you (if you do not do as I direct)' is a certain means of forcing non-members of the society to obey members. Wives are often bullied into silence by the husbands' use of these words, and the oath is also an effective means of putting a stop to quarrelling among women. Women are not allowed to use the oath, nor indeed are any non-members of the society. Even when referring to the oath a circumlocution has to be employed, i.e. instead of saying '*Mmọ lie fa*' a woman must say '*Agbala fa Mmọ*'. Offences against the Mmọ are, or were, regarded not merely as a private matter between the society and the individual concerned, but as a public matter which called for a meeting of all the townspeople and entailed a heavy fine. Women are not normally admitted to the Mmọ society unless they have passed the menopause. But women who have become aware of the secrets of the society may be compelled to join it and required to pay specially heavy fees.[2] Widows also may become members, and thereby save

---

[1] But nowadays the masker merely rubs some of the blood on the dead man's feet and hands. The flesh of the cock appears to be eaten secretly by the members of the society.

[2] In olden days they might have been put to death.

themselves from the many exactions which the society imposes on women.

At Onitsha and numerous other localities that section of the Mmọ society which functions at night is known by the special title of 'Ayaka', the Ayaka being the personators of the ancestors[1] who are believed by the uninitiated to make frequent nightly visits to their living relatives during the dry months of January to March. Membership of the Mmọ society carries with it automatically a nominal membership of the Ayaka society, but active membership of the Ayaka society is confined to those who are physically capable of meeting the strenuous demands entailed by the nightly parades, which include visits not merely to the compounds of the local village but to those of numerous other villages where female relatives are living with their husbands and children.

In December the fields are fired, and it is said that this enables the ghosts to emerge from the nether world. The first flowers that appear in the fields, after the firing, are said to be 'the spoons of Ayaka'. A preliminary warning is given to the people of the annual visit of the spirits. Some days before their arrival the ghostly cry of '*Koko! koko!*' is heard proceeding from the 'bush', and after this signal the members of the society partially block the roads leading to the streams, in order that women going to fetch water may be made aware that the Ayaka season is at hand. Next night, about 9 p.m., the members of the society, or those selected to play the part, secrete themselves in the 'bush' (forest) close to the village or hamlet, and some begin calling in a falsetto voice '*Koko! koko! koko!*', while others reply, in muffled tones, '*Ehei! ehei! ehei!*' On hearing this all women and children hurriedly enter their huts, and if any child is dilatory he will be asked severely by his elders whether he had not heard the voices of the Ayaka.

After making these preliminary cries the personators of the ghosts (many of whom are provided with voice-disguisers which are euphemistically called 'eyes') are joined by the chief dancer of the society, who is known as Ekpuluke-Nwa-Njọma, and wears a skirt of palmfibre, rattles on his ankles, and a fillet of white cloth round his temples. Suspended from his neck is a calabash, covered with a net, which is studded with cowries and nuts. As he joins the others he hums a tune, on hearing which all begin to dance. One of the members whirls

[1] The Ayaka personate only those ancestors who were commoners in their lifetime. Titled ancestors are represented by the tall figures known as Mmọ afia. Masks are not worn by the Ayaka.

a bull-roarer (*odegili-gili*) round his head, and all then sing the following song:

Solo.   *Ora (a)yaka gba nj(e) ogu.*
         (The Ayaka are all assembled here for the fight.)
Refrain. *Agha ebenebe.*
         (Ebenebe war.)
Solo.   *Ndi nwul(u) anwu nagba egu efife.*
         (The dead are holding their midday dance.)
Refrain. *Agha ebenebe.*

This song may be kept up for a considerable time, pending the arrival of members who had been unable to appear sooner, as their wives had been slow in falling off to sleep. But when all have arrived the chief singer salutes them, saying: '*Ora Ayaka nnonu*', i.e. 'Members of the Ayaka society, I greet you': to which the others reply, '*Ogbu-efi*', i.e. 'Cow-killer' (a title of honour). The chief singer then runs through a number of tunes, and at the same time jumps about, peering into every nook and cranny. A procession is now formed, and as it emerges from the 'bush' the members keep grunting '*Mme! mme!*' They visit the various families in turn, singing their ghostly chant outside the hut of the head of the family; and during the chant the chief dancer skips about and the bull-roarer is whirled. The women inside the huts cling to their beds in terror. At the end of the chant the chief singer calls on the head of the family, saying, '*Demegwe*' (a secret summons). But the head of the family must pretend to be asleep. And so the dance is resumed, and once again the chief singer addresses the head of the family, saying, 'My son, have no fear, for it is your forefathers who are visiting you. Answer my call and receive our blessing.' The head of the family coughs in response, and at this all the Ayaka give expression to shouts of joy, while the chief dancer skips about, singing and beating his calabash rattle. Again the chief singer salutes him by name, saying, '*Demegwe*', and the head of the family replies, saying, 'Our father.' The chief singer then bids him bring a gift to the door, lest anything should befall him and his family. In answer the head of the family inquires—'May I then approach?' and the chief singer hums an affirmative. At this the Ayaka disperse in various directions, muttering that '*Izuga*' (a secret name for human beings) have an evil odour. But the real reason for dispersing is to escape the observation of women, who may peer through the door when the head of the family hands out his gift. If a shilling is given it is received by the chief singer with the words 'One goat'. If a fowl is given it is called by some fancy word such as *ajule* or *ọkwọkọlo*.[1]

After receiving the gift the chief singer breaks into the following song:

Solo.   *Onitsha amaro enu aro nwa.*
           (Onitsha does not know what this year will bring.)
Refrain.   *Aye, Aye, Eyem*
           Odezulu Igbo nmehe.
           (Aye, Aye, Eyem, our doings
           are renowned throughout Iboland.)
Solo.   *Ora udi gbakota nu ke eli ude, nmehe.*
           (Companions assemble to give vent to grunts.)
Refrain.   *Nmehe.*
Solo.   *Amozu tilu egede na uhwu akpo, nmehe.*
           (The witch is drumming under the cotton tree.)
Refrain.   *Nmehe.*
Solo.   *Ngakoliko ihwudohwọm oya ka ọbu, nmehe.*
           (Witch, if you overtake me there will be disgrace.)
Refrain.   *Nmehoho.*
Solo.   *Amozu nọ na enu ọji akwachali.*
           (On the top of the African oak the witch is supreme.)
Refrain.   *Ude Mmọ.*
           (The glory of Mmọ.)
Solo.   *De ajuku de egwe mme mme.*
           (Meaning unknown to informant.)
Refrain.   *Ude Mmọ.*
           (The glory of Mmọ.)

After this song the head of the family may present a further gift, the Ayaka signifying their satisfaction by saying—'*Hi! hi!*' through their voice-disguisers. The wives of the head of the family may also present gifts through their husband. If any head of a family were to refuse a donation, the Ayaka, in revenge, would block up, with logs

---

[1] Other secret or fancy words used by the Ayaka are *ogwe* (to signify danger or an obstruction on the road), *eneo* (be silent), *olokpo* (yam), *akpawawu* (goat), *ukala anya ino* (dog). Young members of the society are described as 'useless pots' (*nkpong nkpọ ite*), cowries as 'snails' (*npiolo*), money as 'a glittering thing' (*nmumu liọlio*), iron double hand-gongs as 'tongues of an animal' (*ile ngbada*), and the friction drum used by the Ayaka as 'the leopard of the Mmọ' (*Agu Mmọ*). The friction drum, incidentally, is a pot with the bottom knocked out and covered with a single membrane, with a piece of fibre fastened to the centre of the membrane. In sounding the drum the fingers are wetted and drawn along the fibre, causing vibrations which are communicated to the membrane.

of wood and rope, the entrance to his house, thereby preventing him
from getting out in the morning, until freed by a relative. Stones
and rubbish would also be thrown into his compound, and his name
would be used derisively in the subsequent songs of the Ayaka. In
this connexion it may be noted that the Ayaka have the privilege of
adopting any song sung by women, modifying it to suit themselves.
Thereafter the women must cease to sing this song, and any woman
breaking this rule is said to 'break the heads of the Mmǫ'.

Two hours or more may be spent in the compound of any extended-
family or kindred, and the Ayaka then pass on to a neighbouring
family. Occasionally during the night the chief singer, who is the
master of ceremonies, bids the Ayaka 'go and eat food'. All then rest
quietly as though partaking of some spiritual meal. Some move off to
a distance and, when summoned again by the chief singer, appear back
suddenly as though they had emerged from the ground. During the
interval some of the dancers may skip round the village and shake
their calabash-rattles close to the walls of bedrooms, in order to strike
terror into the women and other non-initiates. The Ayaka must avoid
coughing like an ordinary human being, and it is an offence also to
laugh. If something amusing occurs their laughter must be suppressed,
so that it resembles the noise made by a fowl with the croup. Similarly,
if any one receives an injury, he must stifle all expressions of pain.
The members also assume and use towards each other the names of
dead relatives, so that women who overhear them may really believe
that they are listening to ghosts. One may assume the name and voice
of a dead child, and another those of the child's dead mother. A third
may carry on a conversation with the mother and assert that the child
had suffered from the effects of its long journey to the lower world.
A fourth may play the part of the dead father and rebuke his wife
(the dead mother) for having insisted on accompanying him on the
long journey back to the upper world. When they pass the house of
an inquisitive woman, who might be guilty of prying into their secrets,
the Ayaka make a point of singing out in a falsetto voice, 'The crevices
of the wall—who is the owner thereof?' (i.e. the Ayaka can penetrate
everywhere). Occasionally the Ayaka of one village come across those
of another, and when this occurs each side may endeavour to block
the other's way. A scuffle may result, and if any of the Ayaka has a
packet of *Agbala* powder he may throw the contents over the heads
of his opponents, thereby causing intense itch. Incidentally, it is
said that the blacksmiths of Awka commonly carry a supply of this

powder when they go on their travels, and they dispose some of it
secretly in the beds of rich men, who promptly call for a doctor and
are treated by the smith. The smith not merely receives a fee, but
takes the bed away as well, saying that it must be tenanted by devils!

And so the pantomime continues through the night, until towards
4 a.m. the personators of the ghosts are warned by the cry of the *obu* bird,
and later by that of the bush-fowl, that daybreak is at hand. They hasten
back, therefore, to the 'bush', and there disrobe and betake themselves
home. Women must at this season avoid going to draw water before
sunrise, for if they happened to meet any of the Ayaka returning home
they would be heavily fined and compelled to become members of the
society. In pre-Government days they might have been put to death.

When an important member of a kindred dies, the Ayaka attend
the funeral rites at night, and one of them personates the dead man,
imitating his manner, voice, and even his laughter. Another, speaking
on behalf of the ghosts, welcomes the dead man to the underworld.
They then engage in dancing and singing, and after an interval the
chief singer goes to the hut of the deceased's senior relative and calls
on him to obtain from the female mourners some gift or gifts for the
Ayaka. The relative comes out to obey this command and crosses the
compound to the hut where the female mourners are concealed. As
he does so the Ayaka secrete themselves, but after he has entered the
women's hut they give vent to exclamations of disgust, saying, 'Ugh,
how that *Izuga*, who has passed us, stinks!'

Besides the Ayaka there are sub-societies of Mmǫ, each with functions of its own. Thus there is the society of Onyekulum, a word
which seems to mean 'Who summoned me?' This society operates
during the dry season, and serves a useful social purpose by pointing
out defects in the characters of members of a kindred. A bold agile
person is selected by the society to go at night and hurl abuse in a
ghostly voice at any one whose behaviour has been disapproved. His
confrères, meanwhile, remain at a distance, singing their ghostly
chant. Agility is required by the delegate, for the person abused may
treat him to a shower of stones!

In the Nsukka Division there are two well-known secret societies
which were, and are still to some extent, used as an integral part of
the system of law and authority. These societies are known as Odo[1]
and Omabe respectively.

Odo, personated by a masker, appears from the spirit-world every

[1] Pronounced *ɔdǝ*.

three years[1] in December, and lives among men for a period of seven months. On the first day of his arrival, which corresponds with the time of the planting of yams, he is escorted into the town at midday from his grove in the 'bush', carrying a decorated stick and led by the priest, who keeps beating an iron gong. Surrounded by initiates of the cult, he parades the town with a dancing step, and is saluted by all the people, who go down on one knee and throw dust with both hands over their right and left shoulders. In the evening Odo, speaking in a croaky voice which is interpreted by one of the priest's assistants, informs the people that he has come to reside with them once more, and warns them that all must behave decorously during his stay.

After this preliminary visit he is escorted back to the grove, where he remains for eight days before taking up permanent residence in the town. He is then again escorted into the town, visits the market, and finally takes up his abode in the house of the priest. A general feast known as Nkali-Odo or 'the viewing of Odo' is held, and from that day onwards Odo becomes the object of daily sacrifices and petitions by individuals. He sallies forth regularly in public and visits all the compounds in the town, receiving the greetings, gifts, and petitions of the households. All who fail to make way for him on the road are severely flogged by his attendants. Every one must be on his best behaviour, for it is believed that if people quarrel or misconduct themselves during the visit of Odo the crops will fail and death will invade the town. Those who feel that they have received good-fortune from the hands of Odo use the occasion of his visit to show their gratitude. Thus a woman who had vowed that if she obtained a child she would give a gift to Odo would, if her desire had been granted, take a chicken to the house of the priest. The woman, remaining in the background, would hand the chicken to her husband who would hand it to the priest. The priest would hand it to the masker concealed behind a curtain in his hut. If the woman had been misbehaving, the masker, speaking in a deep voice, would say that he refused to accept the gift of a wanton woman. The priest would thereupon hand back the chicken, but at the urgent appeal of the woman, who would vow that she would mend her ways, the genius would reluctantly accept the gift, with a warning that if she repeated her evil conduct she would meet with a speedy death. A rebuke of this kind was made known to the woman's father, who would use all his authority to see that his daughter behaved herself in future. One of

[1] At Ukehe Odo appears every two years.

the main functions of the cults of Odo and Omabe is the discipline
or even the subjection of women.

At the end of the seven months, when the corn has been harvested
and the new yams are ready for use, the priest offers a sacrifice of new
yams to Odo, and a few days later the genius parades the town in
sorrowful fashion, with his headgear thrown back and his costume
worn loosely and negligently to give the appearance of a sick and
listless deity. He then returns to the house of the priest, where he
bids farewell to all who have been initiated into the cult, saying that
he is returning to the spirit-land but will revisit the upper earth in
three years' time. He turns and dances away slowly towards the
grove, attended by the priest and his assistants, who take with them a
ram, goat, and chicken,[1] and a basket containing the skulls of animals
and feathers of chickens which had been sacrificed to Odo during his
stay in the town. As the genius moves away, all the initiates fall down
on their knees and throw dust on their shoulders, saying, 'Our father
is now leaving us, our father is now leaving us. Protect us, so that we
may be alive when you visit our town again.' After the departure of
the genius all go to the river and bathe, and at sunset shut themselves
up in their houses, for no one may see the priest returning from the
grove. On the following morning they go and salute the priest, who
shaves his head as a sign of mourning for the god. He had remained
unshaven during the whole period of Odo's visit.

Each village, and sometimes each kindred, has its own Odo cult,
and boys are initiated into the mysteries of the cult about the age of
ten or eleven. The boy's father is required to give a gift of thirty
rods to the head of the kindred or village, who divides them up between the elders and officials of Odo. On the day appointed for the
initiation the priest and all initiates are invited to a feast by the
father of the boy, and in the evening the boy is taken to the sacred
grove. The priest opens the proceedings by placing some food-offerings in front of a branch of an ebony tree which is sacred to the deity.
The costume of Odo is then brought out and set beside the ebony
branch. It consists of a headpiece and a skirt of leaves. The headpiece
is a conical basket surrounded with rolled palm-leaves. Porcupine
quills and the feathers of owls and fish-eagles are inserted here and
there. There are openings for the eyes. The priest lays some pudding
and soup on the ground beside the costume, saying, 'This your son
has come in order that he may be known to you and you to him.

[1] These are sacrificed later in the sacred grove.

Protect him and prevent him from disclosing your nature to those who know you not.' The priest then tells the boy to come forward, and says, 'What is this'? The boy peers at the costume and then starts back in fright. He is urged forward again and sees a man, who is well known to him, enter the costume and take it off again. The priest then warns the boy that if he ever reveals to a woman that Odo is a dressed-up man he will be put to death. This sentence was quite commonly carried out and the woman was also killed. If the boy revealed the secret of the cult to another boy who had not been initiated, the other would be initiated at once and the informer would be put to death unless his father were rich enough to redeem him.[1]

It might be supposed that the initiates of such a cult cannot regard it as anything but a pious fraud. But the initiates believe that Odo is spiritually associated with the costume, and the masker himself believes that while he is personating Odo the god is immanent in his person. The shrine of Odo was an asylum for persons who had rendered themselves liable to be sold as slaves on account of some offence. The refugee became the servant of Odo, and as such his person was sacrosanct. He could continue living in his own home, but was at the beck and call of the priest of the cult. Runaway slaves from other towns could also find sanctuary at the shrine of Odo. Persons who thus became servants of the god formed a special caste of their own, into which it was taboo for any one not belonging to the caste to marry. The cult of Omabe is of a similar character, and at Nsukka the deity appears annually in one or other of the villages or 'quarters', each of which has a cult of its own.[2] On his reappearance he mourns for those of his devotees who had died since his last appearance, and when he departs, three days before the rising of the new moon, a wooden gong is beaten.

From this review it will have been observed that the belief in the continued spiritual existence of the ancestors serves many useful purposes. By it social continuity is preserved, hereditary rights are respected, and conduct is regulated in a variety of ways. The belief also serves as a solace to the living in the loss of their dead relatives

[1] Those who disclosed the secrets of Odo were compelled to hang themselves at a particular spot in the 'bush' immediately after the arrival of the god in December. The corpse was left naked at a cross-roads as a warning to all.

[2] The maskers may, during the year in which they personate Omabe, administer thrashings not merely to members of their own group but to members of neighbouring groups. The maskers of the neighbouring groups retaliate in due course. Ill-feeling may arise between two groups if the maskers show excessive zeal.

and friends. In the past the secret societies were, and still are to some considerable extent, a powerful factor in the maintenance of law and order. They provided a useful and necessary disciplinary training for the youthful male members of the community, and for adult males they constituted a strong bond of union, besides fulfilling many of the other social purposes of clubs. On the other hand, they were frequently used for committing brutal judicial murders, and many of the societies have for this reason been suppressed by the Government. Moreover, they were an unfair means of exploiting and bullying women and keeping them in a state of subjection to men. On this account alone the Christian Missions are justified in taking a strong stand against these societies, which are fast losing their power as their secrets are being gradually disclosed.

Witchcraft, Doctors, and Medicines.

Witches and witchcraft do not, of course, exist; but the belief in their existence is one of the most potent in the lives of most African peoples. And it is a belief which cannot easily be exorcised, for it is not an isolated factor, but an integral part of the whole psychological and magico-religious system. And yet not all tribes are equally dominated by the fear of witchcraft, and the Ibo appear to be very much less influenced by witchcraft beliefs than their neighbours the Jukun, among whom almost every death is ascribed to the projected malice of some living human being. In some Ibo groups it was roundly declared that witchcraft was non-existent in their own community, though practised by their next-door neighbours! How far the belief in witchcraft has been weakened recently by the spread of Christian teaching and the opening up of communications would be difficult to determine.

Witchcraft manifests itself in a variety of ways. Witches appear at night as balls of fire falling from the tops of trees (particularly African oaks). If the person who sees the ball of fire is protected by an effective 'medicine', the fire is immediately extinguished. Witches (*amozu*) and wizards (*ogboma*) have also animal counterparts, and so assume the forms of owls, lizards, vultures, and numerous species of night-birds. Consequently, if a night-bird comes and rests on a house, the owner loses no time in trying to drive it away or shoot it; and if he fails he will seize his *ǫfǫ* and call on his ancestors or any local deity to rid him of his enemy. A witch always assails at night. By magic means she attacks the throat, so that the victim is paralysed and cannot move or speak, and in the morning may be found lying senseless and naked outside his hut. Such a one may have to be sent to some distant town before he recovers his health. Or at night a man may meet a tall figure and may run for his life. But if he is brave he may close with the figure, who, it is said, may then turn into a person well known in the village. In this way many witches and wizards are discovered. Persons who talk to themselves may be held to be witches conversing with their fiendish friends; and if a woman in a market-place begins talking as though she were 'seeing things' she may find herself treated as a witch. One informant stated that a friend of his who was a musician was making his way home one night when he was stopped by witches who appeared to be pleased with his music. And so he was held rooted to the ground and forced to play his flute, until a seer happened to come along the road and, discerning the witches, bade them be gone. The musician continued on his road, but was again assailed by the witches, who had flown ahead. And so he stood spellbound once more, playing hard for many hours, until discovered by his father who had come to search for him. The father happened to be armed with witchcraft medicine and was able, therefore, to rebuke the witches and release his son.

Witches can penetrate into a house through the smallest cracks in the wall, and can assume the form of the smallest insect. Flies and other creatures which bite are witches or the agents of witches, and if a person is severely bitten he may consult a diviner, who will order the patient to offer sacrifice to propitiate some witch, and induce the witch to remove the spell by transferring it to some one else. Witches can poison food or infect it with sorcery, and if any one eats a meal cooked by a witch he will become seriously ill or die. Mothers, therefore, advise their children to avoid eating food outside their own homes. Witches are dangerous to women during menstruation. They seize this chance to tie up the woman's womb, and so prevent conception. For this reason many women, particularly the wives of titled men, are confined to their huts during their monthly periods.[1] Witches also can cause sexual impotence in men. A man's own mother may be a witch and keep him impotent as long as she is alive. But when she dies her witchcraft is disclosed, for he suddenly becomes a virile being.

---

[1] But in most of the tribes which segregate menstruous women the reason assigned is not the protection of the women, but the protection of other members of the community from the women, who in this condition are regarded as dangerous. (See my *A Sudanese Kingdom*, pp. 329–31.)

Witches know and consort with one another. They form themselves into clubs or guilds with a view to assisting each other to obtain
victims. By placing leaves in a person's house a witch exposes that
person to attack by the whole company of witches. Or if a witch
points at a man a calabash containing a certain powder that man
will become vulnerable to attack at night by all the members of the
witches' guild. A witch, on initiation into the guild, has to contribute
(in the form of the soul-substance or spiritual counterpart of the
body) a son, daughter, or other close relative, to provide a feast for
the initiates. She discloses to a wizard the name of her victim, who
is thereupon maimed by the wizard's spiritual arrow.[1] The witches
then proceed to divide among themselves the various parts of the
victim's body; and when finally the heart is divided the victim dies.
And so when any one falls sick suddenly, and a diviner declares that
he is the victim of a certain witch, the sick man's friend may go to the
person named as the witch and ask her to desist. The person charged
with witchcraft will deny complicity, but may nevertheless be compelled to march round the village, beating a tin can or packing-case,
and shouting out, 'Members of the guild of witches, I have decided
to surrender our victim. Here is my share. Let her who took the
head restore it; and her who took the legs, and her who took the
chest, and her who took the stomach, and her who took the eyes!
Members of the guild of witches, hear my entreaty; for a goat has
been given to us to replace the human being whom we took.' The
sick person, hearing that he is once more a free man, frequently makes
a speedy recovery.[2]

A witch can cause an innocent person to become a witch by introducing *edi*—a spiritual substance—into his food. After eating the
food the innocent person begins to fall under the influence of the
witch, who then proceeds to administer the powerful medicine known
as *onukpulu agbulu*, a phrase which is said to mean 'may the mouth
be blunt'. Having partaken of this the hitherto innocent person conceives a craving for feeding on his fellow men, and is initiated into
all the mysteries of the guild of witches. He is pledged to secrecy and
told when and where the witches meet at night. The hour of meeting
is indicated by the cry of birds, and on hearing this the witches all

---

[1] Attacks of pneumonia are ascribed to the arrows of wizards. The Jukun belief
is precisely the same. (See my *A Sudanese Kingdom*, p. 299.)

[2] The African Negro, being highly suggestible, is particularly susceptible to the
curative influences of auto-suggestion.

rise from their beds, and, assuming the form of owls or ants or other animals, proceed to the common meeting-place.

The great ally of the people against witchcraft is the *dibia*, or diviner and medicine-man. If any one has been troubled by a series of misfortunes he betakes himself to a *dibia*, who, as he throws his divining-apparatus,[1] keeps asking questions of his client and so ascertains considerable information about his client and the state of his mind. If he perceives that his client suspects witchcraft by one of his neighbours, he may suggest that his client has been bewitched. The client will then take two stalks of the *egbo* tree and, saying that one is so-and-so and the other so-and-so, will breathe on them and ask the diviner to say which of the two stalks represents the witch. The diviner may indicate one of the stalks, or he may avoid giving a direct answer, merely throwing out hints from which the client can draw his own conclusions. The diviner may then instruct his client to procure a goat or fowl, together with certain leaves; and when these have been obtained he may offer sacrifice in the client's compound, burying certain portions of the sacrificial animal in the ground, and saying, 'We have to-day closed the eyes of the witch who is troubling this man.' He will then cut a yam and coco-yam in half, place the two halves in receptacles, made of banana stalks, and leave them on the spot where the sacrifice had been made.

Most heads of families have in their houses 'medicines' or amulets to protect the family from witches. It is said that some headstrong witches, knowing the danger they incur, enter these houses and are caught by the medicine. The witch so caught may endeavour to escape by entering a lizard. She may then turn herself into an owl or into a piece of broken pottery. And, if still unsuccessful, she may lie on the floor in a trance, and remain there until the members of her family procure her release, by paying a sum of money to the owner of the medicine.

On the other hand, witches are said to be able to nullify the effects of many medicines which are used for the treatment of disease. At one time it was even said that the European drugs used at the Church Missionary Hospital near Onitsha had been vitiated by witchcraft (presumably because many patients had died or failed to make a good recovery). But in due course, so it was believed, the European doctor manufactured an antidote, which not merely prevented the witches

---

[1] The apparatus consists of four strings with fish-bone attachments. For a description of the method of divination see my *A Sudanese Kingdom*, p. 326.

from doing any further damage, but led to their 'crucifixion'. Incidentally it may be noted that failure to cure a person who is the victim of witchcraft is often ascribed to the fact that witches make compacts with the ghosts of the dead, by which doctors and diviners are misled into making incorrect diagnoses. A diviner, misled in this way by the ancestors, may ascribe a disease to the action of an ancestor instead of a witch, and so prescribe a useless remedy.

Some witches are more powerful than others. The most dangerous of all are known as *igabi*, and it is said that this class of witch can deal successfully with any medicine-man and the whole of his pharmacopoeia. The witch approaches the medicine of the medicine-man and slyly asks the medicine the nature of its composition.[1] She wishes to know, she says, in order that her medicine and that of the medicine-man may become one, and serve a single purpose. The medicine may dismiss the witch with a refusal and a severe rebuke. But if the medicine-man had been neglectful in offering sacrifice to his medicine, the medicine may succumb to the wheedling of the witch, and, in return for a gift of a fowl and some chalk, reveal the nature of its composition. The witch then jumps for joy, for she can now manufacture an antidote which will counteract the action of the medicine-man's medicine, and expose him and his household to a withering attack. Hence the continual rivalry between medicine-men and the guild of invisible witches. Many medicine-men and heads of families attach bells to their medicines or cultus-symbols, and these are believed to tinkle when witches approach. When they tinkle during the night the owner may rise and, holding his *ọfọ*, call on the ancestors to protect the household. In the morning he may claim to have driven off a witch, when in reality the bell had been tinkled by a rat or other animal!

It is said by some Ibo that a witch cannot kill any one outright, unless she is assisted by a wizard. The wizard kills the victim with his bow, and then the witch and her associates proceed to feed. But wizards themselves never feed on human beings—their food is snails. Nevertheless, most Ibo maintain that wizards or sorcerers need not be feared as witches are feared, for a wizard that causes injury to an innocent person incurs the wrath of Ala (the Earth-deity). A wizard who solicits the assistance of Ala or of the ancestors for the removal of evil, brings about his own downfall, if he himself has been a doer of evil. It follows, therefore, that as Ala metes out automatic punish-

[1] It will be observed that medicines are regarded almost as sentient beings.

ment to wizards who abuse their powers, it is never necessary to
compel well-known wizards to undergo trial by ordeal, which is, or
was until recently, the normal method of dealing with persons suspected of witchcraft.

Witches are revealed in various ways. On her deathbed a woman
may declare that she had for years been an insatiable witch, that she
had initiated others into her black art and had fed on their children
as a fee; or that she had caused hundreds of women to abort by
devouring the babies in their wombs.[1] Or a woman may be classed as
a witch by general consent, because everywhere she goes disaster
follows in her train. Sorcerers may point out witches within the
kindred; or their names may be disclosed by the divining-apparatus.
Or a diviner may make a decoction of leaves which, when poured into
the eyes of a sick man, will enable him to recognize the person whom
he believes to be bewitching him.[2]

A *dibia* or diviner is not always on the side of the law (as we conceive the law). He is often a dealer in 'poison' (*nsi*), using this term
in its magical as well as in its ordinary connotation. The poison may
take the form of concoctions or material objects laid on or buried in
the ground, so that an enemy who crosses over them shall sicken and
die. Certain species of chicken (viz. *aiagare* and *ekpuru*) are commonly
used in preparing *nsi*. Or the *dibia* may provide genuine poisons to
be inserted in food or drink. It is not uncommon, therefore, for a
man who becomes a *dibia* to be sworn by the elders of his family-
group that he will refrain from the practice of illegitimate magic, lest
the magic should recoil on their heads as well as on his own.

A *dibia* can make medicines to counteract or palliate the action of
medicines made by other *dibia*. He relies also on his conjuring skill.[3]
He will dig a hole in a man's compound with the pretence of discovering evil medicines deposited there, and by sleight of hand produce the medicine. He will suck the arms, head, or abdomen of a

---

[1] One informant, a devout Christian, stated that he knew a girl whose mother was
a witch. She suffered from a swollen finger for years. But the day her mother died
her finger became normal.

[2] For a description of the native methods of dealing with charges of witchcraft
see pp. 225 ff. The question of administrative policy regarding witchcraft is discussed
on pp. 344 ff.

[3] It is a mistake to regard a *dibia* as nothing but a charlatan because he resorts to
conjuring tricks. As Dr. Marett has somewhere said, his conjuring is a professional
gesture which is in strict keeping with the official tradition. In order to be popular
all authority must manage somehow to be impressive.

new-born baby in order to remove worms, and will spit the worms out of his mouth. A *dibia* who practises sorcery can, it is believed, cause a person's hair to fall out, or an unborn babe to be exchanged for something else. He can provide a man with the lock and key of another's life. It is believed, therefore, by some, that if a person whom you cannot trust asks you the time by your wrist-watch, you should make some evasive answer. For if you tell him that the hour is so-and-so, he may at once turn the magical lock and you will be dead at that hour on the following day.

A *dibia* is always a leech, and some *dibia* are also possessed of second-sight. A seer, whether male or female, and any one subject to possession (i.e. to a state of dissociation), is known as *amoma*.[1] Possession takes hold of a person, who is subject to it, spontaneously, the subject first showing signs of irritability and then passing over into a state of complete dissociation. But the condition may be induced by artificial stimulants, such as drumming or the drinking of certain concoctions, or by an exciting environment. Possessed persons throw themselves about without suffering injury, or may cut themselves without appearing to feel any sensation of pain. Male *amoma* sometimes climb palms without a rope, and may remain above until their relatives offer sacrifice to Amadi-Oha (the god of lightning). Female *amoma* frequently lose themselves for days in the 'bush', and on their return 'speak with the spirit' (i.e. in a mystical manner).[2] In due course they calm down and become normal, and if any one had become possessed for the first time her relatives establish for her the cult known as Agu-Nsi, the god of divination and second-sight. The symbols of this cult are (*a*) *oha*, *ogirisi*, and *abosse* trees; (*b*) carved wooden images (male and female) which are portable, and (*c*) an *ofo*. On the day of the week known as *Eke*[3] the woman comes before the symbols at sunrise, washes her hands, chews kolas and 'alligator' pepper pods, spits the fragments over the symbols, rubs white or yellow clay round her eyes, beats a tortoise-shell and sings the praises of Agu-Nsi. In this way she becomes a recognized *dibia*.[4]

[1] There are no male *amoma* at Owerri, but there are female *amoma* there, and also in most of the Isu towns. It was stated that there are a number of male *amoma* at Okpala and Udo.

[2] But the 'gift of tongues' attributed in other Nigerian tribes to possessed persons appears to be unknown at Owerri, where this information was obtained.

[3] See footnote to p. 36.

[4] In some cases a sick man will be told by a diviner that his sickness is caused by Agu-Nsi and that it will leave him if he obeys Agu-Nsi by becoming a professional *dibia*.

A man may become a *dibia* in the same way. But a man may also become a *dibia* because his father or mother was one, or by serving a course of apprenticeship to a *dibia*.

If the spirit of possession takes hold of a man, he is escorted to the market by other *dibia*, dancing as he goes along. On arrival in the market he seizes articles exposed for sale—an indication that he has lost his self-control. He is then put into a hole in the ground resembling a grave. Thorns are placed on the floor and are covered over with plantain leaves. The novice's eyes are bandaged with a black cloth, and he is laid on the bed of thorns and covered with plantain leaves. The senior *dibia* present kills a cock, removes the bandage from the novice's eyes, and pours some of the cock's blood into his eyes. The body of the cock is secreted in some spot close by, and the novice is told to find it. It is said that he can declare at once where the cock is, or else follows the footsteps of the *dibia* who had secreted the cock until he finds it. As soon as he finds the cock, guns are fired and all rejoice; for the novice has proved that he is worthy to be regarded as a genuine *dibia*.

In 1927 there was a remarkable outbreak among adherents of the Kwa-Ibo Mission. It took the form of a religious hysteria, and bands of Christian converts, most of whom were women, went about the country declaring themselves to be inspired, destroying objects sacred to the pagans, and torturing those who refused to confess their sins. Some of the victims were bound with thongs tightened with levers, and after water had been poured over them they were left to die. Twenty-nine people who had been trussed up were rescued by the police, and soon the prisons were crowded with prisoners. The symptoms displayed by the missioners were such as are commonly described as 'possession'. The subjects rolled their eyes, contorted their limbs, foamed at the mouth, and fell into a frenzy. The condition appeared to be contagious and a whole village sometimes became affected by contact with a single 'inspired' individual.[1]

Many intelligent Ibo, uninfluenced by Christianity, have no faith in the medicines of *dibia*, but nevertheless keep them in their houses and sprinkle them over their wives and children, believing that the medicines serve a useful purpose by giving or restoring confidence. Some of the medicines appear to have real therapeutic value, independently of any magical character which they may be supposed to possess. Indeed, in spite of the great increase in scientific knowledge, the

---

[1] See Sessional Paper No. 28 of 1930, Annexure I, para. 56.

dibia still continues to fulfil a useful purpose in Ibo society. In the words of Dr. Rattray, 'divination is the African's way of seeking an unbiased answer for his doubts and questionings. It enables him also to place the onus of certain unpleasant but wholesome truths on the shoulders of the spirits, and to fix in the same quarter the opprobrium of carrying out unpopular but salutary measures. It is good psychology and policy, because in nine cases out of ten the soothsayer's wand will bend to the trend of public opinion.'[1]

[1] *The Leopard Priestess*, p. 105.

IV

THE SOCIAL AND POLITICAL STRUCTURE

THE FORMS OF SOCIAL GROUPING

THE system of law and authority among primitive peoples is so closely interwoven with the social and political fabric that in describing the latter we shall also be describing the former. It would indeed be almost impossible to give an accurate account of the former without first analysing the latter, and it is true to say that many serious administrative blunders have been committed in the past through attempts at 'discovering' native authorities by short-cut methods, without first undertaking the arduous preliminary work of studying the various forms of social grouping and the means by which each is held together and controlled. The necessity, moreover, of studying the social structure is proportionately greater among peoples lacking a central form of government, as their modes of regulating conduct are highly complex and by no means obvious to a European observer. I make no apology, therefore, for devoting the next three chapters to the study of a single topic. Our analysis of the social structure must be a close one, beginning with the smallest unit and ending with the highest, and our data will not be derived from a single locality, but from representative localities in three distinct provinces.

The Kindred.

In all Ibo communities the basic social unit is the group of patrilineal relatives who live together in close association and constitute what is known as *umunna*, i.e. the children of a common forefather. The *umunna* may coincide with a single extended-family, i.e. the group composed of a man and his wife and small children, his grown-up sons and their wives and children, and his brothers or cousins and their wives and children. Or the term *umunna* may include two or more distinct but related extended-families, in which case each of the extended-families is known as *onunne* or *umunne*, i.e. children of one mother.[1] In other words, the term *umunna*, which may be con-

---

[1] The expression 'children of one mother' does not imply matrilineal descent in the accepted sense. It indicates that the people using the term believe themselves to have had a common female ancestor as well as a common male ancestor, i.e. that they are descended from the same wife of the male ancestor.

veniently called a 'kindred', includes the term *onunne* or *umunne*, which connotes an undivided extended-family.

The Village-Group or Small Clan.

A kindred occupies an area which, if the kindred is small, may be described as a hamlet, or, if it is large, as a village.[1] Or several kindreds living in close conjunction may form a village. Finally, a number of contiguous villages, which believe themselves to be related, form a 'village-group'.[2] The village-group constitutes a single political unit, usually the highest political unit found. Its unity is based on a sense of common ancestry, the possession of a common territory and home, common customs, and a common shrine of Ala, the Earth-deity. The village-group may, therefore, be regarded territorially as a commune, and socially as a clan, though it is seldom an exogamous unit.

An Ibo refers to his village-group as his *ala* (country) or *obodo* or *mba*. He uses the words *ṅkporo, mbam*,[3] *ogbwe, ebo, onuma, onama*, or *ibeama*, to describe the subdivisions (i.e. villages, quarters, or hamlets) of his village-group. In some localities he refers to his own particular local group as his *nchi*, i.e. 'circle'. His *nchi* may coincide with his *umunna* or kindred, or it may embrace a number of kindreds. Schematically, therefore, the composition of a village-group may be represented as shown (p. 90), the local or geographical terms being shown in roman type and the kinship terms in italics.

The great variety of terms used by an Ibo to describe the social groupings is noticeable. And it is noteworthy that the terms used do not always bear the same precise connotation. Thus *obodo* and *ala* are sometimes used to describe, not the whole village-group, but the speaker's own subdivision. And the term *umunna* may be used loosely to include, not merely the speaker's own consanguineous relatives, but all the members of his village or even of his village-group or clan. This looseness of terminology is really a reflection of the dynamic

[1] But the term 'village' does not necessarily imply a collection of houses closely adjoining one another as in England. The 'village' may include groups of houses or hamlets or even small villages scattered over a wide area, and it is sometimes difficult to judge by the eye where one 'village' ends and another begins.

[2] The term 'village-group' is retained as it has become stereotyped. But just as the term 'village' may be applied to what is in reality a collection of villages, so the term 'village-group' may embrace a number of village-groups. An independent village-group might more properly be described as a commune.

[3] *mbām* = subdivision of town is not to be confused with *mbám* = my town.

condition of society. Villages are constantly breaking away from the parent stock and kindreds growing into clans. Cases came to my notice of (*a*) a village seeking inclusion in a group to which it had not hitherto belonged, on the ground that its customs and interests were identical with those of the group; (*b*) a village being expelled from membership of a village-group or clan because it had resorted to the

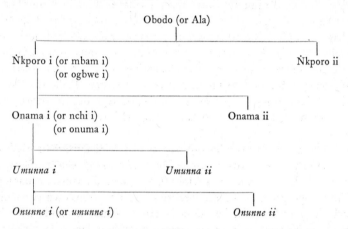

use of black magic or had failed to fulfil its common obligations, such as keeping clear its share of the road leading to the clan market, or failing to contribute to a common sacrifice; (*c*) a kindred which was exogamous a few years ago bisecting itself into two intermarrying groups; and (*d*) a kindred bisecting itself in order to facilitate social and political control. Facts like these are of great administrative importance, in view of the tendency to treat clans and other forms of social grouping as static institutions whose character and composition, once determined, must always remain the same.

The Large Clan.

It has been said that the single independent village-group or commune is usually the highest form of political unity found. Nevertheless, the sense of territorial and social solidarity or clanship may, in point of fact, cover a wider group, even though the ties binding the group together are slender. Thus, in the Okigwi Division of Owerri Province there is a group of close on 50,000 people, the Isu-Ochi, who, besides sharing the same name, have some considerable degree of social solidarity. They consist of two groups, the Eze-Isu and the

Ihite-Isu—a dual organization being, as we shall see, typical of most Ibo communities. The former group comprises five distinct village-groups and the latter four. Between these various village-groups there was in the past little political or social unity. They seldom met together for any common purpose, and each managed its own affairs. But in abnormal circumstances a general meeting would be held at Nkwo-Ago, the most central market. Thus, if there was a rumour that Aro mercenaries were threatening an invasion, all would assemble at Nkwo-Ago, and the head of the senior family of the senior village in the clan would lay his *ọfọ*, or sacred insignium, on the ground, pour a libation of palm-wine over it, and deposit on it the seeds of a kola, saying, '*Ọfọ*, I ask your protection for our lives, even as you protected the lives of our forefathers. We of the Isu-Ochi are faced with danger. If any man of the Isu-Ochi attempts to go against his brother do you, *Ọfọ*, take away that man's life.' The position would then be discussed and arrangements made that all should go to the assistance of the village first attacked—an undertaking which was not always carried out. A general meeting might also be held to settle a dispute between two Isu-Ochi villages, to offer some special sacrifice at the instance of a diviner or an agent of the Aro-Chuku oracle, or to decide whether an Isu-Ochi community which had been charged with some offence should continue to be regarded as one of themselves.

It is apparent, therefore, that in comparatively large clan-groups like the Isu-Ochi, although the sense of solidarity is much less well-developed than in the smaller commune, there is still a sufficient basis of clanship on which to build up some form of clan administration.[1]

The Sub-tribe.

There are still wider territorial groupings than those of the type just described. But in these the bonds of relationship between the constituent elements are so feeble that it is safer to describe the group as a sub-tribe rather than as a clan. Thus in the Owerri Division there are the Oratta and the Isu, the former numbering 35,000 and the latter 96,000. The constituent village-groups of each are wholly independent, they never meet together for any common purpose, and

[1] It is satisfactory, therefore, to record that as a result of the recent investigations among the Isu-Ochi the boundary which split the clan in two has been adjusted and that the clan has been welded together by being given a judiciary and council of its own. This course has been successfully pursued in numerous other groups of similar type.

they do not even claim to be related. And yet there is some sense of kinship based on a certain community of customs. For this reason the Oratta and Isu regard themselves as distinct peoples. The former affect to despise the latter because they (the Oratta) were warriors in the past, whereas the Isu were merely traders. An Oratta man might marry an Isu woman, but no Oratta woman would marry an Isu man. The bride-price was and still is higher among the Isu than among the Oratta, and there are numerous differences in the food customs of the two peoples. The Isu live in more concentrated communities and suffer from a shortage of land—the real explanation of their excessive devotion to trade. In the matter of government, too, there were differences between the Isu and Oratta, due principally to the fact that among the Isu the influence of the Ọzọ society, or the institution of title-taking, was predominant. This institution was one of the principal means of maintaining law and order and served as a unifying force between the various village-groups, thus giving the Isu a greater measure of solidarity than they would otherwise have had.

It is clear, therefore, that even in the larger territorial groupings there is some consciousness of unity and kinship between the constituent elements based on the similarity of culture-pattern. And it is possible and indeed probable that this can be utilized for the purpose of building up federal native administrations, so that in due course groups like the Oratta and Isu will become consolidated units, each with its own executive council, treasury, judiciary, and prisons, and its programmes of medical, educational, and public works services.[1]

FAMILY, VILLAGE, AND CLAN ORGANIZATION (OWERRI DIVISION)

The Village-group.

With this preliminary sketch we may now proceed to examine the constitution and composition of a single independent village-group or commune, analysing its social organization down to the lowest unit. The first example will be of the village-group or 'town' of Owerri, the small community from which an entire province, comprising two million people, has received its name.[2]

---

[1] A movement in this direction had already begun in 1931, when a large group of Isu, known as Ikeduru, demanded separation from the Oratta, and the establishment of a judiciary of their own.

[2] Owerri is the official spelling. But the word is pronounced Owɛrɛ.

Owerri belongs to the Oratta sub-tribe and consists of the following subdivisions, the numbers in each of which are shown in brackets.

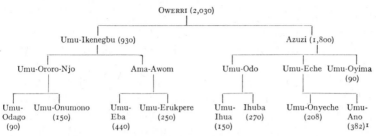

A remarkable feature in this scheme is the obvious tendency towards a dual organization. An apparent exception is the division of Azuzi into three sections instead of two, but this is explained by the circumstance that the Umu-Oyima are recent immigrants from the town of Nekede, who will, it is thought, soon coalesce with the Umu-Eche.

How far this practice of bisection is a blind following of an ancient custom, or is due to social and political factors which are still at work, would be an interesting subject for investigation. In some Ibo communities the custom would seem to have some connexion, direct or indirect, with the practice of exogamy. For at Ama-Imo an instance was obtained of a large exogamous group which had recently split into two sections between which intermarriage is now permissible. In Owerri itself, however, the dual groupings have no apparent connexion with exogamy, as the rule of exogamy covers the entire community, with the exception of the Umu-Oyima and Umu-Ano, both of whom are recent settlers. No native of Owerri, therefore, may marry any other native of Owerri, unless he or she belongs to the Umu-Oyima or Umu-Ano kindreds. There is a further proviso that members of the Umu-Onyeche and Umu-Ano kindreds may not intermarry, as these two kindreds are next-door neighbours. So here we have an instance of two groups coalescing to form an exogamous unit —the exact opposite of the case recorded at Ama-Imo.

It was stated that not very long ago the Umu-Ororo-Njo and the Ama-Awom constituted a single *nchi*, or group, i.e. that the Umu-Ikenegbu group has only recently bisected itself into two distinct social and political groups. The explanation given in this case was that an *nchi* tends to split in two as a result of the increasing separation

[1] Accurate figures for the Umu-Ano group were not obtained.

between two branches of a kindred claiming descent from one man and two wives. The descendants of each wife form a distinct *onunne* (children of one mother), and the two *onunne* so formed tend to become independent of each other, and in some cases even hostile. In due course the *onunne* again subdivides itself, the mode of reckoning descent from the first 'mother' giving place to that of descent from a later 'mother'. This statement may be accepted as a rough mode of explaining how subdivisions arise, but does not explain the frequency of a dual organization rather than a triple or quadruple organization, as there is no reason why the original founder of a family should not have had three or four or more wives instead of two.

The official register of Owerri shows the *nchi* of Umu-Ororo-Njo as consisting of two *onunne* or extended-families, namely, the Umu-Odago and the Umu-Onumono. But an examination of the composition of the *nchi* by the genealogical method proved that in reality it consisted of five distinct family groups, viz. the Umu-Odago, Umu-Onumono, Umu-Mano-Mere, Umu-Nwe-Mere, Umu-Chikwere, and a few strangers. Nevertheless, the *nchi* has formed itself into two groups, one consisting of the Umu-Odago, Umu-Mano-Mere and a section of the Umu-Onumono, and the other of the remainder of the Umu-Onumono, the Umu-Chikwere and Umu-Nwe-Mere. It was said that this dual division had only recently come into being, with a view to simplifying the collection of the Government tax, but this must be considered doubtful, as the *nchi* showed signs of cleavage a good many years ago, when it put forward two candidates for a single vacant chieftainship. However this may be, it would seem certain that, as far as the Umu-Ororo-Njo are concerned, the dichotomy of the group is due to political rather than kinship causes. And as for the Ibo as a whole, all we can say is that, just as it takes two to make a marriage or a quarrel, so the Ibo find that a dual organization is a natural condition of society and an aid to its control.

The Local Group and Kinship.

Confining our attention now to a single *nchi* or local group, we may proceed to analyse the composition of the Umu-Ororo-Njo. This group consists of the following kindreds or extended-families: (*a*) Umu-Odago, (*b*) Umu-Onumono, (*c*) Umu-Mano-Mere, (*d*) Umu-Chikwere, and (*e*) Umu-Nwe-Mere. All these families, with the exception of certain stranger elements, are believed to be related to one another by direct descent from Ekwem Arugo, the traditional

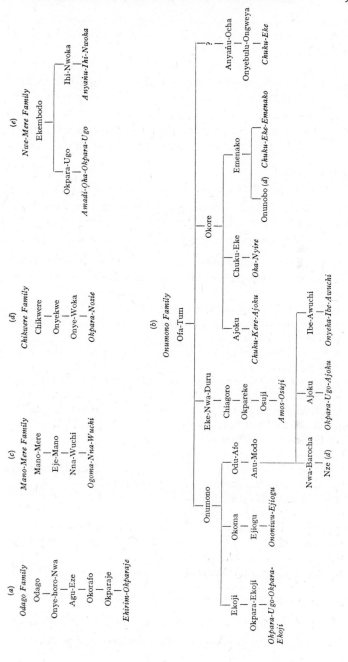

founder of Owerri. The genealogical tables on page 95 show the reputed descent of each family, the names of the living headmen being italicized.

In addition to the above families there is attached to the *nchi* a smaller *nchi* composed of *osu*, or cult-slaves (or their descendants) formerly owned by various members of the free-born *nchi*. There are ten households of these *osu*. In former times the *osu* lived immediately opposite the entrance of the compound of their respective owners, but at the present time they are grouped together in an *nchi* of their own.

The Household.

The *nchi* of the free-born consists of twenty-two *onu-isi-onye* or households,[1] and the following is a list of the heads of households (*obilobi*). The names italicized are those of the Ǫha or heads of families or family-groups. The functions of these will be described presently.

Heads of Households	Onunne (Extended-family)
1. Daniel Agonono (adopted stranger)	Umu-Odago
2. *Ehirim-Okparaje*	,,
3. Ejiogu (adopted stranger, but a distant maternal relative of Ehirim)	,, ,,
4. Nnǫ-Rǫm (adopted)	,,
5. Chuku-Eke-Onyebulu-Ongweya	Onumono (Umu-Okore branch)
6. *Ogoma-Nna-Wuchi*	Mano-Mere
7. *Okpara-Ugo-Okpara-Ekoji*	Onumono (Ekoji branch)
8. Ononiwu-Ejiogu	,, (Okoma branch)
9. Chuku-Kere-Ajoku	,, (Okore branch)
10. Oka-Nyire-Ǫha-Chuku-Eke	,, ,, ,,
11. Thomas (adopted stranger)	,, ,, ,,
12. Chuku-Eke-Emenako	,, ,, ,,
13. Okpara-Ugo-Ajoku	,, (Anu-Modo branch)
14. Ejiogu-Mba (adopted)	Onumono
15. Anyaǹu-Ihi-Nwoka	Nwe-Mere
16. *Amadi-Ǫha-Okpara-Ugo*	,,
17. Onyeka-Ibe-Awuchi	Onumono (Anu-Modo branch)
18. Amos Osuji	,, (Eke-Nwa-Duru branch)
19. *Okpara-Ugu-Iwu-Ala* (adopted)	,, ,, ,,
20. Njoku-Onu-Kwura (adopted)	,, ,, ,,
21. Kamalo-Anyaǹu (adopted)	,, ,, ,,
22. *Okpara-Nozie*	Chikwere

Let us now examine the composition of a single household. That

[1] The 'household' is usually a small 'extended-family'.

of Daniel Agonono will serve as an example. It consists of the following persons:

(*a*) Daniel Agonono, four wives, one son, and two daughters.

(*b*) Ogu-Ebula, one wife, and two sons.

(*c*) Onyemanze, two wives, two sons, and one daughter.

(*d*) Kamala, two wives, two sons, and one daughter.

(*e*) Acho, two wives, two sons, and two daughters.

The relationship between the above will be gathered from the following genealogical table.

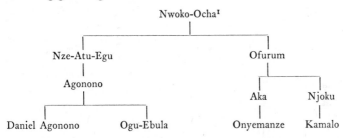

Acho is not shown in this table. He is a half-brother of Daniel Agonono's mother. His father, for some reason, left his own town, and so Acho joined the household of his brother-in-law. In addition to having children of his own Acho is also guardian of the three children of his late brother. It is interesting to note that one of these three children, a male, was married as a small child to a grown-up girl. This girl bore a child by another man,[2] and so Acho's brother's son, though only a boy of eleven, is legally a father.

In the matter of farm lands Daniel holds a plot of land on behalf of himself and his half-brother Ogu-Ebula, who has none of his own. Similarly, Onyemanze holds lands for himself and his brother, inherited from their father Aka. Aka, it may be noted, had received this land from Agonono (Daniel Agonono's father), who had acted as Aka's guardian after the death of Nze-Atu-Egu. Ofurum had died before Nze-Atu-Egu, and the land transmitted to Aka was that formerly held by Ofurum, who had received it from his father Nwoko-Ocha during the latter's lifetime.

Acho holds a piece of land which was given to him by Agonono.

[1] Nwoko-Ocha was a stranger adopted by the Umu-Odago extended-family. His descendants are therefore (it was said) disqualified from acting as head of the Umu-Odago.

[2] This was not a breach of native morality. See p. 276.

H

He can lease this land if he pleases, but he cannot pledge it, as he is not a patrilineal relative. If his family were to die out, the land would revert to Daniel Agonono or his descendants.

It is important to record details of this kind in view of the belief among many Europeans that all lands are held in common. It is sometimes thought also that labour is communal. But every adult male is responsible in the main for his own welfare. Co-operative assistance, however, is given when required. Thus, at the beginning of the farming season, all the members of the household assist in clearing each other's farms, and throughout the season the heaviest forms of work on each man's and woman's farm may be done by joint labour. The farm of an absentee member may even be farmed for him, in return for occasional gifts. In most other respects, also, the adult male members of a household are economically independent, though all help each other in difficulties. The proceeds of a woman's marketing are used for her own requirements and those of her children, though she may give a share to her husband, and possibly even to a co-wife. A woman owns her own cooking utensils, and besides cooking for her husband and children is responsible for collecting firewood and water.

The head of a household has numerous ritual, moral, and legal rights and obligations. He offers sacrifice for the welfare of the family, organizes the exploitation of family land, assigns kitchen-garden plots to wives, rations supplies in times of stress, helps members of the family who have got into difficulties, and bears a large part of marriage, funeral, and hospitality expenses. If the wife of any member of the household bears a child, the head of the household is expected to present her with a cloth and food, and to provide a goat for the naming feast. He himself confers the name. In short, the head of the household is the material and spiritual guardian of the group, and in external matters assumes responsibility for all, as far as he reasonably can.

In return for discharging these duties he receives respect and obedience. And he receives also material tokens of goodwill from any member of the household who has had a good harvest or been successful in some other way. He can claim one day's farm-work in the full eight-day week from each adult male, and he is also entitled to receive from them and their wives one-fourth of the wine obtained from their palms.[1] But when he taps his own trees, the head of the household is

[1] But one-eighth only from a wife who has purchased her palms with her own money.

expected to give one-eighth of the wine to the heads of each section
of his household. Thus Daniel Agonono would give one-eighth of
his wine to Ogu-Ebula and Onyemanze. Kamalo would be given
none, as he would receive a share of the wine given to Onyemanze;
and Acho also would receive none, being a relative in the female line.
It may be added that although Acho is the oldest member of the
household he is debarred by the patrilineal rule from holding the
position of head of the household. He may, however, act as Daniel
Agonono's representative at a public meeting. Most of the members
of Daniel's household are baptized Christians or catechumens.

One other example of the composition of a household may be given,
namely, that of Ononiwu-Ejiogu, who belongs to the Okoma branch
of the Onumono kindred. His household consists of the following
(children not reckoned):

1. Ononiwu and four wives.   5. Nze-Unebu (no wife).
2. Ohiri and two wives.   6. Obodo and one wife.
3. Mba-Ohoro and five wives.   7. Ukunna (no wife).
4. Amadi-Oha-Okpara and one wife.

The following table shows how the members of this household are
related to one another.

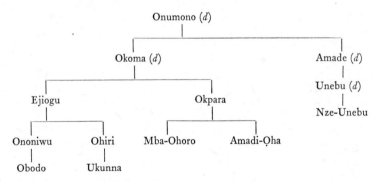

It will be seen that Ononiwu and Ohiri are first cousins of Mba-
Ohoro and Amadi-Oha. But it happens that they are also half-
brothers. This is due to the circumstance that when Ejiogu died one
widow was married to his younger brother, Okpara, to whom she
bore Mba-Okoro and Amadi-Oha. Nze-Unebu's father formerly had
a household of his own, but on his father's death Nze-Unebu joined
the household of Ononiwu, as he was too young to live by himself.

As in other households each married man must provide for himself and his wife, children, and other young dependent relatives. There is no community of stocks, but there is a good deal of co-operation, and it may be said generally of the Ibo household that it is an economic grouping which supplies most of its own needs, men, women, and children all contributing. The large number of wives in Ononiwu's household is an index of its prosperity.

As regards land, Ononiwu holds a portion of land which was given him by his father. This is regarded as his personal property and not as the joint property of his household. He can pledge it to a stranger if he pleases, but before doing so would give the first refusal to members of his own household (in which case the land would become the property or holding of the person who had received it in pledge). Ononiwu also owns a piece of land which he himself obtained in return for a loan of money. Finally, he holds, on behalf of the whole household, a portion of land which he divides out at the beginning of each agricultural year. Ohiri has an individual holding given him by his father, and this he shares with his son.[1] He is also, of course, entitled to a share in the common land of the household. All wives receive a piece of land annually, and there is a tendency for the same piece to be re-assigned and for the wife to pass this on at death to her sons—junior sons if her eldest son has already inherited a portion of land from his father.

Land Tenure.

As the subject of land tenure is of paramount importance for the study of family and village life, it will be advisable to digress here for a few moments in order to give a brief description of the system followed by the Ibo, so far as this could be ascertained in the course of general investigations. There is no subject on which more fallacious views are held by some Europeans, and even among some Administrative Officers of wide experience the belief still lingers that all native lands are 'communal'.

The various types of land may be classified as follows:

(*a*) Lands which are sacred or taboo.
(*b*) Virgin forest.
(*c*) Farm-land held in common by the members of a village, kindred, or extended-family.
(*d*) Individual holdings.

---

[1] Land may be assigned to sons when they are three or four years of age, and worked by the parents until the sons are old enough to work it for themselves.

The first class of lands includes sacred groves surrounding the shrines of public cults (such as Ala, the Earth-deity, and Ekwêsu, the spirit of evil). It also includes the taboo lands or 'evil bush' known as *aja ọfia*. In both these cases the ownership is regarded as vested in deities or spirits, and no one would normally attempt, or be allowed, to use any fraction of such land for farming purposes. It is a sign of the times, however, that cases have occurred in crowded areas of individuals clearing a patch of extensive taboo land in order to plant yams, being prepared to take the risk of being killed by spirits. If a farmer is bold enough to take this step (without interference from the elders), and farms for two years in succession without suffering misfortune, he becomes the owner of the land, which henceforth ceases to be regarded as taboo.

The next type of land is the virgin forest, which has remained un-used for farming purposes because nobody has required it, or because the village has forbidden farming there, lest it should lose its use as a means of defence or as shade or as a source of supplies of wood or fibre. If a piece of uncleared forest is of no obvious use to the village, any one is at liberty to clear it for farming purposes, and the land so cleared becomes his private farm.[1] He cannot be deprived of it, and he can pledge it or transmit it to his children. But if there is any uncertainty as to whether the village may require the uncleared patch, the would-be farmer must first obtain the permission of the local elders.

The third class of land is farm-land held in common by an entire village, kindred, or extended-family, being formally apportioned out afresh each time it is to be farmed.[2] It is land held in reserve for the benefit of the whole group (in addition to individual holdings), and cannot, therefore, be pledged without the consent of the group as a whole. Firstly, as regards farm-land common to the whole village, this is generally known as *ale-ọha* (land of the people) or *ale-nweko* (land held in common). In some districts[3] there are still large tracts of rich lands held in this way, but they are usually at a considerable distance from the village, the farm-lands nearer home being held by

---

[1] Cf. Laws of Manu (India), 'He who clears a piece of land is the owner of it.' (ix. 44).

[2] Unless it is so extensive that formal division is unnecessary.

[3] Thus, at Adâyi (Nsukka Division), land is so abundant that most of it is held communally and the necessity has not arisen for apportioning it out to families and individuals.

individuals or small families. In other districts (e.g. at Ache and Inyi) the only farm-lands held communally by the village or village groups are infertile lands of little use save for growing cassava. The richer lands have long since been apportioned out among the various kindreds and families. In other localities (e.g. at Owerri) there is no farm-land held by the entire community.

Land held in common by a kindred or extended-family is known as *ala-ndichie* or *obozoku* (ancestral land). As already stated, it is land apportioned annually to members of the kindred (in addition to their private holdings) and it can only be pledged to strangers by consent of the whole group. Where the kindred has split up into various branches it will generally be found that the land formerly held in common by the whole kindred has been subdivided among the various branches. Thus, at Owerri, the Onumono kindred, which consists of several branches, has now no land held by the whole group. The land formerly possessed by the entire kindred has long ago been parcelled out among the various branches. One of these is the Umu-Okore (see p. 94). Like the other branches the Umu-Okore received its share of land, but being hard pressed for money it decided to pledge a portion of this land.[1] Some time ago (it is said) the land so pledged was redeemed by the present head of the Okore group and retained by him for his personal use, on the ground that none of the elders of the Umu-Okore had assisted him in redeeming the land. This led to a dispute, and at a meeting of the elders of the local group (Ororo-Njo) it was held that the head of Umu-Okore had acted within his rights. If the other members of the Okore family wish to share the land they must pay to the head of the family some share of the redemption price.

It should be noted that strangers who have joined a local or kindred group have no automatic right to a share in the common land of the group. They may, however, be given a share as an act of grace, and would be expected to give a gift of a few yams at harvest to the senior elder or elders of the group. The same remark applies to slaves. In some villages (e.g. at Itika in Awgu Division) there is an old-standing complaint that land and economic trees[2] lent to slaves have, since the abolition of the status of slavery, become the property of the ex-slaves.

---

[1] The head of a family may have to pledge a piece of family land to pay off a debt left by the previous head, and he may insist on doing so against the wishes of the family, if the family has offered no assistance in paying off the debt.

[2] e.g. Oil-palms, coco-nuts, oil-bean, and mahogany trees.

Some of the former slave-owners, or their heritors, are content to leave their ex-slaves in possession, but others are eager to recover some at least of the land and trees, and to prevent the ex-slaves from pledging the land.

Next, there is the land on which compounds are built, together with the adjoining plots. This land belongs to the household occupying it. If the household removes to another site it retains its rights in this land. By common consent the household may give this land or a portion of it in pledge, but as a rule the household (or it may be an *onunne*) prefers to retain full rights over former sites for religious or, at any rate, for sentimental reasons. To give such lands in pledge would usually be regarded as slighting the ancestors who lie buried there.[1] Sites of former habitations are known as *uhu* or *ukwu* land.

Finally, and most important of all, comes the land which is individually held. This is land handed on by father to son, or acquired by clearing virgin forest or in return for a loan. In many village-groups there is scarcely any land at all within the recognized boundary of the group which is not held by individuals. Land so held can be pledged by the holder without reference to any one, and it is common practice for a man to pledge his land in order to cancel a debt, pay a bride-price, or even to raise the means of paying his tax. Land which has been pledged is normally redeemable at any time at the same rate at which it had been pledged,[2] and there is an Ibo proverb which says, 'A thing which is pledged is never lost' (*ihe ibe efui-efu*). In point of fact, however, pledged land is often permanently alienated. It may be pledged, for example, for a sum far in excess of that normally given, and so may remain unredeemed for generations, and become in fact unredeemable, as all evidence of the original transaction has been lost. In this way rich men have acquired land in perpetuity. In some communities, e.g. at Ama-Imo (Owerri Division), it seems to have been the custom that if a man had received a second loan in respect of a piece of land he had to repay double the total amount of the loan if he wished to redeem the land. In practice this virtually amounted to a sale. The same custom, in slightly different form, was found at

---

[1] Nevertheless, some families, particularly Christian families, do not mind leasing *uhu* land.

[2] But not, of course, until after harvest, if the land is under cultivation. A pledgee at Akabo (and no doubt other localities) is protected against arbitrary treatment by a rule that if the owner of the land demands its return before it has been farmed he has to refund twice the amount of the loan he had received.

Ihe in the Awgu Division, where it is possible for a landowner who wishes to hinder an ill-disposed relative from inheriting his land to fix the redemption price of land he has pledged at double the amount of the loan. In order to formalize this proceeding he demands from the pledgee, in front of witnesses, an additional payment of thirty pieces of the minute iron-hook currency which is still used in parts of the Awgu Division. The value of these thirty pieces is little more than a halfpenny, so that the additional payment has nothing of the nature of a cash sale, but is merely a legal formality serving as evidence of transfer. At Owele, Abo-Ogugu, and various other localities, it is even possible to sell land outright, by demanding from the buyer or pledgee an extra payment of eight yams, one fowl, and twenty pieces of iron-hook currency or some oil and palm fruit. This practice is, of course, uncommon, as no one would permanently alienate land except under great stress. Nevertheless it is increasing, and cases have even occurred in which the pledgee has endeavoured to secure the land in perpetuity by means of a written document.

It remains to add that, just as land may be pledged for a loan, so it may be leased for a season or longer. The rent charged may be nominal. Thus a man may lend a piece of land to a friend free of charge, expecting merely to receive a pot of palm-wine and a feast at harvest. Or, if the plot of land were substantial, he might demand a rental of twenty or thirty yams. In the Awgu Division cases came to my notice of plots of land being hired out to strangers at a rental charge varying from 3s. to 8s. per acre per annum.[1]

The Okpara.[2]

We have seen that the head of each household or small family-group has definite privileges and responsibilities, being at once the governor of the family and its trustee. He receives obedience and tokens of respect, but is expected to spend most of his money on bride-prices, funeral expenses, and assisting members of the family in numerous other ways. Similarly, in the larger family-group containing several households, there is a definite head, namely the *okpara* or 'elder brother' of the group, who, as the oldest member of the extended-family, or the head of the senior branch, is the holder of the family *ọfọ*. The *ọfọ* is a sacred symbol, a portion of the branchlet

---

[1] The question of administrative policy regarding land tenure is discussed on pp. 343–4.

[2] Pronounced *ókpárá*.

of the *Detarium senegalense* tree, a tree believed by the Ibo to have been set aside by Chuku (God) as the symbol of truth. Possibly one reason for its use as a family symbol is that the dead portions of branchlet break off sectionally from the parent branch, just as families break off from the parent stock.

The authority of the *okpara* is based largely on the fact that he is the intermediary between the family and the ancestors, and that to insult him is to insult the ancestors, on whose goodwill the members of the family are largely dependent. The *okpara* offers sacrifice on behalf of the whole family or of individual members of the family. If he is displeased with one or more of the family he may, when offering sacrifice, ask the blessing of the ancestors 'for those of the family who are right-minded', and this reservation would cause disquietude or even alarm among those with whom he had quarrelled. Or if an individual member of the family had (at the instance of a diviner) been instructed to offer sacrifice to his ancestors through the head of his family, the latter might refuse to do so, on the ground that he would imperil his own safety if he performed rites on behalf of one who had insulted the ancestors by insulting himself. (In such cases peace is usually restored by the delinquent giving a small gift to the *okpara*.)

Though the *okpara* is the chief priest and ceremonial head of the *onunne*, and is a unifying force for the component parts, he is not entitled to interfere in the everyday affairs of the households or families composing the *onunne*. Each family-head is responsible for his own family. Nor, if the *onunne* comprises several branches, can he demand farm assistance[1] from the members of all the branches. He is only entitled to assistance from members of his own branch. Thus, if we refer to our genealogical table (p. 95) Okpara-Ugo-Okpara-Ekoji, who holds the senior *ọfọ* for the whole of the Onumono kindred, is only entitled to service from the Ekoji section of the kindred. Chuku-Kere-Ajoku is entitled to service from all members of the Okore branch (including the households of Oka-Nyire and Chuku-Eke-Emenako), and so on.

In addition to farm service the *okpara* of an extended-family has certain rights over animals killed during hunting by members of the family. A successful hunter must bring the dead animal to the house of the *okpara*, who sees that the animal is divided up in accordance

---

[1] Normally four days at the beginning of the farming season, and one day in eight throughout the farming season.

with custom. The *okpara* takes the heart and part of the chest; the hunter receives a leg, and is given another leg for his father, part of the ribs for his wife, sisters, and other women of the family, the jaw for his eldest son, the neck for his sisters' sons, and the head for members of his age-group. One leg is presented to the elders of his group and the remaining leg to the general body of hunters.

Privileges entail responsibilities, and if the head of a kindred or even of a household fails to fulfil his responsibilities, e.g. by assisting those in trouble or by providing wine on the occasion of a marriage, or a goat on the birth of a child, he would lose the allegiance of the members of his family-group. It may be said generally that the authority of the *okpara* of a family is less nowadays than it used to be, partly because the younger members of the family group (or at least those who have become Christians) no longer respect the religious authority of the *okpara*, and partly because they may be rich, while the *okpara* may be poor and incapable of rendering assistance. Even in the olden days the chief executive control of the *onunne* might have been vested in some rich, generous man, rather than in the *okpara*. Of this there will be more to be said presently.

The *ofo* of an *onunne*, together with the *umunne*[1] or cult of the founder of the family, is inherited by the next oldest member of the *onunne*, who thus becomes the *okpara*.[2] It does not pass to the late *okpara*'s eldest son, for it is said that if a family *ofo* passed to the eldest son 'it would be held by the head and not by the tail'.[3] This is the general rule, but there are exceptions in numerous communities (such as the village-groups of Umunoha and Ogwa, Orodo and Atta), where the senior *ofo* passes from father to son. The reason for this difference appears to be that in these communities family seniority is, or was, determined by the order in which families first took the Ozo title. The *ofo* of this title passes from father to son.

The *ofo* of the extended-family is not to be confused with the

---

[1] See p. 63.

[2] But adopted members, relatives in the female line, and persons of slave origin are not permitted to hold the *ofo* of an extended-family. And in some localities the *ofo* of the extended-family is simply the personal *ofo* of the senior member, i.e. there is no hereditary family *ofo*.

[3] Normally when the holder of an *ofo* swears an oath or makes a solemn asseveration he holds the *ofo* by the 'tail', i.e. by the thin end, and strikes the ground with the thick end. But when withdrawing a curse imposed by the *ofo* he holds the *ofo* by the thick end and keeps circling the thin end on the ground, saying: 'Formerly we called down evil upon you, but now we withdraw. May no evil come upon you.'

purely personal *ọfọ* which are inherited by eldest sons, provided they are old enough to assume them. A personal *ọfọ* is originally acquired at the instance of a diviner.[1] The person directed to obtain the *ọfọ* provides himself with a piece of the sacred branchlet, and summons to his house a number of elders previously specified by the diviner. One of these takes the *ọfọ* stick and ties round the head a number of twigs. It is the addition of these twigs that makes the *ọfọ* thicker at one end than the other. While he is fashioning the *ọfọ* the other elders say: 'We are making an *ọfọ* for you that you may hold it for a long time and that it may descend from one eldest son to another. It should not pass to any one who is not entitled to hold it.' A fowl is then killed and the blood is poured over the thick end of the *ọfọ*. One of the elders now takes a kola, chews it, and spits it on the *ọfọ*, saying, '*Ọfọ*, be effective and perform the duty which your owner intends you to perform. Be attentive to him, but do not show violence towards his own kith and kin. For even friends may quarrel—pay no attention to trifles such as that.' The *ọfọ* is then handed to the owner, who receives it with both hands. A fowl is killed and eaten, and the elders receive a small gift (in cowries). The particular elder who made the *ọfọ* is given a special fee. During the ensuing four days the new *ọfọ*-holder addresses prayers to his ancestors and household gods, that he may live long to hold the *ọfọ* and that the *ọfọ* 'may never meet the fate of being thrown away'. (A personal *ọfọ* is thrown away if the owner leaves no sons.)

The *ọfọ* of an extended-family is not carried about in public unless the owner is attending some important meeting at which the *ọfọ* may be required. But the owner of a personal *ọfọ* frequently carries it with him as a charm or as a medium for swearing an oath. If he should suddenly find himself called upon to swear (or to swear some one else), and is without his *ọfọ*, he may take a twig of the *ogirisi* tree and use that as though it were an *ọfọ*. Or he may use his clenched fist. The owner of an *ọfọ*, if he loses anything by theft, may invoke evil on the thief, striking the ground at the same time with his *ọfọ*. Or he may curse the thief, through the agency of his young children, this being considered as efficacious as a curse invoked through an *ọfọ*. The children take a twig of the *ogirisi* tree, and as the father invokes evil on the thief the children strike the ground with the twig. The act of striking the ground with an *ọfọ* (or *ogirisi* twig) is intended to carry the message to the ancestors who are under the earth. The invocation

---

[1] For a parallel account of the procedure followed in Awgu see pp. 63-4.

of a curse is frequently accompanied by an act of striking the ground, and the withdrawal of a curse by circling the *ọfọ* on the ground.

There are two further points of interest regarding *ọfọ*, namely, (*a*) that an *ọfọ* cannot be inherited until the final funeral rites of the late holder have been performed, and (*b*) that if the holder of an *ọfọ* happens to be a young person, as he may very well be, particularly in communities like Umunoha and Ọgwa where the *ọfọ* passes from father to son, he is expected to act on the advice of some elder specially selected for this purpose. On occasions of religious rites, for example, the elder would direct the younger man what to do and say. Another point of administrative importance at the present time is that if the head of an extended-family happens to be a Christian he may refuse to assume the *ọfọ*. In some cases this difficulty is overcome by appointing some non-Christian member of the family to act as the *okpara*'s deputy. But if the particular extended-family happens to be the senior family of the whole village-group, their *ọfọ* taking precedence of the *ọfọ* of all other families, great pressure would be brought on that *okpara* to assume the *ọfọ* personally. It is commonly said that if a man refuses to 'take up' the senior *ọfọ* of a village-group that *ọfọ* will soon bring him to a violent death.

There is a definite ritual in assuming a family *ọfọ*. It is brought in a bag by the late *okpara*'s eldest son, who is careful not to touch the *ọfọ* himself. The bag is handed to the new *okpara*, who takes out the *ọfọ* and touches it with a chicken, saying, 'Ọfọ, I cleanse you of defilement (i.e. of death). I take you into my care, as I am the rightful person to do so. May I hold you for many years.' He then throws the chicken away. This rite is carried out in the presence of four elders of the *onunne* or of the *nchi*.

We have seen that the *okpara* of every extended-family is the holder of the family *ọfọ* and is also priest of the *umunne* or family-cult. In the case of a large kindred, consisting of several branches, the senior *ọfọ* is held by the senior branch (or by the branch which first included in its ranks a member of the Ọzọ society). Thus, in the case of the Onumono kindred, which consists of six branches, namely, (1) Ekoji, (2) Okoma, (3) Anu-Modo, (4) Eke-Nwa-Duru, (5) Okore, and (6) Anyaṅu-Ocha (see genealogical table on p. 95), though the *okpara* of each branch holds an *ọfọ* for that branch, there is one *ọfọ* which takes precedence of all the others, namely, that of Okpara-Ugo-Okpara-Ekoji, who is therefore the senior *okpara* of the entire Onu-mono kindred. The order of seniority of the various branches of the kindred is usually well recognized, and at any general meeting of the entire kindred the various holders of family *ọfọ* lay their *ọfọ* down on the ground in strict order of seniority. Similarly in a small local group or village composed of extended-families or kindreds which may be unrelated to one another, the senior *ọfọ* is that of the family which first came to the locality, or first became ennobled, by obtaining a title. Thus in the Umu-Ororo-Njo *nchi*, the senior *ọfọ* is that of Ehirim of the Umu-Odago, which is reputed to be the oldest family in the *nchi*. In the whole village-group or commune the same principle is followed, namely that the senior *ọfọ* is that of the oldest family, or of the family which had first acquired a title for its leader.

The senior *okpara* is the ritual head of the group, and, as such, at all public meetings is the first to lay his *ọfọ* on the ground and the first to receive a share[1] of all sacrificial[2] foods, gifts, fines, or fees. He is the direct representative of the group before the ancestors. If the meeting had been summoned to settle a dispute, the parties concerned would, on the conclusion of the evidence, call on all the *Ọha* or heads of extended-families, to swear on their *ọfọ* that the decision they were going to give was in accordance with custom, and that none of them had taken a bribe or would show favour because of some family relationship or enmity. The holder of the senior *ọfọ* would then stand up and, holding his *ọfọ* in his right hand, say: 'Our judgement is in accordance with custom and is one therefore by which you must abide. If you refuse to obey the decision may *ọfọ* kill you.' He would then strike the ground with his *ọfọ*, and all the other *Ọha* would follow suit.[3]

---

[1] As great importance is attached by the Ibo to the order observed in 'sharing' anything publicly, it may be of interest to give some examples of the class of things which are publicly shared. In olden days the property of a trader captured because he owed a debt or belonged to an enemy town was divided out publicly. Refugees might be sold and the proceeds shared publicly. A cow or other animal belonging to a public cult may, with the consent of the deity, be killed and the meat divided among the townspeople. Wild pigs or antelopes killed in hunting are shared among the families of the local group. The fees of candidates for the Ọzọ title are shared by the members of the Ọzọ society. At weddings the father of the bride provides the elders and others of the *nchi* with wine (given by the bridegroom) and this is formally shared. Similarly, the goat given by a man to his father-in-law when his wife bears a child is shared out among the members of the group. Fines for offences were shared, and at the present time money given by the Government for public work done is shared.

[2] But if sacrifice is offered to some deity with a priest of its own, the priest receives the first share of the sacrificial foods.

[3] In some communities (e.g. Avuvu) the proceedings at a public meeting are

It may be noted here, incidentally, that the term *Oha* is applicable to the *de facto* heads of families and is not, therefore, synonymous with the English word 'elders'. A comparatively young man may be one of the *Oha* if he is the *okpara* or recognized head of his family. On the other hand, an old man of, say, sixty, would not be classed among the *Oha* if his elder brother or cousin were alive. The general term for elders is *ndi-oki*, and this term includes all heads of households, even if they are still comparatively young. A full court for the decision of any matter includes the *ndi-oki* and *Oha*, but a restricted court consists of *Oha* only. It is considered that a court which consists solely of *Oha* is more inclined to abide by custom and the truth, as they are all holders of powerful *ofo*, which can injure themselves as well as others. But a court of *Oha* may call in elders who are not *Oha* as assessors, if they find the matter one of difficulty. A party to a suit may summon all the elders or only the *Oha*. But any elder or *Oha* may absent himself from any trial in which he knows that a member of his own group has a bad case.

In a large kindred composed of several branches, though the head of each branch may hold an *ofo* for the branch, there may be only a single *umunne*[1] (cult of original ancestor) for the entire kindred, the priest being the *okpara* of the senior branch. In time, as a branch increases in numbers, it may (at the instance of a diviner) set up an *umunne* of its own. In this case particles are taken from the cultus-symbol of the original *umunne* and built into the new cultus-symbol, which represents not the founder of the entire kindred, but the founder of the branch. For a time the members of the branch may continue to offer occasional sacrifice at the original shrine, but in due course they become wholly independent. The religious independence is accompanied, *pari passu*, by a social and political independence.

From our sketch of the *okpara*, whether of an extended-family, kindred, local group (*nchi*), or village-group, it is apparent that he is a ritual head to whom respect is due in virtue of his position *vis-à-vis* the ancestors. If he happens to be a man of substance and strong personality he may dominate his own *umunna* and exercise considerable influence also in all matters of general public importance. But he has usually no individual *executive* authority outside his own family-group. It may be said generally that among the Ibo govern-

opened by the oldest member present. The decision of the elders is frequently announced by the elder considered to be the best speaker.

[1] See p. 63.

ment is based on the family organization, and that the controlling authority is the general body of family heads, the senior *okpara* acting as ceremonial president.

Other Leaders of Society.

In all society the possession of wealth confers power, and so we find that, if in any group there was a personage of outstanding wealth, that personage obtained a measure of authority within the group which overshadowed that of the *okpara*. Such a personage could, if he were able and generous, obtain a position of chieftainship of his local group (*nchi*), and be styled the *Onyisi*[1] or head of the group. He might even be regarded as the *Onyisi* of the whole village-group. He obtained his position for obvious reasons. By rendering services to all he placed all under an obligation. By being able to purchase fire-arms and powder he was not only able to protect himself and his own kindred, but he could offer protection to other kindreds and thus place them in the position of dependants. With him rested the decision whether the group should go to war or not, for he alone could provide the means of carrying on war successfully. Thus he obtained control over the younger age-grades, which readily placed themselves at his service for any purpose. By rendering financial aid to all he was constantly adding to the number of his free-born followers, and by demanding a major portion of captives taken in war (as compensation for his expenditure on arms) he was constantly adding to the number of his slaves. It is easy to understand that a rich, generous man could become the principal judge and centre of authority. When he died his authority was handed on to a brother or son, and thus his family became hereditary rulers. Even if the wealth of the family declined, the people, with their innate respect for heredity, would continue to recognize the head of the family as their *Onyisi*. But if the wealth of the family became so diminished that it could no longer protect and assist, then the members of the group transferred their allegiance to some other individual who had been successful in trade and built up a large family.

To take an example from the Umu-Ororo-Njo, one Anu-Modo of the Onumono kindred was in pre-Government days recognized as

[1] But the term *Onyisi* or *Onyishi* sometimes connotes the *Okpara*. The general term for rich man is *Ogarainya*. The leading *Ogarainya* of an *nchi* may be styled the *onye uku* or 'big man', but if he were a member of the Ọzọ society he might hold the title of *Eze* or 'lord'.

the *Onyisi* of the *nchi*, as well as being one of the principal personages in the village-group of Owerri. He was addressed as *Di Ayi* ('Our Husband') by all members of the *nchi*, because, if any monetary or other trouble overtook the *nchi* as a whole, or individual members of the *nchi*, Anu-Modo bore the brunt. In return for his protection all members of the *nchi* were expected, and in fact required, to render service on his farm when called upon to do so, and any one who absented himself unreasonably from such service was fined by the members of his age-grade. He could summon a meeting at his house for any purpose, and took the principal part in deciding matters of importance affecting the *nchi*. When he died he was succeeded by his son Nwa-Barocha, who became a 'warrant chief' in Government times; and at the present time, though the family of Anu-Modo has lost much of its wealth, his grandson, Ugo-Ajoku, is regarded as the *Onyisi* of the group (i.e. of Umu-Ororo-Njo). The *okpara* of the group is, however, Ehirim, who holds the senior *ǫfǫ*. Ehirim himself admits that in executive matters he has no authority (outside his own extended-family). Ugo-Ajoku, however, respects the religious position of Ehirim, and it was stated that a senior *okpara* of a group may abuse the richest man without fear of retaliation: the latter would merely reply, 'You speak as you do, because it is you,' i.e. 'Your ritual position enables you to take liberties which no other person in the group would dare to take.'

In the neighbouring *nchi* of Ama-Awom, Njemanze occupied a corresponding position, and could command the age-grades of the *nchi* to wage war on some other group, or capture individuals. The captives were held to ransom and, if not redeemed, were sold. The age-grades were rewarded by gifts of dogs or goats. All minor disputes within the *nchi* were normally settled by a council of elders, but difficult cases were referred to Njemanze, whose decision was final. If any man of Ama-Awom got into debt, Njemanze would pay his debt and make the man his servitor. Or if a family of Ama-Awom had a dispute with some outside family, Njemanze would fight on their behalf, and in return would claim compensation in some form or other. It is said that rich men of the kind indicated pursued a definite policy of rendering assistance in order to gain ascendancy over the persons assisted. On the other hand, a family which felt itself to be weak would endeavour to secure the friendship of a rich man by rendering him voluntary services and then persuading him to swear an oath of friendship with them. Nowadays there is less inclination to rely on the rich, as poor people have learned to look to the Government for the protection they formerly sought from the rich. At public meetings, nowadays, the remark will often be heard, 'If it were not for the Government you would not have dared to open your mouth!'

In the commune of Ọgwa one Oginye, and subsequently his son Ejiofo, ruled the sub-division known as Umu-Ebwe. If any man of Umu-Ebwe committed a serious offence he was arrested and handed over to Oginye, and sold or kept in custody until redeemed by his father or brothers. Or he might be allowed to return home, provided he gave an undertaking to pay compensation. If he failed, Oginye might pay the compensation himself and then make the man work for him until he considered that the debt had been wiped out. If a member of another local group, or of a neighbouring town, had a complaint against any man of Umu-Ebwe he took his complaint to Oginye. Oginye decided when the group should go to war, and all heads of enemies taken in war were hung up on a tree outside his house. If a native of Umu-Ebwe were killed in another town, Oginye would order an age-grade to take revenge on that town, and if the murderer's head were brought back Oginye would reward the age-grade with gifts of money or of goats. If a man of Umu-Ebwe lost his life during the fighting, Oginye would compensate his brother by giving him part of the proceeds of the sale of one of the prisoners taken. He was not only the principal judge in his own local group but frequently acted as arbiter in disputes between other groups.

The rich, influential men of one community were well-known to the people of other communities, as (in return for dues) they could offer safe-conduct to travellers or visitors. Their very names served as a passport. When fighting occurred between two groups, the result frequently depended on the length of the purse of the rich men in each group, who, in addition to providing the material resources of war, might hire mercenaries to fight on their side. Nor was the existence of rich men of the type described exceptional. They could be found in almost every village-group. In those districts in which titles were in vogue, as for example among the Isu, they were the leaders of the titled classes, who were 'the heaven-born' of Iboland.

In drawing attention to the powers formerly exercised by men of outstanding wealth, it need hardly be said that there is no intention of justifying the former native court system, by which the court members or judges of the court, who were largely rich men of the type described, assumed (or were forced by the Government to

I

assume) uncontrolled authority in their towns. For in the olden days the rich received authority in return for services rendered, and they lost it if they acted in an oppressive manner. Moreover, in recent years there has been a tremendous alteration of status, due to new economic conditions. Nevertheless it would be impolitic and contrary to native ideas to attempt to exclude rich men of personality from taking an important part in local administration merely because they belong to a class which is no longer in favour with the Government, or because they do not happen to be holders of a senior *ọfọ*. In numerous communities the direct descendants of these rich men are still regarded as the natural leaders of the group, and cases have occurred in recent years of *okpara* being given a position of authority over the heads of these men, to which they had no traditional title. In one instance an *okpara* so advanced admitted that he had no customary claim to any executive authority, but remarked that 'if you put salt in a man's mouth he won't spit it out'!

It may also happen that the recognized leader of an *umunna* or an *nchi* is neither an *okpara* nor a rich man but owes his position to his own ability and uprightness or force of character. Under the old Native Court system each local group appointed a 'headman' or representative, a man of strong character if possessed of no other qualification. 'Headmen' were frequently nominees and henchmen of the Court Member or 'Warrant Chief', but the system of 'headmen' cannot be regarded as having been merely a convenient mode of increasing the court member's authority. It was a definite attempt on the part of society to adjust itself to the new political conditions, which demanded a greater measure of internal orderliness and cohesion than formerly existed. The headmen, to a great extent, took over the former functions of the captains of age-grades or of the *Ikoro-Ọha*, an institution which will be described in due course.[1] It is not surprising, therefore, that though the system of 'headmen' is disapproved by the Government it still continues to function unofficially.

As regards the government of the whole village-group, the centre of control was the general body of *Ọha* or *de facto* heads of families, members of the senior age-grades acting as their executive officers. No single individual could ever claim a position similar to that held in a local group by some individual of outstanding wealth. A feature of Ibo life is the intense jealousy existing between the various villages composing a village-group, and inter-village fighting was a common

[1] See p. 206 et seq.

occurrence. A general meeting of all sections of a village-group was infrequent, being held only when it was necessary to take common action against some external enemy, to offer common sacrifice, to get rid of some 'abomination', or to attempt to settle an internal dispute which, if allowed to continue, would be likely to disrupt the community.

V

THE SOCIAL AND POLITICAL STRUCTURE
(*continued*)

FAMILY, VILLAGE, AND CLAN ORGANIZATION (AWGU DIVISION)

THE concrete examples cited to illustrate the character of Ibo social organization have so far been confined to the neighbour-hood of Owerri. But as considerable variations occur between one district and another it will be advisable to give examples from other localities. In this chapter a review will be given of the conditions found in the Awgu Division of Onitsha Province, and we may begin, as before, with an examination of the composition of a kinship group and the various means used for its control.

The Kinship Group.

In the village-group or commune of Mboo one of the subdivisions in a dual grouping is known as Amudara. This contains two kinship groups known respectively as the Umu-Ago-Kugwa and the Umu-Ano-Kwocha. It is believed that the founders of these two kindreds were 'brothers'. But the relationship between the kindreds is now so remote that if a member of one wishes to marry a member of the other no objection is offered by the elders. Nor do the two kindreds unite to perform sacrifice to their common ancestor, as might be expected had they indeed had a common ancestor: but they do unite to perform sacrifice to the local Ala or Earth-deity which protects them both.

The Umu-Ago-Kugwa kindred consists of about 300 persons, who fall into six groups or extended-families, each with a recognized head. The following table shows the reputed relationship between these heads of extended-families.

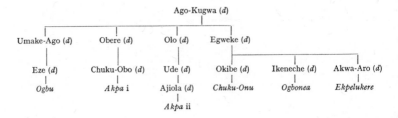

Confining our attention now to a single extended-family, let us select that of Ogbu and see how it is constituted. It consists of twenty-two brothers or half-brothers by the same father (Eze),[1] together with their wives and children and in some cases their deceased brothers' children and widowed mothers.[2] The whole of this group occupies ten compounds, of which seven are close together, the other three being located about a mile away. The compounds or households are as follows:

I. Ogbu, his six wives, eight sons, two daughters, one first cousin (Nwaka—son of father's brother) and his wife, one half-brother (Ngwoosu), and one son's wife. There are thus twenty-one persons in the compound. Ogbu, who is about forty-five years of age, has had thirty children of whom twenty died, i.e. two out of every three children are dead. Of the deceased children twelve died in the first year, five in the second, two in the third, and one in the fourth year of life. He has had eight wives in his lifetime, two of whom died. Six were natives of his own commune of Mboo. Only one of his sons is married, the others being still under age. He has no married daughters.

II. The head of compound No. II is a half-brother of Ogbu, named Nna-Bugu. His full-brother Oji lives with him and also five young sons and four young daughters. Under his care also are nine young nephews and three young nieces, the children of his deceased brother, Ezenta, who was formerly the head of the family. Nna-Bugu became the guardian of these children in preference to Ogbu, as he was the full-brother of Ezenta, whereas Ogbu was only a half-brother. He is responsible for the feeding, clothing, marriage, and proper behaviour of his nephews. He is the custodian of their property inherited from their father, and if he misuses it he is liable to be called to account by Ogbu his elder half-brother, who is the head of the family. When the nephews reach the age of sixteen or seventeen, Nna-Bugu will be expected to give them each a few pounds with which to begin trading. In the meantime the nephews assist their uncle in farming. Oji farms independently of his brother Nna-Bugu, but he, also, may utilize the services of his nephews. Nna-Bugu will be entitled to receive the bride-prices of his nieces. He has six wives and Oji has one.

III. The adjoining compound is occupied by Okori, a son of Eze.

[1] The twenty-two brothers are the offspring of Eze's thirteen wives.
[2] There are also thirteen surviving daughters of Eze. Nine are married at Mboo, three in neighbouring towns, and one is unmarried.

Okori has eight wives, five young sons, and seven daughters. The abnormal number of wives found in this family-group is due to wealth acquired by trade and the practice of divination, for skill in which the family has long been noted. A feature of interest is that two of Okori's daughters bear the same name. This is due to the fact that both are believed to be reincarnations of Okori's mother. It is also of interest that one of his daughters is a surviving twin.[1]

IV. Compound No. IV is occupied by Nwajo, his half-brother, Sokivibe, and half-sister, Nwambo, his five wives, four sons, and three daughters. His full-brother, Ezakata, lives in a separate compound— not because he fails to get on with his brother, but merely as a matter of convenience. The younger brother refers all his difficulties to his elder full-brother, and each assists the other in farming. Half-brothers assist each other less frequently, as quarrels between half-brothers are common.

V. Compound No. V is occupied by Ngwoogo, a full-brother of Ogbu. He has one wife, two sons, and one daughter.

VI. No VI is occupied by Oke, a half-brother of Ogbu. He has three wives and one daughter. He had three sons, all of whom died within three years of birth.

VII. No. VII is occupied by Ude, a full-brother of Okori. He has two wives and two daughters. Two other children (one male and one female) died early.

VIII. Compound No. VIII belongs to Ezakata, a full-brother of Nwajo. His mother lives with him. He has two wives, two sons, and two daughters. It is interesting to note that one of the sons of Ezakata is called Nna-Nwa-Ago, i.e. 'the father of the son of Ago'. The reason for this curious name is that Ezakata is considered to be a reincarnation of a son of Ago, the founder of the extended-family of Ago-Kugwa. Ezakata is, therefore, also called Nwa-Ago (son of Ago). When Ezakata's son was born he was declared to be Ago himself, so that in relation to Ezakata he is Nna-Nwa-Ago (father of Nwa-Ago).

IX. This household is a heterogeneous collection consisting of Ogwa, son of Eze and full-brother of Ngwoosu (who lives with Ogbu), his wife and son, nine half-brothers, and two half-sisters. Of the nine half-brothers only one (by name Kama) is old enough to be married. Kama has two wives. When each of the young half-brothers marries he will found a separate home for himself. The mother of one of the young lads also lives in Ogwa's compound. This compound is that

---

[1] In bygone days twins were killed at birth. See p. 291.

formerly occupied by Eze the founder of the family-group, and Ogwa
has been placed in charge of it temporarily by his elder half-brother
Ogbu, the head of the family-group. In due course Ogbu will himself
take possession of his father's compound.

X. The next compound belongs to Ale-Nwo-Kara, son of Eze,
together with his wife and two sons.

XI. The final compound is occupied by Udumake, a full-brother of
Okori. He has two wives and two daughters.

Coming now to the question of authority within the kinship group,
the general principle is the same as in the Owerri Division. Each
household is controlled or directed by its senior member, and the
group of households constituting the *onunne* or *umunna* is controlled
by the heads of households acting in concert, under the presidency of
the *okpara*, i.e. of the senior elder or head of the senior branch. But
the *okpara* may be merely the ritual head of the kin, the real leadership
being vested in some person of wealth or ability, who may be the
holder of what is known in the Awgu Division as an *aro* or staff of
authority—a staff which was originally the insignium of a titled
society. Thus, in the case of the Umu-Ago-Kugwa kindred, the
senior elder, one Akpa, is merely the ritual head, the executive head
being Ogbu, who, with the approval of the whole kindred, inherited
the position of authority held by his father, a titled man of great
wealth.

Just as the head of a household offers, on behalf of himself and all
the members of his household, periodic sacrifice to his immediate
ancestors, so the ritual head of the kin offers sacrifice on behalf of the
whole kin to the plurality of ancestors, and in particular to the founder
of the kin. He is the holder of the senior *ofo*—an *ofo* being (as already
stated) part of a tree specially set aside by God as a symbol and
guarantee of truth, and a suitable abode therefore for the ancestral
spirits, who are champions of truth. All *okpara* accordingly are expected to be scrupulously truthful, and it is believed that if they
speak falsely, especially when holding their *ofo*, they will be killed
by their ancestors. This is the secret of much of their authority. It
is believed that an *okpara*'s *ofo* can kill all who deal falsely by it, or
deliberately instigate mischief within the family group. Thus it is
said that if a man had committed adultery with a kinswoman, his
guilt would be revealed by the ancestors on the first occasion on which
he dared to take part in rites offered to the *ofo*. In these rites the
head of the kin lays the *ofo* on the ground and speaks as follows: '*Ofo*

of our ancestors, receive our offerings of food. Let not the men of
our kindred die: let not the women die: may the women we marry
bear children, and may the children, male and female, grow up strong
and prosperous and remain long in the world. But bring not to us
any child that will be an "abomination" or a thief or poisoner. Prevent
murder from entering our midst, and avert accidents among us,
whether great or small. May our crops exceed those of other men.'
Having said this he splits a kola and places it on the ground beside the
ọfọ. He then slays a chicken, pours the blood over the *ọfọ*, plucks some
feathers from the chicken, and sticks them in the blood. The flesh of
the chicken is cooked and pieces of the liver are laid on the *ọfọ*. The
officiant also chews a piece of kola, together with some pepper, and
spits the mixture on to the *ọfọ*. Finally, having smoothed the surface
of the *ọfọ* with his hand, he replaces it in his house.

When a kindred decides to offer a joint sacrifice, the elders of the
various component families assemble at the house of the *okpara* in
order to make the necessary arrangements. It is a usual rule that the
cost of the sacrificial animals is divided equally among the extended-
families composing the kindred, irrespective of the size of the family.
The senior elder of each extended-family is held responsible for the
collection in his own group. When a private individual wishes to
offer sacrifice to any deity he may do so without reference to the
senior elder, but on completion of the sacrifice he is bound to take a
piece of the sacrificial animal to the senior elder.[1] Similarly it is
customary for any one who kills a game-animal to give part of the
quarry (e.g. the liver or neck) to the senior elder of his family-group
(though he may refuse to do so if he is on bad terms with him).
Sometimes, if the kindred is composed of two extended-families, the
members of one extended-family give the necks of their quarry to the
senior elder of the other extended-family, and vice versa.

The senior elder or *okpara* of the kindred is consulted on all matters
affecting the welfare of the kindred, and his advice can never be
ignored unless he is so old and decrepit that another elder has to act
on his behalf.[2] He takes immediate steps to stop inter-family fights

---

[1] He may ask the senior elder to sacrifice on his behalf. A man who believes himself to be troubled by the ghost of his dead father or uncle generally appeals to the
senior elder, who goes to the grave of the troublesome relative, plants his staff there,
and asks the dead man to desist.

[2] But even though he is decrepit he may still be called on to offer the customary
sacrifices.

within the kindred and, assisted by the other elders, investigates all disputes and warns those who have misbehaved themselves that if they repeat their misconduct they need not look to him for assistance. If the matter were serious, such as theft, he might have to warn the thief that a repetition of his offence would lead to his being driven out of the kindred or (in the olden days) being sold as a slave to the Aro.[1] He might even order him to be tied hand and foot, and placed on a platform over a smoking fire for two days without food or drink. He might threaten to drive out of the kindred any young man who had shown himself to be lazy and had taken no steps to obtain a wife. He confers a name on all children born into the kindred, and, if he is the holder of an *aro*, all new-born babies have to be presented to the staff.[2]

At a general meeting of the kindred the *okpara* is given ceremonial precedence. If the heads of each family-group have occasion to bring their *ọfọ* to the meeting, the *ọfọ* of the *okpara* is first placed on the ground, the *ọfọ* of the other elders being placed round it. When sacrifice is offered to the ancestors by the whole group his *ọfọ* receives the first offerings of kolas and palm-wine. When a man takes a title he asks the head of his own immediate family to sacrifice on his behalf, but he would also ask the *okpara* of the kindred to sacrifice animals provided by him for the ancestors and the members of the kindred, the blood of the animals being poured over the *okpara*'s *ọfọ* with a prayer for the welfare of the taker of the title. When gifts, fees, or sacrificial foods are divided, the *okpara* takes the first share. When meetings are held to settle disputes, he is usually called upon to announce the decision of the elders, holding his *ọfọ* in his right hand and quoting precedents in support of the decision given.[3] He receives a special fee for his service. Owing to the necessity for being able to quote precedents the family of the *okpara* tends to become expert in legal matters. It is therefore quite appropriate that *okpara* should receive from the Government some recognition consistent with their status. But there should be no misunderstanding as to what their status is. The *okpara* is not normally a 'chief', in the ordinary acceptation of that term. For most practical purposes the families composing a kindred are independent of each other, and the authority of the *okpara* may be purely ceremonial. If he is an able man his

[1] i.e. the traders and slave-dealers of Aro-Chuku.
[2] For the ritual followed see p. 296.
[3] But the duty of announcing decisions may be the privilege of a particular family other than the *okpara*'s.

authority is great: if he is also wealthy he is indeed a chief: if he is neither he is a mere figurehead, and the real leader or chief of the kin—if there is any single individual leader at all—may be some one, not necessarily an elder, possessed of personality and possibly also of wealth, or some one whose father or grandfather had been a man of substance and a senior member of a titled society.

A few remarks may now be made about the legal system within the kindred. It may be said generally that an offence committed by one member of a kindred against a fellow member was settled privately within the kindred as far as possible, and was dealt with much more leniently than a similar offence tried publicly. *A fortiori*, an offence committed by one member of an extended-family against a member of the same extended-family was treated with still greater leniency. A few examples will illustrate the procedure. At the village of Umuhu (Owele) there is a large kindred known as the Eworaga. It consists of six extended-families, viz. (1) Umanoano (120), (2) Umuohagu (45), (3) Umochima Ana (25), (4) Umodafia (45), (5) Umohojo (60), and (6) Umanoke (12). Each of these extended-families is controlled by its elders under the presidency of its senior elder, but the whole kindred of Eworaga recognizes the supreme authority of the senior elder of the Umanoano extended-family, a man named Okerekenta. It so happens that Okerekenta is the most aged elder in the kindred and the holder of the senior *ofo*, but his authoritative position within the kindred is not due solely to these circumstances but also to the fact that his own particular subdivision of the kindred has from time immemorial been a wealthy and powerful family, and a recognized court of arbitration, not merely for the whole of the Eworaga kindred, but for the whole of the village of Umuhu. No important case could be settled at Umuhu without the attendance of the head of this family, who acted as president of the local council and announced its decisions, holding in his hands the *aro* or spear which was the guarantee of his authority. Within his own kindred his influence was so great that it amounted almost to a measure of chieftainship. All serious matters occurring within the kindred were reported to him and settled at his house, and all meetings of the elders of the kindred for any secular purpose, or for making arrangements for a common sacrifice, were held at his house. He represented the kindred in all its external relations.

Nevertheless, each extended-family within the kindred endeavoured to settle its own disputes without reference to Okerekenta. Thus, if a man of the Umohojo extended-family had been caught pilfering from another member of the Umohojo family, the matter was dealt with quietly by the senior members of the Umohojo family, the culprit being warned that, if he were capable of stealing from one of his own 'brothers' and continued in that frame of mind, he would soon make inroads on the property of other families, and involve not merely himself but all the members of his family in the evil consequences. A case of this sort was not even always brought to the notice of the senior elder of the extended-family, lest this would lead to a meeting of elders and the affair become noised abroad by the married women of the compound. It might, therefore, be settled secretly by the two small (or primary) families concerned. But a repetition of his offence would result in the culprit's conduct being reported to Okerekenta, who, with the other elders of the kindred, might order him to be tied up for several days. If, on the other hand, a member of the Umohojo extended-family accused a member of the Umochima extended-family of having pilfered his property, the matter would be immediately brought to the notice of Okerekenta, who would summon a meeting of the elders of the whole kindred to examine it. If the charge were proved, the punishment inflicted would be very much less than if the man had stolen from a member of some other kindred and had had to stand his trial before the elders of the whole village. He might escape without any other punishment than contempt and ridicule and an order to restore the stolen property. And he might also be ordered to give a ram to the owner of the stolen property for sacrifice to Njọku, the yam spirit. If he repeated his offence, and it became apparent that his continued presence within the kindred would be a nuisance to all, he would not again be dealt with by the elders of his own kindred but by the general assembly of the whole village. The reason for this was that the penalty for persistent theft was selling into slavery, and fellow members of a man's kindred were averse to being a party to this extreme measure.[1] Nor would any member of a kindred accept the proceeds of the sale of a fellow member.

[1] But in some cases if a man had become a notorious thief he might be sold to the Aro by his own brother. In others, though a man would refrain from selling a member of his own extended-family, he would have less compunction about selling a member of another extended-family of his own kindred (Oduma). At Awgu the head of a kindred might, at the instance of the elders of the village, order a thief to pack up his things and accompany Aro traders as their slave. Rather than accept this fate many thieves committed suicide.

It does not follow, however, that the authority of the elders of the kindred was ever so great that their decisions were in all cases accepted without demur. Thus if Okerekenta ordered the accused to swear his innocence in a doubtful case, the plaintiff might object on the ground that the accused was a well-known liar who could protect himself by 'medicines' against the effect of the oath. He might insist that the matter should be referred to the decision of a diviner or to the oracle at Umunọha or Aro-Chuku. Or he might insist that the accused's relatives should also swear, knowing that the latter would refuse to do so if they considered the accused was guilty. If the plaintiff and accused were each supported by the members of his own extended-family, Okerekenta and the other elders of the kindred would have no option but to refer the case to a general meeting of the whole village. Normally, however, all cases were settled within the kindred when possible, if only to avoid the greater expense of public proceedings.

It is a common cause of complaint by the elders that their power, and in consequence the family solidarity, has been severely undermined by the present custom of plaintiffs referring every case, however trivial, to the decision of the Native Court.[1] Half-brothers frequently take action against each other in the Native Court, and nephews against uncles, without having previously referred the matter to the elders of their own kindred. Not that disputes between such close relatives were unknown in the past, for jealousy between half-brothers is a feature of polygamous society, and quarrels between young men and the brother of their deceased father were common on the ground that the uncle who had inherited the father's property (on behalf of the sons) had used it improperly. It may be of interest to describe how a case of this kind would have been dealt with in the past.

If a young man had occasion to complain that his paternal uncle had failed to provide him with a wife from the funds of his father's estate, he would report the matter to the head of his extended-family. The latter, in order to avoid any suspicion of partiality, would refer the young man to the senior elder of the kindred, who would summon the elders of the various component families and endeavour to arrive at a satisfactory decision. If they had any doubt about the evidence they would refer the case to a local-group tribunal with the Ala priest, perhaps, as president. Each party would present the members of the

---

[1] This was written in 1931, prior to the reorganization.

tribunal with a pot of palm-wine. The priest would lay the *ọfọ* of Ala on the ground, and, pouring some of the palm-wine into a buffalo-horn, would speak as follows, 'Ala, who protects men and women, come and drink and look into this matter. It is our desire to settle this case in accordance with our custom. You can discern who speaks the truth and who speaks falsely. Arrest the perjurer by causing him to fall sick and eventually to die.' The priest would then pour a libation on the ground and on the *ọfọ*, and all would help themselves to wine. The priest would now rise and counsel the members of the tribunal to give close attention to the evidence. He would then call on the plaintiff to state his case. If it appeared that the uncle was quibbling, the priest might there and then order him to swear on the *ọfọ* that he would indeed provide a wife for the plaintiff. If the uncle protested that he had no money, the plaintiff would take the priest and elders to the uncle's palm-grove, and the priest would there place a knotted palm-leaf or a piece of hide on the trees, as a sign that the trees were now under the interdiction of Ala. The taboo would be kept up until sufficient fruit had been collected by the agents of the priest to provide a wife for the nephew.

Quarrels between husband and wife, which could easily have been settled by arbitration under the old methods, are frequently nowadays taken straight into the Native Court, and result in a dissolution of marriage. Such quarrels might in the past have been settled in the husband's compound, without even the necessity of calling in the wife's relatives. Thus, at Owele, in cases of serious matrimonial quarrels, the wife would summon all the other wives, not merely of her husband's extended-family but of the whole of his kindred, and the husband would summon all the senior men. This joint council would meet in the husband's compound, and if they decided in favour of the husband they would warn the wife to mend her ways—to take more care, for example, in preparing her husband's food. Neverthe-less, they might call on the husband to display more patience. The male members of the council might suggest that the wife should pay a small fine, but this would be opposed by the females on the ground that the wife had been taken away from her parents and protectors. On the other hand, the husband might be ordered to give a gift to his wife. In any case he was required to provide palm-wine to those who had come to arbitrate.

A case occurred recently of a woman bringing an action in the Native Court against her late husband's son for attempting to drive her out of the compound.[1] She had taken no steps to have her case settled in the traditional fashion, which would have been as follows. The woman would have first reported the matter to the senior elder of the extended-family. He, in order to avoid any appearance of prejudice, would have referred her to the senior elder of the whole kindred, who would have decided the matter in consultation with the whole body of elders of the kindred, together with any elders of other kindreds in the village whom the woman had wished to call. This insistence on impartiality is a striking feature of the native legal system, of which there will be more to say at a later stage.

Another well-known feature is the collective responsibility of the extended-family, and to a lesser degree of the kindred, for the conduct of its members. The stock example of this is in cases of murder or manslaughter. Immediate retaliation was made by the kin of the murdered man on any member of the murderer's kin, and the property of the immediate relatives of the murderer was pillaged. In consequence of this rule the murderer was expected *by his own family* to commit suicide immediately, in order to save the whole family from attack and their property from spoliation. If the murderer failed to do this, the whole of his kin had to seek refuge in flight. When the anger of the murdered man's kin had subsided, the kin of the murderer could return on condition that the murderer, or *some other member of his family*, committed suicide. Details will be given on this subject later, and it need only be remarked here that in consequence of this rule the elders of a kindred were wont to warn their young men to keep control over their feelings and avoid the use of lethal weapons. Further, as murder was considered an offence against Ala, the Earth-deity, the crime, if committed against a fellow member of the same family, was not one which could be palliated or settled privately by the family itself. The whole community took action against the murderer, and his own brother might be the first to set fire to his house. Even if a man killed his brother accidentally, he had to fly and remain away for a period of one month. He was then permitted to return, but at the first festival of Ala he had to take a goat, fowl, new basket, cloth, and some yams to the shrine of Ala, where he knelt down and said, 'Ala, I bring these gifts to you. I did not kill my brother by design. I went out hunting like the rest, and killed him by an accident. Ala, spare my life.' The various articles brought were

[1] It was customary at Owele for a man to break down the hut of his father's widow if he suspected her of having appropriated any of his father's property.

left at the shrine. The animals were not sacrificed. The goat became sacred and taboo and was allowed to wander about unharmed. Indeed it was given the right of way on the road. If it bore young ones they also became taboo, being known as 'goats of Ala'. The goat was in fact a scapegoat, for it was stated that the 'evil' which had moved the man to kill his fellow passed into the goat, and that if any one ate the flesh of that goat the inherent 'evil' would cause his death. It is to be noticed that in a case of this kind (i.e. of a man killing a member of his own extended-family or kindred) no blood-money was payable, on the ground that it would be heinous to derive profit from the death of a 'brother' (Oduma).

The collective responsibility of the kinship group is shown also in numerous other ways. Thus (at Oduma), if a man were summoned by the elders of the town to answer some charge, and refused to attend, the elders would send young men to bring him by force. If they could not find him, they would capture any member of the accused's extended-family and keep him a prisoner until the accused appeared. This would induce the elders of the accused's extended-family to bring pressure on the parents of the accused to produce him or disclose his whereabouts. If the accused had run away to some distant town, the members of his extended-family would be called on to pay the penalty of the accused's offence. Similarly, in cases of debt, if the creditor could not induce the debtor to repay the loan, he would go to the compound of any of the accused's relatives who happened to be absent on their farms, and capture goats or any other articles equivalent to the amount of the debt. Later in the day he would send word to the owner of the property, informing him of the reason of his action. The owner in turn would bring pressure on the debtor to pay the sum he owed. If the creditor belonged to another village, he might appropriate property from any one in the creditor's village, the elders of which would then force the debtor to pay. These regulations do not imply that there was any collective ownership of property, or that a person was held morally responsible for the sins of his relatives. They were an obvious method of obtaining redress through those who were in a position to bring pressure. And they were evidence of the strength of kinship and local-group solidarity, which, indeed, they served to cement.

The Local or Village-Group.

A kindred may be so large that it coincides with the primary local grouping known in the Awgu Division as an *ọnuma* (or hamlet). Or

two or three kindreds living in close association may constitute an
ọnuma. A group of *ọnuma* form an *ṅkporo* (village) which in turn is
a subdivision of an *obodo* (village-group or commune).

The affairs of an *ọnuma* manage themselves for the most part. Even
if the kindreds composing the *ọnuma* are unrelated, the bond created
by local association is so strong that all consider themselves members
of one large family. All unite to offer common sacrifice and, if necessary, to take common action against any other *ọnuma*. Thus, if a
member of one *ọnuma* murdered a member of another, and the murderer escaped, the members, not merely of the murderer's kindred but
of all the kindreds composing the *ọnuma*, would be forced to take
refuge in flight. The *ọnuma* of the murdered man, assisted perhaps
by members of other *ọnuma* of the same *ṅkporo*, would pillage the
property of all and sundry in the *ọnuma* of the murderer.

The *ṅkporo* or group of associated *ọnuma* has also a well-marked
individuality. It enjoys indeed a solidarity that the *obodo* or village-
group does not possess. Its units are bound together by (*a*) the common possession of territory and consequently of a common cult of
Ala, and a common necessity for defence and particularly of defending
its farm-lands against encroachment; and (*b*) a sense of relationship
based on the belief in descent from a common ancestor and cemented
by the possession of a common emblem, tutelary genius, or taboo. It
is virtually, therefore, an independent unit, jealous of its own rights
and ever ready to take violent action, if necessary, against any other
ṅkporo. In pre-Government days it seldom referred any matter to
outside arbitration, except (*a*) one which, if it remained unsettled,
was liable to destroy its own solidarity, or (*b*) a dispute with a neighbouring *ṅkporo*. The occasions on which all the *ṅkporo* of a village-
group met in common council were few and far between. The *ṅkporo*
lived its own life and took little cognizance of what happened in other
ṅkporo. Prior to the advent of the British Administration it was
frequently unsafe for a member of an *ṅkporo* to wander outside its
boundaries, as he was liable to be caught and sold as a slave by members of a neighbouring *ṅkporo*. Fighting between neighbouring *ṅkporo* of the same *obodo* or commune was constant, and frequently two
or three *ṅkporo* combined against two or three others. The *ṅkporo* is
not usually an exogamous unit, though the *ọnuma* frequently is.

A group of associated *ṅkporo* constitutes the *obodo* or village-group,
which from many points of view can be regarded as a clan, the sense
of relationship between the *ṅkporo* being expressed figuratively in

the assertion that they are brothers or half-brothers, i.e. the original founder of the town had a number of sons (by the same wife or different wives) each of whom became the founder of an *ṅkporo*. Occasionally one of the *ṅkporo* is described as a 'sister's son' of the others, an indication of the prevalence of intermarriage. Each *ṅkporo* (or its representative) is, at public meetings, accorded a definite order of precedence, according as the founder of the *ṅkporo* is believed to have been the eldest, second, third, or fourth son of the founder of the *obodo*. The original settlement or village is known as the *okpara* or 'eldest son', and the senior member of the senior family of that settlement is the holder of the senior *ọfọ* of the whole *obodo*. At a general meeting of heads of kindreds his *ọfọ* is the first to be laid on the ground, the others following suit in a well-recognized rotation. As there is seldom any dispute as to the seniority of the various *ṅkporo*, it might be inferred that tradition has faithfully preserved the order in which offshoots of the original settlement came into existence. But in many cases it appeared that seniority depended not on descent but on the order in which titles, now a defunct and in many cases a forgotten institution, had been first acquired. In other words the holder of the principal *ọfọ* is the head of the family which had first acquired a title.

Just as the extended-family or kindred is the basis of the social and political system, so the mode by which it is controlled is the pattern of government for the local groupings, whether they be hamlets, villages, or village-groups. In an *ọnuma* or village, for example, authority is vested in the heads of families acting in concert, and supported by the warrior age-grades, as the principal executive officials. The heads of families are on an equal footing, though ceremonial precedence may be given to the senior elder, or to a priest of Ala, or to the holder of an *aro*. Government was therefore government by a body of individuals and not a single individual, though a single individual might attain a position of leadership. It was government by an informal body which had no resemblance to the Warrant-Chiefs or Native Courts of the present time.[1]

The term 'government' is, of course, used in a qualified sense. Public notice was not taken of every case that was a breach of customary law, but only of cases which were (*a*) an offence against religion (or, as the Ibo would say, an 'abomination') and so would bring disaster

---

[1] This refers to the type of Native Courts which existed in Awgu Division at the time of the investigations.

on the community unless the steps prescribed by custom were taken, or (*b*) which were likely to break up the solidarity of the *umunna*, *ọnuma*, *ṅkporo*, or *obodo*. A man might steal from another and be sold into slavery by the owner of the stolen property without reference to the elders or any one else. Or a creditor might recover his debt by appropriating a goat or other property belonging to the debtor, or a member of his kinship, or local group. Or again two parties to a dispute might refer their dispute not to a formal council of the group, but to certain arbitrators chosen by each side. Even in cases where the group solidarity was imperilled, the senate of the group might be powerless to intervene. The elders, in short, were a body of mediators and referees rather than of prosecutors and judges, and the community was a republic in the true sense of that term, i.e. a corporation in which government was the concern of all.

We may now give some examples of leading personages or classes in the Awgu Division. In many communities the priest of Ala was regarded as the father of the community.[1] It is sometimes even said of him that he is the 'owner' of the village and of the people, on the ground that Ala is the 'owner' of men. As one aged informant put it, 'If you do not stand on the ground, where are you to stand?' And so at any public trial or investigation, particularly one dealing with an alleged 'sin' or 'abomination', the priest of Ala might act as president and open the proceedings by pouring some palm-wine or tobacco-snuff on the ground, saying, 'Ala, take this palm-wine (or snuff).' He would then hand some snuff to the elders and say, 'My fellow men, in this matter which we have come to settle, let no one introduce any form of falsehood. May Ala deal with any one who attempts to pervert the truth.' Or he might lay his *ọfọ* on the ground and deposit on it a piece of kola and some palm-wine, saying, 'Ala, eat kola-nut; Ọfọ, eat kola-nut; Chuku, eat kola-nut; Agbara, eat kola-nut, for the life of men and of women. May you and the *ọfọ* take the lives of all who speak falsely in this case.' If the accused denied the charge he might be asked to swear an oath on Ala. The whole company would resort to the shrine of Ala, the accused standing beside the priest, who would take a yam and matchet and speak as follows, 'If this man is guilty (e.g. of stealing) and continues to deny the charge then may Ala take his life. But if he is innocent may Ala spare him.' Or the

---

[1] In these communities the position of the priest of Ala would appear to be the same as that of 'the Master of the Earth' in the Northern Territories of the Gold Coast, as described by Dr. Rattray (*The Leopard Priestess*, pp. 70 and 102).

priest might split a kola and lay it before the cultus-symbol. The accused would say, 'Ala, if I have done this thing may you kill me after I have eaten this kola.' Then kneeling down he would pick up the kola with his lips and eat it. It may be added that it is commonly believed that all the original laws were passed in the name of Ala. The people having decided to pass a law went to the shrine of Ala, and there the priest, after pouring a libation to the deity, said, 'Ala, we of this town have decided that from henceforth no one shall do such and such a thing. If any one contravenes this law, do you, Ala, kill that man.'

These data would seem to support the suggestion of Professor Westermarck[1] that gods come to be guardians of social morality through the practice of making the pronouncement of a curse and blessing take the form of an appeal to the god. And so in time the idea grows up that the god can punish or reward independently of human invocation. Incidentally, Professor Westermarck observes that in Morocco the patron saint of a village is expressly said not to be concerned about the conduct of the inhabitants outside the precincts of its sanctuary. In Iboland, similarly, the Ala of one village-group is unconcerned with sins committed in another.[2]

In some communities the priest of Ala might also be the announcer of decisions, in others he might merely open the proceedings and take no further part in the trial, lest by so doing he might be a party to some wrong decision and so incur the wrath of Ala; in others, again, he might take part in any but murder cases, on the ground that, being identified with Ala, he could not abide parley over the murder of one of Ala's children. At Lokpa-Uku the priest of Ala took no part in any trials except those concerned with land. At Ugbo the Ala priest refused to take part in any proceedings which involved the selling of a townsman into slavery. Indeed any fugitive from justice, except one guilty of murder, could take refuge in the house of the priest of Ala, who, by placing his matchet on the fugitive's head, caused him to become the slave of Ala. In due course such a one might be allowed to redeem himself by providing a goat and chicken which, after being waved round the slave's head, were sacrificed to the deity, with a prayer that the slave might now be allowed to go his way in safety. At Awgu the priests of Ala took no special part in the trial of cases, but always intervened to stop fights between local groups. On such occasions the Ala priest of each contending side, accompanied

---

[1] *Early Beliefs and their Social Influence*, p. 31.   [2] See, e.g., p. 209.

by the elders and influential men, would meet together and would pour a libation to Ala, saying, 'Ala, permit not a thing to continue which will rob you of your sons. For if we are not alive who will remain to provide you with food? But we do not ask your protection for the lives of abominable men, and if any person has introduced among us some medicine to stir up strife, let that man perish by his own devices. Help us, therefore, that our discussions to-day may be smooth and agreeable to both of these contending parties.'

The announcers of decisions were always prominent personages at councils or trials. They had usually to be men of good address and to have a sound knowledge of the customary procedure. They were commonly the holders of the senior *ọfọ*, but if the holder of the senior *ọfọ* was not a good speaker he had to delegate one of his family-group to act as his deputy. In some communities the duty of announcing decisions was not assigned to any particular person or office. Any good speaker would be called on to perform this duty. In other communities certain *aro*-holding families had special rights of announcing decisions, and in some cases these families acted as principal arbiters in all disputes, their *aro* or iron staves being called 'staves of judgement'.[1] These *aro* appear sometimes to have been used as a magical means of testing the validity of a decision. For it was stated in one group that in the olden days the holder of the *aro*, when announcing his decision, planted the staff in the ground and said, 'Give ear to what we are about to say, for life is in the ear.' After quoting precedents he would announce the judgement, and if the staff did not immediately fall to the ground it was a sign that the gods and ancestors had repudiated the decision and that, if a retrial were not held, the elders who had given the decision would meet with divine retribution. Sometimes, the *aro*-holder took precedence of all other elders, because he was the senior member of a titled society or was the direct descendant of the first person to receive a title.

The members of titled societies (*Emume*) exercised bureaucratic authority in many localities of the Awgu Division. Breaches of customary law were reported to the senior member of the society in the local group and he, together with other members of the society, would go to the offender's house and capture or kill one of his goats, pending further investigation of the case. If the offence were small the loss

---

[1] Compare the elders in Homeric times who sat in the assembly holding staves and 'then rose up before the people and gave judgement each in turn'. (*Iliad*, xviii. 497 et seq.)

of the goat might be considered a sufficient punishment, but if it were serious the members of the society might order the man to be sold, and divide the proceeds among themselves. If the culprit had taken refuge in the house of the priest of Ala the members of the society might capture and sell a boy or girl from his family. Fines were imposed on any one who insulted a member of the society, and it is said that people were even afraid of offending a person whose brother was a member of the society. To assault a member of the society was almost sacrilege, and if the culprit was unable to pay the heavy fine inflicted he was sold into slavery. It was an offence for any layman to enter the house of a titled man after dark, and there were special penalties for adultery with the wife of a titled person. Creditors could distrain the property of debtors, but not of debtors who were members of the *Emume* society. The members of the society, moreover, besides taking a principal part in settling disputes, acted as guardians of orphans and of their property, a rule which was found to be necessary, as the relatives of orphaned children had often little compunction about selling the children into slavery. The subject of titled societies will be fully dealt with later,[1] and it need only be added here that in the Awgu Division the most important societies have now completely disappeared. With the advent of the British Government the members of the societies could no longer exercise their most prized privileges.

We may now give one or two concrete examples of individual men in various communities of the Awgu Division who, by reason of their wealth, titles, or ability, attained positions of such outstanding prominence that they might almost be described as chieftains of their group. In the subdivision of Mboo known as Awa-Nabo the authority of one Eguongwu was in pre-Government days so well recognized that every matter of importance was referred to him. Eguongwu was a rich man with many wives, children, servants, and slaves. His wealth was largely attributable to the fact that early in life he had visited the oracle of Aro-Chuku and had subsequently become the agent of the Aro at Awa-Nabo. Eguongwu presided at all trials, which were usually held at his house. At these trials he was assisted by other elders of lesser standing, summoned by himself, and, though the proceedings might in certain cases be opened by the priest of Ala, Eguongwu would usually open them himself, by pouring a libation over his *ofo* and calling on Ala to punish any of the parties or witnesses who spoke

[1] See Chapter vii (p. 165).

falsely, or any of the jury of elders who, through envy or on account of a bribe, gave a dishonest decision. After the case had been heard, the jury of elders withdrew to consider their verdict. Eguongwu as judge remained. If the jury returned a verdict with which Eguongwu disagreed, he sent them out again to reconsider. It was stated that, if the jury persisted, Eguongwu might overrule them, but the informants were unable to recall any example of such an occurrence. It will be observed that, in this instance, there is a close approximation to the English system of trial by judge and jury. It is also of interest to observe that before the trial of any case the elders could by general consent call on any elder of known bad character to withdraw. It was permissible for either party to a case to demand the withdrawal of any elder, on the ground that that elder was an hereditary enemy of his family. There was thus a system of challenging jurors, and the question might be considered whether this right should not be continued in Native Courts at the present time.

In the other subdivision of Mboo one Eze occupied a position corresponding to that of Eguongwu. As a travelling doctor and local agent of the Aro oracle he had amassed considerable wealth and an intimate knowledge of the world. He acquired a title of the highest order, and became a recognized arbiter in disputes, not merely in his own community but in neighbouring communities as well. Thus, if a man of Mboo had been seized by a man of Awgu on account of a debt, Eze would send a request to some rich, influential personage at Awgu that the captured debtor should not be sold into slavery, pending a settlement of the debt. Eze would then call on the members of the debtor's family to pay the debt through himself and so secure the debtor's release. Or he might in the first instance pay the debt himself and endeavour to recover it from the debtor's family later.

In the commune of Owele there were three or four individuals of outstanding importance. There was the senior priest of Ala, who took a leading part in the settlement of disputes which were likely to lead to inter-village fighting. All cases of exceptional difficulty were referred to a public assembly in the market-place where the central shrine of Ala was located, and the priest of Ala would, if necessary, call on one or other of the parties to the dispute to swear an oath by Ala.[1] He might also announce the decision of the arbitrators, or offer

---

[1] The *aro* or spear of Ala was brought out and planted in the ground. A circular hole was dug in front of the *aro*. One of the parties then called on the other to swear, and might Ala kill him if he swore falsely! The priest then poured some palm-wine

a sacrifice to purge the offence. If two kindreds or local groups were likely to be drawn into a bloody quarrel which had arisen in consequence of one side having accused the other of having used poison or black magic, the elders of the contending parties might summon the senior priest of Ala to come and allay the dispute by pouring a libation to Ala and calling on the parties to desist from further fighting. The parties would regard this as an order from Ala, and the injured kindred or group would be absolved from the disgrace of not following up the secret murder of one of their number. Normally, however, the priest of Ala did not permit himself to take part in cases connected with homicide, poisoning, or kidnapping, on the ground that participation in trials of such matters would lead to his consorting with persons abominable to Ala. It is noteworthy, therefore, that when he intervened in order to prevent bloodshed his peroration contained a covering formula, namely, 'Ala, I have said what the elders told me to say, and if their decision is not good in your eyes may you, Ala, not vent your anger on *me*.' The priest of Ala might also in exceptional cases intervene to save a convicted person from being sold into slavery. His house was an asylum for criminals who succeeded in reaching it before capture. It might be thought that this would tend to encourage crime, but the refugee became a slave and lost his wife and property, and the right to marry a free woman. Even his former children ceased to be regarded as his and were adopted by relatives.

For the everyday conduct of public affairs, however, the most important personages at Owele were not the priests of Ala but the heads of certain large and wealthy families. Thus, it is generally agreed that before the advent of the Government there were three men of outstanding authority in Owele, namely, Ago-Ani of the Uhu-Nanyi section of Amebo village, Okerekenta of the Umanoano kindred of Umuhu village, and Onoha-Ngoke of the Ozam section of Amebo. Each of these men owned numerous slaves, and exercised so much authority in his own group that no important step could be taken without his consent. He summoned meetings, took the principal part in trials, and announced the decision. It is said that even in criminal cases

into the hole, and if the wine immediately disappeared the swearer was pronounced guilty. If not the swearer went down on his knees and drank some of the wine. The oath was thus a form of ordeal. The *aro* used was an iron spear with a round shaft and pointed butt. Immediately below the blade a bundle of fibre was fixed to the shaft. This fibre was said to have been obtained from a stinging plant, with the idea that liars should be 'stung'.

in which the injured party was entitled to sell the culprit automatically into slavery, no one would exercise this privilege without reference to this leader of his group, who might himself redeem the criminal. In this way he came to be regarded as a protector of the community. With the assistance of his bodyguard of slaves he was in a position to enforce his will, and to provide safe conduct to members of his own village who wished to visit other villages, and of members of other villages who wished to visit his. He was the acknowledged representative of the village in all important external relations. He often acted as guarantor in other ways. Thus, if a man were accused of theft and repudiated the charge, he would ask this rich leader of his village to provide a cow in order that beef might be presented to the villagers (the elders, in particular, who would try the case). This was the customary guarantee of good faith pending the trial. If the plaintiff lost his case he had to pay the cost of this cow and also hand over another cow to the defendant. Public meetings of importance were commonly held at the house of this rich personage, who summoned the elders by beating a drum of special pattern.[1] He sat on a special stool, and as a symbol of his authority carried an *aro* or spear.[2] As an indication of the wealth of such personages it may be remarked that the roof of the hut in which Ago-Ani lies buried is lined with the skulls of one hundred cows and two hundred goats.

In each village of the commune of Ache there was a family the head of which held an *aro* of judgement, i.e. had the hereditary right of announcing decisions. The *aro* ordinarily used was the iron staff of a titled society (*Emume*), and in announcing the decision of the tribunal or assembly the spokesman planted the *aro* in the ground, and, holding his family *ofo*, said, 'Ala, come and eat kola; Achihi,[3] come and eat kola; Chuku-Kere-Mado,[4] come and eat kola; Igwe-Ke-Ala,[5] come and eat kola; Omeje,[6] come and eat kola; Ndichie (ancestors), come and eat kola. If what I am about to say is not the decision of the elders, and is contrary to our custom, then may you, Ala, follow me; may you, Achihi, follow me; may you, Chuku-Kere-Mado, follow

---

[1] It had a single membrane braced by strings made fast at the centre and kept in position by graded slats of wood.

[2] Ago-Ani's spear was that formerly used by holders of the Ihuji title. The shaft was 5 ft. 3 in. in length and the blade 9 in. The spear of Okerekenta, which was 6 ft. long, had a polished shaft decorated with brass spirals and an iron-pointed butt (1 ft. long). The blade was 18 in. long.

[3] One of the principal cults at Ache.   [4] Chuku, creator of men.

[5] The spirit of the oracle at Umunoha.   [6] The personification of custom.

me; may you, Igwe-Ke-Ala, follow me; may you, Omeje, follow me; may you, Ndichie, follow me.' He then struck the ground with his ọfọ and placed kola seeds beside it. Having done this, he would announce the decision and quote precedents, saying that he had been told by his father that on a certain occasion a similar case had arisen and had been decided in the same way. But there were other *aro*, sacred spears held by certain families. On these oaths might be sworn, the officiant standing before the spear and saying, 'Ala, come and drink, for you are the senior. Chuku, come and drink. Igwe, come and drink. Ọfọ and Aro, come and drink. This man is about to take an oath on you. If he has done an evil thing and persists in denying it then may you take away his life.' The officiant poured a libation on his ọfọ and on the ground beside the spear. After this the accused person extended his hands towards the *aro* saying, 'Aro, if I did this thing then may you take away my life.'

The office of spokesman was not, at Ache, considered to be one of much importance, the most influential members of the community being one or two rich men who had acquired wealth by trading slaves and cattle to Bende, Umunọha, Ozakole, and other distant towns. On the other hand, these rich men are not to be regarded as the principal *executive* officers. The principal executive officers in the Awgu Division were the Ndishi-Uke (sing. = Ishi-Uke), who were the captains of the adult or warrior age-grades[1] in each local group. And so, if a person had cause to charge another with some offence, such as setting fire to a kola or bread-fruit tree, or of having dug up his yams, or cut his yams' tendrils, or of having stolen palm-wine from one of his trees, he would report the matter to the Ishi-Uke of his village, to whom he would give an initial gift of some palm-wine. The Ishi-Uke would then direct the 'head-getters' or members of the warrior grades to capture a goat or pig from the defendant's house or from any member of the defendant's family. A panel of elders, among whom the Ishi-Uke would be included, would next investigate the charge, having received from both parties gifts of kolas and palm-wine. They would first inquire of the plaintiff if he wished the captured goat to be killed. If the plaintiff were at all doubtful of his case, he would ask that the goat should not be killed, and if he lost his case the goat would be immediately restored to the owner. If he had given his consent to the killing of the goat, he had to pay the cost (which was usually assessed by the owner at considerably more than its

[1] *uke* = age-grade.

value!). But if he won his case, and the goat had been killed and eaten by the elders and villagers, the defendant had to bear the loss of the goat as well as pay compensation for his offence.

This was the procedure in cases where both parties belonged to the same village and the case was tried by the elders of that village. But if the plaintiff wished to mulct the defendant heavily, he could lay his complaint before the elders of the whole village-group. In this case the animal seized and killed was a cow. In all cases of this character the winner was required to pay a fee of rods to the elders who had tried the case, the number of rods varying with the importance of the matter at issue. The Ndishi-Uke received a large proportion of this fee.

From this review it will have been gathered that, although certain personages were assigned special duties of a public character, these duties were primarily ceremonial, and did not usually carry with them any definite form of personal authority. The community was governed by the whole body of the people represented by the heads of families. In such a body special respect might be accorded to the priest of Ala, but the dominating personages would be those of dominating character or of outstanding wealth. Comparatively young men might, therefore, exercise greater influence in the community than many of the elders. This has been instanced in our remarks on the government of the kindred. The real leader of the kindred was not necessarily the senior elder or holder of the senior *ọfọ*, but might be some capable rich or generous young man who would be the prime mover in all matters and would, with the consent of the whole kindred, deal with any trouble in which the kindred had become involved. At public meetings, also, an elder was frequently accompanied by a capable son who would, if necessary, speak on his father's behalf. It is a cause of complaint that under the present judicial system if some old man is making a mess of his case his son is fined if he attempts to speak on his father's behalf. In olden days the son would have been permitted to conduct his father's defence. In olden days, moreover, if a dispute arose between two villages it was not uncommon for the elders of each village to appoint delegates to deal with the matter. The delegates chosen were the most capable men, irrespective of age. There is justification, therefore, in native custom for allowing *young* capable men some share in administration. For there is a real danger now that, with the swing of the pendulum and the discovery of the importance of *okpara* and heads of families, administration may become wholly centred in the aged, and thereby fossilized.

VI

THE SOCIAL AND POLITICAL STRUCTURE
(*continued*)

Family, Village, and Clan Organization (Nsukka Division)

Family Organization.

OUR final examples of the social and political organization are taken from the Nsukka Division, in the extreme north of Onitsha Province, and we may begin with a brief description of an extended-family. In the village-group or commune of Nsukka there is a family known as the Ori-Ada, consisting of ninety persons. This family is one of six related families which together form the Amokwa kindred, the Amokwa kindred being in turn one of six kindreds which form the hamlet known as Umu-Kaka. Umu-Kaka and three other hamlets form the 'quarter' or village of Ihe, which is one of the four 'quarters' or villages composing the 'town', or village-group or commune of Nsukka. The following diagram illustrates the position:

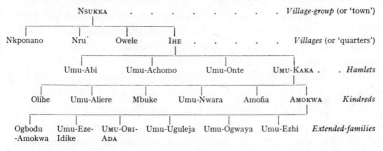

The Ori-Ada extended-family consists of the following adult males, wives, and children:

		Wives	Children	
			M.	F.
1.	Asogwa-Oyeze	1	2	3
2.	Atâwe-Eza	2	2	2
3.	Ugu-Ata-Weeza	1	..	..
4.	Ugwoke-Eza	2	..	2
5.	Ezugori-Weeza	2	2	2
6.	Ugwoke-Ugu-Amoke	3	2	2
7.	Agbo-Eza	2	1	..
	Carried forward	13	9	11

	Wives	Children M.	F.
Brought forward	13	9	11
8. Agbo-Asogwa	1	..	1
9. Uguja-Ezede	1	1	1
10. Omeeja-Weezede	1	1	2
11. Asado-Ogbene	1	..	1
12. Ugu-Weezema	2	..	1
13. Ugu-Ezema	..	..	..
14. Eze-Ngwata	2	..	2
15. Ugu-Uku-Eze	4	5	3
		(5 of the 8 are adopted children)	
16. Ezugu-Weeza	1	..	..
17. Asadu-Weeza	2	2	..
18. Ugwoke-Ugu	2	4	3
19. Eke	2	2	3
20. Eze-Ngwabo	2	..	2
21. Ugwai-Yagbo	1	1	..
	35	25	30

The common ancestor of this extended-family was one Ori-Ada. Ori-Ada had three sons, viz. Asogwa-Ugu, Ezegu-Ndaba, and Oshinoko. With the exception of Ugwoke-Eza, who is a descendant of Oshinoko, and of Eze-Ngwabo and Ugwai-Yagbo, who are descendants of Ezegu-Ndaba, all are descended from Asogwa-Ugu. The table on the opposite page illustrates the relationship of all the members.

The members of the family enumerated above do not all live together in the same area. Numbers 1–13 form a single group; number 14 lives by himself two miles away from the main group, as he wishes to be near his farm; numbers 15–19 also live by themselves about two miles from the main group because, in pre-Government days, they, in company with members of other kindreds and groups of the commune, were posted on the outskirts of Nsukka to act as a picket against attack by neighbouring villages; and numbers 20 and 21 live a mile away from the main group, simply because they wish to live by themselves.

Though the extended-family is not wholly localized, all the members recognize the authority of Asogwa-Oyeze as head of the family, and any serious disputes between members of the family would be referred to him. All the members meet at feasts in his compound, and he performs sacrifice to the common ancestor, Ori-Ada, on behalf of all. Any of the family who wishes to acquire a public title must

GENEALOGICAL TREE OF THE ORI-ADA EXTENDED-FAMILY *(living members italicized).*

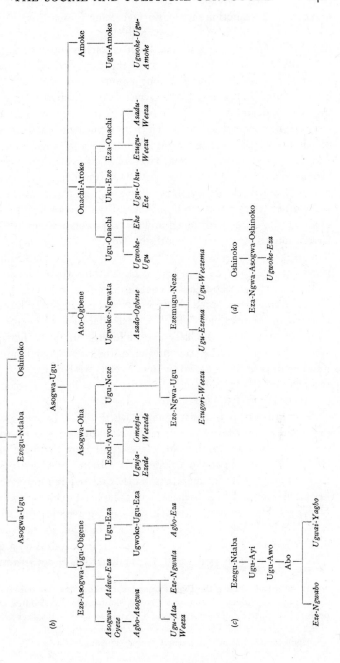

first obtain the sanction of Asogwa-Oyeze and present him with gifts. Asogwa-Oyeze holds himself responsible, and would be held responsible by the Government, for tax due from each member of the family.

It will have been observed that in this extended-family there are thirty-five wives distributed among twenty-one husbands. This is a high proportion. Seven of these wives were inherited from deceased brothers (elder or younger). A further point of interest is that the twenty-one husbands had between them formerly twenty other wives, of whom twelve died and eight abandoned their husbands. Ugu-Uku-Eze, who now has four wives (two of whom he married as virgins, one of whom was married before, and one of whom was inherited from a deceased younger brother), had also at various times three other wives, of whom one died and two ran away. He is a man of about fifty-three years of age and has had seven wives in his lifetime. Cases came to my notice of youths of twenty-two to twenty-four who had had already as many as three wives. The average number of wives that an Ori-Ada man had in his lifetime worked out at 2·6.

The twenty-one households contain fifty-five children. But six of these children are adopted children, having been begotten by deceased brothers of householders.[1] Each householder has an average of 2·33 living children. Of the fifty-five children thirty are females and twenty-five are males. Dead children of the twenty-one householders numbered twenty-eight, of whom twelve were males and sixteen females, i.e. twenty-eight out of seventy-seven children born are dead, or a proportion of 36·36 per cent.

As an illustration of the manner in which the household groups are organized we may take the unit represented by numbers 15–19 on the list. As already stated, this group lives apart from the main group, as they were sent in pre-Government days to act as an outpost. For this reason we find that members of other related and unrelated families are living intermixed with them. The head of the group is Ugu-Uku-Eze. His compound, which was occupied by himself and three wives[2] and one son, contained (a) the hut of Ugu, (b) the three huts of Ugu's wives, (c) the hut of Ugu's son, (d) a kitchen, (e) a granary, (f) a sheep and goat pen, and (g) a small garden of coco-yams.

---

[1] It is not usual among the Ibo, as among many other Nigerian tribes, for a man to hand over one of his children to a relative who has none. A childless old man is helped on his farm by all the members of his extended-family. But they avoid giving him direct gifts lest he should become wholly dependent on them!

[2] Ugu's fourth wife lives in a neighbouring compound.

The hut of Ugu was designed as follows:

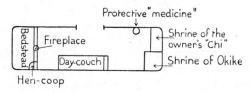

The shrine of Okike, i.e. the Creator, contained one stone and four upturned pottery dishes, representing Ugu and his four wives. The front of the shrine was covered with a curtain of palm-leaves. A single pot symbolized the *chi* or accompanying soul of Ugu and his wives, and the wall forming the back of the *chi* shrine was plastered with bunches of feathers of chickens. The day-couch was a mud platform with a mud head-rest at one end. The bedstead was a mud platform with a fireplace underneath (in the centre) and a chicken coop at one corner. It was covered with a mattress of palm-branches, and, parallel to the outside edge of the bed, a log of wood was fixed to prevent the occupant falling out. Over the bedstead was a shelf made of palm logs. The roof of the hut was made of stick-rafters, covered with split palm-branches, to which the leaves still adhered. These, in turn, were covered with a grass thatching. On the outside of the roof, over the entrance to the hut, six skulls of horses were fixed. Four of these horses had been killed at the final burial rites of Ugu's father, and the other two at the final rites of his mother. There were also two skulls of cows (one killed in honour of his father and one in honour of his deceased brother), and numerous skulls of pigs which had been killed for the feasts of the tutelary genius known as Omabe.[1] It may be added that the few pigs in the compound slept at night in Ugu's own hut.

The huts of Ugu's wives each contained a mud bedstead with a fireplace underneath, and a mattress of palm mid-rib. There was no furniture except a square wooden stool and a vertical loom. There were several pots of water, and a pear-shaped basket made of woven twigs. The outside of the basket was smeared with mud to render it waterproof. This basket was used for storing coco-yams. The porch was used as a kitchen, and over the hearth was a shelf made of palm mid-ribs and woven pieces of *akpa* creeper. In another part of the compound there was a separate kitchen for general use. Built on

[1] See p. 78.

to the end of this kitchen, underneath the eaves, was a mud platform containing a mill.

Close to the huts was a small thatched granary mounted on wooden posts. The walls of the granary were made of woven straw. This was used for storing yams. In the centre of the compound was the ancestral shrine. It was rectangular in shape, and contained four stones representing Ugu's grandfather, father, and two paternal uncles. The back wall was dotted with bunches of palm leaves, into which were stuck the feathers of fowls which had been offered to the ancestors. The skulls of one or two goats were fixed to the back of the wall. It may be remarked that of Ugu's four wives three belonged to Nsukka and one to Opi. Two had been married before, and two not. Of the former, one, who was the mother of five children, had been inherited from a younger brother, while one had abandoned her first husband, leaving her son behind. As already stated Ugu had had three other wives at various times. But none of these had borne children.

The compound adjoining Ugu's was occupied by two brothers belonging to the extended-family of Umu-Idike, which forms part of the same kindred as the Ori-Ada family (viz. Amokwa). Their mother lived with them and also one of their father's widows, an old woman who had no son of her own to look after her. Each of the two brothers had an Anyañu (Sun) shrine, and a shrine of Agu, the spirit of divination.

The next compound was occupied by Ezugu-Weeza and Asadu-Weeza, two brothers belonging to the Ori-Ada extended-family. Ezugu had one wife and no children, and Asadu two wives and two children. Their mother lived with them. Each had a shrine of Anyañu. Though they were brothers by the same mother, each farmed on his own account, but they helped each other on special occasions. The adjoining compound was occupied by Ugwoke-Ugu. His half-brother, Eke, did not live with him but occupied the neighbouring compound together with his mother, wives, and children. Ugwoke had a grown-up son, who had begun to make a compound for himself, as he was about to take a wife. The final compound was occupied by a man who was not a member of the Ori-Ada extended-family, nor yet of the Amokwa kindred. He belonged to the Umu-Ise kindred which had delegated his father to join the outpost group (known as 'Obilage'). Some distance off there were other groups of 'Obilage', who belonged to various kindreds of Nsukka.

Turning now from the organization of the extended-family to that of the higher social unit, namely, the kindred, it has been said that the Ori-Ada family is one of six related extended-families composing the Amokwa kindred. These six families are (a) Ogbodu-Amokwa, (b) Umu-Eze-Idike, (c) Umu-Ori-Ada, (d) Umu-Uguleja, (e) Umü-Ogwaya, and (f) Umu-Ezhi. All these families are believed to be related genealogically, but it was not possible to obtain a reliable table proving this relationship. It was stated that all were descendants of one called Ezoka, and that the founder of two of the families (viz. Umu-Eze-Idike and Umu-Ori-Ada) were brothers by the same father and mother.

The Amokwa kindred might almost be described as a small 'clan'. It is an exogamous unit, but the question is being discussed whether intermarriage between the less closely related families of the kindred should not now be allowed. It is noteworthy, moreover, that, although intermarriage between the various extended-families of the kindred is forbidden, it is not an offence if sexual relations occur between two unmarried members of different families of the kindred, provided those families are not too closely related. If the girl were to conceive as a result of such intercourse the child born would be claimed by her fiancé. If she had no fiancé the child would be claimed by her father, who would bring it up as an ordinary member of his family. No deep sense of incest or pollution, therefore, is attached to the idea of marital relations between the extended-families of the Amokwa kindred. But the idea of marital or sexual relations of any kind between members of the same extended-family is utterly abhorrent. A man breaking this taboo would be poisoned by the members of his own extended-family. It would be, they said, as though he had outraged his own mother. There will be more to be said on the subject of exogamy later,[1] and it need only be added here that there is no form of totemism associated with the exogamy at the present time. But formerly it was taboo for any Amokwa man to eat bulrush-millet.

The kindred of Amokwa has a definite headman or Onyishi,[2] viz. the senior elder, irrespective of the particular extended-family to which he belongs. His authority is sustained by the fact that he has charge of the shrine of the original forefather Ezoka, to whom he

---

[1] See pp. 259 ff.

[2] The word Onyishi or Onyisi is a contraction of onye = man and ishi (or isi) = head.

offers regular sacrifice once a year on behalf of the whole kindred, and irregular sacrifice on behalf of individuals of the kindred who for any reason are ordered by a diviner to sacrifice to Ezoka. As chief priest of the clan he can bring any recalcitrant member to heel by the mere threat of refusing to offer sacrifice on his behalf. To insult him is to insult the ancestors who are regarded as immanent in his *ọfọ*, and any one guilty of such conduct would be ordered by the elders of the kindred to hand over a chicken, some kola-nuts, and a pot of palm-wine, that sacrifice might be offered to the ancestors. It may be remarked that for the annual sacrifice all householders assemble at the shrine of Ezoka with supplies of food, and the Onyishi kills a fowl and allows the blood to drip over the symbol, which consists of a mud pillar surrounded with sticks, one of which represents Ezoka, while the others represent the founders of the various extended-families. The Onyishi calls on the ancestors to protect them all, and a feast is then held. Sometimes a cow is sacrificed, and when this is done the expense is borne by all the families composing the kindred, according to their numbers. When a child is born and has cut its lower teeth it must be brought by its mother to the Onyishi to be presented to Ezoka and the ancestors.[1] The Onyishi deposits a kola-nut before the shrine and calls on the ancestors to protect the child, who is verily their son as he has cut his teeth in the proper way. The mother then takes the kola and eats it. If she refused, it would be tantamount to a declaration that the child was the offspring of an adulterous union. The Onyishi has thus a strong hold on the wives of members of the kindred. If the child cuts its upper teeth before the lower, it is not taken to the ancestral shrine as it is not considered to be a bona-fide member of the kindred. In former days such a child was sold, and the proceeds of the sale were divided up between the senior Onyishi and other elders, together with the titled members of the kindred who were known as Asogwa and Ndishi-Iwu.[2] There was an Asogwa and Ishi-Iwu for each extended-family, and they acted as the executive officers of the Onyishi.

The Onyishi of the kindred is the final authority in deciding all disputes and questions of custom within the kindred, and in pre-Government days could, with the approval of the other elders, order the punishment of any member of the kindred for any offence, unless the offence was of such gravity that it called for the intervention of

---

[1] But normally babies are presented to the head of the compound in which the parents live.   [2] *Ndishi* is the plural form of *Ishi*.

the whole community. Thus he could order a member of the kindred to pay a debt to another member of the kindred, or to a member of another kindred, and if the debtor refused or was dilatory he could compel him by placing a taboo on his farm (in the form of a knotted palm-leaf). If the debtor still refused to pay, the Onyishi would direct the Asogwa and Ndishi-Iwu to go to the house of the debtor, accompanied by a masker personating the genius known as Omabe, and pillage the debtor's property. We shall see later that in most towns of the Nsukka Division the Omabe or Odo society was freely used to enforce authority.[1] The Onyishi of the kindred could punish any member of the kindred for insulting or 'polluting' Omabe, or for committing adultery, assault, or theft. In cases of adultery by a fellow member of the kindred, the accuser laid a complaint before the Onyishi, who summoned the accused and heard the case in the presence of the other elders of the kindred. If the evidence was sufficient for summary conviction, the guilty man was fined the value of one cow, and the proceeds were divided among the Onyishi and other elders and titled men (i.e., the Asogwa and Ndishi-Iwu) and the aggrieved husband. He was also required to give a goat and chicken to the husband, that the latter might sacrifice to his ancestors. The guilty wife had to give her husband a chicken for a similar purpose.

But if the person charged with adultery denied the charge, and there was no clear proof of his guilt, the Onyishi of his kindred would call upon him to prove his innocence either by (a) undergoing the sasswood ordeal, or (b) swearing an oath by the ancestors of the kindred or by some well-known deity. If he chose the latter course the oath was sworn in the presence of the Onyishi, who fixed the time limit within which the oath should be effective. The aggrieved husband would demand that this time limit should be one year, the maximum allowed by custom, but the Onyishi, out of consideration for his kinsman, might declare that a limit of three months was sufficient. The person taking the oath remained unshaven throughout the period fixed, and, if he did not die within that period, he came to the Onyishi and showed that his innocence had been proved. He then shaved and paraded round the market-place. If the accused demanded trial by ordeal, so that the case should be decided instanter, the matter became one of public concern, and the sasswood was administered by the senior Ishi-Iwu of the whole local group (Ihe),

[1] See pp. 150, 152; also 75-8.

in the presence of all the elders and titled men of all the kindreds in the group.

Even if the accuser and the accused belonged to different kindreds, the case might be settled privately by the kindreds concerned without reference to a public tribunal, the Onyishi of the accused's kindred compelling him to give satisfaction in the manner described above. If the two kindreds failed to agree, the dispute would be referred to the village tribunal, if the kindreds concerned belonged to the same village. If the kindreds belonged to different villages the dispute would be referred to a tribunal of the whole commune; but sometimes the kindred which had felt itself to be injured would decide to punish the other summarily, by preventing the women of the other kindred from attending their market.

Local-Group Government.

The system of local-group government in the Nsukka Division does not differ in principle from that of Owerri and Awgu, though it has certain characteristic features of its own, the most noteworthy being the powerful influence still exercised by the title-conferring societies. Authority is, or rather was—prior to the introduction of the alien system of 'Warrant Chiefs'—primarily vested in the heads of families or kindreds, and most matters were settled locally in the kindred or hamlet concerned. There was no strong central organization. Thus, if a man had shown disrespect to a masker of the Odo society,[1] he was summarily dealt with by his fellow villagers, without reference to any higher authority. He would only be brought before the tribunal of the whole village-group if he had refused to pay the fine imposed, or if his offence had been so grave that it called for his public execution—if he had, for example, disclosed the secrets of the Odo society to a woman. A general council of the whole village-group might also be called to deal with cases of kidnapping, homicide, or disputes between subdivisions; to discuss measures of defence in the face of threatened attacks by other village-groups; to consult diviners in cases of severe epidemics; to make rules regarding the taking of titles, the control of markets, and the time for burning the 'bush'; to pass laws such as that the penalty for stealing at night should be (e.g.) one cow, and for stealing in the daytime one chicken and one hundred rods; that no one must export food during a time of scarcity, or visit a town where there was an outbreak of smallpox, or fire guns

[1] See pp. 75–8.

at burial rites if smallpox was raging locally, or tap palms for wine immediately before the celebration of some public festival.

The general council, composed of heads of families, was usually presided over by the Onyishi or the head of the family which had first settled in the district, or had first introduced the Ǫzǫ title, or from time immemorial had provided the priests of the most important local deity. The executive officials of the council were a body of men of the warrior or titled grades, of whom a dozen or so were selected from each village by the elders of the village. It was the business of these to collect fines and preserve good order generally, especially in the market. They sometimes used the maskers of the local secret societies to enforce their authority, but usually relied on their own physical powers and on the authority of the elders. Laws were promulgated through these executive officials, each of whom announced the law or rules, after ringing a bell, to the members of his own immediate group. The public priests were also an adjunct to administration, as they were guardians of public morality and could refuse to sacrifice on behalf of any one who had disregarded 'custom' or the decisions of the elders.

Thus, to take a few examples, in the village-group of Nsukka itself the senior member of the group council was the Onyishi of the Nguru kindred, who, as Atama or priest of the principal cultus, was regarded as the father of all Nsukka. He could, through the executive officials known as Ndishi-Iwu, summon a general council or assembly of all heads of kindreds and members of titled societies. At the meeting he would explain the reason of the summons, and on its conclusion the senior elder of each subdivision would send a messenger round the subdivision, announcing the decision of the council. The titled members of society were at Nsukka mostly known as 'Asogwa' and formed a bureaucratic society, with the Ndishi-Iwu as their lieutenants. It would seem that the Ndishi-Iwu often abused their authority, bullying the weak and appropriating without cause small articles of property. Any protest would be met by an accusation that the protestant was insulting the Asogwa, and he might accordingly be haled before the Asogwa and fined.

The Ndishi-Iwu were the principal officers of the law[1] in numerous other groups. Thus, in the commune of Neke, if any one broke a rule, such as that oil-beans were not to be plucked until they were ripe, the Ndishi-Iwu went to his house and placed a knotted palm-leaf on

---

[1] *Iwu* is almost synonymous with our word 'law'.

the roof, thereby interdicting the owner from touching anything until he had made a formal appearance before the Ndishi-Iwu. If at the investigation the accused denied the charge, the matter was settled by giving sasswood to a dog, which had been selected as the proxy of the accused. In flagrant cases where no investigation was called for, the Ndishi-Iwu, led by an Ishi-Iwu of the culprit's kindred, went to the culprit's house and pillaged his property. In cases of murder the property of the murderer's kin was also pillaged. The Ndishi-Iwu might impose fines summarily without reference to the body of elders, and the moneys so obtained were set aside to provide the sacrificial animals required for the public cults.

In the village-group of Opi, also, the Ndishi-Iwu were the police-magistrates of the community. They arrested and fined people at the instance of the council of heads of kindreds, or they could take summary action on their own account, sometimes using the maskers of the cult of Omabe as their penal authority. It is said that the maskers frequently appropriated live stock wandering on the road and shared the proceeds with the Ndishi-Iwu. On the other hand, it was stated that an Ishi-Iwu could be suspended by the elders for flagrant misconduct, and that the Onyishi of Opi, holding his *ọfọ* in his hand, could fine him. The fines imposed by the senior Ishi-Iwu for all major offences had to be divided out in his house in the presence of the Onyishi and Eze of Opi, and of the other heads of kindreds and holders of important titles. When the fines took the form of live stock, the animal was sacrificed by the Onyishi of Opi, some of the blood being poured over the *ọfọ* of all *ọfọ*-holders present. The flesh of the animal was then divided. But in certain classes of offences involving pollution to the community, the animal taken as a fine was sacrificed by the priest of the principal cult, and he received the finest share of the flesh.

At Adâyi each village of the commune had an 'Onyishi' or headman who was rather more than *primus inter pares* in the village council. He held this position not because he was the oldest member of the council, but because he was the head of a particular kindred which alone had the right to appoint the Onyishi. A rule of this kind tended towards a heightening of authority, and so at Adâyi the position of the Onyishi was not unlike that of a mayor in England. On nomination he had to pay dues to all the heads of kindreds in his village, and it was also a rule that no one could be appointed 'Onyishi' of a village until the 'second-burial' rites of the late Onyishi had been completely carried out.

There was also at Adâyi an Onyishi of the whole commune, who was chosen from a particular kindred in each village by rotation. He was chosen by divination from a number of candidates and so was not necessarily the senior elder of the kindred. He had to be a man of means, as his nomination entailed the payment of numerous dues, including a feast to all the most important members of the commune. His appointment carried with it the presidency of the local titled society, and gave him the right to exact dues from the Ndishi[1] of villages on their appointment, and from all other candidates for titles. Some of his duties were of a ritual nature. Thus, at the yam harvest he would preside at the rites, placing offerings of kolas and palm-wine on the staves of heads of kindreds and holders of titles, and calling on the ancestors to accept the offerings and bless the people. Or, if the Onyishi of a village had been advised by a diviner to sacrifice to his ancestors, he would bring his staff to the Onyishi of the commune, who would plant the staff in the ground, spit some chewed fragments of kola over it, and, holding a chicken in his right hand, would say, 'Staff, and So-and-So (naming the ancestor of the Onyishi whose spirit was believed to tenant the staff)—you lived and died and left your son to succeed. He has come to make an offering to you. Grant him prosperity: may his children and crops increase: and may peace reign in his kindred and throughout his village.'[2] He would then kill the chicken and pour the blood over the central bulge of the staff. Next, plucking some wing feathers, he would stick them in the blood as it congealed. The chicken would be cooked and small pieces of the flesh deposited on the staff.

The constitution of the commune of Ubolo was similar to that of Adâyi. Each of the five subdivisions had a headman or Onyishi who was assisted by titled 'Asogwa'. In addition there was a senior Onyishi and a senior Asogwa. All cases of murder were reported in the first instance to the senior Asogwa, who reported them to the Onyishi of Ubolo. The latter sent a number of Asogwa, headed by the senior Asogwa, to the kinsmen of the murdered man, counselling them to refrain from hasty action likely to cause the death of many. At the same time the murderer's kin were advised that it was their duty to assist the kin of the murdered man in arresting the murderer. The murderer, when arrested, was handed over to the senior Asogwa, who

---

[1] *Ndishi* or *ndi-ishi* is the plural of *onyishi* or *onye-ishi*.
[2] Nowadays he might add, 'And may we all live in peace with the Government, and with one another.'

took him to the compound of the Onyishi of Ubolo. The latter summoned all the elders and Asogwa, and tried the accused, who, if found guilty, was taken to the site of execution and ordered by the senior Asogwa to hang himself. The body of the dead murderer was removed from the tree by a man of another town hired by the murderer's kin for the duty, as most Ibo are unwilling to be a party to the execution of a fellow townsman, lest they should render themselves liable to the vengeance of the dead man and of his ancestors. Any one revealing the secrets of the Omabe society to women was, after trial by the Onyishi and the commune council, handed over to the 'Esato' or maskers of the cult. He was taken to the market-place and shot by the maskers, all women having previously been driven away. Edicts of the Onyishi and the commune council were regarded as having the sanction of Omabe, and many of the penalties were enforced in the name of this spirit. The maskers of Omabe were indeed likened to the court messengers of the present régime, and Omabe himself to the British District Officer. The maskers were under the immediate control of the Asogwa and went to make arrests, inflict fines, or pillage the property of a recalcitrant member of the community. The approach of the masker caused terror to the culprit who, if he were wise, hastened out of his compound to meet the masker and buy himself off as cheaply as possible. Falling down before the masker, he saluted him by putting his hand to the ground and then to his forehead four times, murmuring 'Ata, ngwa, ala, Ata, ngwa ala', i.e. 'Father, owner of the land'.

The Asogwa were active agents of the law in numerous ways. They summoned the elders to meetings by ringing their bells, they were sent by the Onyishi to stop quarrels between kindreds or local groups, to inspect and report on land under dispute, to trace kidnapped children, and to collect fines. They were directly responsible for the control of the markets, a number of them being deputed to supervise the market on each market-day. They could arrest and fine disputants whose conduct was likely to cause a break-up of the market. The fines imposed in such cases were their own perquisite. If a person lost any article of property he reported the loss to the Asogwa, paying them an initial fee of eight iron rods. The Asogwa then employed a diviner to 'smell out' the thief. The diviner would first, it is said, be drawn in the direction of the thief's palm-trees, then to his yams, and so to the thief himself. The person so detected or suspected was taken before a tribunal, and if he admitted the theft was required to pay compensation to the owner of the property, and a fine, which was divided equally between the elders and Asogwa. If he denied the theft, he had to produce a dog, to which sasswood was administered by the senior Asogwa. If the dog died the person charged was considered guilty, and he might either be fined or have his property looted by the Asogwa. It may be remarked that this mode of detecting thieves has been abandoned, as a person so charged by a diviner might, under present conditions, bring an action for defamation of character. Thieving has, therefore, it is said, enormously increased. The Asogwa inflicted summary fines on any one who set fire to the 'bush' in the dry season before the appointed time, i.e., before the people had time to collect grass for thatching, and nowadays it is the Asogwa who turn out the people for Government work, and take a principal part in the collection of taxes. In many of the Native Courts some of the members are, quite properly, Asogwa, but in some communities the Asogwa are discontented with the present limitation of their powers and the inadequate recognition they receive from the Government. Asogwa receive their title by payments of from seven to ten pigs to the members of their society.

In numerous communities of the Nsukka Division, and indeed of many other parts of Iboland, the leading personage of the local group holds the title of Eze[1]—the highest form of title obtainable. If it is held that the conception of chieftainship is wholly unknown to the Ibo this would be an exaggeration. For the very word Eze implies lordship, and it is the name which the Ibo of these parts apply to the Supreme Being, in the expression Eze Chukwoke—the Lord God the Creator. It is not contended, however, that the Eze of any of the communities of Nsukka Division was ever so autocratic that he could disregard the other titled officials and heads of kindreds, who were his coadjutors. And in some communities the Eze (or Ezes—for there may be more than one) was not even the leading personage. Nevertheless the title usually connotes some measure of chieftainship, even in the autocratic sense in which Europeans are accustomed to interpret this term, and it is for this reason that claims to Eze-ship have been one of the commonest causes of political disputes in Iboland. It is significant that many of those 'Warrant Chiefs', who were mere nominees of the British Government and had no traditional claim to authority among their own people, often sought to acquire this

---

[1] This word is pronounced *èzè*.

authority subsequently by taking the title of Eze. Eze-ship, indeed, can be regarded as a direct link between the institution of title-taking and that of chieftainship.

In the village-group of Nkpologu the Eze was the head of the community, the Onyishi being second and the Asogwa third. The Eze was always chosen from a particular family, and the Onyishi from one of two families. The Asogwa also belonged to a particular family and was chosen by divination. The elders of the kindred submitted a number of names to three diviners who were first sworn to divine honestly. The diviners, working with the two divining strings, had to agree with one another, and, when the choice was finally made, the Asogwa-elect was taken to the shrine of the head of the kindred, who offered sacrifice on his behalf, beseeching the ancestors to protect and guide the new Asogwa. He then bestowed on him the iron staff and gong which were the insignia of his office.

The Eze exercised certain priestly functions and was also head of the Ọzọ society. Any one taking the title of Ọzọ was required to give a goat to the Eze and Onyishi, a dog to the Asogwa, and seven cows to the other members of the society. The Eze was also head of the judiciary. In trials by ordeal he was the administrator of sasswood. Any one guilty of murder, if he escaped with his life, was required to pay a fine of one goat to the Eze and Onyishi, a dog to the Asogwa, and a fowl to the chief priest. He was then sent into exile, and his family was required to compensate the family of the murdered man by presenting them with a girl. Persons charged with grave sacrilege were tried in the house of the chief priest, in the presence of the priest, Eze, Onyishi, Asogwa, and elders, and if convicted were placed in a hole in the ground and speared by maskers. Any one who, by carelessness or design, set fire to the shrine of the local deity was fined one cow, which was divided between the priest, the Eze, and other men of title. An habitual thief was sold as a slave, the proceeds being divided between the Eze and the senior officials. If cases of assault were brought to the notice of the Eze, he sent the Asogwa to plant his iron staff in the compound of the man who had committed the assault, and this taboo could not be withdrawn until the man had been tried by the Eze, Onyishi, and other elders. If found guilty he had not merely to compensate the person assaulted, but had also to pay a fine of one cow. The Eze and other men of title also acted as arbitrators in disputes between individuals, kindreds, or local groups, and were given gifts of kolas for their trouble. Although the litigants were not bound to accept the decision, they had at least to treat the arbitrators with respect. A case was cited in which the head of a kindred who was dissatisfied with the judgement given by the Eze and his coadjutors ate some of the kolas he had brought as dues and scattered the rest on the ground. For this affront he was called on to pay a fine of one cow and, after much bickering, complied.

In the village-group of Nibo, also, the three principal personages were and still are the Eze, Onyishi, and Asogwa. The kindred to which the Eze belongs has a traditional connexion with Nri, a town in the Awka Division famous for its priest-chiefs and as the birthplace of titles.[1] It is said that the founder of the Eze's kindred at Nibo left Nri in order to avoid having his face cicatrized with the *ichi* marks of the Ọzọ society. And so it is taboo for any Eze of Nibo to meet any person of Nri face to face. The traditional forefather brought with him from Nri the cult known as 'Agbala', the symbol of which is an iron staff covered with cloth. Before this staff the Eze offers frequent sacrifice. Taking a kola he breaks it and speaks as follows: 'Agbala, I come to offer you the daily service which my fore-fathers were wont to offer. If I am the duly appointed Eze of this community receive the offering; but if I am not then spurn it. Protect my life and the life of my people, and grant us an increase of children. Enable me to rule my people well and long.' During these rites a wooden gong is beaten by one of the Eze's sons, and this gong is also beaten during the Eze's meals, which he must eat unseen by any save the wife who had cooked the meal and children under the age of puberty. He may not eat food in the open air nor in any other house save his own. Before he begins his meal the Agbala staff is placed beside him, and, after he has finished eating, he deposits small offerings of food on the ground beside the staff. These offerings are subsequently eaten by small children. He may not leave the town, for to do so would provoke the anger of Agbala and the spirits of former Ezes, who are regarded as living in close association with the staff.

When an Eze of Nibo dies his body is laid on a shelf in his room. The shelf is covered with mud plaster with holes inset, so that the effluxes of the body, which is subjected to fumigation, may be able to drip through to the ground. Women, chosen by divination, keep a fire burning day and night under the shelf for a considerable period. At the end of this period the body is placed in a canoe-shaped coffin,

---

[1] For further information on this subject see the article entitled 'The Divine Umundri King' by Dr. M. D. W. Jeffreys, in *Africa*, July 1935.

with a lid working on hinges. The coffin is then deposited in a shaft-and tunnel-grave, resting on a bier. Succeeding Ezes are buried in recesses of the same grave. No new Eze may be appointed until the late Eze has been buried. The present Eze holds no official position, but is represented on the bench of the Native Court by his son.

The village-groups of Ozala, Ibagwa-Ani, Edem, Obukpa, and Erọ were also governed on the same bureaucratic system, the titled members of the community being the centres of authority. At their head was an Eze, assisted by the senior Asogwa of each village. All matters of importance for the whole community were brought before the Eze, sitting in council with the Asogwa (and any heads of kindreds who were not Asogwa). The Eze was president of the council and when it was necessary to decide a case by ordeal he was the administrator of the sasswood. He acted as arbitrator in disputes between sub-divisions, and received a gift of a goat from each of the subdivisions for his services. With the authority of the Asogwa and heads of families he could sell persons guilty of certain offences such as kidnapping, or the theft of goats, dividing the proceeds with the Asogwa and the leaders of age-grades who acted as executive officials. He could sell children who cut the upper before the lower teeth, and sell or hold to ransom a child born to a woman before her previous child had been weaned. He could impose a fine (of one cow) on any one who interfered with a stranger coming (under promise of safe-conduct) to visit a friend. A person convicted of murder was ordered by the Eze and Asogwa to hang himself in the presence of the relatives of the murdered man. Male adulterers were fined and required to give a fowl or goat to the wronged husband for sacrifice to his ancestors. A rain-maker who consistently failed to make rain was fined one cow, which was sacrificed to Ifijiọku, the yam spirit. A person accused of stealing yams, and denying the charge, had to drink sasswood prepared by the Eze, and if he died his family had to produce one of their number to be sold as a slave, the proceeds being divided between the Eze, Asogwa, and the victim of the theft. If the person offered were a female, the Eze might take her to wife, paying a reduced bride-price which was divided between the Asogwa and the victim of the theft. The Eze and Asogwa acted as a court of appeal in all disputes about the ownership of land. The Eze also decided for or against war, and in the former case provided the powder. The Asogwa were the directors of military operations. They, with the Eze, selected the companies fit for fighting, issued powder, gave orders for the construction of defences, and determined who should form the attacking party and who should be left behind to guard the town.

If any one refused to obey the order of the Eze's tribunal the Eze sent his staff to be planted in the culprit's compound at sunrise, and if the culprit failed to appear by midday the Eze, accompanied by the Asogwa and some members of the warrior age-grades, went to the culprit's house, and exacted a heavy fine or pillaged his property and drove him from the town. The property of a kindred which had refused to hand over a murderer was also pillaged.

The Eze and Asogwa did not, however, take cognizance of every form of offence, or dispute. In many cases they delegated their authority, explicitly or implicitly, to the leaders of the age-grades. These persons acted as justices of the peace and settled many cases in a summary manner, being assisted, when necessary, by bodies of young men or by maskers of the cult of Omabe. Moreover, it was in the interests of individuals, kindreds, and local groups to settle differences among themselves without reference to the central authorities, who were always inclined to put off the decision of cases, with a view to lining their own pockets. It was stated at Obukpa that when a case was referred to the Eze and Asogwa both sides had to give gifts before a date was fixed for the trial. On the first day of the hearing proceedings were stopped after a few cursory questions, on the pretext that additional witnesses were required. The court would meet a week later only to find that, owing to the (intentional) absence of an important member, a further adjournment was necessary. And so on until the members of the court had been able to collect as many fees or bribes as possible. In many cases no decision was given at all, as the members of the court had promised the verdict to both sides.

The Eze usually belongs to a particular kindred which has held the title from time immemorial. Thus, the Eze of the village-group of Erọ is always appointed from the Ugbene kindred, after having paid the prescribed fees to the elders of his own kindred, to the heads of all other kindreds, and to all the other titled people of Erọ. On appointment his head is shaved by the senior elder of his kindred, and a circular tuft is left on the crown of the head. (This tuft must remain until his death, when it is shaven off and placed in his grave.) The senior member of his kindred then fixes the royal bracelets on the Eze's wrists and hands him also the *aro* or staff, which at Erọ is four feet long and is covered over with brass foil. He is also given a stool, on which no one but the Eze or his full brother or sister's son may sit. Thereafter he goes into seclusion for one month. The Eze offers periodic sacrifice to Dim-Eze, who was the first Eze of Erọ. When an Eze dies he is buried in a shaft- and tunnel-grave in a special graveyard for Ezes. An *ibodo* tree is planted over the grave of each Eze. There are nine of these trees to be seen to-day, so that there have been at least ten Ezes of Erọ.

The village-group of Ogurte is distinguished by having a female Eze. She is saluted as 'Agamega' or 'Female leopard'. It is not an Ibo custom, as far as I know, to confer authority in public matters on women, though (as we shall see later) the women known as Umada sometimes intervene as arbiters in quarrels between kindreds or local groups. But among the Igala and some other tribes of the Northern Provinces women are occasionally invested with public authority. The present Eze of Ogurte is the first woman to hold the title, which she purchased[1] with the consent of her own family and of the whole group, who, incidentally, are said to be of Igala origin. Her grandfather and great uncle were Ezes, and she succeeded the latter after an interval of about fifteen years. She stated that in former times it was customary for any one seeking the title of Eze to give one of his daughters to the Ata of Ida, and she claims that the grandmother of the present Ata was a daughter of her grandfather.

The Eze-ship of Ogurte is not confined to a particular kindred. Any one in Ogurte is eligible for the title, if he or she can pay the dues. Nor does the Eze-ship confer any great measure of authority, for the present Eze stated that in all important matters she was bound to consult the senior elder or Onyishi of Ogurte, who is regarded as the father of the community and offers annual sacrifice to the traditional founder of the group. Even in her own section of Ogurte (Umu-Ida) she cannot take any important step without obtaining the sanction of the local Onyishi. When dues are payable to the controlling authorities (e.g. when fees are paid for titles or when animals are given as gifts to celebrate final funeral rites) the first share is taken not by the Eze but by the Onyishi of Ogurte. The Eze takes the second share, and the rest is divisible among the senior elders of the various sub-sections.

The present Eze, being a woman, is the chief arbiter in all disputes between women, and takes a prominent part in settling matrimonial differences, recovering runaway wives and remonstrating with hus-

---

[1] Her title cost her £20, one cow, and three horses, paid to the senior elders of her own kindred and of the various subdivisions of Ogurte.

bands who ill-treat their wives. She makes the arrangements for the public sacrifice which the women offer periodically in the market-place to the 'Umada' or deceased 'mothers' of Ogurte. She does not offer the sacrifice in person, as this duty is always performed by the oldest woman of the community. The Eze, who is a member of the Native Court, is unmarried, as her family insisted, as a condition of helping her to attain the Eze-ship, that she would divorce her husband and refrain from re-marrying. Their reason for this was to ensure the safe return of their capital (with interest). For in this part of Iboland a husband has a claim on the property of his deceased wife.

All Ezes carry an iron staff, an ọfọ stick, and a piece of buffalo bone, with which they tap their dishes of food before partaking of a meal. The Asogwa, in addition to their whisks made from buffalo tails, carry, slung from the shoulders, bags made of the skins of wild cats.

Atama.

Finally, there are the 'Atama', who, as high-priests of the community, exercise considerable authority. In some cases their authority is purely priestly, like that of the priests of Ala elsewhere, but in others the Atama ranks as a nobleman as well as a priest, and it would seem that the office had been introduced as part of the religio-titular system disseminated throughout Iboland from Nri (near Awka).

In the commune of Amala there is a priest-chief of this character. He is known as the Atama of 'Ezugu' and, assisted by the Onyishi of Amala and four special heads of kindreds known as Ọnọdu-Ọha, exercises a controlling influence throughout Amala. It is said that in former times Amala was 'ruled' by an Eze, but that the office of Eze fell into abeyance when the spirit of Ezugu made it known to the last Eze, whom he is believed to have killed, that he, Ezugu, was the one and only Eze or 'ruler' of Amala. It is instructive to note the recurrence of this belief that the real rulers of the town are the ancestors or spirits, and that living persons who act as rulers are merely the agents of the ancestors. This doctrine is the basis of priestly-chieftainship, and the divine kingship which is found among the Jukun, Igala, Yoruba, and Bini tribes.

The Atama-ship of Amala is confined to two particular kindreds. The origin of the office is given in the following story. Once upon a time a spirit called 'Ezugu' appeared at Amala and went to the house of one Amanachi and asked for water. Amanachi refused this request, so Ezugu repeated his request to two of Amanachi's wives, who were half-sisters.[1] The wives immediately complied, and in his gratitude Ezugu told them that in the morning they would find something at the threshold of their hut which, if they tended it, would help them in all their troubles; for that thing would be himself, as he, Ezugu, was a spirit. When darkness fell Ezugu vanished from their midst, and the women became afraid. But in the morning they found a piece of iron outside their hut. They took it, planted it in their hut, and began to make to it offerings and requests. In consequence they won great prosperity and bore numerous children. When the women died the spirit of Ezugu fell upon one of their sons. The possessed child fled to a hill, and after spending seven native weeks there without food or shelter returned to the town, where he was immediately acclaimed in the market-place as the new divinely-chosen priest of 'Ezugu'. He was allowed to appropriate anything he saw in the market, including a maiden who became his wife without the payment of a bride-price. She was given the title of Orocha and it became her duty to cook the sacrificial foods. The Atama-designate then proceeded to the shrine of Ezugu where a servant of the cult took a chicken, pressed it against the face and body of the Atama, broke its beak, and threw it into the 'bush'. The intention of this rite was that the human soul of the Atama might enter into the chicken and be cast away, making room for the divine spirit of Ezugu, who now took complete possession of the Atama. The Atama then offered a goat in sacrifice to Ezugu, saying, 'I have returned to be your servitor for ever. Do you guide and protect me well.' After this sacrifice the young Atama lived a life of semi-seclusion for a year, avoiding contact with all save young boys and girls and aged men and women. At the end of the year he went to the shrine and shaved his head, leaving the tuft of hair which, among many tribes of Nigeria, is the characteristic symbol of priesthood and of chieftainship. He sacrificed a cow, pouring the blood over the symbol, at the same time informing Ezugu that he had shaved his head and was now proof against contact with persons defiled by sexual intercourse.

The Atama performed sacrifice to Ezugu every second day at sunrise. He had first scrupulously to wash his hands, face, and feet, and his wife had to sweep the shrine 'to remove all footprints'.[2] Kneeling before the symbol of the cult he touched the ground with his fore-

---

[1] It is not taboo, as among most tribes, for a man to marry a half-sister of his wife.

[2] The intention in removing footprints is discussed in my book *A Sudanese Kingdom*, p. 158.

head, and then touched his left wrist with his right hand. Taking a kola he said, 'Ezugu, I bring kola-nuts to you. Do you protect me and give me length of life and prosperity. Increase my intelligence and enable me to speak the truth, and to rule my people without favour. Prosper also my people.' He then split the kola and placed the fragments on the ground before the symbol. A libation of palm-wine was also poured. He concluded the rites by touching the ground twice with his forehead.

This was the regular ritual, but he might sacrifice also at any time on behalf of individuals who had been directed by a diviner to give a gift to Ezugu. Twice a year also (at the Ongwenu and Ongwesa festivals) he offered sacrifice publicly in the presence of all the elders, asking for protection for all the people of Amala and in particular for those who had contributed gifts in the market-place for sacrifice. Incidentally, there were four women known as Adugu (i.e. daughters of Ugu) attached to the cult, whose duty it was to collect chickens and kolas in the market on the day before these public rites. These women were chosen for their office by divination from among women who were subject to nervous crises.

There were a number of taboos connected with the Atama-ship. Thus, the Atama might not eat in the presence of any but members of his own family; he might not eat coco-yams, or yam-peas, or dog's flesh. He might not enter certain villages, and he might not meet the Atama of Amube face to face.[1]

On the death of an Atama his tuft of hair was shaved off and placed in his grave, which was of the shaft and tunnel (and not the usual rectangular) pattern. His bracelet was removed and given to his successor. The body, covered with a cloth and mat, was laid on a bed which was placed inside the tunnel. It was customary also to kill a slave and place the body at the foot of the bed. Some time after burial another slave was killed and buried outside the grave. Before his execution the slave's hands and legs were tied, and kolas were placed in the palms of his hands with the instruction that he must deliver the kolas to the dead Atama. It is believed that when an Atama dies he becomes reincarnated as the Ata of Ida, and when an Ata dies he becomes reincarnated as the Atama of Amala. It was the custom for a new Ata of Ida to send a goat and chicken to the Atama of Amala for sacrifice to Ezugu, the Atama in return sending to the Ata some of the magical chalk of Ezugu.

[1] The present Atama has ceased to be bound by these taboos.

M

Amala was governed on the same principle as other village-groups, i.e. each village managed its own affairs as far as possible. But matters of outstanding importance were referred to a public meeting at the Atama's house, which included the Onyishi of Amala, the four Onodu-Oha, the other heads of kindreds, and the Asogwa who were the principal executive officers.

The present Atama of Amala is a young man of twenty-one. He stated that the spirit of Ezugu had fallen upon him some time before the age of puberty. He cannot remember anything of the onset, beyond finding himself on the top of the sacred hill of Ezugu, and during his stay there seeing numerous leopards which had been sent by Ezugu to protect him. Had he not indeed been the chosen of Ezugu the leopards would have killed him. He had not kept any tally of the number of days spent on the hill, having merely remained there until the spirit had moved him to return home. He clearly believed his own account of what had happened, and we can only conclude that fasting and exhaustion had created a state of hallucination, the form of which had been fixed by tradition.[1]

The most noteworthy Atama in the Nsukka Division is the Atama of Amube in the commune of Enugu-Ezeke. This Atama is regarded as the 'father' of the whole commune. He is chosen by divination from one of three kindreds in rotation, wears a red gown and a red cap with ear-flaps. Into the front of the cap are fixed four bustard feathers, together with a large number of porcupine quills and the red feathers known as *awo*. These partially cover his face. In the centre of the feathers there is a circular mirror of European make. His footgear is of leather and he carries in his left hand an iron staff with a knob handle, a red feather being stuck into the knob. The upper half is covered with cloth, and the lower half with brass wire. A number of bells are attached to the centre. In his right hand he carries the *ure*, which corresponds with the *ofo* of most Ibo communities. It is a wooden stick of bulbous appearance due to the accumulation of sacrificial blood. The handle is surrounded with brass wire. The Atama is always followed by a small boy carrying his stool. When he sits no one else may sit, except on the ground. It is taboo also for any one to mention corn in the Atama's presence, or to speak of relieving nature. If any one breaks these taboos the Atama takes a twig known as *aroro* and touches his forehead, right and left shoulder,

---

[1] But compare the account of a state of 'dissociation' given in my *Tribal Studies in Northern Nigeria*, vol. ii, p. 260.

chest, knees, and feet, and then his iron staff. When he appears in public he is accompanied by a drum and flute band, and his followers sing or shout laudations such as:

'God owns you, God owns you, and you own mankind, Leopard!'

'The leopard kills a goat and leaves the stick to the owner of the goat; when the owner of the goat comes he thanks God that the leopard had not killed him also.'

'Owner of the land, hold your land well, for other things you will eat—do not spoil your land (i.e. you will attain higher things if you rule well).'

This ascription of the title of 'leopard' to the Atama is noteworthy, for in most tribes this title is confined to chieftains. The Atama claims the right to all leopards killed by the people of Enugu-Ezeke, Ihakpo, Ihoro, Amakpo, Ihaka, and Ovoko, and states that he was accustomed to give a gift of four brass rods to the slayer of the leopard, two rods to each of the men who had brought the leopard's carcass to his house, and one rod to the head of the kindred of the slayer. He distinguished the leopard-slayer by placing in his hair the feather of an eagle and *awo* bird. He himself appropriated the skin and claws of the leopard, while the flesh was handed over to the members of his kindred to eat. Some of the villages mentioned repudiate the Atama's claims in this matter.

The Atama offers private sacrifice every second day to Ugu, and to Ugulemie the wife of Ugu. He also offers public sacrifice three times a year (in March, May, and September). All the elders of Enugu-Ezeke attend the rites, and sometimes also the elders of Ihaka, Ihakpo Amakpo, Ihoro, and Ovoko. It is customary also for any one who wishes to establish a family-cult to go to the Atama with a goat and fowl which the Atama sacrifices to Ugu, saying, 'This your child has come to offer sacrifice to you, and to tell you that he wishes to set up a shrine for the service of his father. Permit him to do so, and protect him and all the members of his family.'

The Atama is the keeper of the calendar for the whole district. The Ibo year is a seasonal or solar year reckoned from the time of planting yams. But the moons are also a factor in reckoning time, and are numbered consecutively from the time of planting. As a lunar year of twelve moons falls short of a solar year by eleven days, there may be some uncertainty every few years whether the moon which has appeared about the time of planting is to be reckoned as a thirteenth moon of the old year or as the first moon of the new.

At Enugu-Ezeke it is the Atama's business to determine such and kindred matters. A moon which overlaps the planting season is known as *ongwefu kefu* or 'the nameless moon', and during such the Atama, in bygone days, was wont to visit each kindred in Enugu-Ezeke and receive gifts of cloth, goats, yams, and chickens. On these occasions he was invited to adjudicate on family disputes which the heads of kindreds had been unable to settle themselves. He also presided at trials by ordeal, and was the chief administrator of oaths. As the keeper of the calendar he worked in close conjunction with the rain-maker, with whom he conferred in secret regarding the date at which rain-producing or rain-stopping rites might be performed with a probability of success.

Summing up, we may say that in the Nsukka Division government was, as elsewhere, the business of the whole community, that it was based on the family organization, and that authority was in consequence widely distributed. But the system of titles, which was bound up with the possession of wealth, tended to cut across and frequently even to eclipse the family organization, establishing the richer families at the expense of the poorer, and a form of polity which, if more centralized and effective, was also more bureaucratic. On this there will be more to say in the ensuing chapter.

VII

TITLES

THE system of title-taking is one of the most characteristic features of Ibo society. There are various types of titles. There are those which confer a political as well as a social status, those which are public and recognized throughout the community, and those which are private, having no significance outside the owner's own kindred, those which are hereditary and those which are not, those which are confined to certain families and those which are open to all except slaves. In some localities the institution of title-taking is still an essential feature of the social life, amounting almost to a system of caste; in others it is fast losing its former prestige; while in others again it is already dead, having failed to maintain itself in the face of new standards of value.

In the Nsukka Division title-taking is, as we have seen, still of considerable political and social importance, particularly as regards the highest title of Eze, which has tended to become identified with 'Warrant Chieftainship'. The most important titles there are divided into two groups known respectively as 'Ama' and 'Ọzọ',[1] the former system being followed in some communities and the latter in others. A man may proceed to take any of the senior titles at any time, provided he is rich enough and his kindred has the right to take the particular title sought. There is no restriction as regards age, and a father may obtain a title for a son who is a mere boy. There are numerous Asogwa who have not yet reached the age of twenty. A son, on the other hand, may, if he has acquired wealth, provide his father with the means of taking a title. One reason for this is that sons are not allowed to take titles which are equal to or higher than those borne by their fathers.

As a rule most young men acquire a number of junior titles before proceeding to take a senior title. These junior titles are of little value and are easily obtained. Thus at Umufu one Ezeako, the present Eze, began climbing the social ladder by taking, at the expense of a horse, cow, and other gifts, the minor titles of 'Jebile' and 'Itegina'. He then proceeded to take the so-called 'drum title' known as 'Egede'. To do this he had to give a gift of two horses, one cow, and four goats

---

[1] Both vowels in this word are open. The phonetic spelling, therefore, is Ɔzɔ.

to the elders of the Ozam and Amofia kindreds (who jointly own the 'Egede' drum), and also to all the members of the 'Egede' society. In order to obtain seniority among those who had previously taken the title he gave a further gift of one horse. It may be remarked that this 'Egede' title is found also at the town of Unareze (or Umalo), where it is said that the drum, which is regarded as sacred, was introduced from Nri (in Awka Division). There is a drum priest known as the Eze Egede who offers sacrifice to the drum periodically. The priest had to pay seven horses for his office, and he and the others associated with the cult recoup themselves by hiring out the drum for considerable sums at the final funeral rites of all important people.

Ezeako then obtained two further titles, namely, 'Ozo-Odo' and 'Ozo-Opienya'. He stated, possibly with some exaggeration, that the latter cost him seventeen horses, which were sold, the proceeds being divided among the elders of his own kindred, all heads of families in his village, and all fellow members of the association. Finally, he approached all the most important elders in his group in order to ascertain whether they would support him if he became a candidate for the title of Eze. When they assented he began making his payments by presenting the elders of his kindred with three goats. A series of feasts was given to each group in Umufu, and gifts of rods were distributed to the guests. Special gifts were given to the *oha* or members of the senior society. Nine hundred rods were distributed among the various age-grades of Umufu, and fifty rods were given to each of the guilds (blacksmiths, dancers, palm-tappers, hoe-handle makers, and midwives). Four hundred *aka* beads, valued at forty pounds, were distributed as a final gift among the *oha*. These assembled at his house, where the senior elder of the Ozam kindred sacrificed a cow (provided by the candidate) at the Anyaňu or Sunshrine of the candidate, with a prayer that his (Anyaňu's) child, who was taking the title of Eze, would be prospered in all his doings. He was then given the insignia of his office.

At Ukehe the three principal titles are (1) 'Ele', (2) 'Owa', and (3) 'Ozo'. But a number of minor titles may be taken before proceeding to these. Thus a man may receive the title of 'Emume-Enyinya' as a recognition of the fact that he had killed a horse to celebrate the funeral rites of his father. He may be entitled 'Emume-Isi' if he has killed a man, bush-cow, or leopard. 'Ifijioku' is a public title obtained by paying 300 rods to the other 'Ifijioku' of the group. The title of 'Ele' is obtained at a cost of about four pounds payable to the other

'Ele' of the group, while that of 'Owa' costs a pound or two more. The final title of 'Ọzọ' or 'Ichi' is only obtained after the distribution of large sums among all holders of the Ọzọ title throughout the commune. The sign of this title is the so-called *ichi* markings.[1] These marks are inscribed with an elaborate ritual. The candidate is made to lie down with his head resting against two sticks set over a hole in the ground, into which the blood from the cuts flows. A medicine is buried underneath the hole, with the intention of safeguarding the candidate from bleeding to death. Another medicine is placed on his chest to give him courage during the painful ordeal. While the marks are being incised all holders of the title sit round the candidate blowing the ivory horns which members of the society alone may use. On the completion of the operation the candidate lives a life of seclusion for fifteen days, attended by one of the order. On emerging he offers sacrifice to Ala, the Earth-deity. But he remains unshaven for a year and may not attend any market. On the completion of the year he shaves his head, appears in the local market, and again offers sacrifice to Ala.

At Nsukka if a man wishes to obtain the title of Asogwa (one of the senior titles in the 'Ama' grade) he has first to receive the approval of the head of his kindred, who would withhold approval if the candidate's character were considered unsatisfactory. The candidate first presents the head of the kindred with a goat which is sacrificed to the ancestors of the kindred, and he then gives a further gift of 50 to 100 rods. He has also to provide a liberal feast for all his kinsmen, among whom he distributes 200 rods. Having satisfied the demands of his own kindred he has then to secure, by gifts of rods, pigs, goats, kolas, palm-wine, and salt, the goodwill of all the local members of the society, and also to provide four public feasts. Finally, the senior titled member of his group confers on him the buffalo-tail which is the hall-mark of an Asogwa. In former times a newly appointed Asogwa was accorded the right of seizing and selling a boy from a kindred which had no right to membership of the Ama society. The new Asogwa kept one-third of the proceeds of the sale, and handed the balance to the other members of the society.

Atama or priests of public cults have also to pay for their titles. Thus the Atama-Aji or 'Priest of the yams' at Agamede (one of the villages of Eha-Amufu) had to secure by gifts the goodwill of the

---

[1] These markings are peculiarly disfiguring, being multitudinous and extending over the eyelids.

children of the former Atama-Aji and to give 1 cow to the elders of his kindred; 1 cow, 1 goat, and 100 rods to the elders of the village; 100 yams to the two senior elders; 1 goat and 1 fowl to the blacksmiths; and 90 yams to each holder of a yam title. He had also to give a cow for sacrifice to the spirit of the wooden gong which is beaten when yam titles are conferred. As the yam priest of Agamede is considered the principal yam priest in the whole village-group of Eha-Amufu he had to give gifts varying from 40 to 100 rods to the elders of each of the other villages of Eha-Amufu. In the dry season, after providing a feast for the whole village-group, he was formally appointed by the Atama-Aji of Umuhu (representing the Atama-Obum) and was given the title of 'Ongwu Debo' which means 'The Moon is not two', i.e. 'There is one yam priest and one only'.[1] At the same time he was informed that he must observe certain taboos (e.g. avoid drinking from anything but a pot, or relieving nature in the 'bush'). The Atama-Aji recoups himself for all this expenditure by taking a large share of the fees paid by those who take any of the yam titles. There are three grades of yam titles at Eha-Amufu. The first, known as Jebile, is obtainable by a gift of 100 yams to the Atama-Aji and of one ram and a feast to the elders and other holders of yam titles. The second, known as Itegina, is obtainable at the cost of one cow and one horse. The cow is sacrificed and the skin, head, liver, and one leg become the perquisite of the Atama-Aji, the rest being shared by the elders and holders of yam titles. The horse is sold and the Atama takes one-third of the proceeds, the elders another third, and the holders of yam titles another. The third title, namely, that of Iyareya, is so expensive that there are only two holders of the title in the whole of the village-group.

Reference may be made to three other titles which are common in the Nsukka Division, as elsewhere among the Ibo. These are (1) Ogbu-Madu, given to a man who had killed an enemy or slave, (2) Ogbu-Efi or cow-killer, and (3) Ogbu-Anye or horse-killer. An example may be given of the manner of obtaining the Ogbu-Efi title (at the town of Adâyi). The candidate makes a substantial gift of yams to the Onyisi of the local group, who divides them amongst the other elders. All then proceed to the candidate's house, where a cow is killed by the candidate, while the Onyisi offers a prayer at the shrine of Ifijioku for the candidate's welfare. He breaks a kola and deposits a fragment on

---

[1] Actually each quarter has an Atama-Aji of its own. But there is only one Atama-Aji whose priestly authority extends over the whole village-group.

the stone-symbol of the cult, eats a fragment himself, and gives a piece to the candidate. The candidate is then entitled to wear the string anklet which is the insignium of the title. A woman may take the Ogbu-Efi title, and in this case the procedure is slightly different. The Onyisi, accompanied by the elders, proceeds to her compound, in the centre of which he plants his iron staff. Then, taking a kola, he chews it and spits some fragments over the staff, calling on the woman's ancestors to protect her. The woman provides a feast for her guests, some fragments of the food being first deposited on the staff.

Apropos of the taking of titles by women, reference may be made here to the class of senior women known as Umada. These obtain their title by giving gifts and a feast to all the matrons of their local group. They are then invested with the *osha* or pumpkin rattle which is the symbol of their status. They exercise considerable authority in the community, for not only are they the arbiters in quarrels between women, but they sometimes intervene to settle quarrels which the male authorities have been unable to settle. They often play an important part in preserving the peace of the market. Thus, if one woman accuses another of having purloined some of her stock, the Umada may hear the case and order the accused to swear her guiltlessness on the symbol of the market-genius. They may have a cult of their own, by virtue of which they may compel debtors to pay their debts, and slanderers to pay a fine. They may fine widows who anoint their bodies before completing the mourning period, and mothers who become enceinte before their last child has been weaned. They perform annual rites in honour of their deity, and may exact dues for these rites from all traders attending the market. Any one repudiating their authority would be regarded as guilty of sacrilege, and would be punished by the priests and titled officials to whom the Umada would report the offence.

In other divisions, also, women have their own clubs or feasting societies. A banquet is given once a fortnight during the slack season by each member in turn, and the person whose turn it is to provide the banquet receives contributions from the others. The club has a number of executive officials, some of whom are empowered to impose fines for small unconventionalities. The money thus obtained may be used for offering sacrifice, or for buying 'medicines'. One of the commonest medicines used is for the purpose of preventing squabbling among themselves.

In the Awgu Division at the present time titles confer little political status, and their social value is steadily decreasing. In former times
all men of influence and affluence took titles, and we have seen that
some of these titles conferred public privileges and duties. At Ache,
for example, the holders of senior titles constituted a bureaucratic
class and no one could insult a member of their order without laying
himself open to a fine. But with the advent of the Government most
of the privileges attached to these senior titles became illegal and the
titles have therefore gradually disappeared. Such titles as have remained merely confer a social dignity, so that a non-titled man would
be slow to contradict one who had a title, and a junior titled brother
might in some communities take precedence of a senior non-titled
brother in most family matters. On the other hand, no one would
attach any importance to the opinions of a titled man who was
considered lacking in discretion, and a young titled man would hesitate to contradict an elder who had no title.

The titles are few and simple. They are obtained by giving a feast
to the people of the group, and paying dues to those who already
hold titles. Thus among the Isu-Ochi the title of 'Nnọ' is granted
to a man who, having had an exceptionally good yam harvest, provides a feast to all kinsmen and holders of the title. This feast entails
the killing of one cow and nine goats, and the candidate is also required to present the members of the order with 100 brass rods.
When the title is conferred an *ọfọ* is conferred with it. All holders of
the title assemble outside the candidate's compound, and pile their
ọfọ on the ground. The senior member present then cuts a section
from a branch of an *ọfọ* tree and lays it on the pile of *ọfọ*. He chews a
piece of kola-nut and spits the fragments over the *ọfọ*, saying 'Ọfọ,
take kola-nut and eat.' Next he takes a chicken (provided by the
candidate) and speaks as follows: 'Ọfọ, give ear. This man is taking the
title of 'Emume',[1] and we are about to confer on him the *ọfọ* of the title.
May you, Ọfọ, secure to him length of life that he may enjoy the
advantages of the title for many years to come.' Having said this he
cuts the chicken's throat and allows the blood to trickle over the *ọfọ*,
including the new *ọfọ* of the candidate. Some of the chicken's feathers
are stuck in the congealed blood. The new *ọfọ* is then handed to the
candidate, who is required to give a further gift of eighteen lumps
of salt to the title-holders. The initiate is henceforward known as
Onye-Nnọ (i.e. the man of 400 rows of yams).

---

[1] Emume (= feast) is a generic term for titles.

At Ihe one who has killed a cow in honour of his wife is known as 'Owanobo'. At Ngbwidi the title of Omenihunnaya (i.e. doer in presence of her father) is conferred on a woman whose husband has given a gift of a cow to her father. This is a compliment to a beloved wife who has borne a male child. Before killing the cow, the woman's father speaks as follows: 'Chuku (the Supreme Being), Ala, and Ancestors, this cow has been given to me by the husband of my daughter. I thank you for having spared my life to partake of these good things. Grant that my daughter may bear many children who will grow up into men and women before my eyes.' At the ensuing feast the principal guests are the wives of the husband's relatives and of all the local titled men. A leg of the cow is presented to the husband.

It may be of interest to describe in some detail the procedure followed in taking one of the most common titles such as that of Ogbu-Efi (cow-killer) or Maze (or Ogbu-Inyinya = horse-killer). The example given is taken from the town of Ngbwidi. The candidate's first step is to inform the head of his extended-family that he is desirous of taking the title of e.g. Maze. If the head of the family has no objection to the proposal, the candidate seeks the first opportunity of buying a horse. Having done so he goes to the local priest of Ala and asks him to offer sacrifice on his behalf. The priest takes a chicken (provided by the candidate) and waves it round the candidate's head, saying; 'Ala, this man has bought a horse in order that he may take the title of Maze. Protect his life and the lives of all who will participate in the ceremony. Grant that no ill-disposed person may attend the ceremony and cause a dispute. May all the proceedings be brought to a peaceful conclusion.' After this prayer the candidate returns home, and the priest kills and eats the chicken at his leisure.

The candidate then invites to his house all the holders of the Maze title in his own local group, and informs them that he intends, with their sanction, to take the title of Maze, and that he has already bought the horse. The senior member of the society then takes a chicken and calls on Ala and the ancestors to protect the candidate and to protect also the horse until the time arrives for parading it in the market. He presses the fowl against the horse's head, saying, 'Horse, take this fowl.' The fowl is then killed and eaten by all present.

A few days later the candidate gives a banquet to the members of the society, and after the banquet the horse is led in procession to the local market-place. The procession is headed by women—the wife of the candidate, the wives of his relatives, and the wives of all holders of the Maze title. These are followed by the title-holders themselves, in order of seniority. All parade round the market, singing songs and firing guns. The procession then visits other neighbouring markets.

On the following market-day all the title-holders again assemble at the candidate's house, where the senior amongst them is presented with a goat, the others being given a lump sum of money (amounting at the present time to about 30s. or £2). The brother of the candidate kills the horse, and when this has been done the priest of Ala goes to the threshold of the compound, and, holding a gourd of palm-wine, speaks as follows: 'Chuku, Ala, and Ancestors, our brother who has now killed this horse has done well in inviting the people to come and eat the flesh. Protect his life and the lives of all present.' Having said this he pours a libation on the ground.

A number of young men are detailed to cut up the flesh of the horse, which is divided out as follows. Half of the liver is given to the head of the candidate's extended-family, and half to his father's sister. One leg is given to the relatives of his father's mother, and one leg to the relatives of his wife. A special piece of meat is given to his father's eldest brother, and the offal goes to his sisters. The remainder is divided amongst the various members of the society in order of seniority, and small pieces of meat are also given to any other guests present.

If the taking of the title is associated with the final funeral rites of the candidate's father (or mother), it is customary for the senior member of the candidate's extended-family to take a small piece of the horse's liver to the gate of the compound and speak as follows (addressing the deceased): 'Your son has killed this horse to-day in honour of your final funeral rites. Protect him: allow no trouble to overtake him; and do not trouble him yourself, so as to keep him continually offering sacrifice to you. He has killed this horse in order to show that you have a living grown-up son. Reward him, therefore, by giving him a full measure of prosperity.'

In former times the title of Ogbute was, at Ngbwidi, conferred on any man who had killed and decapitated an enemy in war. The *ikoro* drum was beaten to announce the feat, and the head-getter immediately smeared his right leg and arm with camwood, his left leg with yellow dye, and his left arm with chalk. In his hair he stuck an eagle's feather. He then appeared dancing with the other head-getters and holding the head in his left hand on a pointed stick: in his right hand he brandished his matchet. He buried the head for three native weeks, to clean it of flesh. The skull was then dug up, and one half was smeared with camwood and the other half with yellow dye. A dance of all head-getters was held in the market-place. On the conclusion of this dance the head-getter took the skull to the village of his mother and laid it down at the threshold of the hut of his mother's father (or brother), saying: 'Greetings to you—whose daughter has borne a brave man.' His mother's father would provide a feast in his honour. If his means permitted he would even kill a cow, and if this were done the head-getter would in future be known as Oriefiogo, i.e. 'eater of war-cow'.

It was customary for a head-getter to undergo rites of purification, for he was regarded as infected with the spirit of Ekwêsu[1] and was unable, therefore, to go near his barn or farm—to do so would entail pollution to his yams, and be an offence also against Njǫku, the yam-spirit. He was escorted, accordingly, by the head-getters to the grove of Ekwêsu, taking with him a pullet and a pot of palm-wine, which had not come in contact with the ground (and so caused pollution to Ala). The senior head-getter, standing before the symbol of Ekwêsu, spoke as follows: 'Ekwêsu, we have come to offer sacrifice on behalf of this man who has taken the head of his enemy. We do this in order that his right arm (*ikenga*) may remain unimpaired. Grant that nothing of what the relatives of this man's enemy would like to do to him may have effect, and do not allow the dead man's ghost (*obi*) to pursue him.' He then cut off the pullet's head with a single blow and allowed the blood to pour on the ground. The flesh of the fowl was cooked and shared by all.

The head-getter was then conducted to a river. Entering the water he faced first towards the direction from which the river came, and then towards the direction in which it went. Then, throwing some water over each shoulder, he said: 'I wash away the blood of the man I killed. May this river carry it away.' He was then given a piece of *akǫro* creeper and a leaf of the *opete* tree, and with these he washed the right side of his body, then the left, then the abdomen and then the forehead, repeating the words: 'I wash away the blood of him whom I killed.'

The holder of a title cannot as a rule be deprived of his title. But he may, for any gross misconduct, be ostracized by his fellow titled-men and refused his share of dues. In some communities the holder

---

[1] See p. 39.

of a title may, if he is in straitened circumstances, pledge his title, i.e. he may, in return for a loan, assign his title and all the benefits thereof.

As regards the procedure in sharing dues or gifts, this is done by seniority, and the senior men usually receive a larger share than the junior. Apart from all questions of titles, if a gift is given to a village as a whole, it is divided up equally between the local groups and again subdivided equally among the kindreds, irrespective of the numbers of the kindreds. When kolas are presented by litigants to the elders who act as arbiters, they are handed to the most senior man present, who would keep one and hand the others to his fellow elders. He would split the one he had kept and throw the seeds on the ground, saying: 'Ancestors, Ajana, and Chuku, come and eat kola and assist us in our deliberations.' He would retain one section of the kola, and hand one to the person who had presented it. The latter would first eat his section, to show that it had not been poisoned. Similarly, if a householder is visited by friends or relatives, it is customary for him to present a kola to the most senior of the visitors, first licking it to show that it has not been poisoned. The senior visitor hands the kola to one of his juniors to split. The junior then hands the split kola back to his senior, who in turn hands one section to the host. The host eats his section first. The senior visitor then eats his section, or part of it, and hands the other sections to his companions.

Turning now to the Owerri Division, the institution of title-taking seems to have had no place in the social or political life of Owerri itself, but among the Isu the Ọzọ society played an important part in administration in pre-Government times and operated also as a centralizing agency. Indeed, it is true to say that the sense of solidarity possessed by the Isu is largely due to the unifying influence of the Ọzọ society. As the society is still in existence in a number of communities I studied it in some detail, with a view to assessing its present administrative possibilities.

In the olden days the taking of a title was a costly and elaborate affair, extending possibly over a number of years. The ritual varied in the different towns, and it is not easy to give an accurate general account, owing to the forgetfulness of the old men who took the title in pre-Government times, their tendency to exaggeration, and the confusion caused by later modifications of the old rules. The following account is based mainly on the ritual observed at Mbieri.

Any man of sufficient means could present himself as a candidate

for the Ọzọ title, with the approval of the members of the society
who resided in his own local group. Unless he bore a notoriously bad
character no opposition was offered to his candidature, as the members of the society were only too glad to receive (in the form of the
new candidate's fees) interest on the capital which they themselves
had expended in obtaining their titles. The local members of the
society were entertained by a preliminary banquet given at the house
of the candidate, who was also required to present gifts of a specified
character.[1] A feature of the preliminary rites was the planting of a
branch of an *ururu* tree in the compound of the candidate.[2] This was
done by a member of the society indicated by a diviner, and as he
planted the branch he said: 'May you and your wives and children
live to a good old age.' Offerings of palm-wine and cassava mixed with
oil were deposited beside the branch, and the blood of a fowl sprinkled
over it. Some of the blood was sprinkled on the *ọfọ* of the members
of the society, who left their *ọfọ* lying on the ground until they had
each received a gift of a few cowries. The person chosen to plant the
tree received a special fee of 400 cowries.

Later, another banquet was given to the members of the society,
and gifts consisting of 8 pots of cassava mixed with oil, cooked oil-
beans, 8 pots of palm-wine, 9 yams, 1 pot of oil, 16 kola-nuts, 8 balls
of *edo*, and 4,800 cowries. The candidate then provided himself with
the *mpata* or stool of the society, and the members of the society were
again invited to a feast at which one of the members planted eight
cuttings of *ogirisi*, *abosse*, and *ọha* trees, saying as he did so: 'May the
candidate and his family and all holders of the title live long. May he
be able to obtain all the fees necessary for his title.'

The next stage was known as Ọkpọrọm Ọzọ and consisted of

[1] 4 alligator peppers, 8 kola-nuts, 8 balls of *edo*, 4 parcels of cooked oil-beans,
and 1 pot of palm-oil. At Ubomiri the preliminary gifts were said to be 4 pots of
wine, 2 fowls, 16 kola-nuts, 16 'bitter kola-nuts', 32 bundles of kolas and bitter kolas,
and cowries to the value of £2. Seven days later the candidate again summoned the
members and entertained them, presenting them with 4 pots of wine, 2 goats, and
a large sum in cowries. Seven days later he again presented them with 2 fowls, 8 jars
of wine, 160 kolas, 160 bitter kolas, and a further sum in cowries. Some say that the
total expenses amounted to £100, others that they did not exceed £40, and others
£20.

[2] At Umunọha at the preliminary rites (*Ekwem Ọzọ*) the Onyisi-Ọzọ took a goat,
cock, axe-handle, palm-stalk, and branches of *ururu*, *abosse*, and *ngu* trees and walked
round the candidate's house, saying, 'May you live long and obtain the means to take
the title.' He then planted the trees and poured over them the blood of the goat
and the cock.

another feast (with gifts),[1] accompanied by the planting of another group of tree-cuttings. Then followed a feast known as *Ekwem Ǫzǫ*,[2] and after that the feast or rite known as *Onye* at which two branches of a *mboto* tree were planted and two others laid crosswise over them. On this occasion the senior members of the order placed a necklace (provided by the candidate) on the candidate's neck, saying, 'May you live long and continue patiently to fulfil the remaining duties of title-making.' The fees for this rite amounted to 9,600 cowries.[3] Soon afterwards rites in honour of Anyaṅu (the Sun) were observed. A branch of the *otinne* tree was planted. The top end of the branch was split and four pepper-pods were introduced. Young palm-leaves were hung round the end of the branch. Cuttings of *ogirisi*, *ǫha*, *abosse*, and *ururu* trees were then set in the ground round the *otinne* branch. The senior member of the society took a chicken and, looking up to the sun, said: 'Anyaṅu, be pleased to bring wealth to the candidate and all of us assembled here.' The cock was killed and the blood poured over the symbol. The Anyaṅu rite was followed by another known as *Mbata* (Enter), for which branches of the *ururu* and *ǫha* trees were planted outside the door of the candidate's house, with the sacrifice of a cock and hen, and the presentation of further gifts.[4]

The next rite was known as *Emwaia akan ala* or 'The putting of the hand in the ground', and was performed after sunset. A small tunnel was dug in the ground and into this the senior member of the society poured the blood of a cock and hen. He also placed in the tunnel some of the feathers of the fowls. He then took the right hand of the initiate and thrust it into the hole, saying, 'May the Ǫzǫ title prove to be a thing of value to you.' When the candidate extracted his hand, smeared with blood and feathers, he touched his breast. The left hand was treated similarly. No explanation of this rite was obtained. The fee payable was 16 pots of palm-wine, 16 pots of cassava mixed with oil, 40 kola-nuts, 16 balls of *edo*, 20 alligator pepper-pods, 1 pot of oil, and 1 ball of salt.

Some of the above rites were unknown in other groups than Mbieri,

[1] 8 yams, 8 pots of cassava mixed with oil, 8 pots of wine, 8 kolas, 1 pot of palm-oil, 1 ball of salt, 8 balls of *edo*, 4 packets of cooked oil-beans, and 4,800 cowries.

[2] This entailed the following gifts: 4 fowls (2 cocks and 2 hens), 16 pots of wine, 16 pots of cassava, 16 kolas, 1 pot of oil, 9 yams, and 9,600 cowries.

[3] But in some groups the conferring of the necklace formed part of the final ceremonies.

[4] 18 yams, 8 balls of *edo*, 8 kola-nuts, 4 pepper-pods, &c. A special fee was given to the senior and second senior members of the society for sacrificing the fowls.

but the following ceremony, known as *Onumono*, appeared to be essential in all groups, and was attended by all members of the society throughout the commune.

On the evening before the rites the members of the society assembled in the candidate's compound, and one of them (selected by divination) built a small platform of mud beside the wall of the house, in which he planted four camwood sticks. This became the symbol of the new *chi* or guardian spirit which a person was believed to obtain on being initiated into the society. It was known as *chi Ozo*. After the completion of the symbol the officiant killed a goat and hen, poured the blood over the symbol, stuck some of the hen's feathers in the blood, and offered a prayer for the initiate's welfare. The next morning a mound of earth was built, and four branches of an *ogirisi* tree were planted on one side of the mound and four on the other. To each of these a bundle of *oboro* grass was attached. The senior member of the society then took eight branches of an *ururu* tree (which had been obtained by young children of the candidate's family)[1] and, having waved them round the initiate's head, planted one of them in the mound of earth. The remaining seven were planted by other members of the society, so as to form two lines (four in each line). Thirty-two pieces of camwood stick, which had first been dipped in a solution of *edo*, were also passed round the candidate's head and planted in the mound.[2] The senior member of the society then killed a goat and cock and sprinkled the blood over the symbols, saying, 'May this title prove to be a cold thing and not a hot,' i.e. may it bring peace and not trouble. A banquet was provided for all (including women), and was followed by dancing, the members of the society blowing their ivory horns at intervals. During the evening the senior member of the society (i.e. the Onyisi-Ozo) set the candidate down on a specially woven mat, and all the members sat round him, holding their *ofo*. The Onyisi-Ozo then called out, 'May the new member live long to enjoy his title!' The others called out, '*Eba!*' (Yea!) and struck the ground with their *ofo*. The Onyisi again called out, 'May the new member derive wealth from his title,'

---

[1] Children were chosen because of their purity.

[2] At Ubomiri some of the sticks planted in the mound were said to represent deities, e.g. *abosse* or *ururu* sticks were planted symbolizing the sun, and *oha* sticks symbolizing Amadi-Oha (lightning). At Umunoha 8 pieces of camwood were fixed in the ground and surrounded by a rope across which a bundle of wooden images (representing Ikenga, Nshi, Agunsi, Ihu, Omako, Okunije, and Umôe) was laid. The Onyisi-Ozo then killed a goat and cock and sprinkled the blood on these images.

and again the others shouted '*Eha!*' and struck the ground with their
ọfọ. As the evening wore on they fell asleep, it being customary for
the members of the society to spend the ensuing night in the new
member's compound. Just before sunrise the Onyisi-Ọzọ raised the
candidate from his mat, led him outside the compound, and planted
a branch of an *ogirisi* and *ururu* tree. The new member was made to
sit down on his mat with his back against these branches, and his
hands placed on the *Ọzọ-ọfọ* of his father.[1] He was then ceremonially
washed by the Onyisi-Ọzọ with water in which leaves of the *onono*
creeper and four palm-nuts (without the kernels) had been soaked.
When the initiate rose after this baptism he placed his *ọfọ* against his
breast, while the Onyisi-Ọzọ chewed some alligator-peppers and kola-
nuts and blew the fragments over the *ọfọ*. The Onyisi-Ọzọ then said
to him: 'Your new name is Duru.' New names were also given him
by (*a*) his eldest son, (*b*) his eldest daughter, and (*c*) another member
of the Ọzọ society. The new member thus obtained four new names
and no longer answered to his old name. He was henceforward known
as *Onye-Nze*, or nobleman. The Onyisi-Ọzọ finally placed the Ọzọ
cap,[2] adorned with four eagle feathers, on the head of the new
member, who was congratulated by all, drums being beaten and
guns fired.

After these rites the new member went into seclusion for a period
of eight days[3] during which he smeared his body regularly with camwood oil. When he emerged, the Onyisi-Ọzọ again placed the cap of
the society on his head and led him by the hand to the market, where
he was congratulated by all, and given gifts. During the day he
danced some of the steps of the Ọzọ dance.[4] Four days later the
Onyisi-Ọzọ placed the copper or string anklets of the society on his
legs, saying: 'You have now performed all the duties of initiation into

---

[1] A brass ring was attached to the *ọfọ* to show that the son had taken it over from
his father.

[2] At Umunọha the initiate was (in addition to the woollen cap) given a European
opera-hat!

[3] At Irette and Orogwe (Umu-Nwọha group) a rite known as *Ikpo* followed the
Ọnumono rite. A mud throne was built for the new member, and when he first sat
down on this the Onyisi-Ọzọ killed a goat and sprinkled its blood on his head. After
this rite the new member received his cap and went into seclusion for twenty-eight
days. At Umunọha branches of the *mboto*, *ngu*, and African ebony were planted in
the throne, together with an old pestle and a piece of iron. The period of seclusion
was three months.

[4] Any non-Ọzọ man imitating the steps of the Ọzọ dance was liable to a fine.

the Ozo society; may you live long to obtain fees from other initiates, whereby you may recoup yourself for your own expenditure.'

These final rites of *Onumono* were said to cost the initiate anything from £10 to £20. But the fees were reduced by one-half if the initiate's father had been a member of the society. By making small payments the initiate's wife was also automatically ennobled. She was made to sit down on an *mpata* stool by the Onyisi-Ozo, was given a pair of anklets, and received the title of Lolo. In some groups[1] it was customary for the special marks known as *ichi* to be incised on the faces of members of the society. This operation was performed after the completion of the final rites, at a time indicated by a diviner. The new member lay down with his head resting on a plank laid over a hole in the ground (to receive the blood). Charcoal mixed with water was rubbed into the incisions. The operation was generally performed by men belonging to the Umu-Dioka commune, who were expert at the work. A feast was given before and after the operation. In the Umu-Nwoha commune *ichi* marking was not practised, and no Ozo member of the commune would eat in the company of a man so marked.

The burial rites of members of the society differed in some details from those of commoners. When a member of the society died, his fellow members were required to fast until he was buried. In the grave the body was laid flat (face upwards) on a plank covered with a mat and supported by sticks. Planks were fixed alongside the body, which was also covered by a plank, the whole presenting the appearance of a coffin. There was apparently no process of desiccating the body (as in the case of titled persons in certain other Ibo localities). Before burial all the tree symbols of the deceased were uprooted or cut down by young men of the deceased's family. The members of the society (*Ndi-Nze*) had to be present while this was done, and when the operation was finished the Onyisi-Ozo placed kola-nuts, *edo*, and palm-wine on the stump of the trees. He then took a fowl and some *akoro* creeper and placed them against his neck, saying: 'I am not responsible for your death. May you obtain a share of good things in the spirit world, as we obtain our share in this.' The Onyisi-Ozo next handed the fowl and creeper to all the other members of the society present in turn, each of whom made a similar declaration. The chicken and grass were handed back to the

---

[1] Facial marks can still be seen at Akabo, Ngugo, Ihuo, Atta, Inyishi, Ama-Imo, Ikembara, Eziama, Amakofia, and Avuvu.

Onyisi-Ọzọ, who placed them in a split piece of bamboo, which he planted in the middle of the spot formerly occupied by the trees.

The members of the society now laid their *ọfọ* on the ground in a row, and the *ọfọ* of the dead man was brought and placed beside them, but with the head pointing downwards. The Onyisi-Ọzọ killed a cock and a hen and poured the blood over the deceased's *ọfọ*, saying, 'We are taking away your *ọfọ*—you are no longer one of us.' The dead man's *ọfọ* was then handed to his eldest son, who held it close to his breast, while the Onyisi-Ọzọ blew fragments of kola-nut, *edo*, and alligator-pepper over it. The son then deposited the *ọfọ* in his bag and carried it into the house. For performing this rite the members of the society received a fee, but they in return contributed gifts for the funeral feast.

According to other accounts the ceremony of handing over the *ọfọ* of the deceased to his eldest son was only performed after the final funeral rites known as 'Ekwa-Ozu' or 'the crying for the dead', rites commonly known to Europeans as 'the second burial'. At these rites the members of the society came to the gate of the deceased's compound and sounded his name with their ivory trumpets. For this they received gifts from the deceased's heir, and were further rewarded for sounding his name within the compound, at the site of the deceased's Ozuzu shrine,[1] and at the door of the deceased's hut, where they broke a calabash of water over the head of the deceased's eldest son, who was then given formal possession of his father's *ọfọ*. The deceased's stool (*mpata*, or *okuku*) was in some groups thrown away into the 'evil bush' immediately after burial, but in others was retained by the eldest son.

It will have been observed from these rites that many of the typical features of initiation and installation rites are found in title-taking. The candidate undergoes a death to his former self and rebirth into a higher state. He goes into seclusion, is ceremonially washed, and receives a new name. His person becomes sacrosanct henceforth, he is affiliated with the gods (symbolized by the planting of trees), he may not be seen eating (except by members of the society), and when he dies he is given a special form of burial (which will be described later). The Ọzọ society was thus not merely a secular institution. It was a means of obtaining a measure of supernatural grace, and so making its members intermediaries between the gods and men.

---

[1] An Ọzọ cult (at Ubomiri).

The persons of members of the society were sacred,[1] and if any one struck or pushed or abused a member, or even a member's wife, he was liable to a heavy fine or to a raid on his property (conducted by the members of the society and their followers). The killing of an Ozo man had to be made good by the surrender of four[2] of the slayer's family, who were sold into slavery. If any one removed the cap of an Ozo man he was heavily fined. Neither the Nze nor their children could be seized on account of debt (like commoners), and no one dared place evil 'medicine' on land belonging to a member of the society, for it was believed that the 'medicine' would return to kill its owner. Members of the society could stop fighting between two groups by placing palm-leaves between the combatants and summoning the leaders of the groups to appear before them on an appointed day. They took a special part in settling land disputes, as the disputants were afraid to fight in their presence. They also acted as debt collectors and impounded the property of those who refused to pay. The house of a titled man was a sanctuary, and commoners going to a distance to farm would leave their domestic animals for safety there. Persons charged with offences would fly to the home of a member of the society pending the investigation of their case. Travellers between one village-group and another could secure immunity from attack by borrowing (in return for a fee) the ivory horn of the society. There were special penalties for committing adultery with the wife of a member of the society. The Nze also performed special functions in connexion with the purification of widows. They took a prominent part in all public affairs, and any one who interrupted them while speaking was liable to a fine of a fowl. A commoner was not allowed to stand between two Nze men at a meeting, and if a commoner wished to address a public assembly he first folded his hands and bowed to the Nze present. But a member of the society who committed a serious offence, such as stealing or poisoning, was degraded from the society, his cap being taken from him.[3] He lost his right to a share of the fees of candidates. He might, however, be readmitted, if the society thought fit, but in such cases it was customary to make

[1] Even the persons of those who had only paid some of the preliminary fees were sacred. Such were known as *Umegamega*. They were not entitled to receive any share of the fees of new candidates, and if they died before the completion of the *Onumono* rite all their previous payments were lost.

[2] Eight in the Umu-Nwoha group and sixteen at Akabo.

[3] In the 1929 disturbances the women rioters demanded the caps of 'Warrant Chiefs' or judges of the Native Courts.

him pay half the amount of his former fees. Any commoner who committed an offence of similar gravity was sold into slavery. The rich, important men of most groups were usually members of the Qzọ society.

At the present time in the Owerri Division the institution of title-taking has fallen into a general state of decadence, even in the Isu and Umu-Nwọha groups, where formerly it was a governing factor in the social life of the people. It has either been given up altogether or continued in a form which confers little status and no privileges of any importance. This form may consist merely of one of the pre-liminary rites, such as *Ekwem-Qzọ*, which is carried out with the implied condition that the remaining rites necessary for the full title will only be performed if means permit. As few, nowadays, consider themselves sufficiently wealthy to take the title in full it is seldom taken, except possibly at Mbieri and in a few other communes where strenuous efforts are being made to keep the flame of life flickering. Those who take titles in the restricted sense mentioned above are usually sons (or nephews) of former holders of the title, who have been instructed by a diviner to take the title or to take over their fathers' *Qzọ-ọfọ*, lest they should incur their fathers' ill will. The man so instructed summons the elders of his extended-family or members of the Qzọ society, if there happen to be any still alive. These plant an *ọha*, *oruru*, and *ogirisi* tree in the compound of the candidate, who sits on a *mpata* stool while the senior elder, followed by the other elders in turn, passes a chicken round his head. The chicken is then killed and the blood sprinkled over the trees, together with offerings of corn and beans mixed with palm-oil, pepper, and salt. As he makes the offerings the senior elder says: 'This man has brought all these things and has promised to take the Qzọ title. He will do so when his forefathers have enabled him to obtain the neces-sary means.' A feast is then held. A person taking over his father's title in this manner may also receive the stool, anklets, and cap of the society, together with a new name, and he may even observe the custom of going into seclusion for a period. But even in the few communities where the title is still taken with the full ritual, the fees have been reduced and the facial marks of the society are no longer inscribed.

The reasons for the decadence of the Qzọ society are threefold. In the first place the Government now gives the security which was formerly given by the Qzọ society. The roads are safe for all, and if

any one has a complaint he takes it to the Native Court. The society
has, therefore, lost its former source of revenue derived from travellers' fees and the settlement of cases, particularly land and debt
cases. And it is no longer able to take action for offences against its
members, for all are equal in the eyes of the law. The persons of
members of the society are no longer sacrosanct, and nothing has
caused greater offence and injury to the society than the fact that
members can be and are arrested and imprisoned just like the meanest
commoner. So strong is the sense of outrage when a member of the
society has been imprisoned for some political or technical offence
that he undergoes a rite of purification as soon as he is released. A
senior member of the society takes a fowl and presses it against the
body of the ex-prisoner, saying: 'This is to remove the impurity of
the handcuffs.'[1]

The second reason for the decadence of the Qzọ society is that all
the Christian missions have from the outset forbidden their converts
to become members, on the ground that title-taking involves religious
rites inconsistent with Christianity. Particular objection is taken to
the custom of tree-planting, which savours of the idolatry denounced
in the Old Testament. The missions can hardly be blamed for their
attitude, but had a less uncompromising view been taken towards this
ancient institution a good deal of hostility might have been avoided.
It might have been possible to effect an arrangement by which
Christians seeking to take the title could be exempted from those
parts of the ritual which were considered objectionable. Or a system
of taking the title by proxy might have been devised. It would appear
to be too late for anything to be done in this direction at the present
time. In some village-groups it was naïvely stated that the modern
ceremony of being married in church was regarded as conferring more
social status than membership of the Qzọ society.

The third reason for the decadence of the society follows automatically from the first two. Membership of the society was, apart
from the social status it conferred, a form of insurance. Though
admission entailed heavy expenditure, this was recoverable from the
fees and feasts provided by subsequent candidates. But owing to the
dearth of candidates in recent years a new member would have no

[1] As manual labour is taboo to members of the Qzọ society it was considered an
outrage to their order if any member of the society was compelled, as sometimes
happened, to engage in the work of making or repairing roads. In this connexion
see p. 7 n.

hope of receiving any adequate return on his capital. People can employ their capital nowadays to much greater advantage. A well-built modern house, for example, is considered a better investment, and it confers more social prestige than membership of the Ọzọ society. The rising generation are inclined to jeer at Ọzọ as a foolish waste of money. If it were thought that the Government was anxious to preserve the society as an adjunct to administration many of the richer classes would not hesitate to join it. But the general mass of the people regard the society as an outworn institution which should be allowed to die a natural death.

These remarks apply primarily to the Owerri and Awgu Divisions. But we have seen that in many communities of the Nsukka Division title-taking is still closely linked with administration. In the Awka and Onitsha Divisions also the most prominent men in public affairs are frequently members of the Ọzọ society.[1] Furthermore, in those areas of Iboland in which the institution of title-taking is now moribund, seniority and authority are still commonly based on the title-system of former times. Numerous instances of this have already been given, but as a final illustration we may quote the case of a mere boy at Orodo (Owerri Division) who exercises unquestioned authority over his local group by virtue of the fact that he is the direct descendant of the first person in Orodo to receive the Ọzọ title. Though only twenty years of age at the time of my visit, he could command the attendance of all male adults at his house by merely beating a drum, and any one who failed to appear was fined. Disputes were settled at his house, and the elders stated that they felt no difficulty in rendering obedience to one so young, for they regarded him as the mouthpiece of his distinguished forefather.

It will be apparent, therefore, that, whereas in some localities the title-system can be safely ignored by the Government, in others it must be treated with respect, as long as it continues to be respected by the people and to fulfil a useful purpose. The general policy, however, will be to encourage the spread of the new standard of values, which is already causing many thoughtful Ibo to view title-taking with the same contempt as is felt by Englishmen for the buying and selling of 'honours'.

[1] Generally speaking, the position in many parts of Iboland resembles that found by Dr. Rivers in Melanesia, namely, that while there is nothing in the nature of chieftainship, the place of chiefs is taken by men of high rank in the titled societies.

VIII

KINGSHIP[1]

KINGSHIP is not and never was a feature of the Ibo constitution. Where it occurs it is clearly of exotic origin. But as it does in fact occur in one or two communities it must be described. And for this purpose a brief account may be given of the constitution of Onitsha, which, though a small community, has played no small part in the opening-up of Nigeria.

The kingship at Onitsha was derived from Benin. It is confined to two kindreds, viz. the Umu Eze-Arole and the Umu Dei, whose leaders agreed on their arrival from Benin that each should take it in turn to provide a ruler. It is common in African states, in which the kingship is supposed to pass from one kindred to another, to find that the theoretical rule is readily set aside by any kindred which is strong enough to do so; and this is what happened at Onitsha. The Umu Eze-Arole provided six kings in succession until 1900, when the kingship returned to the Umu Dei kindred in the person of Okosi. Throughout his long reign of thirty-two years Okosi had to contend with the continuous intrigue of the kindred which had been displaced, and it is almost true to say that every political difficulty experienced at Onitsha in recent times has been due to the jealousy existing between the two kindreds. For this reason it may be advisable, and indeed necessary, to modify the traditional method of appointment.

In days gone by, when a king or Obi of Onitsha died and his death had been publicly proclaimed, the kindred whose turn it was to reign, or who were strong enough to insist on reigning, announced the name of the person chosen as successor. The king was not selected from any family of the kindred, but from the particular families which had formerly supplied kings. He was usually, during the latter half of the nineteenth century, the eldest son of a former king (the kingship having become confined to the Arole group). The general body of the populace had no say in the matter, except in cases where disputes over the kingship led to civil war.[2] But it was usual for the

---

[1] The information contained in this chapter was obtained during a short visit of six weeks to Onitsha in 1931.

[2] Fifty years ago one Elendo attempted, with the assistance of a number of Igala, to make himself king. Civil war ensued and ended in the death of Elendo. In Anazongwu's reign one Ijomma of the Alossi family, having been given the title of

candidate to secure the goodwill of as many of the 'Ndichie' (or holders of senior titles) as possible. He had himself to be the holder of an Ọzọ title, but was not necessarily one of the Ndichie.

Immediately after his nomination the king-elect gave a banquet to the elders of the Asele kindred. After the banquet the senior elder of the kindred placed in the hands of the king-elect the royal *ọfọ*—the symbol of 'divine right', as it were—saying: 'So-and-So, from to-day onwards you are the Obi of Onitsha. We of the Asele kindred conferred the *ọfọ* on your father, who ruled over us and went his way, and we conferred it also on your grandfather and all former Obi of Onitsha. As we have now conferred it on you there can be none to gainsay your right. May the previous kings who reigned and died help you to govern the town in peace.' All present then came and bowed before the king, saying, '*Obi*, *Eze* (Lord), *Igwe* (Sky).'

Some days later the king was escorted by members of his own family and of the Ọbiọ kindred to a shrine on the Owerri road known as Udo. Here he had to sleep beside an ant-hill, with the intention that by so doing he should notify his ancestors, who had performed a similar rite, that he had assumed the kingship, and with the further intention that his body should become dynamized by the spirits which haunt ant-hills (an ant-hill being regarded as a porch of the underworld). Next morning the king was shaven by the senior elder of the Ọbiọ kindred, who, as he placed the razor on the king's head, said: 'Udo, I am about to perform the rite of shaving the Obi. May it not entail his death or mine. His father was Obi and was shaven by my father, and all was well. May this Obi live long and govern his people in peace.' A tuft of hair was left at the side of the king's head. This was in former times a sign of royalty, but may now be worn by any person of title.

The shaven hair of the king was then deposited in the ant-hill, together with his old loin-cloth, which had been removed by the senior elder of the Ọbiọ kindred. A new loin-cloth was conferred on the king, with the words, 'Eze, you have now removed the cloth of suffering and poverty'. The king repeated, 'I have now removed the cloth of poverty and suffering'. A slave was then killed by one of the king's attendants, and the blood was allowed to flow over the ant-hill. The rites were concluded by the shouldering of the king, who was carried home to his palace, where slaves were sacrificed to all his

Oba, began to assume some of the prerogatives of the king and had to be removed by the British.

cults (including his *chi* or accompanying spirit) and also to his granary
and washing-place.

The king was not allowed to leave his palace except at the annual
festival known as Ọfọ-Ala. At this festival, which is held in October,
the king appeared in all his regalia and received the plaudits and contributions of his people.[1] For the rest of the year the king was not
permitted to appear in public, though he might receive visitors at the
palace. He was obliged to observe strictly the following ritual:

At 5 a.m. a gong was sounded, and after the king had performed
his ablutions (which were to some extent a ritual act), he proceeded
to the hut where his *ọfọ* was kept. Taking this in his left hand and a
kola-nut in his right he spoke as follows: 'Chuku (God), and my
ancestors, protect my life and the life of my people. May they and I
live at peace with one another. Prosper their crops, so that they may
be able to provide me and themselves with food.' Then striking the
ground with the *ọfọ*, he placed the *ọfọ* on the ground, split the kola
and deposited fragments on the *ọfọ*. This rite had to be performed at
sunrise under all circumstances, even, it is said, if the king's own son
had died a few hours previously. The king acted as priest on behalf
of the people, and it was owing to the necessity for performing these
rites at the proper time and in the proper place that the king was
not allowed to sleep anywhere but in his own palace.

The king also was required to eat his food ritually, and always
between sunrise and sunset. His food was cooked and served by a
young boy who had not reached the age of puberty.[2] During the
meal the boy retired, for no one could see the king eating. In fact
it was taboo to say that the king 'ate', for he was regarded as an
embodiment of divinity. He began his meal by depositing a few
morsels of food on his *ọfọ*, and when he had finished he summoned
the boy attendant by ringing a bell. It was permissible for the
attendant or young children of the king, but for no one else, to eat
the remnants of the food.[3] It is said at the present time that the
reason for the secrecy of the king's meal was to ensure his food
against poison and black magic. This may be so, but the meal seems

[1] The festival corresponds in all respects with the Puje festival of the Jukun.
See my *A Sudanese Kingdom*, pp. 144 ff.

[2] Compare the Ancient Egyptian rule that the medium in spirit-gathering had to
be 'a boy pure, before he has gone with a woman' (*Book of the Dead*, chap. C, rubric).

[3] Among the Jukun it is believed that the remnants of the king's meal are charged
with a divine dynamism which would kill any one, but an insulated person, who ate
them.

also to have been a ritual communion with the ancestors and gods. The king himself was 'a son of the gods', and was addressed by the title of 'Igwe' or 'Sky'.

It is said that the king of Onitsha is called the Obi because he is the 'court' (*obi*) of the people. He had the power of life and death and was referred to as *Ogbu onye mbosi ndu na gu ya*, i.e. 'He who kills a man on the day he desires a life'. There was a royal executioner known as Agwagu, and it is said that before the Agwagu performed the duties of his office the king rubbed some white chalk on his arm as a sign of his sanction for the execution.[1] The king was also saluted as 'Nkpu' or 'Ant-hill', for just as an ant-hill has innumerable apertures so the king has innumerable eyes, being aware of everything that occurs in the town. His counsellors saluted him as 'Leopard', one of the commonest titles of African kings. Leopards are the brothers of kings, and if any one killed a leopard he had to surrender the corpse to the king.[2] The king was also entitled to the carcasses of hippopotami, 'bush' pigs, buffaloes, manatees, and fish-eagles. Runaway slaves from other towns, if recaptured at Onitsha, had to be handed over to the king. Any one who succeeded in obtaining the head of an enemy killed in war had to show the head to the king, who inscribed a chalk mark on the head-getter's arm and placed an eagle's feather in his hair. At harvest all farmers were expected to present the king with gifts of yams, the number of which varied with the status of the farmer.

When the king died his death was kept a secret, and his body was subjected to a form of mummification by fumigation. It was first smeared with a lotion of tobacco juice or seeds and wrapped in a mat of palm-fibre in order to keep off flies. It was then placed on a platform which was coated with clay and perforated with holes, in order that the effluxes might be able to drop into a well in the ground below. Or alternatively the body was fixed in an erect position over a circular hole in the ground which was covered with a flooring of sticks, the body being kept in position by means of four stakes which met over the head and were tied with a rope to one of the rafters of the roof. Fires were kept burning round the corpse day and night, and were tended by sisters of the dead king. The period of fumigation varied from one month to four months according to circumstances, i.e.

---

[1] When the executioner had fulfilled his duty he slew a cock and rubbed his face in the blood to purify himself.

[2] The jaw-bone only was given to the hunter.

until the family of the deceased had been able to collect the means necessary for the burial and a decision had been reached regarding his successor.

The dead king's skull was not removed. His body was placed in a coffin and buried in his own house by members of the Alossi family. It was customary also to kill a slave and place the body in the royal grave. Two other slaves were also killed and buried separately. This custom was carried out last at the burial of Akazue.

The king ruled his people mainly through the titled officials known as Ndichie. Indeed, in many respects he was not so much a king as president of a bureaucratic society. There were (and are) three grades of Ndichie, namely, (a) the Ndichie-Ume, (b) the Ndichie-Okwa, and (c) the Ndichie-Okwa-Araze. The senior grade, namely, the Ndichie-Ume, consisted of six persons who acted as the king's counsellors and chief executive officers. They bore the following titles in order of seniority: (1) The Onowu, who is saluted as Iyasele; (2) the Aje (or Ajie), who is saluted as Esagba; (3) the Odu, who is saluted as Osodi; (4) the Onya, who is saluted as Ozoma; (5) the Ogene, who is saluted as Onira, and (6) the Owele, who is saluted as Osowa. It is said that these titles were originally conferred on those who had specially distinguished themselves in war, and not on account of money payments as at the present time. This is hardly credible as no African king ever conferred a title without receiving some form of payment. In any case it is clear that the Onitsha titles are modelled on those held by the Eghaivbo nobles at Benin, and some of the titles are in fact identical. Thus, the Onowu's title of Iyasele is obviously the same as that held by the senior noble at Benin, viz. the Iyashere. The Aje's title of Esagba corresponds apparently with the Benin title of Esogban, which was held by the second senior noble.[1] The Odu's title of Osode is no doubt the same as that of Oshodi, who was head of the Eruherie quarter at Benin. The titles of Osuma (Ndichie-Okwa) and Isama (Ndichie-Okwa-Araze) are both found at Benin. The word Araze would seem to be the 'Arase' of Benin.[2] A curious feature of the Onitsha system of titles is that the forms of salutation have a Yoruba rather than an Edo (or Bini) flavour. Thus, Orowu or Olowu is typically Yoruba, and Ogene is clearly the same title as is borne by the Oni of Ife (viz. Ogenni).[3] This may be due to the fact that the kings of Benin were of Yoruba origin, or it may be due to a

[1] See Talbot, S.N., vol. iii, p. 584.
[2] See ibid., vol. iii, p. 585.   [3] See ibid., vol. i, p. 156.

later association between the people of Onitsha and Yoruba-speaking groups.

In Benin all tribute was paid through the Eghaivbo nobles, and no one could approach the Obi save through them. The same system was followed at Onitsha. The Ndichie ruled the subdivisions and settled all cases which could be disposed of locally, but all serious cases, and any cases in which the Ndichie had failed to secure agreement, were referred to the king, whose decision was final. Thus, to take a few examples, if a dispute arose about a bride-price the elders of the families concerned would endeavour to settle the matter privately, and if they failed they would refer it to the Ndichie of their subdivision or subdivisions. The decision might be left to the oath. It would seldom be left to the king. If a woman were charged with adultery, the charge would be investigated in the first instance by the *Ada*, i.e. the elder sisters of her group, and if there were any doubt about the matter the decision would be left to occult powers. The senior Ada would take a fowl, and say: 'If you had connexion with that man may this fowl die when I split its beak: if not may it live.' She would then split the fowl's beak and lay it on her *ọfọ*.[1] If the fowl died, the man named as the partner in the woman's adultery might offer to pay damages to the husband. But if he refused, the case would be reported to the Ndichie and elders of the group who would summon the accused and, after investigation, would absolve him or order him to pay damages or to swear an oath. The accused might repudiate the decision of the local Ndichie and appeal through the Onowu to the Obi, who would hear the case in his palace in the presence of all the Ndichie. An official known as the Okugba stood behind the king and secured silence, by flogging if necessary.

A debtor who refused to pay, after his case had been heard by the local Ndichie, would be haled before the king, to whom the creditor would have to present a preliminary fee of a bottle of gin. Land cases were usually settled by the Ndichie without reference to the king, but the fees obtained had to be brought to the king who, after taking his own share, assigned the rest to the Ndichie. If the fees payable were large the king might direct that a portion should be set aside for sacrificial purposes. It is worth noting that, when cases were tried by the Ndichie, it was customary for the Onowu to open the proceedings by splitting a kola (presented by one of the parties concerned)

---

[1] The senior Ada of each quarter is the holder of an *ọfọ*. It is unusual among the Ibo for women to be the possessors of an *ọfọ*.

and calling on the gods and ancestors to help them to arrive at a right conclusion, punishing all who gave false evidence or a false decision.

In cases of murder, if the murderer escaped the vengeance of the murderer's family, the matter was brought immediately to the notice of the king, through the Onowu. The king summoned all the senior Ndichie, and the heads of all the principal families in Onitsha, together with the parties concerned. If it appeared that the homicide was accidental, the king ordered the relatives of the manslayer to give a woman as wife to the brother of the man slain. Otherwise the guilty man was directed to hang himself. It may be said generally that the king was bound to take cognizance of all cases which were likely to cause defilement to, or disturb the peace of, the town, or lead to disputes with neighbouring towns. He had to call a general meeting, also, in order to decide the measures which should be adopted for driving sickness and witchcraft out of the community, or for carrying out warlike operations against neighbouring communities.

The king was not surrounded by a large number of executive officials. The principal executive officers were the members of those age-grades which happened to be at the prime of life. The following is a list of the grades in recent times:

(a) 'Ejiji akpa' = 'Bag-holders', the most senior grade.
(b) 'Uchichi' = 'Night', i.e. fearless at night.
(c) 'Iwonofu' (a personal name).
(d) 'Akirika' = 'Grass'.
(e) 'Ochoku' = 'The Quarrelsome'.
(f) 'Edomani' = 'Peace-makers'.
(g) 'Akpali' = 'The Akpa people'.
(h) 'Ikusi' (a dance name).
(i) 'Omekome' = 'The unheeding ones'.
(j) 'Akakama' = 'Hands excel matchets'.

When youths reached the age of 20–24 they were banded together to form a society sworn to obey their own laws and to have 'no father or mother other than the Society'. They appointed a leader and could, with the approval of the king and Ndichie, frame rules or laws (e.g. that the bride-price must not exceed a certain sum). They had a summary jurisdiction in cases of breaches of their own rules, and collectively the grades acted as police on behalf of the Obi and Ndichie. They used, however, the Mmọ (or maskers personating spirits)[1] and

---

[1] See pp. 66 ff.

not the king as their legal sanction, i.e. they enforced their authority
in the name of the gods and ancestors. Thus, to take an example, it
was reported (many years ago) that a catechist (C.M.S.) had disclosed
to a number of women of Onitsha that the Mmọ was nothing but a
dressed-up man. The king, on hearing this, summoned the Ndichie,
and they together directed that the age-grade known as Ochoku
should deal with the matter. The members of this grade came, with
the masker, to the catechist's compound and compelled him and his
family to pay a heavy fine. Again, if a man had refused to refund a
bride-price after being ordered to do so by the Ndichie, the king
might, on hearing of the matter, direct one of the age-grades to arrest
the man and bring him to his presence. He might also direct the
age-grade to seize the woman concerned and carry her back to her
husband's house. But he did not always employ an age-grade to
carry out his orders; normally he would use his own servants or
messengers. And if these wished to serve a summons effectively, they
would deposit a knotted palm-leaf on the roof of the house of the
man summoned. In this case also the ultimate legal sanction was not
the king but the Mmọ, for the knotted palm-leaf was a symbol of the
Mmọ, and a refusal to obey amounted to a repudiation of the 'gods'.

Another dignitary of whom some mention should be made was
the Ọmo or queen of the women—the king's official mother. At
Onitsha, as in many African kingdoms, no one could be appointed
king whose father or mother was alive, for the king was regarded as a
divine being above the position of having earthly parents. If, therefore, the parents of a king-elect were alive they were (in ancient days)
either put to death or secretly removed to some distant town. A
woman of good family was chosen as the female counterpart of the
king. She had her own court and could take part, together with the
Ndichie, in any council held by the king. She was subject to many of
the taboos imposed on the king, and in addition was not permitted
to wear any parti-coloured garment. Her house was an asylum for all
who had incurred the anger of the king, and she also exercised certain
priestly functions. The office of Ọmo has now fallen into abeyance,
as the last Ọmo (in Anazongwu's reign) had acted in an autocratic
way which gave offence both to the Obi and Ndichie.

As the Ndichie-Ume were the chief ministers it will be necessary
to give some account of the method by which these dignitaries obtained their titles, more especially as this question has been frequently
used to foment ill feeling between the two rival royal groups.

Before any one can join the ranks of the Ndichie he must first have become a member of the Ọzọ society. And in order to do this the candidate is obliged to undergo nine different rites of initiation, each involving a money payment to the members of the society. It is possible, however, to combine all the ceremonies and payments, and obtain full membership without delay. In pre-Government times the total cost of membership was estimated at about £50, but in 1906 the amount had risen to about three times this sum. At the present time (1931), owing to the scarcity of money, the entrance fees have been reduced, and they are likely to be reduced still further owing to a dearth of candidates. Indeed it is probable that, unless the society assumes a new form, it will disappear altogether within the next decade, as there is no longer any security for the return of capital invested.

In order to obtain one of the Ndichie-Ume titles the candidate, having secured the approval of his own kindred,[1] approaches the king, who, if he is living on good terms with all the Ndichie-Ume, would first obtain their consent before accepting the candidate. It is contended by the present Aje, and the faction of which he is the leader, that the king has no right to appoint unless all the members of the order are agreed. But this would appear to be an overstatement. The Obi has the prerogative of appointment, just as the Oba has at Benin. Nevertheless no discreet Obi would attempt to make an appointment against the wishes of a majority of the Ndichie-Ume. Nor would he attempt to veto the candidature of all save members of his own kindred or kindreds friendly to his own. The present Obi's[2] action in appointing his own brother to be the Onowu or principal minister has proved to have been impolitic. But it was hardly unconstitutional, for although at Benin the king was not supposed to give appointments to his brothers, or indeed to have any full brothers at all, this rule was not always observed.[3] In fact it is not uncommon in African kingdoms for kings to appoint brothers to the highest offices. On the other hand, in most states the principal minister is regarded as the people's representative *vis-à-vis* the king, and for

---

[1] But cases have occurred of candidates offering themselves in opposition to the wishes of some sections of their kindred. In Akazue's reign a man whose candidature had been provisionally accepted by the king was displaced by his brother on the following day. The present Aje disapproved of the title of Onya being conferred on his own nephew.

[2] i.e. Okosi, since deceased.   [3] See Talbot, vol. iii, p. 578.

this reason is seldom chosen from the king's own family. Indeed, he is often a person of slave origin. At Benin the Iyashere, who corresponds to the Onowu at Onitsha, was formerly chosen by the king from one of his mother's slaves.[1]

The king signifies his approval of a candidate by a rite known as *Ibunye-Ewu* or 'the killing of the goat'. The approved candidate, having paid a preliminary fee of £5 to the king, takes a goat to the palace and kneels before the royal cultus-symbols. The king takes a kola and speaks as follows: 'Chuku (God), and my ancestors! This man is about to take the title of Ndichie-Ume. Do you help him to look after his people well and to rule them in peace. Protect his life and my life and the life of all the Ndichie.' Then, splitting the kola, he places the seeds on the cultus-symbols, and hands a section of the nut to the candidate, who eats it. He gives pieces also to the Ndichie[2] and others present. He then cuts the throat of the goat and allows the blood to drip over the symbols. The flesh of the goat is divided out and eaten by all present (except the king). Finally the candidate kneels before the king, who speaks as follows: 'I confer on you the title of Onowu (or Aje, &c.). Take it and go home and rule your people in peace. See also that you take steps to complete the payments due.' The candidate is conducted home by his friends, whom he entertains to a banquet. Even though he has not completed his payments he is permitted to assume his title, but he is not permitted to assume the regalia. He is still a novice, but his title cannot be taken from him and given to another. If he dies before completing his payments his heirs must make up the deficiencies; otherwise the final funeral rites would be withheld.

The first payment is made to the king, and in olden days took the form of three slaves, which nowadays are reckoned at about £30. The candidate had then to give one slave and a goat or two bottles of gin to each of the Ndichie-Ume. He had also to provide a feast for the Ndichie-Ume on three separate occasions. Having done this he was able to go to the king and receive his regalia by a rite known as *Nwocha* (= washing white). He knelt down before the king, who placed a red fez on his head, a staff in one hand, and a fan and bell in the other. Having received these he returned home and gave a final banquet to all the Ndichie and his friends. On this occasion he

---

[1] See Talbot, vol. iii, p. 583.

[2] The candidate must, before the rite, notify all the Ndichie, who would all (under normal circumstances) attend the ceremony.

was expected to give a gift of £10 to the Ndichie-Okwa and Ndichie-Okwa-Araze (jointly), and one of £2 to the Ọzọ society. The new member had henceforth to be attended, wherever he went, by a boy carrying a bell, and he was required also to eat his meals in private like the king. When he died his body was mummified by fumigation, to allow his family time to raise the funds necessary for the expensive funeral rites with which he was buried.

It is clear from this brief account that the kingship at Onitsha did not in its main features differ from that found all over West Africa and described in detail in my recent book *A Sudanese Kingdom*. The king was less of a ruler than the sacred repository of the people's prosperity and the custodian of their customs. What, then, is to become of his office now that its magico-religious basis has been undermined? For the people of Onitsha have adopted Christianity in no uncertain manner, and the Obi himself has become a Roman Catholic.[1] All that remains to him of his old prestige is the presidency of a society which functions feebly, and a certain sentimental regard by the people, which can only be galvanized into a genuine loyalty by an Obi of very exceptional personality.

The question of building up a Native Administration at Onitsha on the basis of the former organization has never been seriously considered. A Native Court has long been established at the Waterside and has jurisdiction over a number of neighbouring villages, in addition to the town of Onitsha. The Obi is a member of this Court, but none of the Ndichie-Ume are members. On the other hand, each of the tribal groups at the Waterside (Hausa, Kakanda, Nupe, Yoruba, and Ibo) is represented on the bench by a judge who has also functioned as the executive head of his group. Although the Obi is admittedly chief of the Waterside in addition to the Inland Town, it has been customary to carry on the administration of the Waterside independently of the Obi. The Court members, and *ipso facto* the executive heads of the Waterside, have been selected by the groups concerned, without reference to the Obi. They obtained the sanction of Government direct, and the Obi was compelled to give his formal approval.

Another factor that has operated against the building up of a Native Administration on traditional lines has been the inclusion of Onitsha within the jurisdiction of the British Supreme Court. This has tended not merely to encourage defiance of the Obi's authority

---

[1] This refers to Okosi, who has since died.

and that of the Native Court, but also to add fuel to the fire of local faction. Thousands of pounds have been spent in litigation in the British Court by the two contending groups. Had the Supreme Court never been established, and had some attempt been made at an early stage to organize a native administration on progressive lines, giving offices of responsibility to the leaders of both parties, the political condition of Onitsha in recent years might have been a great deal happier. As it is the Government is faced with a delicate problem. Can it revivify the ancient constitution so as to meet the new conditions and secure general goodwill, or is the kingship and title system so moribund that it should be abandoned altogether? Might not the Obi still function as the president of an executive council composed of the Ndichie-Ume and the heads of immigrant groups, all orders being issued through the Obi? The members of the council would act as the executive heads of quarters. In this way it might be hoped that the leaders of both factions would, by association in the common work of administration, lay aside their differences. The executive council might also function as a native tribunal which would not, it may be hoped, be boycotted like the present Court.

An alternative scheme would be to admit the elective principle as regards membership of the Council and Court, on the ground that this principle has long been recognized by the Government and that the offices of Ndichie-Ume are merely a matter of money. In this latter connexion it should be remembered that the whole system of title-taking is regarded with disfavour by a large section of the Christian population, and if the possession of a title is to be a qualification for office many worthy members of the community will be disqualified from taking their proper share in the conduct of public affairs.

The domestic affairs of Onitsha are of little interest beyond the confines of Onitsha itself, and are only discussed here by way of illustrating the variety of the problems with which the Government is confronted. What is suitable in one area may be unsuitable in another. In the past Onitsha differed signally from the rest of Iboland in the character of its political constitution. At present it is a centre of progressive ideas and many of its inhabitants are well-educated and highly cultured persons. It will be interesting to see how far they will be able to devise for themselves a constitution suited to their immediate needs, or whether they will continue to throw the entire onus of this on the shoulders of the Government.

IX

AGE-GRADES

THE next social institution that calls for some description is the age-grade organization, by which all male members of society are classified in groups or companies of approximately the same age. As a general rule the groups remain unorganized until the members reach the age of fifteen to eighteen. Boys form their grade automatically and informally through playing together at night or engaging in wrestling bouts. In the same way a group of boys in one *nchi* or village comes to know a corresponding group in another. There is no ceremony of initiation into the grade, but it is customary for a father to give a feast to his son's grade, when the son begins to wear clothing.

When the age-class reaches the age of fifteen to eighteen it may take a name and appoint some senior man as its captain. The following are some examples of names assumed in the Nsukka Division. One grade may call itself *Egbara*, the name of a prickly seed. The idea is that if any one interferes with the members of the grade he will get scratched. Another may be *Ajoro* or 'Fly-whisks', i.e. the members of the grade will not suffer annoyance from any one. Another may be *Okampu* or 'The Hornets', another *Enyimu* or 'The Endurables', another *Ola* or 'Brass' (i.e. the fine-looking ones), another *Anumu-Achogo* (= 'I want to fight'), another *Igbo kwe* = 'If Ibo allow' (us to stay and prosper), another *Igbo Nemegina* (= 'What can other Ibo do?'), another *Ebugbo* = 'If we see Ibo' (we'll kill them), another *Ekpa*, or those who shoot at funerals. An age-grade of females may call itself 'The Basins' or 'The discreet ones' or 'The navels of Ekpe' (a genius).[1] In some communities, however, the age-grades are not named, possibly because in former times a grade was not considered entitled to a name until it had performed some deed of prowess which would now be illegal (such as raiding a neighbouring town). In other communities the ancient qualification has been modernized, and age-grades will be found bearing names which indicate that they have taken part in road or railway construction on behalf of the Government. A case was reported recently of

---

[1] The Ekpe secret society is well known in some parts of Iboland. I had no opportunity of studying it. Details will be found in Dr. Talbot's *Peoples of Southern Nigeria*, vol. iii, pp. 779 ff.

an age-grade, which had visited a commercial centre as carriers of
Government loads, deciding to call itself by the title of the manager
of the European trading-firm, namely, 'Agent'. Soon afterwards
another age-grade was found to be using the same description, and
each demanded that the other should change its name. A sharp
controversy ensued and was only settled after lengthy proceedings in
the Native Court!

The age-grade organization is in the first instance a convenient
means of differentiating seniors from juniors, in a society where
seniority is of great social importance. Respect must be shown to
those older than oneself, and it is indecorous therefore for a person
to use joking or familiar language to one of a senior grade. Similarly
the senior age-grades can command the junior. The age-grade institution, therefore, provides a suitable means by which public duties can
be performed by those to whose age such duties are appropriate. An
age-grade of a local group could be commanded by the elders, or
might of its own volition undertake, to clear a path, to cut down
forest, to carry yams from one place to another, to plant yams for an
important rich man or the holder of a senior ofo, to act as market
police, to mount guard over the town in time of war, or to go out
and ambush enemies. Any member who failed to obey was fined by
his fellows.

But the age-grade organization had an even more important function, viz. of guarding public morality. For each age-grade was a
censor morum for its own members. It took common action against
any of its members who committed an offence or behaved in an unseemly manner. Thus, if any one had committed a theft, he would be
called on by his grade to restore the stolen property and pay to the
grade a fine of one goat. The elders of the village might consider this
a sufficient penalty and take no further action. If a member of the
grade kidnapped a child, it was the duty of his fellows to force him to
surrender the child or report his offence to the elders. If a man committed murder or was accused of poisoning, the members of his age-
grade were expected, and indeed required, to arrest him and hand
him over to the elders for trial. Or if any one had struck his father or
mother, or used insulting language to an elder, or had had sexual
relations with the wife of a fellow-member, he was fined by the
members of his grade. Each grade was careful of its own good name,
and did not hesitate to punish those who had disgraced it.

But each age-grade was also a society for companionship and mutual protection. If a person had been captured by some unfriendly group, the strongest force that operated for his redemption was his own age-grade. An age-grade assisted a member to recover a runaway wife or collect a debt (by arresting the debtor or seizing his property), or to carry out the heavier forms of farm-work (in return for a feast). It functioned as a wrestling team, a dancing club, and a dining-society. Banquets were provided by members on special occasions: e.g. if a wife had borne a child the husband was expected to invite the members of his grade to the birthday feast, known as *Umugwo*, which was held twenty-four days after the child's birth, and provide them with seven gallons of wine and some goat-flesh, they in return presenting gifts of cowries. Every owner of a wine-producing tree was expected to give a small gift of wine annually to the members of his age-grade. When a man died the members of his grade attended the funeral feast,[1] and contributed a dog, if the deceased had one wife, or powder[2] if he had two. Should a man have decided to emigrate, he was expected to present his age-grade with a dog if he were wifeless, a dog and a goat if he had a wife and no children, and a dog if he had a wife and child (provided he had already given a birthday banquet—otherwise a dog and goat). In this way he repaid the age-grade for the various banquets to which he himself had been invited. Absentee members of an age-grade were expected to send small annual contributions to the age-grade. New-comers to a town became members of the local age-grades by giving a feast to the grade they wished to join.

A number of age-grades grouped together and composed of grown-up men acted as police or executive agents of the council of elders. These were (and are still) known as the *ebiri uku* or big age-grades, and they took automatic action in cases of alleged stealing or of 'abominable' offences, by seizing some property of the suspect (or of one of his relatives) and holding it as surety for his appearance at a public investigation by the *Ọha* or elders. They collected fines imposed by the elders, retaining a proportion for themselves. The *ebiri uku* also exercised legislative powers. For instance, if it became apparent that stealing was on the increase throughout the village-group, the *ebiri uku* would meet and decide to increase the penalties for this offence, and their decision would be accepted by the elders. Or they might pass a law fixing the rate of rent for land, and the price of

---

[1] But nowadays many who are Christians refuse to attend funeral rites carried out with pagan ritual.   [2] For firing off guns.

palm-wine. (If the price of palm-wine had been fixed and a woman sold it at a higher price the *ebiri uku* would seize one of her chickens.) Or an age-grade, or group of age-grades, might represent to the elders that the bride-price was too high, or that burial-rites involved an excess of expenditure. Or, observing that palm-fruit was being cut before it was ripe, they might make an order that the fruit was not to be cut before a certain date.

The executive powers of the age-grades have been greatly curtailed since the introduction of Native Courts, but in some village-groups the grades continue to effect arrests, or seize the goats of a person suspected of stealing, pending his appearance before the elders. The elders frequently deal with cases of theft without reference to the Native Court, imposing a fine of two goats and requiring the thief to hand over to his victim twice the value of the stolen property. If the thief refuses he is arrested by members of his age-grade and taken before the Native Court.

In difficult land cases, also, the combined age-grades may attend to see that the elders do not inadvertently give a wrong decision (just as in any other case a young man may accompany his aged father to see that his father is not befogged by the evidence, and does not swear to an unjust decision which would expose the whole family to the wrath of the ancestors). The age-grades continue, therefore, to function not merely as a social institution but as an executive body; and local councils should be encouraged to use this ready-made institution rather than paid officials, and so to foster the old idea that government is the concern of the whole community. By laying public duties on the age-grades, which were in the past the very foundation of the State, the younger members of society will from an early age be incorporated into the political and social life of the community instead of growing up into individualists concerned solely with their own careers.

Women are also in some communities organized into age-grades, the members of which select leaders and subscribe periodically to a common fund which is used for the purpose of holding feasts and assisting each other in difficulties. They are not organized in any other definite manner (that I could discover).[1] But if things appear to be going wrong senior women may call a general meeting of women

---

[1] Close inquiries on this subject were inadvisable at the time of my visits, as women were still sensitive about the events of 1929. Some further information on women's societies has been given at p. 169.

and decide to draw the attention of the elders to the matter. Thus, if the harvest had been bad, they may ascribe it to the fact that adultery was being committed on farm-lands, and they may call on the elders to take drastic action to prevent this pollution of the soil. Or they may draw attention to the fact that the young male age-grades have not cleared the roads or the 'bush' surrounding the village. They may become so annoyed by the constant failure to clear the roads that they may decide to do it themselves and remain outside the village until the men come and bribe them to return. Or they may threaten to leave the village in a body, if the men continue to refuse to build a bridge over a river or a main market road. The women of a community may swear to support one another in a common policy, such as the secret poisoning of cattle (usually owned by men) which interfere with their crops. They may join also to offer a sacrifice through some public priest, holding a general meeting to determine the procedure and manner of raising the necessary funds. In many towns (e.g. Ama-Imo) a woman may be tried and fined by the other women of her local group for stealing, fighting, committing adultery, having sexual relations with a husband's brother, or with an *osu*, speaking lightly to males about matters of childbirth, or listening to the conversation of a husband and co-wife who are spending the night together. Women show great loyalty to one another, and it is *infra dignitatem* for a woman to inform a man of his wife's intrigues. If she did so she might be summoned before the women of the extended-family, presided over by the *Ada* (or senior female member of the family), and subjected to a fine.

The women's riots of 1929, which arose in consequence of the belief that women were to be taxed, were a signal example of sex solidarity and of the political power which women can exercise when they choose to do so. These riots will be described in the final chapter, and it need only be remarked here that huge meetings of women were summoned without difficulty at selected points all over the country by leaders who displayed high gifts of oratory and organization. Women who refused to join the rioters were assaulted as traitresses to their sex. Nor were the 1929 riots the only example of feminist disturbances in Iboland. In 1925 a movement of religious origin arose at Atta in Owerri Province. In answer to what was believed to be a miraculous message from Chuku (God) bands of women marched up and down the country proclaiming that, in order to increase the birth-rate, the people must return to the customs of olden times. A check must be put on prostitution, and more attention paid to sanitation. As the movement spread other points were added to the programme of reform. No one was to use British currency, and market-prices were to be fixed. Women were henceforth to wear their clothes in a prescribed manner. At Umu-Ahia a crowd of elderly women entered the market and tore off the clothes of all unmarried girls. At Awgu it was proclaimed that henceforth cultivation of cassava was to be confined to women; that disputes were to be tried by village-councils and not by Native Courts;[1] that bride-prices were not to exceed a certain sum and were to be paid in native currency; and that married women were to be allowed sexual intercourse with other men than their husbands. It was also announced that, as all Europeans were leaving the country, the Native Courts should be abolished. At Isu the Native Court buildings were actually destroyed.[2]

It may be of interest at this stage to make some general remarks on the status of women. It is a fallacy to suppose that a woman is a chattel in the hands of her husband, merely because the husband has paid a bride-price on her account. A wife can leave her husband at will, and would be removed by her relatives from a husband who had consistently ill-treated her.[3] She may abandon a husband who had become a thief, and may summon a meeting of her own and her husband's people to correct any form of misbehaviour on the part of the husband. A husband must provide his wife with a hut for herself, a piece of land for her farm, and clothes. If she is a bride he must provide her with food, until she is able to obtain supplies from her own farm.[4] But a wife must cook for her husband. If a man has more than one wife, each wife cooks for her husband for four consecutive days (and sleeps with him for four consecutive nights). If she brings with her from her own home a supply of seed-yams the product of those yams is her own, and if she leaves her husband she can take her yams with her.[5] Goats, dogs, and fowls brought from her own home

[1] And so forestalled the Government's own proposals.

[2] See Sessional Paper No. 28 of 1930, para 60 et seq.

[3] But though a husband may ill-treat his wife and drive her away he is entitled to the refund of his bride-price.

[4] Mothers contribute towards the feeding of their children, particularly between July and October, when the species of yam cultivated by men is not available.

[5] But this old rule is now modified. If she had male children she must leave the yams for the children. She might also leave some of her yams with the husband in return for any help he had given her in farming the yams.

remain her own property. Any money she makes by her own efforts (e.g. by trading or selling part of her farm produce) belongs to her entirely. Many wives in fact are richer than their husbands, and cases occur of wives supporting the husbands instead of husbands supporting the wives. In former days many women owned slaves; and rich mothers, instead of fathers, might provide their sons with wives. Women could also hold titles, and instances occasionally occur at the present time of women belonging to the highest grades of titled societies and of being selected by the community to sit as judges in the Native Courts.[1]

Women cannot inherit land, but they may be given the usufruct of a piece of land by their father or husband. In the latter case they can transmit the land to their male children, but if they have no children the land reverts to the husband or the husband's heritor. Women may also obtain rights over land from any one, in return for a loan of money, and the land remains their own until it is redeemed. A woman's property is inherited by her children, but the children may allow their father a share. In the absence of children the woman's property is, nowadays, claimed by her husband. In religious matters women are dependent for the most part on the services of some male priest or elder. But it is not unusual for women to place offerings personally at the village shrines, and in most communities there are deities special to women which are the objects of periodic rites. In the dances which sometimes accompany these rites, particularly during the annual festival held in the seventh month, feminist songs are frequently sung.[2]

With the general rise in the standard of life the position of women has improved enormously in recent years. Indeed, it would seem that the economic demands of women on their menfolk have become excessive, and that this is one reason for the great increase in the numbers of unmarried women and of divorcées.[3] Incidentally also, children, like those of European countries, are making greater demands on their parents, and giving very much less in return.

As we are dealing with questions of status it may be of interest to say something about the cult-slaves known as *osu*, to whom reference has already been made.[4] An *osu* is a person who has been bought and dedicated to the service of the owner's cult. Or he is the descendant of such a person. He differs therefore from an *ohu*, who is a slave in

---

[1] See pp. 158 ff. [2] e.g. 'Is it a shame if we refuse to give ourselves to men?'
[3] But see pp. 342–3. [4] See p. 31.

the ordinary sense. An *osu* is both despised and feared, his person being taboo; but an *ohu* is not. Any free-born person, whatever his position, may marry an *ohu*'s daughter, but no free person would marry an *osu*. To do so would be 'abomination', and if a free-born person were to marry an *osu* he would himself become an *osu*.[1] An *osu* can only marry an *osu*.[2] An *ohu* could be redeemed, but an *osu* could not. The owner of an *osu* could only sell an *osu* with the consent of the deity served by the *osu* (the consent being given by means of divination). If an *osu* were sold he had to be replaced. A master might inherit the property of an *ohu*,[3] but in no case would he take that of an *osu*. Free-born persons avoid buying seed-yams from an *osu*, and people are even afraid of buying seed-yams in a market, lest they should have been grown by an *osu* and so infected by the deity he serves. Persons who pawn themselves acquire the status of an *ohu* until redeemed, and the children of unredeemed persons are also regarded as *ohu*. The children of an *osu* can never be anything but *osu*, but the children of an *ohu* by a free woman have the full status of free-born persons (with the exception that they cannot inherit the *ọfọ* or any of the cults of the master's family).

The owner of an *osu* must provide him with a piece of farm-land,[4] seed-yams, and also a matchet and gun (for war purposes). The *osu* then works on his own account and is entitled to the products of his labour. He may assist the master on the latter's farm for two days in each eight-day week.[5] The master may, at the instance of a diviner, provide the *osu* with a wife (the daughter of another *osu*); or the *osu* may marry a wife on his own account, the master assisting him to obtain the bride-price. But the owner of an *osu* woman cannot accept a bride-price on her account. The bride-price would be receivable by an *osu* of her own household. An *osu* could be punished by his owner, but only with the permission of the deity served by the *osu*, the permission being given by a diviner. In no case could a master put an *osu* to death, for fear of the vengeance of the deity. An *osu*

[1] It was even taboo for a free-born person to have sexual relations with an *osu*.

[2] The ordinary rules of exogamy apply, i.e. an *osu* male cannot marry an *osu* female who is closely related. But two *osu* attached to the same household or extended-family may marry, if they are not related, and no bride-price would be demanded.

[3] When an *ohu* dies his property is inherited by his eldest son (if grown-up). Otherwise it is at the disposal of the *ohu*'s master.

[4] On the death of the *osu* this land passes to his heir.

[5] Nowadays *osu* frequently refuse to assist their owners, saying that they are not *ohu*.

must always continue to serve the deity to whom he has been dedicated. He cannot dedicate himself to some other deity. But nowadays
he may re-dedicate himself to his own deity, and so earn a substantial
fee. He may even re-dedicate himself to a deity in another town
which bears the same name as that of his own.

This section may be concluded by a few remarks on the pledging of
the person on account of a debt or in return for a loan, a custom which
is still practised to a considerable extent.[1] If an unmarried man
pledges himself in return for a sum of money or even for a wife, he
must live with and work for his creditor-master every day in the week,
the master providing him with food. He may find time, however, to
plant yams on his own account, and the master will usually give him
the opportunity to cultivate a farm so planted. He will also allow
the debtor to visit his home occasionally. If the debtor is married,
he and his wife work for the master three days in eight, and they are
provided with food on these three days only. When he is able to
redeem himself by repaying the loan, plus 50 per cent., he is expected
to present his master with a goat, a hen, twenty yams, a jar of wine,
a pot of palm-oil, a bunch of seasoning leaves, and four kola-nuts.
The master gives a banquet to celebrate the occasion, and as a prelude
he sacrifices a chicken to Anyañu (the Sun) or Mbatako (deity of
wealth), as a thank-offering for the repayment of the loan.

A girl may be pledged by her guardian (father or brother, uncle or
cousin) and remains with her master or mistress under the same conditions as those described above for an unmarried man. She may be
redeemed before reaching the age of puberty, or she may remain after
puberty as the wife of a member of her master's household, the
difference between the bride-price and the amount of the loan being
adjusted. She cannot be given in marriage by her master to a man
in another family than his own. To mark the termination of her
condition as a pledge it is customary for her relatives to present the
master with a goat, which is killed and eaten together by both sides.
This practice of pledging girls still continues to some extent, though
it is discouraged by the Government and is resented by the girls as
savouring of slavery.

[1] Many cases have occurred of men pawning themselves or their children in order
to obtain money to pay their taxes.

X

LAW AND ITS ADMINISTRATION

IN the chapters dealing with the social and political structure the general principles governing the legal system have already been outlined, and we have seen how law begins, as it were, at home, in the extended-family or kindred, whose mode of regulating the behaviour of its members is, or was in the past, the pattern for all other forms of grouping. And we have seen also that some disputes and offences were dealt with privately and some publicly; that some were disposed of by summary executive action, while others were brought before a panel of judges; and that in some circumstances the judges were no more than arbitrators, while in others they were armed with the fullest penal authority. These principles require further illustration by concrete examples, dealing both with legal procedure and with substantive law, and in addition it will be necessary to say something on the subject of legislation.

By way of preliminary some description may be given of an institution which has not previously been mentioned and existed in some communities only.[1] It is known as *Ikoro-Ọha*.[2] In all communities the principal governing authority was the body of elders or *Ọha*, which included the heads of families, rich influential men, members of the *Ọzọ* society, and priests of important public cults. The *ebiri uku* or senior age-grades acted as the executive. But in some communities there was a class of younger elders known as *Ikoro-Ọha*, who represented the *Ọha*, and exercised executive authority on their behalf. The head of each *onunne* or family-group would, with the general consent of the householders or *obilobi* of the *onunne*, appoint an energetic young elder to represent the *onunne* in all its external affairs. Or the *onunne* might be represented by two such men, one chosen by the head of the *onunne* and the other by the *obilobi*. If any matter arose which concerned the whole of the *nchi* (local group) or the whole of the village-group, the various *Ikoro-Ọha* would meet, and, if the matter were a simple affair, they would deal with it summarily, reporting their

---

[1] Of the Owerri Division. In many respects, however, the *Ikoro-Ọha* of Owerri Division correspond with the *Ndishi-Uke* of Awgu Division (see pp. 137 ff.), or the *Ndishi-Iwu* of Nsukka Division (see pp. 149 ff.) or generally with captains of age-grades.

[2] The phrase seems to mean 'The gongs (i.e. heralds) of the titled elders or heads of kindreds'.

action to the *Ọha*. But if it proved to be one of importance, they would report to the *Ọha*, leaving it to the latter to decide at a general meeting of the *Ọha*, who would invite the *Ikoro-Ọha* to attend. If, for example, a child had been seized by a man of his group, and the father of the child had complained to the *Ọha*, then the *Ọha* would direct the *Ikoro-Ọha* to investigate the case. If the *Ikoro-Ọha* found that the man who had captured the child had done so for some trifling grievance against the father, then they would order its immediate release. But if they found that the child had been captured because his father had done some grievous injury to the other (e.g. had undertaken to effect the sale of the other's disobedient daughter and then embezzled the proceeds),[1] then they would refer the whole matter to the *Ọha* of the group, who in due course would summon both parties to state their case.

Again, if a member of one local group had been seized by a member of another on account of a debt, the *Ikoro-Ọha* of the debtor's group would go to the *Ikoro-Ọha* of the creditor's group and ask for his release, in return for an undertaking that, if the debt were proved, it would be paid. The *Ikoro-Ọha*, acting in conjunction, were collectors of debt, receiving for their trouble fees proportionate to the amount of the debt. If a debtor refused to pay, the *Ikoro-Ọha* would seize one or two of his goats.

If two parties had a dispute about their farm boundaries, and had referred the matter to the *Ọha*, the latter would send the *Ikoro-Ọha* to visit the area under dispute and decide the question there and then. If the *Ikoro-Ọha* were unable to come to a decision, the *Ọha* would summon the parties and call on one or the other to swear an oath that his claim was just. Or they might call in a diviner to decide the matter by supernatural means. Each party would bring a stick or other object from what he considered was the true boundary, and the diviner, after looking at the objects and twirling his divining-instrument, would declare which of the two was speaking the truth. Or he might declare that both were wrong, and he would then indicate the true boundary by specifying certain trees.

Again, if one local group had had a dispute with another, and the *Ọha* on both sides had become so irritated that they had decided to settle the matter by force of arms, they would instruct the *Ikoro-Ọha* to warn the age-grades to prepare for war. The *Ikoro-Ọha* would

---

[1] It was not uncommon in the olden days for disobedient children to be sold into slavery.

themselves act as leaders during the war operations. In cases of stealing or sacrilege, the *Ikoro-Ọha* arrested the offenders and compelled them to pay compensation to the injured party or the offended deity. No one could be sold for any offence without the permission of the *Ikoro-Ọha*. If, for example, an *onunne* wished to get rid of an undesirable member, it would first report its desire to the *Ikoro-Ọha* of the *onunne*, who would then obtain the sanction of all the other *Ikoro-Ọha* of the group. Nevertheless, in all cases, an appeal lay from the decisions of the *Ikoro-Ọha* to the *Ọha* themselves.

The procedure in the cases quoted was not invariably followed in every community which had *Ikoro-Ọha*, but the instances given illustrate the general character of the institution. It may be observed that in the institution of *Ikoro-Ọha* there is a precedent in native custom for the system of so-called 'headmen', provided these 'headmen' are the accredited agents of the *Ọha* and not the mere tools of the judges of the Native Courts. It would be quite in accordance with native custom that a kinship or local group should be represented in its external relations by a young elder chosen by the *Ọha* of the group. Whether the community had the *Ikoro-Ọha* system or not, it was customary for kinship and local groups in the past to send as their representatives to a public meeting one or two of their ablest men, even if they did not happen to be heads of families; just as in the family-group, if a money collection were being made for any purpose, the money collected was handed, not necessarily to the official head of the family, but to the person considered the most trustworthy. In choosing the personnel, therefore, of councils and courts considerable latitude should be exercised; for if the Government adopts a hard-and-fast rule of selection, the people will circumvent it, when necessary, by misrepresenting the position of their nominee.

Examples of the procedure in dealing with specific classes of cases may now be given, and it will be observed that practice was not always uniform.

Homicide.[1]

To commit murder was an offence against Ala, and it was the concern of the whole community to see that the steps prescribed by custom were carried out. If the murderer hanged himself forthwith (which he frequently did from remorse at having killed one of Ala's

---

[1] Other instances of the law of homicide have been given at pp. 47, 126, and 151.

children, or to save himself from being beaten to death with sticks, or to save his family from attack and the loss of their property, or merely because he was expected to do so), his brother was (at Owele) required to offer sacrifice to Ala before burying the body of the murderer. He took eight yams and one chicken to the priest of Ala who, standing before the cultus-symbol, spoke as follows: 'Ala, this chicken and these yams have been given to you by the brother of the man who killed your child and then hanged himself. He beseeches you to accept these gifts and to refrain from pursuing the brothers and children of the murderer. He who killed a fellow-man has also killed himself. Let his crime, therefore, follow him to the next world.' It will be observed from this rite that the family of the murderer was considered as sharing in the responsibility of the crime, unless it took steps to dissociate itself from the murder. It had to provide a cow, goat, fowl, two yards of cloth, and a keg of powder for the funeral-rites of the murdered man.

If the murderer did not immediately hang himself, but took refuge in flight, his family had also to fly,[1] for the kin of the murdered man (including maternal relatives) immediately made a raid on the compounds and property of the kin of the murderer. In this raid any members of the local group might join. The compounds of the murderer's family were burnt to the ground, their yams were uprooted, and their palms cut down.[2] All property found might be appropriated, but in some communities it was taboo for the patrilineal relatives of the murdered man to keep any of the raided property, on the ground that this would be 'eating blood-money'. But relatives in the female line might do so, as their Ala was not concerned with the death of men in other local groups.

The family of the murderer remained in exile for a period of at least one month,[3] when they might be invited by the elders of their town to return, the consent of the kin of the murdered man having first been obtained. The murderer himself continued to remain in

---

[1] If the murderer and murdered man belonged to different local groups, the whole of the murderer's local group might be forced to fly, or a state of war might arise between the groups.

[2] At Mmako, in cases of accidental homicide, a relative of the deceased went to the compound of the man-slayer and cut down one palm-tree and one bread-fruit tree only.

[3] The priest of Ala and elders usually at the end of twenty-eight days called on the kin of the murdered man to desist from making further raids on the property of the kin of the murderer, lest a continuance should lead to another murder.

exile. In some communities (e.g. at Oduma) the following rite was performed before the return of the exiled family. The senior *Ada* or female relative of each of the kindreds concerned went together to the compounds of the exiled family and swept them out thoroughly. They then took a cock and a hen, tied them together with a palm-leaf, and walked round the compounds saying, 'Ala, do not permit such a thing to occur again. Ala, be not angry with us.' They then collected the sweepings of the compound and threw them and the two fowls into the 'bush of evil'. This rite of purification is known as *Eza fu ntu ochu*, i.e. 'The sweeping-out of the ashes of murder.'

On the return of the exiled family[1] a public meeting would be held to inquire into the matter and decide what atonement must be made by the murderer's kin. This meeting might be held in the compound of the priest of Ala, but the priest usually took no part in the discussions, lest he should make some mistake for which Ala would punish him. In some communes meetings connected with a murder were always held in an open space clear of all houses, lest the pollution of the murder should affect the houses. The meeting was conducted principally by the so-called *aro*-holders who in many communities had special authority to deal with cases of homicide.[2] The *aro*-holders would consider all the circumstances of the case, and elicit whether the homicide had been accidental or deliberate, and if the latter whether there were any extenuating circumstances. If it appeared that the homicide had been accidental, the man-slayer might (at Oduma and Nengwe) be allowed to return after twenty-eight days, and on his return would be required to offer sacrifice to Ala. But in some communities there was no difference in the penalty for accidental homicide and murder, owing to the belief that if a man killed another by what we should term an accident he must at some previous time have committed an act abominable to Ala. If there were extenuating circumstances he might be permitted to produce a substitute to be publicly killed. The substitute was often some notorious thief of whom the community wished to be rid. The execution would be carried out by a hireling from another community, as it was considered

---

[1] In some cases the family of the murderer would not be permitted to return until they had produced the murderer or a substitute, who would be required to hang himself publicly.

[2] It is noteworthy that in all investigations into homicide the judges refused to accept any form of preliminary gift such as snuff or palm-wine or kola, lest they should incur the anger of Ala.

an offence against Ala to slay a fellow townsman. Some time later the murderer was required to go through the form of dedicating a person to the service of Ala, as a substitute for the man he had killed. He obtained a hireling from another community and took him, together with a tortoise, an *aiagare* fowl, a piece of *ọfọ* wood, a pottery plate, and a pot to the shrine of the priest of Ala. The hireling was stripped naked, and the priest spoke as follows: 'Ala, this man has been brought to you as a substitute for your son who was killed.' The murderer added, 'Ala, let me go free and be not wrathful with me again.' The hireling then knelt before the shrine. He did not apparently remain permanently as an *osu*[1] or slave of Ala, but was allowed to return to his own community.

Whether there were extenuating circumstances or not, the murderer might in some communities be called on to hang himself if he reappeared in the town. Or he might be required to produce some member of his family-group to hang himself in his stead.[2] But if a substitute hanged himself the murderer (at Owele) had to make atonement by the following rite. He summoned the priest of Ala to his house and presented him with a white chicken and a yam. The priest roasted the yam, and holding the chicken and yam in his hand said: 'Ala, I am giving this fowl to you to appease your wrath against this man. Ala, I am going to give this man a yam to eat, and I beseech you that you will refrain from taking his life when he partakes of anything which has been touched by a fellow-villager.' The murderer was then given the yam to eat. The fowl was appropriated by the priest.

At Ache a murderer was permitted to return to his town after the lapse of a year, provided he compensated the family of the murdered man by giving in marriage one of his own female relatives, together with thirty bars of iron, one goat, two chickens, and one pot of palm-oil. He had also to undergo a purificatory rite at the shrine of Ala. The priest took a chicken (provided by the murderer) and waved it round his head, saying, 'Ala, this man who killed one of your children has returned and offers a gift to you to appease your wrath. Ala, whenever he eats of the products of the Earth, do not destroy him.' The priest then cut the fowl's throat and allowed the blood to trickle

---

[1] See pp. 203 ff.

[2] If the murderer were a person of high social standing, the kin might ask that one of their less useful members should be killed or allowed to kill himself in the murderer's stead. It was not uncommon for the brother of a murderer to hang himself as a substitute.

over the symbol. Having cooked the fowl he deposited small offerings of flesh on the symbol and ate the remainder by himself.

At Lokpa-Uku the relatives of the murdered man might also accept some form of compensation, but most of this was used for the burial rites of the dead man and for purchasing a slave to be dedicated to Ala. If the slave were not dedicated to Ala the anger of the deity would be incurred, because the family had derived advantage through the death of one of her children.

At Ngbwidi the murderer's family had to pay compensation of two cows, but the family of the murdered man gave one of the cows to the family of the mother of the murdered man and one to the family of his father's mother. The murderer had to wear old clothes and remain unshaven until these payments were made—as a sign of mourning for the man he had killed. He had also to pay a fee of nineteen rods to the *aro*-holders through whose offices he had been allowed to return to the town. There was also at Ngbwidi a rite of reconciliation between the family of the murderer and that of the murdered man. The former provided a sheep, goat, tortoise, palm-nut, yam, coco-yam, and coco-nut; the latter a fowl. They met together on common ground and summoned a *dibia* or 'doctor' to make a 'medicine'. The animals provided were killed and cooked. A small tunnel was made in the ground, and the *okpara* of the murderer's family stood at one end, while the *okpara* of the murdered man's family stood at the other. The former then passed a cooked yam and some of the 'medicine' through the tunnel to the latter. The *dibia* took some of the 'medicine' and touched the forehead, chest, and feet of each person present, saying, 'I have quenched the evil words and anger. Henceforth, if you eat together, you shall not die.' After this rite both families ate a meal together. Had they eaten food together prior to this rite they would have been killed by Ala. The 'medicine' is known as *efojo obo*, i.e. 'the quencher of vengeance'.

It may be noted, in conclusion, that no person who had been guilty of homicide was allowed to take part in any festival of Ala. During such a festival he had either to absent himself from the town or else sit on a platform, as contact of his person with the ground was regarded as a pollution of the Earth-deity.[1] No one would eat in the company of a murderer and he was usually abandoned by his wife. It is also to be noted that it was permissible to kill a man caught in the act of burglary.

---

[1] For the idea of homicide as a pollution of the land see Numbers xxxv. 31 f.

No general inquiries were made on the subject of the procedure in cases of attempted murder. But it was stated at Lokpa-Uku that if a man who attempted to commit murder had a notoriously bad character he was sold as a slave to the Aro. Otherwise he was merely tied up by his relatives, while inquiries were made of a diviner in order to ascertain what it was that had induced him to attempt a crime so 'abominable'.[1] He was required to purge himself by a sacrifice to Ala. He then took palm-wine and other gifts to the man whom he had attempted to murder, and both ate a meal together.

Suicide.

In cases of suicide it was usual to employ a man from some other town to remove the body of the suicide from the tree on which he had hanged himself. For suicide was classed as an 'abominable' offence, and the suicide's relatives would be defiled if they touched his body. The body was buried in 'the bush of evil', and a diviner was consulted with a view to ascertaining the cause of the suicide and the best means of appeasing the anger of Ala.

Assault.

In cases of assault the *lex talionis* was the guiding principle. The brother of the injured man might retaliate on the injurer, or on one of the latter's brothers, and this might lead to a general fight between two kindreds or two local groups. To put a stop to this the elders of the whole town might intervene and inquire into all the circumstances. They would order the person who had injured the other to pay all expenses entailed by the other's illness, i.e. expenses of treatment and the cost of animals sacrificed (by order of a diviner) to secure his recovery. If he refused to do so, which would seldom occur, the relatives of the wounded man would seize some of the assailant's property or wound him in the same way as he had wounded the other.

Theft.

Stealing was a grave offence, and it made little difference whether the victim was rich or poor, free-born or a slave.[2] But the procedure

---

[1] In cases of murder both the relatives of the murderer and murdered man might go to some distant oracle such as Igwe-Ke-Ala at Umuṇoha to ascertain what offence they had committed against the gods that murder had entered their midst.

[2] It appeared, however, that an *osu* who committed a crime was often allowed to go scot-free, as no one was willing to prosecute, lest he should incur the wrath of the *osu*'s deity. Even at the present day some Native Court judges are afraid of sentencing an *osu*.

varied according to the nature of the article stolen, whether the theft had been committed within or outside the kinship group, and whether the thief had committed similar offences previously.

In the Owerri Division, if a member of one *onunne* stole from a member of the same *onunne*, the theft would be quietly reported to the head of the *onunne*, who would warn the thief and direct him to restore the stolen property. A repetition of his offence might lead to his being sold by the head of his household, in order to forestall the consequences of the man committing thefts elsewhere. If the thief were a married woman she would be sent back to her own home, and the bride-price would be reclaimed. If a member of one *onunne* stole from a member of another in the same *nchi* (local group), the elders of the two *onunne* might agree to an amicable settlement, taking care that the theft did not become known to the *nchi* as a whole. But if the two *onunne* were not on friendly terms (as commonly happened) the victim of the theft would report the matter to one or two leaders of the *ebiri uku* (senior age-grades), who would beat the special drum used for announcing cases of theft, and would then dispatch a dozen or more strong men to go and catch a number of goats belonging to the household of the accused. If the members of the accused's *onunne* had reason to believe that the accused had, in fact, been guilty of stealing, they would send their *okpara* or representative to recover their goats, with an undertaking that the customary satisfaction would be given. The culprit, or his family, would be made to compensate the victim by restoring the equivalent of the stolen property, plus an additional sum, according to the standard tariff existing between the two *onunne* (as each *onunne* had its own tariff for each other *onunne*). The culprit would also be required to present a gift of two goats to the elders and *ebiri uku* of the local group. If these payments were not made the *ebiri uku* would again seize the goats and kill them, thus compelling the culprit to reimburse his own immediate relatives, viz. the owners of the goats. If the culprit had no means of reimbursing his relatives, he might be called on to pledge his person, until the value of the goats had been recovered.

No public trial was necessary in a flagrant case of this kind. But if the accused denied the theft, the case would be heard at a public meeting held outside the house of the *okpara* or of a rich man who was recognized as the leader of the local group. The judges would be the general body of elders, assisted by the leaders of the *ebiri uku*. If the evidence were inconclusive the accused would be called on to swear his innocence. He could either invoke evil on his own person, or on one of his domestic animals. The oath was given a year in which to work, and if nothing happened to the man or his animals the accuser had to pay damages. Heavier damages were exacted if the man had invoked evil on his own person than if he had done so on one of his domestic animals, and for this reason an *onunne* which was satisfied of the guiltlessness of its accused member would generally insist that the accused should choose the former of the two methods (i.e. invoke evil on his own person).

The stealing of yams was an offence not only against the owner, but against the gods, and the gods had, therefore, to be propitiated. Thus, if a man were proved to have stolen yams from a barn, a chicken had to be sacrificed to Ajọku, the yam deity, with the following statement: 'This fowl is given to you, Ajọku, to purify you from the pollution of defiled hands.' Stealing yams in the ground was an offence against Ala, the Earth-deity, and the thief (or his family) had to provide a sheep, hen, or tortoise, in order that the *Ọha* of the *nchi* might perform sacrifice to Ala-Ubi, the protector of farm-land.

At Mmako it was an offence to fail to report to the elders a theft of yams, even if the thief were a member of one's own family. For concealment would bring down the wrath of Ala on the whole community. The elders made the thief hand over five goats, which they ate in company with the priest of Ala. They also ate the stolen yams. In this act of propitiation to the Earth-deity the person who had suffered the loss was not permitted to take part.

At Oduma, if a man were accused of stealing from a member of some family of his own group, the accuser would report the matter to the father of the accused who would, if not satisfied of his son's guilt, call on the senior elder of the group to summon a meeting of elders and titled persons to investigate the case. If the accused were manifestly guilty he would be allowed to redeem himself from being sold as a slave by handing over two cows or 200 currency rods to the owner of the property. Or, if the two families were permitted to intermarry, he might hand over his daughter to his accuser. If the matter were doubtful, both the accuser and accused might agree to refer their dispute to the oracle at Aro-Chuku. If the accused were pronounced guilty, he became the slave of the Aro; if innocent, he was entitled to compensation from the accuser (one goat, two yards of cloth, and one hat). Even if the accuser and accused belonged to two different local groups an attempt would be made by the father of the accused to settle the matter privately. If he failed, he would call on the most influential man in the town to summon a meeting of those elders who were accustomed to act as arbiters in such cases.

At Nengwe matters might be arranged privately by the thief paying the owner of the stolen property compensation equal to three times the value of the article stolen. But otherwise he was sold to the Aro. To escape this fate he might hang himself. A notorious burglar might, when caught, be buried alive in the presence of every one in the group (including children). His brother would give permission for the execution by touching the burglar on the shoulder. His hands would then be tied by his own relatives, and he would be ordered by the senior *aro*-holder of the group to step into a circular hole and lie down. Every one would then throw earth on him and beat it down tightly with sticks. Later the corpse would be removed and thrown into the 'bush of evil'.

At Awgu, if a man of one group had been arrested by a man of another on a charge of theft, the elders of the accused's kindred went to the elders of the accuser's kindred and they jointly investigated the matter. Each side was accompanied by any other elders it chose to summon. If it appeared that the accused was guilty, he was sold to the Aro. Or he might be allowed to redeem himself.[1] But if it were clear that he was guiltless he was entitled to demand a slave as compensation. If the accuser failed to pay the slave, the accused and his family sought an opportunity of catching the accuser and selling him. Or they might catch and sell any member of his local group. In this way a state of warfare might arise between the two groups. If the matter remained doubtful after investigation, the accused was asked to swear an oath, and, if no evil befell him within a year, he became entitled to compensation (one slave). At Ugueme the compensation payable was the equivalent of the article which the man was supposed to have stolen.

At Isu, if a man of one group stole a yam or chicken from a man of another, the owner of the stolen property had the option of deciding whether he would sell the thief or call on him to hang himself. But though he might call on the thief to hang himself the thief might refuse, provided his kindred supported him and was strong enough to defend itself. In this way fighting between two groups might result,

---

[1] But if the two men belonged to the same kindred or *ọnuma* the convicted thief had merely to give a goat and fowl for sacrifice (e.g. to Njọku in cases of thefts of yams).

and would continue until the elders of the whole commune, accompanied by the priest of Ala, intervened. A general meeting would then be held to investigate the whole affair, and if it were clear that the man charged with theft had been justly charged, the spokesman of the assembly would declare that, if the thief's kindred continued to protect him, then all must conclude that he had been delegated by his kindred to steal on their behalf! The thief's kindred would thus be forced by public opinion to call on the thief to hang himself. Any one caught red-handed stealing yams, palm-produce, a sheep, a goat of the species known as *idiri*, or a child, was expected, and would normally be required by his family, to hang himself, as all these things were considered to be the property of Ala, and, if the thief did not hang himself, Ala would take vengeance on his family. But if the article stolen were a cow or some species of goat other than *idiri*, or some other article, the penalty was merely that the thief should compensate the owner by paying double the value of the stolen article.

At Abọ, if a man were charged with theft, the Ishi-Uke or holder of the senior *aro* sent his representative to place a knotted palm-leaf on the accused's farm, as a sign that the latter's yams were taboo pending the settlement of the case. The senior *aro*-holder presided at the subsequent trial, and if the council of elders found the accused guilty, all spat in his face and he was ordered to leave the community as a slave of the Aro. His yams became forfeit to the *aro*-holders of the commune.

In cases where a thief was allowed to remain in the community, his punishment was not confined to the payment of damages or fines. He became an object of contempt and was jeered at in public, particularly by the women. Even before a charge of theft had been proved the women would go about singing, 'Who harbours a thief shall die: who defends a thief shall die.' If the person charged were convicted, the people ever afterwards reviled him by saying, 'Uu! thief!' every time they met him. If the thief were a woman, all the women of the group would go to her house and call on her to come out and be spat on. Ridicule has often driven criminals or other offenders against custom out of the community or caused them to take their lives.

At Ngbwidi it was stated that if a man stole an article from a member either of his own kinship or local group he was merely subjected to ridicule and contempt. When people met him on the road they would say 'Uu! thief!' If he were the holder of a title he would no longer be accorded any share of dues received. Even if he repeated his offence he might (in some groups) escape being sold, on the ground that in former times an epidemic had invaded the group as a consequence of selling a close kinsman. But one caught red-handed stealing from a member of another local group was sold automatically by the owner of the stolen property. Under certain circumstances he might be allowed to redeem himself. For if on some previous occasion a man of the thief's kindred had caught a man of the other kindred in the act of stealing his property, and had refrained from selling him, then it was incumbent on the other kindred to act with similar generosity on the present occasion.

Adultery.

The procedure in cases of adultery (and incest) differed fundamentally from that in most other classes of offences in that, if the offence had been committed within the kinship group, it was usually treated with much greater severity than if committed outside. Adultery within the kinship group was an 'abomination', an outrage on Ala, and therefore a matter of public concern. But adultery outside the kinship group was usually, but not always, a private injury with which the general public were unconcerned.

Thus, at Ngbwidi, if a man were charged with having committed adultery with the wife of a member of his own *umunna*, the matter was reported to the priest of Ala, who summoned all the elders of the town to a meeting in the market-place. The priest asked the accused couple if they admitted the act, and if they did he took a kola-nut and said: 'Ala and ancestors, if such a thing as this occurred in the past it was not concealed. For this reason we have called this couple, for they have done an abominable thing. Ala, be not angry with us. Ancestors, be not angry with us. These two have committed abomination, and we will rid the land of their presence.' He then split the kola and threw it on the ground. The male adulterer was ordered to leave the town as a slave of the Aro, and the female to return to her own people.

At Mmako, if a man were found to have committed adultery with the wife of a member of his own kindred, the kinsmen had to take 300 yams, 1 calf, and 1 chicken to the priest of Ala.[1] The priest tied a knotted palm-leaf round the neck of the calf and the legs of the chicken, as a sign that they had become taboo. Then, taking the

---

[1] At Ukehe the male adulterer provided a goat, and the female a dog for sacrifice to Ala.

chicken in his left hand and leading the calf with his right, and followed by his sons with the seed yams, he paraded round the compounds of the kindred, saying, 'I am removing pollution from the
land.' He then went to 'the bush of evil' and left the animals and
yams there. The guilty couple were banished from the commune.

At Onitsha, also, adultery with the wife of a kinsman was an offence
against the gods and ancestors. And if any one were believed, on good
grounds, to have committed this abomination his conduct was reported to the Mmọ society.[1] Maskers of the society thereupon invaded the compounds of the culprit's kindred and seized or killed
all the live stock they could lay their hands on. The kinsmen made
the culprit repay them fully for their loss, or else sold him into
slavery.

With regard to adultery in which the partners did not live in the
same kinship group, this was normally regarded as a private injury
which should be settled by the parties concerned, aided if necessary
by a board of elders acting as arbitrators. But in some circumstances
adultery so committed might be a public offence and be dealt with
publicly. Thus, adultery committed on farm-land was considered to
be a pollution of Ala, and a danger to the crops of all. Persons believed
to have committed this 'abomination' were accordingly tried in a
public assembly, and if found guilty were sold as slaves, sacrifice being
offered to Ala to purge the land. Similarly, public notice was taken
of adultery committed between a slave and a free-born woman. The
slave was sold. At Onitsha it was a capital offence for any one to have
sexual relations with a wife of the Obi, and one convicted of adultery
with the wife of any of the titled order known as Ndichie was called
on to pay a fine of one goat to each member of the order. We
have seen elsewhere[2] that throughout Iboland the members of titled
societies exacted special damages from those who interfered with
their wives.

As far as commoners at Onitsha were concerned procedure was
elastic and depended on circumstances. Thus if a woman made a
confession of adultery (as many women do under the duress of illness)
her husband might be satisfied if the paramour paid damages at the
recognized scale of one goat and twelve pots of wine. If the paramour
refused to pay the damages, the husband and his friends might lie in
wait for him, and assault him, or would endeavour to seduce or even
violate women belonging to the paramour's group. In a doubtful

[1] See pp. 66 ff.   [2] See, e.g., pp. 133 and 181.

case the procedure would be different. Thus, if a woman were charged with adultery and denied the charge, the case might be investigated by the senior 'sisters' of her husband's local group, and, if there were any doubt about the matter, the decision would be left to supernatural powers. The senior sister would take a fowl and say: 'If you had sexual intercourse with that man may this fowl die when I split its beak. If not may it live.' She would then split the fowl's beak and lay the fowl down on her *ọfọ*. If the fowl died, the man named as her paramour might offer to pay damages to the husband. But he might refuse and demand that the case be investigated by the Ndichie and elders of the groups concerned, who would either absolve him, or order him to pay damages, or to swear an oath of innocence.

Sometimes the illness of the husband might lead a wife to confess that she had committed adultery, believing that her adultery might be the cause of his illness. The husband might then send word to the paramour's family that his blood was on their heads, and they would accordingly bring gifts, that sacrifice might be made to Ala for his recovery. It will be seen, therefore, that adultery committed outside the kinship group was, in some communities at least, regarded as a sin, though not such a heinous sin as when committed within the kinship group. For this reason it was customary in many communities for the townspeople to insist that any one proved to have committed adultery must give one of his goats to be sacrificed at the central shrine of the Earth-deity.

Some husbands condone a wife's adultery, and some settle the matter by assaulting the paramour. But sometimes the paramour will attempt to forestall assault by apologizing to the husband, presenting him with a gift, and promising to put an end to the liaison. But an adulterer caught red-handed might well be killed, and the husband's action would be excused as far as the general community was concerned, though it might lead to a blood-feud between the two family-groups. At Obeago a man caught in the act of adultery was kept under arrest by the husband until some friend (belonging to a different kindred) went surety for his appearance at a trial of the case by elders of both quarters concerned. If convicted he had to pay three goats, one dog, one chicken, and one bar of currency to the husband, who, however, handed all the articles over to members of his *umunna*. At Owele if a man were caught red-handed in the act of adultery he was required to pay compensation now assessed at £5 to the husband, if he were a member of the husband's group, but £7 if he belonged to a different group. If a man were suspected of adultery it was customary for the husband to report the matter to the Ishi-Uke[1] of his group, who would send young men to kill a cow belonging to any one in the group of the person charged with adultery. The cow would be shared by the husband, his family, the Ishi-Uke, and the young men who had killed it. After that the case would be heard by elders of both the groups concerned, and if the charge were proven the adulterer had to pay the cost of the cow. Otherwise the accuser had to pay. It is to be noted that in all cases of adultery outside the kinship group it was not customary in most communities to inflict public punishment on the guilty woman, on the ground that her seducer was principally to blame. But in some communities (e.g. at Mboo) an adulteress might be fined by the women of her group, and if she or her parents refused to pay the fine she would be placed under a ban. No one would provide her with fire, carry her load, or have anything to do with her. In addition to having to pay a fine she was required also to give a chicken to the senior matron, who passed it round the legs of the adulteress, saying: 'Let the spirit which seduced you to do this evil depart from you, so that you may never again commit a similar offence.' The fowl was then killed, cooked, and eaten by women who had passed the age of child-bearing. The company of matrons might also inflict a fine on any other woman who had acted as an agent or procuress.

At Ngbwidi, if a woman were believed to have committed adultery and to be pregnant by her paramour, and if the person believed to be the paramour denied the relationship, both sides would refer their dispute to a board of elders selected from each of the local groups concerned. A fee of eight currency rods would be paid by each party. The priest of the village of the male accused would open the proceedings by calling on Ala and the ancestors to assist them in trying the case in accordance with custom, and to deal with either of the parties who refused to accept their decision. The woman would be called first and questioned by the senior priest of Ala. If she confessed, and was clearly enceinte in consequence of the adultery, the male adulterer would be called on forthwith to pay two cows as compensation to the husband. The husband would hand the cows over to the elders of his kindred, as it was taboo for him to derive personal advantage from his wife's infidelity.[2] If the adulterer failed to pay the compensation, his

---

[1] See p. 137.

[2] At the present time, however, many husbands connive at their wives' adultery in order to obtain damages in court.

property would be raided by the husband and his relatives, assisted
if necessary by young men of the village. It may be noted also that,
at Ngbwidi and in numerous other communities, a woman who conceived a child in adultery might be compelled to bear and wean her
child in the home of the adulterer. Or she might bear the child in
the home of her parents, who in this case would claim a fee of one or
two goats from the adulterer, to meet the cost of their daughter's
confinement.

At Awgu, if a wife appeared to be misbehaving herself she would
be warned by her husband. If she disregarded the warning the husband might tie her up and send for her parents. If she confessed to
adultery her husband would take her to the adulterer's house and
force her to make a formal charge against the adulterer. He would
then report the matter to the head of his kindred, who would in
turn report to the elders of his local group. If both parties belonged
to the same local group, and the person charged were found guilty,
he would have to pay two cows as compensation to the husband. If the
parties belonged to different local groups, the elders of the plaintiff's
group would summon the elders of the defendant's group, and they
would decide the matter between them. If the defendant refused to
pay the stipulated compensation, the members of the husband's kindred
would take the first opportunity of violating a woman of the defendant's
kindred. This might give rise to such a state of enmity between two
groups that inter-violation of women might be carried on for a long
period. Or the men of one village might forbid the women of the
other to attend their market. But cases of adultery might at Awgu,
as elsewhere, be settled privately either by the adulterer paying
compensation to the husband or by the husband inflicting physical
injury on the adulterer.

At Lokpanta, if a man had admittedly committed adultery with
the wife of a member of his own local group (other than a kinsman)
he was required by custom to hand over two goats to the husband's
family. The husband could not eat any of the flesh of the goats, for
it was believed that if he did so he would be killed by his ancestors for
having derived advantage from his wife's adultery. The husband's
sisters[1] shaved the head of the guilty woman, who was required to
give them one chicken for this service. Before resuming marital relations the guilty wife had, in the presence of the husband's senior sister,
to pass a chicken round her legs and then throw it into the taboo

[1] In the classificatory sense. (See p. 300.)

'bush'. There was no public trial unless the man charged with adultery denied the charge, and in this event the trial was, as we have seen, less of a trial than a mode of publicly swearing his innocence. But if the husband and adulterer belonged to different groups of the commune the matter was usually settled by the husband assaulting the adulterer. If the woman confessed that she had conceived by the adulterer the latter was required by custom to pay seven goats to the husband's family and also to keep the woman until she had delivered the child. If he refused to hand over the goats the husband's relatives would endeavour to capture the goats. This might lead to a fight between the two groups, and the elders of all Lokpanta would then have to intervene.

At Owerri, if a man had reason to believe that a fellow member of his local group had committed adultery with his wife, he might take his wife to her paramour and call on him to marry her, by refunding the bride-price. The paramour might agree to do so, telling the husband to send the woman to her parents' home (as he could not marry her direct from the late husband's home). Or the husband might forgive his wife and make her swear on some cultus-emblem that she would give up the liaison. At the same time the husband would send a message to the paramour, through the elders of his *onunne*, to the elders of the paramour's *onunne*, that he must desist from further dealings with his wife. There would be no form of trial in such a case. But the alleged paramour might deny that there had been any adultery, and might call a meeting of his own elders and those of the woman's husband, in order to swear to the truth of his statement. If, however, the alleged paramour did not deny the relationship, and continued it in spite of the warning, he laid himself open to assault, and if an assault occurred it might lead to an investigation by the elders of both sides. But this would be a trial for assault, rather than for adultery *per se*.

If a man of one local group committed adultery with the wife of a man of another local group, the husband would in this case also send word to the adulterer to desist. But the latter might assume an independent attitude and send back word that the husband should keep his wife at home! Cases of this kind frequently led and still lead to assault and inter-group fighting.

Incest and other Sexual Offences.

It was forbidden, and in fact an 'abominable' thing, to have sexual relations with any close consanguineous relative, and it is said that breaches of this law were almost unknown. If a case did occur both the culprits were killed or sold, after an investigation by the Ọha of the whole village-group. If the relatives of the guilty parties were exceptionally strong the punishment inflicted might be modified. But in any case they were required to provide a tortoise, a sheep, and a hen for sacrifice to Ala. If a father discovered that one of his sons was having sexual relations with one of his (the father's) wives, he would tie up the lad and the wife, and then summon a meeting of his extended-family and the wife's relatives. If no defence could be made to the charge, he would return the wife to her own family after the bride-price had been refunded. If the wife's family were unable to refund the bride-price her husband would sell her to some slave-trader. The lad also might be sold.

A case recently occurred of a man reporting to one of the Ọha that a certain woman of his local group had had sexual relations with a farm-labourer in the 'bush'—a heinous offence. All the Ọha of the group immediately went to the woman's house and seized a goat belonging to her husband. A friend of the husband secured the return of the goat by guaranteeing that, if the woman lost her case, he would himself pay the cost of the goat. On an appointed day the Ọha of the group investigated the charge, and as the husband was able to disprove the truth of the charge, the false accuser was called on to pay compensation to the woman. In pre-Government times, if the woman had been found guilty she would have been put to death or sold.

Other 'Abominable' Offences.

In all Ibo communities twins were regarded as abominable and destroyed.[1] It was also abomination for a woman to conceive before her last child had been weaned, and when the child was born it was thrown away. The reason for this was stated to be that a mother cannot nurse two children. It may be concluded, therefore, that one reason for killing twins was the difficulty of nursing two children.[2] Cripples, children born with teeth, children born feet first, and children which did not cry soon after birth were destroyed. Children who cut the upper before the lower teeth, or had begun to walk before they had cut any teeth, were destroyed or handed over free of charge to Aro slavers. A child who was unable to walk before it reached the age of three was regarded as having committed a grievous

---

[1] See p. 291.   [2] But it is improbable that this was the *original* reason.

offence against Ala in its former life and was destroyed or sold. A girl who donned a cloth like a male, or menstruated before she had taken to wearing a cloth, was considered 'abominable', and was handed over to Aro traders. All relatives and friends of the girl wailed on hearing the news, and four days after the girl's departure her mother shaved her head. For an evil thing had fallen on her head and had to be removed. If there were any doubt in the matter the case was referred to one of the local or distant oracles. Another act calling for retribution and expiation was for a woman to climb a palm or kola tree.

Black Magic and Witchcraft.

A charge of using black magic was one of the most serious charges that could be brought against any one. If, therefore, one man accused another of e.g. burying 'medicine' in his compound or farm, the person charged would (at Owele) immediately report the matter to the Ishi-Uke of his local group, who would order young men to capture a cow from the group of the accuser.[1] The cow would be killed and eaten by all members of the accused's group (women and children excepted), the heart and head being the special fee of the Ishi-Uke. A day would then be arranged for hearing the case, and the elders of both quarters would meet in some open space. Women and young men might also attend. The Ishi-Uke of the accused's group would open the proceedings by saying: 'If any one has a quarrel with another which does not concern the case in hand, let him not intrude it into these proceedings. We are met here to discover the truth with regard to the particular quarrel between these two men.' The accuser would then make his statement, and the accused would reply by offering to swear on any recognized medium produced. The elders would retire to consult, and on their return might order the accused to go to Ache and summon the priest of the cult of Nnemmiri to bring some object from the shrine of that spirit. On his return (accompanied by the priest) a public meeting would again be held, and the elders would inquire carefully of the accuser the formula of the oath which he required the accused to take. They would then instruct the accused to follow this formula. The accused would kneel down before the cultus-symbol and, stretching his hands towards it, would say: 'If I put evil medicine in this man's compound then may you, Nnemmiri, kill me. But if I did

---

[1] The owner of the cow would feel no resentment, as after the trial he would assess the value of the cow at an amount considerably above the market value.

not do so then spare my life.' The oath was given one year in which to work, and during this period the two families concerned were not allowed to eat together. If they did so Nnemmiri would leave the guilty man alone and assail the innocent. The accused was required to pay the cost of the proceedings (viz. one kid, and two fowls) to the priest of Nnemmiri, but if he lived through the year he could claim damages from the accuser, who would also have to compensate the owner of the cow.

Incidentally it appeared that in the Owele district it was an offence for a woman to place a taboo on any form of property.[1] If a man had occasion to complain of an infringement of this law he took his complaint (at Ogugu) to the Ndishi-Uke, who would send a company of young men or head-getters to interview the woman's husband. If the latter expressed his regret, and undertook to remove the taboo, the matter would be disposed of. But the husband would be required to give sundry gifts to his visitors. If he refused or answered the young men roughly, the Ndishi-Uke would direct the young men to kill any cow they saw in the husband's quarter. The flesh of the cow would be divided out among the townspeople of each village of the commune, but the Ndishi-Uke and young men who had killed the cow would receive an additional share. If the woman had stated that she was prepared to swear that she had not placed any taboo on the property she would be given the skin of the cow.

The case would now have become a public matter, and a day of trial would be fixed by the principal elders. On the appointed day the elders would meet at the compound of the woman's husband, and if it became clear that the woman had in fact placed a taboo on the plaintiff's property she might not be allowed to swear to the contrary, even if she had offered to do so. For the elders might take the view that if they permitted her to swear she would certainly be killed by the spirit by whom she swore, and her blood would then be on their heads. The woman would be ordered to pay the cost of the cow, and the elders who had tried the case would retire to the house of the successful plaintiff, who would reward them with a gift of wine.

Witchcraft is considered the most loathsome of all 'abominations'. There are many ways of detecting witches. They can be seen and pointed out by sorcerers or witch-doctors. Their names can be discovered from the divining-apparatus, or diviners can, by a decoction

---

[1] This rule was possibly made in the first instance to prevent women laying a claim to the property of their deceased father or husband.

of leaves poured into the eyes, enable patients to see for themselves the witches who are feeding on their souls. Some people are obviously witches, as they are always talking to themselves or else are continually dogged by misfortune. Others again have made a death-bed confession that throughout their lifetime they had fed on the soul-stuff of their fellow men.

At Onitsha any person who was believed to be a witch was reported to the Mmọ society, and if the leaders of the society considered the evidence sufficient they ordered a masker of the cult to summon the suspected woman to a public trial by ordeal. The masker went at cockcrow to the woman's home and called her out of her hut, in the squeaky voice used by maskers to simulate the spirits. The woman would be told that she had been accused of being a witch and must be prepared therefore by daybreak to stand her trial by the sasswood ordeal. The masker would then depart, leaving a deputy to see that the woman did not drink any oil, as oil was believed to negative the action of sasswood. If the woman refused to undergo the ordeal, she would be driven out of the village, and her husband would divorce her and refuse to accept the return of his bride-price. If she accepted, the trial was held in the Obi's compound. The accused sat down on a small bedstead, and was given a calabashful of sasswood, which had to be drunk up there and then. The accused might die within a few minutes, and if so her body was taken out to the taboo 'bush' and buried head downwards, with the feet protruding above the surface. But, if she merely became sick, she was taken home and kept under observation to see that she did not drink oil. If she were still alive at the end of twenty-eight days she whitened her body and went to the market, singing her innocence, and being greeted by the people. 'Chuku is marvellous,' they would say, 'you were accused of witchcraft, but Chuku knew your innocence and brought you out unscathed.' 'Yes,' she would reply, 'they wanted my life for nothing, but my *chi* refused.' She would present her friends with chalk, and in return would receive numerous gifts of food, clothes, and money. A banquet would be given in her honour, and for a whole month she would strut about the village triumphantly. The person who had charged her with witchcraft would be required to pay the sasswood fee of 7,800 cowries, a provision which prevented people from making indiscriminate accusations.

It is said that the officiants at sasswood trials might be bribed either to secure the death of the accused or her immunity. If the accused were to be saved she would be given a dose of oil secretly. But if she were to be killed, other poisons, such as cactus juice, would be added to the sasswood. Sometimes the accused might be represented at the trial by a fowl as proxy.

Those who are interested in witchcraft beliefs in Nigeria and the methods of dealing with witches will find additional information on pages 79–84 of this work and also in my other works, *A Sudanese Kingdom* and *Tribal Studies in Northern Nigeria* (see Indices). The question of policy regarding breaches of the law at the present time, arising out of witchcraft beliefs, is dealt with in the concluding chapter of this book (pp. 344 ff.)

Land.

The rules governing land tenure have already been described,[1] but it may be of interest to give an example of legal procedure in a case connected with land. Let us suppose, for example, that a man had cleared a piece of forest-land some years previously and had farmed it. No objection had been made, and so he now proceeded to clear a fresh piece. This was noticed and reported to the *Oha*, as it was felt that if any more forest were cut down the community would lose its supply of fibre and firewood. The *Oha* would warn the farmer to desist, or they would take a knotted palm-leaf and hang it up on the cleared spot. In the latter case the farmer might summon one or two of the *Oha* to his house, provide them with beer, and inquire why a taboo had been put on his farm. They would say that they did not wish him to continue clearing forest-land, and might even order him to refrain from farming the land already cleared. If the farmer disregarded this order, the *Oha* would send some young men to capture one of his goats, and if the farmer did not redeem the goat by a cash payment the goat would be killed and eaten. A continuance of the offence would cause the *Oha* to come in a body and sleep in the farmer's compound for one night, or even longer if he did not give an undertaking that he would desist. For the *Oha* to sleep in a man's compound was a severe punishment, as the householder had to keep them liberally supplied with food and beer. If he failed to do so, the *Oha* would seize articles of his property, and, if the group possessed a number of rich and influential men who were recognized as leaders,[2] the *Oha* would report their treatment to these men, who would send their servitors to assist the *Oha* in punishing the offender.

---

[1] See pp. 100 et seq.   [2] But such men would normally be *Oha* themselves.

In some communities land disputes were commonly referred for settlement to the body of men who had obtained heads of enemies in war (i.e. to the warrior age-grades). Thus, at Mboo, the plaintiff in a boundary case would send a gift of salt to the leader of the head-getters, with a request that they would come and investigate the matter. The head-getters would inspect the boundary and decide the matter there and then, the winner of the case being required to pay a fee of twenty brass currency rods. This privilege enjoyed by the head-getters was said to have been accorded to them as an induce-ment to young men to acquit themselves bravely in war, and obtain an enemy's head. But the obvious reason for leaving the decision of land disputes to the head-getters was that they were the people best able to deal with the physical violence commonly displayed by parties to a land dispute.

Land disputes are said to have increased in recent years. In the olden days no one but the land-owner would have dared to perform the sacrifice known as *iru ani*, and the performance of this sacrifice was, therefore, good evidence of ownership. But in recent times sophisticated persons, laying claim to land which was not theirs, have not scrupled to back their claim by offering spurious sacrifice. In this and other illegitimate ways many rightful owners have, often with the connivance and assistance of 'Warrant Chiefs', been robbed of their ancestral lands.

Trespass.

One of the commonest causes of litigation is that of damage to crops by live stock. It may be of interest, therefore, to record the following example of a decision given recently over a claim made by a man whose goat had been killed by a farmer on account of damage done to his farm. The spokesman of the council addressed the farmer as follows: 'We have consulted together and weighed up the matter, and we find that you did wrong in killing your brother's goat because it ate a few of your yams. You should have caught the goat and sent for the owner to come and see the amount of damage done. Or you should have taken the half-eaten yams to his house and asked him to pay you the value. But you did not do so: you killed his goat. We require you, therefore, to sell the meat of the goat, and with the proceeds, together with such additional money of your own as may be necessary, purchase another goat and give it to the plaintiff. The plaintiff will then give you the number of yams which his goat ate.'

Then turning to the elders he said: 'Is not this what we have decided?' And all the elders assented.

Inheritance.

Disputes over the inheritance of property were usually settled by the elders of the *onunne* concerned. Thus, if a man who had inherited his brother's property failed to provide the latter's sons with wives, the sons would lay a complaint before the head of the *onunne*, who, backed up by the other elders, would call on the defaulter to fulfil the demands of custom, and might require him to swear on his *ofọ* that he would do so. If the defaulter refused, the elders might place a taboo on his property, thereby compelling him to hand over goats and yams sufficient to provide the necessary marriage expenses. But if the case presented some difficulty it might be referred to the *Ọha* of the whole local group. The general rules governing inheritance will be found on pp. 319–324.

Insulting Behaviour.

To curse any one is a very serious matter, and the person cursed will usually be very ill at ease, until the curser has been induced by apologies or bribes, or by the influence of the elders, to withdraw the curse. Defamation is also serious, though for social rather than religious reasons. To a Negro, living as he does in a circumscribed area, his good name is everything. To take it away is almost to rob him of his life. Any one, therefore, who has been defamed will, if innocent, take swift steps to bring his traducer before the elders and mulct him in heavy damages.

Mere abuse is not a deadly sin, and one may often see two Ibo reviling each other in the strongest language for several minutes, and then bursting into laughter as they walk away. But it would be a different matter if a young man were to use insulting language to an elder. The elder would then be entitled to report the young man to the head of his household or extended-family, who would order him to offer an apology. In making his apology the young man would present the elder with a pot of wine. If the young man refused to apologize and continued to be offensive, the elder would call on some young men of his own family to assault the offender. Or he might ask the best wrestler of his extended-family to challenge the offender to a bout of wrestling, or to fight him should the offender refuse to wrestle. To abuse one of the *Ọha* was more serious than to abuse an ordinary elder, and the Q̧ha concerned might, in such a case, invite the other Q̧ha to take the matter up and fine the offender. It may be noted that any member of a household, extended-family, or local group, whose conduct had been consistently offensive might be sold as a slave, the proceeds of the sale (together with his land) being given to his legal heir.

An old man who had been insulted by a junior might deal with the offence himself, by merely pointing his finger at the young man and saying: 'Very well, never mind, you will see!' The young man might go off care-free, but on the very first occasion on which any misfortune or illness overtook him he would ascribe it to the old man's spell, and would ask his parents to intercede with the old man, presenting him with an egg and saying 'Ono lolo'.[1] The old man, now appeased, would blow on the egg and say: 'What I said to the youth was not intended—may it pass away!' Then putting his hand on the young man's head he would say, 'Nothing shall happen to you. I have cleared my heart of vexation, and if I continue to harbour ill feeling may Ani (i.e. Ala) take away my life!'

Debt.

The procedure in cases of debt was usually somewhat as follows. Let us suppose that a man had borrowed £1 from a member of his own local group, and had allowed the debt to accumulate without showing any sign of repayment. The creditor would come to the debtor's house, accompanied by his sons and brothers, and make a formal demand for the payment of the debt. If the debtor failed to give satisfaction, the creditor would ask the elders of his *onunne* to call upon the debtor to pay forthwith, and if the debtor professed inability to pay, the creditor and (or) his relatives would enter the debtor's compound and seize some of his goats or even one of his wives or children. (But a first wife or eldest child could not be seized.) The confiscated property would be returned to the debtor if some person of standing went surety for the debtor's appearance at the hearing of the case before the elders of the group. Later the elders would, at the debtor's invitation, meet at his house, and, after being given some food and wine, would send for the creditor. If the creditor refused to come to the debtor's house the venue would be transferred to some open space, where the elders would be given refreshment by

---

[1] I was unable to ascertain the meaning of this Onitsha phrase.

both parties.[1] Any one of the elders might then rise and say, 'We have gathered together to inquire into a dispute between A and B respecting a debt; and we advise both parties to avoid any attempt to mislead us. Let them bear in mind that, as we are all members of the same group, some of us may already be aware of the circumstances.'[2] If the debtor denied the debt, the creditor would be called on to swear. If he refused to do so the debtor would be invited to swear, and if he did so would win the case. But if one of the parties considered that the other had no respect for an oath, or possessed some 'medicine' which would nullify the effects of an oath, then he would insist that the oath should be sworn by the other's brother or son, a custom similar to the old English practice of 'compurgation'. If both parties refused to swear, the case would be dismissed. Witnesses might be heard, and if necessary called on to swear to the truth of any part of their evidence.

After hearing all the evidence the elders would withdraw to consider their decision in private, having first ascertained (if necessary) whether in the past the debtor's family had been accustomed to demand the full rate of interest on loans given to the creditor's family, or, whether, in the absence of precedent, the creditor wished to establish a precedent, by exacting the full interest in the present case. Having arrived at agreement the elders would reappear, and the decision would be announced by the holder of the senior *ǫfǫ* or any capable speaker.

If the plaintiff and defendant belonged to different local groups, the plaintiff would in the first instance lay his complaint before the head of the defendant's *onunne* and let the matter rest for the time being. Or, accompanied by some of the elders of his local group, he might go to the compound of the defendant and call on him to pay up the debt. If the defendant refused or failed to pay, the plaintiff would, at a convenient opportunity, seize some person from the defendant's household, or failing that, from his extended-family or even his local group. The defendant would then ask the elders of his local

---

[1] Each party to a case had to supply the elders who tried it with four calabashes of wine and a leg of meat. In important cases there might be a special 'decision fee'.

[2] It may be said generally that there is not much difficulty about evidence. The people live at such close quarters that every one's doings are known to all. One objection to the unreformed Native Court system is that the judges for the most part belong to foreign communities and are without the local knowledge which would assist towards an equitable decision.

group to invite the elders of the plaintiff's local group to come to his compound and hear what he had to say. The elders of both groups would fix a day for hearing the case. Pending the hearing the head of the defendant's extended-family would demand the return of the captured person, himself going security for the appearance of the defendant at the trial. The rest of the proceedings would be as described above, but either of the parties might veto the presence of any elder, on the ground that that elder was the father or brother of his opponent, or was an open enemy of his family.

If the elders of the two local groups could not come to an amicable settlement, the case might by common consent be referred to the elders of the other local groups of the commune. Or fighting might arise between the two local groups. Indeed, failure to repay a debt was one of the commonest causes of fighting between two kinship or two local groups.[1] In such cases the *ebiri uku* of the disinterested sections of the commune would rush in between the combatants, and two of their leaders would cross their guns as a signal that the fighting must cease, pending the hearing of the case at a general meeting of the commune in the market-place. All the elders would bring their *ọfọ* to this meeting, and would call on their *ọfọ* to kill any one who restarted the fighting. If any one disregarded this warning, the combined age-grades of the whole community would pillage his compound.

Debt disputes also led to fighting between different communes, or between a local-group of one commune and that of a different commune. Thus, some years ago, the Umu-Ojeche *nchi* of the commune of Nekede seized (on account of a debt) a woman of the Umu-Eche *nchi* of the commune of Owerri. The men of Umu-Eche chased the assailants with guns and killed one man. On the following day all the warriors of both communes turned out and fought. The loss was considerable on each side, and both communes decided to leave the dispute to the particular local-groups concerned. Thus Umu-Ojeche and Umu-Eche carried on a private war of their own for a number of years, the fighting taking the form of intermittent raids on the persons or property of the other side. This state of strife was brought to an end by the neighbouring commune of Iheagwa, who placed two emblems of their cult, known as Okporogo, on the land between the warring groups. The priest of Okporogo then visited each group in

[1] Local fights were generally begun with sticks and matchets, but frequently ended with guns.

turn, calling on them in the name of his deity to desist from fighting, and to reckon up their losses. To this they agreed, and as it was found that Umu-Ojeche had suffered rather more loss than Umu-Eche, Umu-Eche handed over to Umu-Ojeche a young man, who was forthwith executed. Each of the warring groups then swore an oath that they would henceforth live in peace. The oath-procedure was as follows. Deputations from both sides met together and placed on the ground two of their cultus-emblems. Then each of the men who had been primarily concerned in the quarrel took some *ogu* grass and passed it round the head of the other, saying, 'If you do anything to continue this quarrel may the deities represented by these emblems destroy you.'

There are one or two final points relating to the law of debt. Firstly, in many groups, the principal part in the settlement of debt cases might be taken by some rich influential man. But in some cases which presented no difficulty the debtor might be dealt with summarily by the *ebiri uku*. Secondly, the normal interest chargeable on a loan was 100 per cent. per annum, at compound interest, and loans at this annual rate were known as *omunruwa afọ*. But loans (for trading purposes) might be arranged for short periods, e.g. one week (8 days), three weeks (24 days), or on the basis of a commission for each market attended by the borrower. This system was known as *omunruwa ego-ezoahia*. In the Native Court records there are many instances of claims being made and allowed at the old compound-interest rate. For example, a man who had borrowed £1 five years previously was called on to repay £15.[1] But recently a rule has been made limiting the interest to reasonable rates. Thirdly, if a debtor were unable to meet his debts, it was, and is still in many areas, permissible to sell or hand over to the creditor the debtor's palms or even his farm land. Or the debtor might have to pawn his person or that of one of his family. To this reference has already been made.[2] Lastly, on a man's death, his principal heritor (i.e. his eldest son as a rule) became responsible for the payment of debts. But if a creditor did not give notice of the debt before the conclusion of the final funeral rites he lost all claim to repayment.

---

[1] Some communities have earned an evil reputation as money-lenders. Thus many of the people of Nkwerre (Owerri Province) are said to be hangers-on of Native Court judges in numerous localities and to foment litigation by advancing sums of money to litigants at exorbitant rates.

[2] See p. 205.

Oaths.[1]

At public trials and investigations the proceedings were frequently opened by an appeal to the gods and ancestors to punish any elder who, from malice or because of a bribe, would express a dishonest opinion, and any witness who would give false evidence. In some localities, also, the plaintiff and defendant might, at the outset of the case, each make a solemn asseveration that he would speak the truth. Taking a pot of palm-wine he would pour some into a gourd and then speak as follows: 'Ndichie (ancestors), come and drink. Ala, come and drink. Ajala, come and drink. Chuku, come and drink. Igwe, come and drink. What I am about to say is true, and it is in accordance with the custom of our ancestors and not an invention of my own. Let the guilty be guilty and the innocent be innocent. Let evil follow an evil thinker and good follow a good thinker.' He would then pour a libation on the ground. Whether this occasional practice of swearing a general oath at the beginning of a trial is a genuine Ibo custom or the result of European influence, I was unable to discover. Normally among the Ibo, as among most non-European peoples, oaths are only sworn on particular points that arise during the proceedings. Thus, during the proceedings, one of the parties might offer to swear by some cult. He might swear by Ala, and it was not necessary for him to go to the shrine of Ala in order to do so. The priest of Ala might pour a libation to Ala there and then, and call on the deity to take the life of the swearer if he was guilty. He would then pour some wine into a dish. This the swearer would drink after calling on Ala to take his life if he were speaking untruths. Or he might be sworn on a yam or the skull of an animal which had been offered to Ala. He might be sworn by his opponent on numerous objects one after the other.[2] The swearer would squat before the object while his opponent would speak as follows: 'Your name is so-and-so' (This is said with the intention of informing the spirit of the man's name). 'You said you did not steal my goat. May this (yam) kill you if you have stolen it.' He would then wave a piece of palm round the swearer's head and place it on the object used as the medium.

The *ǫfǫ* of the priest of Ala or of the senior elder present is sometimes used as a medium for swearing. Thus, if the opinion of the elders were adverse to a litigant, and the litigant hotly maintained

---

[1] See also p. 43.

[2] The opponent would produce the medium for the oath, but would himself have to swear that the medium was not one which would kill an innocent man.

the truth of his assertions, the elders might call on the litigant to
swear on the *ọfọ* of the senior elder. They would sit round the *ọfọ*,
while the litigant would stand in the centre and say: 'Ọfọ, I am guiltless in this matter. If I am guilty may you and the "countenances" of
the elders here assembled deprive me of my life. But if I am innocent
may my life remain with me.' Or an unsuccessful litigant might
challenge the elders to assert on their *ọfọ* that, if they were in his
position, they would accept the decision given. The senior elder or
priest of Ala would then say: 'Ọfọ, you have heard what this man has
said. If the decision which we have given is not in accordance with
our custom then may you take away our lives. But if we have tried
this case in accordance with the precedent set by our ancestors, then
may you, Ọfọ, spare our lives.' The man would then usually agree to
do as he had been directed. It may be noted, also, that if any of the
elders, sitting as judges, appeared to be expressing an unfair or parti-
san opinion during the proceedings he might be called on by the
others to swear on his *ọfọ* that he really believed what he had said,
and that he could quote a precedent for his attitude.

Sometimes an unsuccessful litigant would leave the assembly shouting out that he would not abide by the decision. In such a case the
elders, led by the priest of Ala,[1] might proceed to his house on the
following day, and on arrival would keep tapping the ground with
their staves. This would cause the man serious alarm, and he would
ask them to desist, saying that he would carry out their behests. But,
as the conduct of such an one had been an insult to Ala and the
ancestors, the litigant would ask the priest to perform the rite known
as *Imfo jo Ala* or 'The appeasing of the anger of Ala'. The priest would
tell him to bring an egg, oil and some *ọha* leaves. The priest would
pour the oil on the ground, break the egg over the oil and mix in the
juice of the leaves. All the elders would join in mixing up the ingre-
dients, saying, 'Ala, we now seek to appease your wrath. Our hearts,
which were angry against this man, are now cool, and so let your heart
be cool. Do not pursue him or his wife or his children, as he has
agreed to do our bidding.' The priest would then put a little of the
mixture on the forehead, chest, and feet of the man, saying: 'We have
appeased the anger of Ala'. He would sprinkle the rest of the mixture
on the man's house, saying, 'Ala, let no evil overtake this man'.

In some communities the elders might endeavour to enforce their
authority by saying to a litigant who had refused to accept their

[1] Or in some communities by the holder of an *aro* (see p. 136).

decision, 'If you repudiate our decision then may you henceforth meet difficulties greater than your present difficulty and so be under the necessity of calling upon us continually'. This would amount to a curse, which would only be withdrawn when the litigant had apologized and paid a fine of twenty brass rods.

On the other hand, an aggrieved party who had referred his case at the outset to a few selected arbitrators was not, in most communities, bound to accept the decision of this court of first instance. He might ignore the decision or go round the village beating a drum and shouting out that an 'evil thing' had been done to him. This would be tantamount to an intimation that he wished to refer his case to the higher court of the village assembly, a proceeding which entailed an initial gift of one goat to the villagers.

In the Native Courts at the present time many objects are used as a means of swearing oaths, but few are considered effective. At Owele[1] the media for oaths are a diviner's ọfọ and paraphernalia taken from him when he was convicted of some crime, the skull of a goat which had been stolen from a shrine of Ala (to whom it had been dedicated), and the cloth of a madman (with the intention that madness should pursue any one who swore falsely by the cloth). When any one is to be sworn, a Court Messenger takes one of the objects (without naming it) and says: 'If you tell lies may this kill you.' He then touches the man on the head and chest with the object. The man then swears on all the objects collectively. Such oaths have little value, as none of the objects used (except perhaps the ọfọ) command the respect or awe of the people. Moreover, it is essential that before a man swears an oath he should know the name of the deity immanent in the object. For, if he swears an oath and nothing happens to him within the time appointed, he is required to offer a sacrifice to that deity. It is contrary to native practice to swear on a collection of objects. The medium for an oath should be a specially sanctified object, and the oath itself administered by a particular individual according to a prescribed formula. There is a further objection to requiring litigants to swear on objects of which they have no knowledge, namely, that one

---

[1] In the Ache Native Court the media used for swearing are (a) the skull of a horse sacrificed to Achihi, the principal guardian spirit of Ache, and (b) figurines of Agu, the spirit of divination, together with the ọfọ of the *dibia* or diviner from whom the figurines were taken. The skull is considered an effective medium for swearing oaths, but the figurines are regarded lightly, especially as their former owner was sent to prison.

of the objects may be believed to have the power of injuring innocent persons. In the olden days the people of the Owele district used to go to Ache to swear oaths by the spirit known as Nnemmiri, but, following the example of many neighbouring communities, they gave up the practice, having come to the conclusion that Nnemmiri was a friend of the wicked and an enemy of the good. It may be said generally that oaths administered by the Native Courts have little value except when sworn on one or other of the local deities.

Negroes are often afraid of giving evidence against any one belonging to their own kinship or local-group, particularly in serious cases. For this reason many criminals escape. On the other hand, it must be remembered that the belief in supernatural punishment is still so great that those who have done wrong frequently make confession of their own accord, and pay damages for the injuries inflicted. With the spread of Christianity the validity of the old forms of oath has been weakened, and in some cases completely destroyed. But they are still a potent force in most parts of Iboland. Christians are not, of course, required to swear an oath in pagan fashion, but many do so, regarding it as a mere formality.

A Trial.

As a final example of legal procedure an attempt will be made to give a complete account of a trial, such as might have occurred some twenty-five years ago. The account is based on well-tested data obtained at Ngbwidi, in the Awgu Division.

A man named Ehirim, of the village of Ngbwidi, seized and tied up one called Ezedu of the neighbouring village of Agunese, on a charge of having stolen one of his yams. Leaving his prisoner in the custody of his brothers, he walked over to Agunese and informed the priest of Njọku (the yam deity) that Ezedu was a prisoner at his house, having been caught red-handed stealing the complainant's yam (an offence which was little short of sacrilege). The priest of Njọku immediately reported the matter to the priest of Ala and other important elders, including the elders of Ezedu's kindred, and all made their way to Ehirim's house, where it was agreed with the priests and elders of Ngbwidi to thresh the matter out in the market-place on the following day. Next day there was a general assembly in the market-place, and when the elders had piled their *ọfọ* on the ground in two groups the priest of Ala at Agunese rose, holding a gourd of palm-wine, and spoke as follows: 'Ancestors and Njọku, we have met here to inquire into an accusation of yam-stealing. For in such cases it was the custom of our forefathers to hold a public investigation. Help us to try the case impartially, and assist us when we endeavour to find examples of the procedure in former times. If the accused has indeed stolen the yam do you constrain him to confess.' He then threw some kola seeds over his *ọfọ* and placed pieces of kola-nuts on the ground. Next he poured some palm-wine on his *ọfọ* and on the ground, saying, 'Ala, come and drink.' The priest of Ala at Ngbwidi did likewise, and was followed by the Njọku priest of Agunese, who said: 'Ala, come and drink and eat kola-nut. Chuku, come and drink and eat kola-nut. Njọku, come and drink and eat kola-nut. Ancestors, come and drink and eat kola-nut. Ọfọ, come and drink and eat kola-nut.[1] I was told by a man of Ngbwidi, one named Ehirim, that a man of Agunese had stolen his yam, and so I summoned the priests of Ala and *aro*-holders and elders in order that we might inquire into the matter. I called them, even as my father, who was priest of Njọku before me, used to do. If any of these men, who have come to try the case, deal falsely in the matter, or if the accuser or accused or any person called to give evidence tells falsehoods, then do you Ala, Chuku, Njọku, Ancestors, and Ọfọ, deal with that man.' He then poured a libation of palm-wine over his *ọfọ* and the *ọfọ* of all the elders of Agunese, saying: 'Life of men and of women—protect us all.' The Njọku priest of Ngbwidi followed his example.

The Njọku priest of Agunese then rose again and said: 'It is now your duty to call the complainant and defendant and ask them what occurred, that we may know whether Ezedu really did steal the yam, or whether he has been falsely accused.' At this all the elders murmured, '*Imena!*', i.e. 'Quite right!'. Thereupon the priest of Ala at Agunese got up and asked Ezedu point-blank: 'Did you steal this yam?' Ezedu replied, 'It is a lie.' 'Very well,' said the priest, 'then let the man who accuses you stand up and say how he caught you.' At this point the priest of Ala at Ngbwidi rose and said: 'Fellow townsmen, you have heard what the men of Agunese and the accused have said.' Then addressing Ehirim he said, 'Get up and say how you caught the accused.'

Ehirim then rose and addressed Ezedu, saying, 'Do you indeed deny taking my yam? I was not the only one who saw you—there are others. If I am asked to swear, these others will forbid me to do so, for they are prepared to swear themselves.' On this the elders of

[1] Note that in this case the *ọfọ* is given a separate personality from the ancestors.

Ngbwidi exclaimed, 'Sit down, my son, you have stated the matter clearly. Let us see how he is going to refute the charge. Ha! A fellow who was caught red-handed is going to put up a defence! Ha! We shall see.' Some of them held up both hands and started cracking their fingers and saying, 'This man is a liar.' Others raised their feet off the ground and held up their hands, saying, 'May I be delivered from abomination!' Others again picked up a pebble, touched their right and left shoulder, right and left thigh, and having circled it round their head threw it away, saying: 'Ala, do not permit abomination.'

At this stage general confusion reigned, but presently some of the most important elders on both sides rose and, clapping their hands, said: 'Keep quiet—we do not yet know whether he is guilty or inno-cent. We shall know when we have heard him.' The onlookers shouted out 'Quite true!', and calm was restored. A very old man of Agunese now rose and said to Ezedu: 'My son, you have heard what he says—that there were others who saw you. If this is so, speak the truth. You would not be the first man to have stolen a yam, and you would not be put to death on that account.[1] It will be a shameful thing if you deny the theft, and then others come and prove that you are a liar.'

But Ezedu merely remarked that he had said all he was going to say, and, kneeling down, touched the earth, saying: 'Ala, if I stole this yam then do you take away my life.' This act encouraged the elders of Agunese to believe that Ezedu was innocent, and one of them accordingly rose and said: 'You see that our man denies the charge and is ready to swear.' An elder of Ngbwidi then got up and said to Ehirim: 'You said that you could call others to prove the theft. Now is the time to do so.' Ehirim pointed to one of his witnesses, who was then addressed by an elder of Ngbwidi as follows: 'My son, the com-plainant says you saw him at the time he arrested the defendant. We want you now to tell your story, but you must not do this in a spirit of envy or hatred, for you may be called upon to swear.'

After hearing the witnesses all the elders (excluding those of the interested kindreds) withdrew to consider their verdict. One of the Ngbwidi elders said to the elders of Agunese: 'We are of the opinion that our man caught yours red-handed. But your man's oath by Ala makes us a little hesitant. What kind of character does he bear?' An elder of Agunese replied: 'There is nothing against him that we know

---

[1] But actually he might be put to death.

of, and, as you say, he has sworn by Ala. Under the circumstances we had better leave the decision to Igwe (the oracle at Umunọha) or Chuku-Abiam (the so-called 'Long Juju' at Aro-Chuku).'

Having agreed to this the elders returned to the assembly, and there the priest of Ala at Ngbwidi rose and addressed the men of Agunese, saying: 'As your son keeps on denying plain facts are you ready to tell him to produce the necessary fees in order to go to Igwe or Chuku? We will ask our son to do likewise.' On this the elders of Agunese turned to the head of the accused's kindred and said: 'My friend, have you heard what they have said? Give us your answer.' The latter replied: 'We agree.' The priest of Ala at Ngbwidi then said: 'If we go to Igwe, and Igwe proves your man to be a thief, what will be the consequences?' The head of the accused's kindred answered: 'We will do what custom prescribes.' An old man now rose and said: 'Let Agunese and Ngbwidi choose two delegates to go to Igwe, and see that they do not belong to the kindred of the accuser or accused. Then let them be sworn.'

After some discussion the respective delegates were chosen. The Ngbwidi delegates were sworn by the priest of Ala at Agunese, and the Agunese delegates by the priest of Ala at Ngbwidi. The priest split a kola and placed the pieces of nut on the ground before the delegates, saying: 'You are going to eat these kolas. Ala, give ear. If these men go to Igwe, and conceal or falsify what Igwe tells them, may you, Ala, Chuku, Ancestors, and Ọfọ take away their lives.' Each delegate then knelt and said: 'Ala, Chuku, Ancestors, and Ọfọ, if I conceal aught of what Igwe-Ke-Ala may tell me then may you take away my life. But if I truly report all that Igwe says then may I remain alive.' Bending down his head he took the kola in his mouth and ate it.

The journey to Umunọha and back took the best part of a week, and, when the delegates returned, another general meeting was held, at which the senior delegate rose and, shaking a rattle, spoke as follows: 'Igwe-Ke-Ala of Umunọha, what I am about to say is what you told us. Anyaṅu (the sun), what I am about to say is what Igwe told us. Chuku, what I am about to say is what Igwe told us. Ala and Ancestors, what I am about to say is what Igwe told us. Before we left our town for Umunọha we swore an oath that we would truly tell what Igwe declared to us. Igwe-Ke-Ala of Umunọha, if I conceal what you told us, then begin your life-taking by taking my life. And in this do you, Anyaṅu, Chuku, and our Ala, take a share. Igwe-Ke-

R

Ala of Umunọha—Ala give ear—you told us that Ezedu is innocent, and that in bringing this charge Ehirim and his relatives wished to revenge themselves upon the kindred of Ezedu, because once upon a time one of Ehirim's kindred had been found guilty of stealing from one of the kindred of Ezedu. On the present occasion Ezedu did not steal any yam. The whole affair is one of spite. If this is not what Igwe told us then may the oath we took rob us of our lives. Brother delegates have I not spoken the truth?'

After this announcement, which was received with wild delight by the people of Agunese, the Agunese delegates danced forward to greet their fellows, and in order to keep up appearances the Ngbwidi delegates also danced towards the men of Ngbwidi. When the meeting had broken up Ezedu asked the head of his kindred whether he was entitled to compensation. The latter replied that, once in the past, one of their kindred had made a false charge against a member of Ehirim's kindred and had not been called on to pay damages. And so the matter was dropped. But otherwise a claim would have been preferred, and if it had not been paid after two requests it would have been permissible for Ezedu's kindred to have captured the equivalent of the penalty from any member of Ehirim's kindred or local-group. A cow, or even a weaned child, might have been captured in this way, and held to ransom.

The Law of Warfare.

Warfare among the Ibo was more a matter of affrays and raids than of organized campaigns. And it was waged not with the object of winning markets or annexing territory, but with the purely practical purpose of keeping one's neighbours in order. Wars were, in fact, reprisals for injuries received, and were therefore an integral part of the legal system. For in the absence of any strong central authority the best method of preventing outrage is to let every one see that you will give as good as you get. It will appear, moreover, that in spite of all the barbarities of Negro warfare there were certain rules which had the binding force of law for both sides. There was, for example, a recognized system of compensation at the close of the war, and there were rules prohibiting the use of lethal weapons in certain circumstances.

Fights between two kindreds or two local-groups of the same village-group were common occurrences, for numerous reasons, such as debt or adultery. One of the commonest causes of fighting was the refusal or failure of the parents of a wife who had abandoned her husband to refund the bride-price. This frequently led to reprisals by the husband's kindred, and in due course a state of open hostility might supervene between the village of the husband and the village of the wife. In such fights the usual weapons employed were matchets and sticks, the intention being to wound and not to kill. The use of firearms was, indeed, forbidden, and any one breaking this rule was liable to be tried subsequently by the *Ọha* of the village-group. In point of fact, however, the rule against the use of firearms was frequently broken, and in many communities it was considered right and proper for a combatant to use firearms against another who had, with a matchet, killed his brother or first cousin. Even when matchets alone were used a number of combatants might lose their lives, and it was customary, therefore, on the conclusion of the fighting, for each side to reckon up its losses, and for the side which had fewer losses to hand over girls, free of bride-price, to the other side.

Fights between two separate village-groups, or between a section of one village-group and a section of another, were also constant occurrences throughout Iboland in pre-Government times. Thus, if a member of one commune slew a member of another, an immediate state of warfare usually arose. The fact of the homicide was made known by the wailing of the murdered man's kin, and by a whistler who went round the commune summoning the warriors, by whistle, to set out for the commune of the murderer next morning. No formal arrangements were made in a case of this sort. At daybreak the warriors set out for the enemy villages in a disorganized mass, and proceeded to kill any one they saw. If the fighting became general it might be carried on from day to day, the warriors fighting in age-grades, each led by some experienced warrior. The principal weapons used were dane-guns, cap-guns and, occasionally, rifles. Matchets were carried for hand-to-hand fighting, and also for clearing paths. Hoes were used for entrenching.

Every warrior endeavoured to obtain the head of an enemy. Having killed his man he cut off his head with a matchet, and then licked from the blade a little of the dead man's blood.[1] It was said that the slayer thereby became identified with the slain, and so was made safe from pursuit by the dead man's ghost. If, on the conclusion of peace,

---

[1] Cf. 'It is stated that in the Italy of to-day the Calabrian who has used his dagger in a quarrel will lick the blade in the hope of going scot-free.' See Dr. Marett's *Head, Heart and Hands in Human Evolution*, p. 186.

he attended a feast at the dead man's village, he could drink wine, with impunity, which had been made from the dead man's palm-trees! It was even asserted that, by licking the dead enemy's blood, the enemy would become reincarnated as the slayer's son, and would thus become an ally instead of an avenger.[1]

On returning home the head-getter took the head to the grove of Ekwêsu (the war-god), where the priest boiled the head and buried the flesh. He poured a libation on the skull, saying: 'Let not your ghost (*nkporobia*) worry the man who killed you.' Then, cutting a yam in two, he waved the pieces over the skull, and threw them on the ground, saying, 'Take this yam and eat it.' Or the priest might perform this rite with a chicken, and then fix the chicken in a cleft bamboo, where it was left to die. The head-getter shaved his head and smeared himself with camwood. He then went to the market and danced round, holding the skull in his left hand and his matchet in his right. After the dance he hung the skull in the roof of his house.

If one side suffered more than the other, it would ask a diviner or 'medicine-man' to provide them with some charm, and direct them when and where to make the next attack. The charm would be laid on a path leading to the enemy villages. Or a losing side might sue for peace, by sending to the enemy commune an unarmed representative, holding a palm-leaf in his right hand and wearing a palm-leaf tied round his neck.[2] He would go to the house of the most important man (the richest man usually) who would summon his fellow villagers by drum, amid general rejoicing. The victorious group would demand a fee as an inducement to their warriors to lay down their arms. Priests were commonly used as ambassadors. Thus, in the commune of Opi, the priest who controlled the wind and rain was commonly used as an ambassador in time of war. He would proceed to the boundary and meet the deputy of the enemy community, who would also be a priest. The two would then take cuttings of their hair, lay them on the ground, kill a goat, pour the blood on the cuttings and bury them, at the same time declaring that the quarrel between the

[1] Dr. Marett, op. cit., p. 185, says, with reference to Orestes and the biting off of his finger, 'for thus to make a blood covenant with a ghost . . . was bound to convert the avenger into an ally'.

[2] Palm-leaves are carried by messengers in times of trouble. In the 1929 disturbances the women were called out by messengers carrying a palm-leaf. For the use of palm-leaves as a means of imposing a taboo see, e.g., pp. 125, 149, &c. Also Westermarck, *Early Beliefs and Their Social Influence*, p. 10.

two communes was buried for ever, and that any member of one commune who attacked and slew a member of the other would be called on to hang himself, or to hand over a female of his family as compensation to the family of the other.

In the Awgu Division, when both sides began to weary of their war, they would lay down their guns and strike two matchets together over their heads. One side would then direct its war ambassador (*onyishi-ago*) to go to the war ambassador of the other side, in order to arrange a general meeting to discuss terms. At this meeting the warriors would remain in the background with their arms on the ground, ready for action if the proceedings broke down. The elders of both sides would meet, and the business of peace-making would be begun by one of the ambassadors taking a gourd of palm-wine and speaking as follows: 'If any one attempts to play any trick in these proceedings, and so hinder the conclusion of peace, then let that man be the first to be killed in the ensuing fight. Obasi-Idinenu (Lord God), you are witness to my words. We are about to swear an oath, and if any one breaks that oath do you take his life. Ancestors, you are witness to my words. Ala, you are witness to my words. If I myself commit a breach of my oath, and the war continues, then may my people suffer defeat.' During this speech he would keep pouring small quantities of palm-wine on the ground, and on its conclusion would completely empty the gourd. The *onyishi-ago* of the other side would then do likewise.

Each ambassador would now take a kola-nut, split it, and, standing before the cultus-emblem which he had brought from his commune, would speak as follows: 'If this spirit, by whom the other side is going to swear, is one which kills people who do not break their oath, then may it kill me. But if not, then may I remain alive.' He would then cast the seeds of the kola on the cultus-emblem. The other ambassador would do likewise to his cultus-emblem. Next, each ambassador would go and stand before the cultus-emblem of the other side, and, with his hands uplifted, would say: 'If I repudiate what is about to be said (i.e. the formal declaration of peace) then may you (i.e. the spirit) kill me.' The two ambassadors would now stand facing each other, and each would cover the other's eyes with his left hand, and place a piece of kola in his mouth with his right hand. They would then embrace each other. (The covering of the eyes was said to symbolize the blindness which would follow a breach of the oath, and would prevent those who had broken the oath from being able to shoot). Some of the pieces of kola would then be thrown on the ground, as an offering to the ancestors. Other pieces would be passed from one side to the other, and palm-wine would also be exchanged. The senior or most important man of one of the communes would then address the men of the other commune, saying: 'Men of (e.g.) Awgu, you have heard what has been said. Henceforth there is no more war between us, and you can visit friends in Mboo as in days of peace.' The most important elder on the other side would speak likewise. This would constitute the formal declaration of peace, and the warriors, accordingly, would fire their guns in the air.

Sometimes a disinterested commune intervened to stop fighting between two other communes. It would send uterine relatives of the combatant communes to lay a palm-leaf at the threshold of the compound of the leader of each side. A losing side frequently asked a disinterested commune to intervene in this way. This palm-leaf could not be removed by the combatant side, which had immediately to cease fighting or run the risk of finding the disinterested commune ranged on the side of the enemy. But if one of the combatants did not wish to cease fighting, it would request the disinterested commune to come and remove the palm-leaf, and this would be done.

As already noted, it was customary on the conclusion of a war for the elders of both sides and of a disinterested commune to meet and reckon up the number of their dead, with a view to compensation, which was assessed not merely on the numbers killed, but on the social status of those killed. Thus the loss by one side of a man who had three wives was not balanced by the loss on the other side of a man with one wife. A sum of money had to be paid to make up the difference. The loss of a rich important man was balanced by handing over a young man or woman, plus a large payment in cash or kind. The loss of a cult-slave was reckoned at a small sum only, and the side which had killed the cult-slave could not replace him by handing over one of their own cult-slaves, as this would offend the deity of the cult. In reckoning the compensation the elders of the disinterested commune were the recognized arbiters, and this principle might be utilized more freely at the present time, in cases involving disputes between two communes, or two villages of the same commune.

These remarks on warfare may be concluded with the observation that even in times of peace it was usually unsafe for an inhabitant of one village-group or commune to visit another, unless the visitor had a friend in the other. Even so he was liable to be captured and sold before the friendly family could intervene. The friendly family would at once demand the captive's release, and if this were refused a fight might occur. But safe conduct was always accorded a stranger who had been invited to attend any final funeral rites. For it was believed that the dead man would take immediate vengeance on any one who interfered with one who had thus come to do him honour. In pre-Government times many litigants and seekers after divine assistance undertook the journey to Aro-Chuku in order to consult the famous oracle. But the roads were so unsafe that a journey which can now be accomplished in a few days might take as many weeks. Before setting out, the pilgrim had to seek the assistance of some local personage who was able to arrange for a village-to-village escort, through the mediumship of friends of similar standing in the various villages. These personages were not necessarily direct agents of the Aro. They were enterprising traders who added to their wealth by means of this system of 'conducted tours'.

Legislation.

Laws were passed in an assembly of all the elders of the commune and were sometimes given a divine sanction by a sacrifice to Ala or some other deity. Thus, if it became apparent that market brawls were becoming frequent and likely to lead to murder and intra-kindred or intra-group fighting, the elders of the commune might meet together and decide that, if any one in future engaged in fighting in the market, he should be heavily fined. Having arrived at this decision they would buy a goat and take it to the priest of Ala, who, holding the goat by a rope, would say: 'Ala, the elders of the commune have brought this goat to you, in order to inform you of their wishes touching the market. They say that it is not their desire that fights should occur in the market, lest this should lead to loss of life. Ala, it is not your desire that men should kill one another, as we are your children. They declare that if any one breaks this rule he shall pay a fine of fourteen currency rods, and they ask you, Ala, to enforce this law by dealing with any one who refuses to pay this fine. Ala, when the elders call upon you (to assist them in dealing with a law-breaker) do you answer their call (by bringing misfortune upon him).' He would then turn to the elders and say: 'Is not this your wish?' They would all reply: 'Ala, this is our wish.' The priest would then kill the goat, and as he put the knife to the goat's throat would say:

'Take the life of this goat and spare our lives.' The flesh of the goat would be cooked and divided, and morsels of the heart, liver, and kidney would be deposited by the priest on the cultus-symbol.

The elders would then go home, and each would inform the members of his kindred of the passing of the law. If any one subsequently broke the law he would be arrested by young men and handed over to the head of his kindred, who would be instructed to collect the fine and bring it to the market on the following market-day. On that day the elders would walk round the market, beating their matchets and saying, 'Fellow-villagers, come and take what is yours.' The head of the culprit's kindred would then hand the fourteen rods to the senior elder, who would say: 'Fellow-villagers, you have seen that the fine has been paid.' They would reply: 'We have: let it be handed over to the keeper of fines.' The rods would then be handed to a man delegated by the elders to receive fines and hold them until they were required for some general sacrifice. The culprit would be escorted by the elders and priest of Ala to the shrine of Ala. He would hand a pot of palm-wine to the priest and then squat down before the cultus-symbol. The priest would pour a little of the wine into a buffalo-horn and pass the horn round the culprit's head, saying, 'Ala, I and the elders of the commune have brought this man before you to tell you that he has paid his fine for "breaking" your market. He has brought this wine to appease your wrath. Pursue him not. A man's child may offend his father, but is forgiven when he repents.' He would then pour the libation, and the remainder of the wine would be drunk by all present, the culprit included.

The religious sanction was not always Ala. When a law was made the elders might call on the priest of any cult to bring some material object from the shrine. The priest and elders would then say: 'We have made such-and-such a law. If any one breaks this law may this spirit kill that person.' The priest would then strike the ground with the object. If the law were broken the punishment might be left to the spirit. But the law-breaker might forestall punishment by going to the priest, who would perform sacrifice on the man's behalf, saying: 'So-and-so admits that he has gone against you, and he comes now to redeem himself.'

In most cases rules were made without being given any form of religious validity. Thus the elders might announce in the market that wood was not to be cut in a certain area, under the penalty of a fine of one goat. If a man were reported for breaking this rule the elders would send young men to catch a goat from his kindred or local group. If the accused redeemed the goat, the money obtained was divided out among the elders, and there the matter ended. But if he did not redeem it, the goat would be sold or killed, and if the accused lost his case he would be called on to pay two goats to the owner of the goat. If the accused won his case his accuser had to pay the cost of the two goats. If the accused were a woman her fine was payable by her husband or son. Or it might be payable by her parents through the person who had acted as middleman when her marriage had been arranged.

Other instances of legislation are (*a*) that no one should visit a neighbouring town during an epidemic; and (*b*) that women should not visit the market of an unfriendly commune. The elders might post young men on the roads to see that these rules were observed, and the young men were authorized to confiscate the property of any one who attempted to break them. Rules might also be made forbidding the cutting of sticks (to be used for training yam-tendrils) before a certain date.

Legislative powers were not confined to the elders—they might also be exercised by the senior age-grades. Thus, if it had become apparent that stealing was on the increase throughout the entire village-group, the senior age-grade in each village might hold a meeting to discuss the matter, and might decide to increase the penalty for this offence. Their decision would be reported to and accepted by the elders. Or they might pass a law fixing the rate of rent for land, or the price of palm-wine. Or, observing that palm-fruit was being cut before it was ripe, they might make an order that no one was to remove the fruit before a certain date. In these instances the senior age-grades not only made the laws, but also punished those who broke them. But other matters, which did not admit of summary executive action, or required long and careful consideration, would be referred to the elders for their decision. An age-grade or group of age-grades might in this way represent to the elders that the standard bride-price was too high, or that the excessive cost of burial-rites was involving many families in bankruptcy.

Women, also, were not powerless in the matter of legislation. For, although they had no well-developed age-grade system like the men, they did not hesitate to hold a meeting in order to discuss any matter of public importance, and the decision of the meeting would be formally transmitted to the council of elders. Instances of this have already been given[1] and it need only be remarked here that women made numerous by-laws for themselves, and inflicted their own punishments for offences such as pilfering, brawling, adultery, having sexual relations with a husband's brother or an *osu*, speaking lightly to males about matters of childbirth, or being disloyal to their sex in any other flagrant way.

A few concluding observations may now be made on the indigenous system of administering law. First of all it is worthy of notice that, unlike the practice now followed in the Native Courts, persons who brought charges which they could not substantiate were not allowed to go scot-free. Thus, if a man of one local group accused a man of another of having stolen his sheep, and the case came up for trial before the *Ọha* of the two groups, it might be agreed that, if the accused were found guilty, he should be handed over to the other group to be sold, but that if he were found guiltless his accuser should be handed over to the opposite group. If the accuser were handed over and sold for, say, £10, the accused would receive £5 as compensation, the rest being divided among those who had taken a leading part in the settlement of the case.

Secondly, it should not be supposed that proceedings were always conducted in a dignified and formal manner. Although the elders of both groups might (after hearing the evidence) swear on their *ọfọ* that they would be impartial in their judgement and not favour their own man, the two sides frequently disagreed, and the meeting broke-up in an uproar, followed perhaps by a period of inter-group fighting. Or a decision of elders might be received by the general public with shouts of derision or screams of protest, and there the matter would end, without any form of settlement. Frequently, also, the proceedings were interrupted by members of the general public. Such interruptions might be dealt with by some capable elder. Or the holder of the senior *ọfọ* might rise in indignation and say that if any one interrupted again he would call on his *ọfọ* to kill that man. This would usually be nothing more than a threat, and in the case of further interruption the holder of the senior *ọfọ* would merely ask the interrupter to leave the meeting, or call on the head of his family to keep him quiet. In some cases, at the outset of the proceedings, the holder of the senior *ọfọ*, or any elder of superior standing, might say: 'If any one interrupts these proceedings then may Ọfọ kill him.' The *Ọha*

[1] See pp. 200 ff.

would then all strike the ground with their *ǫfǫ*, and this would usually ensure a reasonable amount of order throughout the hearing. It should be noted, however, that any person, whatever his status, was entitled to speak at a public meeting, provided he had first obtained permission from the elders of his group.

Sufficient has now been said to indicate the lines on which law and authority operated. It may be said generally that the administration of the law was not a matter of regular fixed courts which took cognizance of every class of case. It was an elastic system, and though the *Ǫba* played the principal part and were the final court of appeal, law was an affair of the whole community. The elders were regarded as the repository of custom and the mouthpiece of the ancestors and the gods, who were the ultimate legal sanction. But in most cases the elders were referees and mediators rather than prosecutors and judges, and their decisions were judicious rather than judicial. With the advent of the Government and the prohibition of many forms of barbarous procedure, the spread of Christianity and consequent weakening of the legal sanctions which were basically of a magico-religious order, the declining respect for elders, and the growth of individualism, it would be quite impossible, even if it were desired, to restore the old system of administering justice, in any recognizable form. Many of the conditions that called the former code into existence have now ceased to exist. Nevertheless, the restoration of the local group-councils, with a personnel modified to meet existing conditions, will once again make law the business of all, and thus enable the people to adjust their rules of behaviour to their changing environment. There will be more to be said on this subject, and on the general question of administrative policy, in the concluding chapter of the book.

XI

THE LAW OF MARRIAGE

Totemism.

TOTEMISM is the assertion of kinship between man and a species of animal, or of some other animate or inanimate thing. In its strict sense it has a dual character, being at once a form of social organization and a magico-religious practice. Society is divided into groups, each of which has a mystic relationship with some particular species or totem. Totemism, therefore, is not the same thing as the imputation of a sacred character to animals, which, though a wider principle in the religious sphere, constituting as it does the basis of all hunting magic and the propitiation of dangerous animals, has no necessary connexion with a group organization of society.

Among the Ibo there is no typical totemism, and the religious character of such 'totemic' beliefs as they hold overshadows the social. Nevertheless, as many of their social groups are in fact associated with some particular species of animal, and are also frequently exogamous, it may be as well to say something here about these beliefs, though the subject might have been more properly dealt with in the chapters relating to religion.

A certain species of animal may be sacred and taboo to an extended-family (which is invariably an exogamous unit), to a kindred (which, consisting as it does of two or more related extended-families, is usually but not always an exogamous unit), and to a village or village-group (which is not usually an exogamous unit). In some cases we may even find that a species of animal is respected throughout an entire district composed of numerous unrelated social groups, between whom there is free intermarriage.

Thus, at Lokpanta leopards are sacred to the kindreds known as Um-Ago, and Um-Ohe, and, if any member of these kindreds were to kill a leopard or eat its flesh, he would, it is believed, soon come to an untimely end. It is believed, also, that any member of these kindreds can turn into a leopard, and in this guise steal the goats of any one he dislikes. The very name of one of the kindreds, namely Um-Ago, means 'The children of leopards'. Each of these kindreds is an exogamous unit, but there appeared to be no prohibition against a man of the Um-Ago marrying a woman of the Um-Ohe. At Eha-

Amufu the members of the Um-Ezudu kindred regard leopards as their brothers, and for this reason they are known alternatively as Um-Ago. If any one of them were to kill a leopard accidentally, he would have to sacrifice a goat to the spirit known as Ekweesu.[1] If he were to come across the dead body of a leopard he would beat a hasty retreat, and if he were to enter a compound where the flesh of a leopard was being cooked he would seek to disinfect himself by picking up some dust and throwing it over his shoulders. The Um-Ezudu kindred is an exogamous unit.

At Ngbwidi the Umuche kindred, which is exogamous, has an association with leopards. The members of this kindred refrain from killing leopards, as leopards are their counterparts. If their farms suffer damage from the goats of strangers they will warn the owners of the goats that they, in the guise of leopards, will kill the goats, should any further damage be done. It is said that if a leopard is killed by a member of another kindred or village, and a man of the Umuche kindred believes that leopard to be his counterpart, he lies down on the ground as though he himself had been killed. A shroud is placed over his body and drummers are summoned. The music of the drums is said to cause the *obi* (or heart-soul) of the man to leave the body of the dead leopard and return to the man, who then becomes associated with another leopard. Were these rites not performed the man would die. Others stated that if the leopard were shot his human counterpart would vomit the bullet.

The whole population of the village-group of Mbala respect leopards, on the ground that leopards are the children of Ube, the protecting spirit of Mbala.[2] If a man were to shoot a leopard accidentally he would have to report the matter immediately to the priest of Ube, who would order the dead body to be brought to the grove of Ube and buried in a rectangular grave, just as though it were a human being. The man who had killed the leopard would then take a goat and a cock and hen to the priest, who, standing before the shrine of Ube, would speak as follows: 'Ube, this man comes to you as a suppliant. He did not kill your child by design. He did so by pure accident. He grieves for the death of your child. He has buried him and brought to you these gifts. Absolve him and pursue him not.' The

---

[1] See p. 39.

[2] In the commune of Obibi-Ezana leopards are, in one subdivision, sacred to Ala, and in former times if any one of the subdivision killed a leopard accidentally he had to buy a slave and consecrate him to the service of Ala.

priest would then kill the goat and chickens, but the suppliant would not be permitted to eat any of the flesh of the sacrificial animals. He would remain unshaven and unwashed for twelve days, just as though he were mourning a relative. He would live in seclusion and refrain from all farm-work. At the end of the twelve days he would be shaved, and would then go to a stream and wash. No Mbala man would knowingly enter the house of a man of another town where leopard's flesh was being eaten, and before eating in the house of any stranger he would ask his host to wash carefully all the dishes, if leopard's flesh had been eaten there recently. Mbala is not an exogamous unit.

It was stated that at one time the entire Isu-Ochi clan, of which Mbala is a member, respected the leopard, and that most of the constituent villages continue to do so. The taboo extends to a number of neighbouring villages which, though not classed as Isu-Ochi, contain Isu-Ochi elements. Thus at Qrọ, a village near Mbala and containing a number of Isu-Ochi families, there is a general belief that each inhabitant has a leopard counterpart, and that in former times every one had the power of turning into a leopard. If a man sees the dead body of a leopard he must report the matter to the priest of the family of Ile-Mbala, the name of a local spirit to whom the leopard is sacred. Dead leopards must be buried by the priest in the grove of the spirit. If a hunter were to shoot a leopard accidentally, he would have to bring the dead leopard to the priest for burial, together with a mat, cloth, eagle, parrot, and chicken. The dead leopard would be placed in a rectangular grave lying on the mat and cloth. The eagle and parrot would be placed on the leopard's body.[1] After the grave had been filled in, the hunter would be taken by the priest to the shrine of Ile-Mbala, where a chicken would be sacrificed and a petition offered for the hunter's forgiveness. The hunter's gun would become forfeit to the priest.

At Abo-Ogugu (Awgu Division) the kindred known as Um-Owo respects brown monkeys. They are an exogamous group of consanguineous relatives, and their name means 'The children of brown monkeys'. The people of the village-group of Awgunta (Awgu Division) also respect brown monkeys, and if any one finds the corpse of this species of monkey he must take it to the priest of Ala, who wraps

---

[1] Feathers of an eagle and parrot are sometimes stuck into the caps which are placed on the heads of dead members of the Qzọ society, prior to burial. See N. W. Thomas, *Some Ibo Burial Customs*, p. 172.

it in palm-leaves and places it in a branch of some tree of the grove of Ala. The finder has also to sacrifice to Ala through the priest, who, holding a fowl and squatting down before the symbol of Ala, says, 'Ala, this man found your child; he did not kill him. Here is the fowl with which he leads your child home to you.' He then cuts the chicken's throat, prepares and cooks the fowl, and deposits morsels of the flesh on the symbol of the deity. Awgunta is not an exogamous unit.

At Mmako the species of monkey known as *utobo* is sacred to the group known as Eziobodo, because the war 'medicine' of this group was prepared from this monkey. One extended-family of the group (the Umu-Ojota) is believed to have the power of turning into monkeys. A man of this family stated quite seriously that if he were in a hut with some people, and the door of the hut were blocked with a transparent curtain, the people inside the hut would suddenly miss him, and would then see, outside the door, a monkey which would turn into himself. He stated that many years ago two of his brothers who had been captured by some men of Nengwe succeeded in making their escape by turning themselves into monkeys.

In numerous communities the fish in the local river are sacred and taboo to every one. They are regarded as counterparts of the people, with each of whom a particular fish shares a soul.[1] There is a concomitant belief that the fish are the ancestors of the people. The taboo extends usually to all species of local fish, but at Okpanko it appears to be confined to the species known as *nkere*.

At Ama-Imo (Owerri Division) white snails are taboo to the family-group called Ndembara, because these snails are sacred to Amadi-Oha, the god of lightning. The taboo does not apply to the related family-groups of Umu-Dimuma, and Amobo, with whom the Ndembara are not permitted to intermarry. At Ubomiri, also, white snails are taboo to all members of the hamlet of Amoboro, and it was said that if any man of Amoboro ate a white snail his face would swell and his nose fall off. Amoboro is not an exogamous unit. At Orodo and Ifakala white snails are taboo to all, being regarded as sacred to Eze-Ala, the Earth-deity.

At Awgu the members of the small local-group known as Uhuenye respect civet-cats, ostensibly because these are sacred to the local Earth-deity. If a member of the group were to kill a civet-cat accidentally, he would have to go to some other town and capture two

[1] See p. 38.

civet-cats of opposite sex and take them to the priest of Ala, together with the necessary sacrificial offerings. The priest would beseech Ala to forgive the man for having killed his child, and to accept the two cats as a substitute. The man himself would add: 'Ala, the thing I did was done accidentally. Do not be angry with me. And I beg you that when I go hunting again you will not permit me to kill one of your children.' The priest, after pouring a libation and placing food-offerings on the symbol of Ala, would then allow the two civet-cats to run off into the grove of Ala.

The villagers of Ngbwidi and Mboo also respect civet-cats, and intermarriage between these two communes is taboo. There appears to be a kind of blood-brotherhood between Ngbwidi and Mboo, and it is said that in the past they never fought each other. If a member of one group drew blood from a member of the other he had to offer a tortoise, kid, and chicken to the Earth-deity of the other group. But within each group intermarriage is permitted between kindreds which are not close consanguineous relatives.

At Ogugu (Awgu Division) members of the Um-Anogwo extended-family avoid as food the flesh of civet-cats. But there is no taboo against killing civet-cats. Wives of members of the family may eat the flesh of civet-cats. But it is said that if a pregnant wife eats it and vomits she will bear a male child. The oil of the species of palm known as *ojuku* is also taboo as food to male members of this family. There is no taboo, however, against cutting down the trees or preparing and selling the oil. Wives of members of the kindred may use the oil as food, but it is said that, if a wife who is enceinte with a male child drinks the oil, sores will appear on her mouth. At Nengwe also the civet-cat is taboo as food to a number of kindreds, between whom marriage is permissible. At Itika there is a group (Amakoro) which respects civet-cats, badgers, and brown monkeys, and it is said that if any one killed one of these animals his teeth would drop out.

The most widely respected animal in the Awgu Division is the species of harmless snake known as *aka*.[1] These snakes are regarded as the children and messengers of Ala the Earth-deity. If a man were bitten by one he would immediately consult a diviner, who might either declare that Ala had caused the snake to bite him in order to save him from some danger, or on account of some offence which the man had committed and must atone for by sacrifice to Ala. If a man

---

[1] This snake is taboo to all at Ngbwidi, Ugueme, Mboo, Awgu, Okpanko, Abọ, Awgunta, Oduma, Obeago, and the entire Isu-Ochi clan.

were to kill an *aka* snake accidentally, he would (at Oduma) return home crying out that he had killed a child of Ala and would immediately consult a diviner to discover the reason for his misfortune. The diviner might declare that so great was the love of Ala for the man that she had given the life of one of her own children in order to draw the man to herself and save him from meeting sudden death.[1] The man in gratitude would offer sacrifice to Ala, asking her forgiveness and thanking her for her favour.

In most of the communities which respect the *aka* snake it is incumbent on any one who sees the dead body of this snake to summon the priest of Ala to his house. The priest, taking a gourd of palm-wine, into which he drops the fragments of a split kola, says, 'Mother Ala, please look on your son, who, by the wayside, met the dead body of one of your children. It was not he who was responsible for the death of your child; but you have made him responsible for the burial rites. He has brought these yams (32) and these pullets (2), in order that the rites may be suitably performed. Reward him with good, and protect his life and that of all the members of his household.' Having poured the libation on the ground, the priest accompanies the man to the spot where the body of the dead snake lies, and together they carry it to the grove of Ala and bury it in a rectangular grave. The priest then returns to the man's house and takes away the yams and chickens, which are, later in the day, sacrificed at the shrine of Ala.

At Ugueme, if a man kills an *aka* snake accidentally, the knife or stick with which he had killed it becomes forfeit to the priest of Ala. When the priest has performed the rites he mixes some of the sacrificial wine with dust, and rubs the mixture on the man's head, chest, and feet, saying, 'You have now settled with Ala, whose anger is no more upon you.' The man takes home some of the mixture and smears it on the various huts of his compound, saying, 'Ala, I have come into agreement with you. Do not allow such a misfortune to overtake me again.' At Okpanko, when an *aka* snake is buried, a mat is laid in the grove and covered with a cloth. The snake is then laid, belly upwards, on the cloth, which is rolled over the snake's body. After burying the snake the man who had killed it bursts into tears and shaves his head.

At Ngbwidi and in a number of other communes[2] respect is shown

---

[1] In former times if warriors set out to raid a neighbouring town and met an *aka* snake on the road, they regarded that as a warning from Ala and immediately returned home.   [2] e.g. Ezere, Awgunta, Nkwe.

to a harmless river snake known as *osugwo*. It is said that if this snake comes out of the river it is a sign of the sickness of some old man. If the snake meets any person and returns to the river the old man will recover. But if it insists on passing the person the old man will die. This belief is parallel with that held by the people of Tilla in the Northern Provinces, who regard the crocodiles in Tilla lake as their spiritual counterparts. When any one at Tilla is about to die his crocodile-counterpart leaves the lake and crawls to its last resting-place.[1]

Pythons are respected by the Enugu-Aka group at Ache, and by the Oboovia group at Awgu, and if a python is accidentally killed it is formally buried by the priest of Ala. A chicken is sacrificed and laid on the top of the grave. Gunpowder is laid beside the grave and is then fired, in imitation of the firing of guns in the final funeral rites for human beings.

There are numerous other animal and plant taboos, such as the *obu*[2] and *asha*[3] birds, rams,[4] hares,[5] water-tortoises,[6] *ube*-pears,[7] and cassava. It is noteworthy that cassava is sometimes taboo as food to members of the Ọzọ society, and this probably accounts for the fact that in some kindreds cassava may be eaten by females but not by males.

In some cases no explanation could be given of the origin of the various taboos, but in others it was stated that the founder of the family, having fallen sick after eating the animal, forbade his descendants to eat it. In most cases the taboo animal was associated with some cult, particularly that of Ala, the Earth-deity. When cults or 'medicines' are obtained, certain taboos are usually obtained with them. They apply primarily to the priest, but may become extended to the priest's family, and in some cases to the whole local-group, if the priest's cult is an important public cult. There is no obvious connexion, therefore, between the 'totemism' of the kindred and its exogamy, and relationship between kindreds cannot be postulated on grounds of sharing a common animal emblem. On the other hand, it is quite possible that many family-groups originally adopted some

[1] See *Tribal Studies in Northern Nigeria*, vol. i, p. 167.
[2] Sacred to the Egbada group at Ubomiri.
[3]   ,,   ,,   Umu-Eze group at Uzu-Aba.
[4]   ,,   ,,   Ogbuabom group at Obeago.
[5]   ,,   ,,   Um-Aro kindred at Lokpanta.
[6]   ,,   ,,   Um-Akuma kindred at Oduma.
[7]   ,,   ,,   Ngorodo kindred at Amowere.

animal as a family emblem and a means of emphasizing brotherhood. Thus, like the rule of exogamy, and often in conjunction with it, the association with an animal species has been a unifying force within the kinship group. But at the present time the younger people are inclined to regard the old taboos lightly, and Christian converts sometimes show their contempt by deliberately breaking them. But others continue to observe an outward respect, lest any illness or misfortune that might assail them should be ascribed to their own wanton behaviour.

Endogamy and Exogamy.

Endogamy, or the rule which prohibits a person from marrying outside his own social group, exists only in one form, namely, that the class of slaves known as *osu*, that is, slaves dedicated to the gods, together with their descendants, must intermarry among themselves. This rule appears to be due to the belief that it is dangerous to have anything to do with things or persons belonging to the gods, as these become charged with a dynamism which is liable to kill any one who is not insulated. There is the further idea that the gods are jealous of their property. It is even taboo for any male who is not a member of this caste to have sexual relations with any female of the caste, and in some towns any man breaking this rule was, in former times, put to death. .

Exogamy, or the rule prohibiting the marriage of an individual to any person belonging to the same social or local group as himself, is in some degree or other almost universal throughout Iboland. Except in a few localities marriage with close consanguineous relatives is totally taboo. Hence the social group described as an extended-family is almost invariably an exogamous unit, and in many cases the rule of exogamy applies also to the larger group which we have called a kindred. In some cases it may extend to a hamlet or village composed of unrelated kindreds; and occasionally an entire village-group or commune may be found to be exogamous.

A few instances will illustrate these variations. One of the six subdivisions of the village-group of Ukehe is known as Ekwete. Ekwete in turn consists of four local groups, one of which is called Emeze. Emeze comprises seven small extended-families, with a total population of 93. Of these seven families two form one kindred and the remaining five form another kindred. Each of these kindreds is an exogamous unit. At Ibite the average number in the exogamous unit was found to be 84, and at Ọjọ the exogamous unit varied in size from one of 17 persons to one of 137. At Eha-Alumona one of the villages showed exogamous groups varying from a small family of 5 to a large kindred of 372. At Unadu the community consists of two divisions, one of which is known as Ohomo. Ohomo comprises four kindreds, viz. Okele (153 persons), Nwata (97), Agada (55), and Oyijewo (76). The first three of these are believed to be related to one another, and they are known jointly as the Um-Aba. Intermarriage is not allowed between the first two kindreds, but is permissible between either of the first two kindreds and the third. The reason given for this differentiation is that, whereas the founders of the first two kindreds were full-brothers, the founder of the third was only a half-brother. At Erọ there was an interesting example of local exogamy. Three kindreds occupying a common area were found to constitute a single exogamous unit. It was stated that the kindreds were not related and used to intermarry, but gave up the practice owing to repeated epidemics, which they regarded as an intimation that intermarriage with close neighbours was displeasing to the gods. *Per contra*, at the neighbouring village of Asaba,[1] one of the local-groups contains three kindreds which are now allowed to intermarry, but formerly were not. It was stated that, as the local-group increased in numbers, the elders decided to allow intermarriage between the three kindreds composing it, a goat being sacrificed to secure the permission of the ancestors. These examples are an illustration of the dynamic nature of social institutions.

In the Awgu Division a small local-group at Isu was found to comprise four extended-families containing 11, 14, 15, and 25 persons respectively. Each of these was exogamous, but there was no bar to intermarriage between the families. On the other hand, a group at Owele, consisting of six extended-families with a total population of over 700 persons, constituted a single exogamous unit. They claimed to be descendants of a common forefather and called themselves the Umunna (kindred of) Eworaga. In a group so large it is quite impossible to prove by genealogies that there is any relationship between the constituent extended-families, and so the Umunna Eworaga can be described as a 'clan'. In the village-group of Mbala one of the villages (Umbwelu) consists of four extended-families, all of which are believed to be descended from a common forefather. The first

---

[1] An Igala village.

two families may not intermarry, but either may intermarry with the third and fourth, and the third may intermarry with the fourth. It was said that numbers one and two had a common mother as well as a common father, whereas numbers three and four were descendants by different wives. This mode of stating a sense of relationship need not be accepted at its face value.

Sometimes cases occur in which the members of an extended-family in one local group may not marry members of an extended-family in another local group, on the ground that both families had a common ancestor. Thus at Lokpa-Uku the Amankela family of Amuburi village may not intermarry with the Amebo of Uru village, and the Amachioha family of Uru may not intermarry with the Amachioha family of Amuburi.

In the Awgu Division there are three village-groups, viz.—Ache, Inyi, and Awlaw, in which, though marriages are normally contracted with persons belonging to different social groups, there is no strict rule against consanguineous marriages, marriage between relatives as close as first cousins being permissible. Instances were even obtained at Ache of a man marrying his sister's daughter.

At Inyi instances were obtained of marriage between (a) a man and the daughter of the brother of his paternal grandfather, (b) a man and his sister's daughter, (c) a man and the daughter of his father's brother's daughter, (d) a man and the daughter of his father's sister. The commonest form of cousin marriage practised at Ache, Inyi, and Awlaw is the cross-cousin marriage, i.e. marriage with the daughter of the father's sister or mother's brother; and it is worth noting that this form of marriage does not involve any breach of the rule of kindred exogamy as the parties to the marriage belong to different kindreds. Marriage with parallel cousins seemed to be quite exceptional and was, in some of the villages of these groups, regarded with definite disfavour. Moreover, it was stated at Inyi that, though a man might marry his sister's daughter, he could not marry his brother's daughter. This is in accordance with the normal rule of kindred exogamy. At Ache the following reason was given for marriage between a man and his sister's daughter. It is common for a man to claim the female child of his sister in lieu of a part or the whole of a bride-price. He can use her as he likes. He may marry her himself, or give her in marriage to his son, or he may keep her in his house, allowing her to have lovers and claiming any children she may bear. It is even not uncommon at Ache and Inyi for a man to discourage his daughter from marrying, in order that she may bear children promiscuously, which her father adopts as his own.

It was stated that the custom of consanguineous marriages at Ache, Inyi, and Awlaw was not due to any recent foreign influence but had been practised from time immemorial. But this seems improbable in view of the fact that groups of Aro, who practise some forms of consanguineous marriage, have settled in this locality. Moreover, it is customary, when such marriages are contracted, for the parties to undergo a rite known as *Inriba.* They, with their parents, go to the house of the head of their kindred, who kills a chicken, which is then cooked. Each party to the marriage places a piece of the chicken's flesh in the palm of the hand. They then place their hands together and each eats from the hand of the other. It is clear that this custom is intended to negative the supernatural dangers to which the parties to consanguineous marriages are ordinarily exposed.

It is hardly necessary to state that the above marriage-customs of the peoples of Ache, Inyi, and Awlaw are regarded as abominable by most other Ibo communities of the Awgu Division, who say that the people of these groups respect neither gods nor men. It is interesting, however, to observe that even at Ache and Inyi many parents refuse to sanction consanguineous marriages, because they tend to disrupt the kindred or extended-family every time the husband and wife have a quarrel. It was remarked also that in such marriages a husband could not thrash his wife when necessary, as he would be thrashing his own 'sister'!

In the Owerri Division exogamy is the normal rule. Thus, to give some examples, the village-group of Ama-Imo consists of two divisions, viz. Obodo and Umuri. Obodo contains five local groups, viz. (1) Amuzo, (2) Umu-Eze, (3) Umu-Ọfọ, (4) Umu-Shie, and (5) Umu-Lọlo. Of these each of the first four constitutes an exogamous unit. Umu-Lọlo comprises the following extended-families: Umu-Eze-Alambra, Umu-Ochameze, Umu-Eze-Alodu, Ndembara, Umu-Di-muma, and Amobo. Of these the first two and last four constitute exogamous units. It was stated that formerly Umu-Lọlo formed a single exogamous unit, but, having become populous, it split into two groups between which marriage became permissible. The Umuri subdivision of Ama-Imo consists of Umu-Ebo, Ndọhia, Umukwu, Umuwọdu, Ndururu, Amukwa, Umumboke, and Umunkpe. Of these the first six and last two constitute exogamous units.

One of the divisions of the village-group of Mbieri is known as

Amike. This division contains eleven subdivisions, one of which is known as Awo. Awo comprises the following family groups:

1. Umu-Dafo   (population about 190 persons).
2. Umu-Dimobia (,,   ,,   110   ,,   ).
3. Umu-Okperede (,,   ,,   100   ,,   ).
4. Umu-Abo   (,,   ,,   120   ,,   ).
5. Umu-Orioji   (,,   ,,   20   ,,   ).
6. Amudam   (,,   ,,   115   ,,   ).
7. Obiruhu   (,,   ,,   210   ,,   ).
8. Umu-Duregwu (,,   ,,   270   ,,   ).
9. Obilubi   (,,   ,,   180   ,,   ).

Of these the first five (comprising about 540 persons) constitute a single exogamous division. But any of the five may intermarry with any of the remaining four. As final examples we may take the village-groups of Okolochi and Owerri. The former is wholly exogamous, and so is the latter, with the exception of two small kindreds who are recent immigrants. At Owerri, therefore, the rule of exogamy covers a group of over 1,500 people.

If an Ibo were asked to give an explanation of his custom of exogamy, he would be unable to say anything more than that it was immemorial practice. But from the evidence cited it is clear that exogamy is practised because marriage within the group is liable to introduce disharmony. Quarrels between husbands and wives who are relatives or belong to the same group lead inevitably to the taking of sides within the group. And if the marriage is a failure and has to be dissolved, a state of tension is caused when the bride-price is reclaimed from one's own kith and kin. Exogamy, therefore, operating as it does in the interests of unity and brotherhood, is an ally of law and authority. And the study of the subject is not one of mere academic interest, but is of considerable importance from the administrative point of view. For exogamy is a test of the continuance of kinship or 'family' solidarity, and the exogamous unit can thus be used as a basic administrative unit. If two or three extended-families of the same kindred have begun to intermarry, it is a sure sign that the kindred solidarity has been broken down and that each extended-family has become an independent unit and must be treated as such. But if a number of extended-families composing a kindred are still united by the bond of exogamy it will be found that they are united also in numerous other ways and can usually be treated as a single entity.

As regards the penalties for breaches of the law of exogamy it may be said generally that in bygone days deliberate infringement of the law was almost unknown, as a man and woman who might otherwise be attracted to each other would, if they belonged to the same exogamous unit, regard their union as repulsive or at any rate as fraught with certain disaster both for themselves and for all other members of their group. Moreover, as marriage is a matter of long drawn-out arrangement, not merely between the two individuals primarily concerned, but also between the respective families, it would be impossible for a marriage which was regarded as incestuous to be celebrated in a legitimate manner. It might be possible for two distantly related people to contract a marriage without being aware that their marriage was unlawful, but in this case, when the facts became known, the marriage would either be dissolved or legalized by means of a sacrifice to the ancestors. In some communities the rule of exogamy may, as we have seen, become relaxed, so that what was before a single exogamous unit may, by general consent, become split into intermarrying moieties. In others, again, it may become so relaxed that marriage with close relations may become permissible. But even in such a case the parties will usually observe the precaution of obtaining, by sacrifice, the sanction of the ancestors, and so also of their fellow citizens. In recent times young Christians have occasionally married in defiance of the rule of exogamy and thereby caused disquiet among their pagan relatives and friends. But such marriages are now discouraged by the Missionary societies as well as by the Government. Parties applying to be married under the Marriage Ordinance are now required to show that their marriage would not be incestuous according to native law.

It remains to add that the rule of exogamy applies not merely to patrilineal relatives, but also to matrilineal. But the taboo against intermarriage with matrilineal relatives is not usually carried beyond the third or fourth generation. It is to be observed also that sexual intercourse is not permitted between men and women of the same exogamous group, and it is taboo also for any but their own husbands to have sexual relations with stranger women who have joined the group. A breach of this rule may be punished by a fine or even expulsion from the group. In any case it would be necessary for the delinquent male to provide a goat to be sacrificed to Ala or the ancestors. Some further remarks on this subject have already been made in the section dealing with incest and other sexual offences.[1]

[1] See p. 223.

Types of Marriage.

The normal system of contracting a marriage among the Ibo is by means of a bride-price. Exchange marriage in the strict sense of the term does not exist as a regular social institution, except in a few communities, such as Enugu-Ezeke, where it has been introduced by groups of the Okpoto tribe. But, elsewhere, loose forms of exchange-marriage may be practised sporadically. Thus two men may agree to exchange their sisters (or cousins or daughters) as brides; though, when this is done, it is usual also to exchange some small amount of material property, in order to formalize the marriage, as it is felt that if gifts or money are not also exchanged the relationship set up would be one of concubinage rather than of marriage. Isolated cases also occur in which two men agree to exchange their wives (with the wives' consent), the difference in the amount of the bride-price being adjusted. And formerly it was not uncommon for a female slave to be given in lieu of a bride-price, though, if it were intended that the slave should have the full status of a free wife, a small sum of money was paid over on her account, to provide the banquet which would serve as evidence that the transaction had been in fact a marriage.

In the Enugu-Ezeke district marriage by exchange coexists with a bride-price system. It is usually arranged by a boy's father when the boy has reached the age of puberty, but it may be arranged earlier if the boy's father has a female child which can be used as an exchange. But, if a baby girl is given as an exchange for a grown-up woman, an additional gift of from one to two hundred currency rods is demanded. If the father has no daughters he may use a brother's daughter, but he would in such a case have to compensate the brother by a cash payment equal to a bride-price receivable for a daughter born subsequently. A man may use a sister as an exchange either on his own behalf or on that of a son. If there are several brothers, and only one sister, the eldest full-brother is the one entitled to use the sister as an exchange.

After the exchange has been arranged the young man is required, during the years preceding the formal conclusion of the marriage, to give periodic gifts of yams and palm-wine to the mother of his fiancée, in order that she may offer sacrifice to her *chi*. He also presents gifts at the annual festival known as *Ongwenu*, and fires off guns in the compound of his future parents-in-law, in order to advertise himself as a person of some consequence. He is expected to assist his parents-in-law in farm work, in gathering palm-nuts, and in repairing their houses. During these years the girl is at liberty to cancel the engagement, and if this is done the lad receives no compensation for his gifts and his various services. He may demand the return of his exchange 'sister' if he discovers that the engagement had been annulled at the instance of the girl's parents and not of the girl herself, but otherwise he is content to accept a bride-price on her account—the amount received by the girl's parents from the suitor who has displaced himself.

If the engagement has not been annulled, the lad may, at Enugu-Ezeke, demand his bride as soon as her breasts have begun to develop (i.e. a year or so before puberty). But at Ete[1] a bride cannot be claimed until after her first menstruation. The lad makes his request to the girl's father, to whom he gives a gift of a pot of palm-wine and two rods. The father refers the lad to the girl's mother, who is given a similar gift. Gifts must also be given to the senior members of the girl's kindred, to her father's sisters, her mother's sisters and mother's brothers. The girl's brothers are given three rods each; but the brother who is going to marry the bridegroom's sister receives one rod only. A special gift of ten rods is given to the bride's sister, who has the duty of assisting the bride's mother in preparing the bride's outfit. A series of feasts, provided by the boy and his parents, follow. One is given to the girl's parents, a second to the girl's father and paternal relatives, and a third to the girl's mother and maternal relatives. A day is then fixed for the bride to proceed to the bridegroom's house. She goes accompanied by her mother, various relatives, and a girl-friend, who acts as a companion to the bride for the first month of her married life. They arrive with numerous gifts and utensils, pots, plates, baskets, thread, cloth, salt, millstones, yams, a goat, a fowl, forty rods, and sometimes a cat to keep rats out of the bride's hut. All the visitors are entertained to a feast and then return home, leaving the bride and her companion. A few days later the young husband buys a pot to serve as the symbol of his wife's *chi*. He places it beside the symbol of his own *chi* and offers sacrifice with the prayer that the *chi* of both of them may protect them, help them to obtain children, protect their goats, pigs, and fowls and assist the young wife in her trading.

Marriage by exchange can be dissolved by mutual agreement, i.e. each husband reclaims his exchange-sister. But one pair only may

---

[1] Ete is an Okpoto village close to Enugu-Ezeke.

wish to dissolve their union, and in this case the husband does not reclaim his exchange-sister but receives compensation equal to the amount of a bride-price. There are no rules (as in some tribes) by which the more fruitful couple have to hand over children to the less fruitful.

Turning now to the general mode of marriage, namely, by means of a bride-price, it is hardly necessary to remind readers that this well-established term[1] does not imply that a wife is purchased from her parents and becomes a mere chattel of her husband. The main purpose of a bride-price is to regularize and give permanence to the union of a man and woman, and so to distinguish marriage and the foundation of a family from a mere paramour relationship and the promiscuous begetting and bearing of children. Among the patrilineal Ibo it guarantees that the husband shall have the custody of any children born; for in the absence of a bride-price a woman's children are claimed by her family. And it guarantees also that a husband shall have the continuous services of a wife for himself and of a mother for his children; and that a wife and her offspring shall be provided with a permanent home, and supported and protected by her husband. As for the moneys paid over as a bride-price, a large proportion of the share received by the bride's mother is expended in providing her daughter with yams and household utensils, while that received by the father is usually expended in providing a wife for his son. So that what is received on the swings is spent on the roundabouts! It is clear, therefore, that marriage by bride-price is far from being a mere mercenary transaction. The cash received is speedily spent in fulfilling numerous duties. If, therefore, the marriage proves a failure, and the bride-price has to be refunded, the wife's family may be seriously embarrassed.[2] The bride-price accordingly acts as a stabilizing influence by constraining the wife's relatives to use all their influence to promote good relations between her and her husband. It prevents wives from leaving their husbands for some trivial cause.

One of the commonest charges brought against the bride-price

---

[1] I use the term 'bride-price' rather than the new-fangled expression 'bride-wealth', because 'bride-price' suggests a fixed customary sum, whereas 'bride-wealth' is a vague term which may easily be confused with the property of the bride or her 'dowry'. The Ibo term for bride-price is *ako nwanyi* or 'wife-money'.

[2] Unless, of course, the wife speedily finds a new husband, who will refund the bride-price to the former husband.

system in Iboland is that it allows a husband to commit adultery, but penalizes a wife; and if the marriage is dissolved the wife loses custody of the children, even though she may have done no wrong. But these defects are not due to the bride-price system as such, but to the unfair method followed in Iboland of applying it solely or mainly in the interests of the husband. To this, reference will be made later, and it need only be added here that the modern view of marriage as a contract between two free and equal individuals is being widely adopted among Christian converts. The mass of the people, however, still consider that a wife for whom nothing has been paid is worth nothing, and, indeed, hardly deserves to be called a wife.

Some description may now be given of the ceremonial observed in arranging a marriage under the bride-price system. But as procedure varies in different localities and cannot be generalized, I propose to give an account of the custom followed at (a) Mboo (Awgu Division), and (b) Owerri. At Mboo, if the father of a boy is fairly well-off, he takes early steps to secure a wife for his son.[1] On hearing that the wife of a friend or acquaintance has borne a female child he goes to his friend with a pot of wine and asks that the latter's daughter may be betrothed to his son. The father of the girl, before giving his consent, would first consult his wife and the members of his extended-family. His wife may object, because she dislikes the boy or his mother or father; or the head of the family may object because the suitor's family is too nearly related to his own, or is considered socially inferior, or bears a bad reputation, or at one time or other had incurred their enmity. If there are no obvious grounds for objection, the father and mother of the girl may consult a diviner in order to assure themselves that all will be well, and if a favourable reply is received the subsequent visit of the boy's father is greeted in a friendly manner, and the father of the girl, or his elder brother, pours a libation of palm-wine at the threshold of the compound, asking the ancestors to protect the girl and the boy, to avert anything that would prevent the marriage, to enable the boy's father to make the necessary payments, and to render the marriage fruitful and a blessing to all

---

[1] Fathers commonly use the bride-price obtained for daughters in providing first wives for sons, or younger brothers. Or brothers may use the bride-price obtained for sisters. But in order to obtain a second wife most youths have to rely on their own economic efforts, such as extra farm labour, working palms or herding goats for others (receiving the offspring as payment).

concerned. All then drink palm-wine together. The wine for this rite, which constitutes a formal betrothal and precludes the acceptance of any other suitor, is provided by the boy's father, who on his departure leaves the pot behind. On the following day the pot is brought to him by the girl's mother and other women of the girl's family, who thank him for his gift. The gift of wine may be accompanied by a gift of a few yams, and the boy's father may throw a cowry into the girl's drinking-water as an earnest of the bride-price which he intends to pay on his son's behalf.

Some ten days later the above rite is repeated in the presence of all the members of the girl's kindred. On this occasion the father of the boy presents a gift of seven pots of palm-wine. The mother of the girl, holding her baby daughter, kneels on the ground facing the threshold, while the head of the kindred makes a prayer and pours a libation in the manner already described. But he reserves some of the wine, and hands it to the most powerful young man present to drink, the young man being the symbol of the vigour that leads to fatherhood. Another cup is filled and given to the mother of the girl, who sips some of the wine and makes her baby daughter sip some also. She then hands the cup to the boy, who empties it, if he is old enough to do so; otherwise he hands the remainder to his father. This rite is regarded as creating a sacred bond between the boy and girl. If any one were subsequently caught making advances to the girl he would, in former times, have been liable to a fine of one cow.

A few days later the father of the boy again visits the father of the girl, and, after they have drunk wine together, the former invites the latter to come with the elders of his kindred to his house in eight days' time, in order to settle the amount of the bride-price. On taking his departure he hands a sum of 10s. to the girl's father to be distributed among the elders of his kindred, with a view to securing their good will. At the subsequent meeting, after food and drink have been served to the guests, the father of the boy inquires of the girl's father the amount of bride-price expected. The girl's father may say 'Twelve cows'. Both then shake hands, not as a sign of final agreement but as an expression of hope that they will come to an agreement. The father of the boy will then state that his means only allow him to offer four cows. The girl's father may say that he is prepared to accept eight, but the boy's father would reply that seven are the limit of his capacity. At this the senior men present will say: 'Enough of this, as you are going to be "in-laws" to one another. Seven cows is the amount of the bride-price.'[1]

A wooden dish containing oil and salt is then brought, together with a fried bush-rat. The senior elder in the boy's kindred cuts the rat in two and gives half to the senior elder of the girl's kindred. The latter addresses the former, saying: 'Here is my daughter. You must look after her well. If you ill-treat her, I will take her away and refund your bride-price.' The head of the boy's kindred replies: 'We thank you. What you have said is fair. If you take away the girl for no reason you must refund all our payments.' The head of the boy's kindred then dips his piece of rat's flesh in the salt and oil, and places it in the mouth of the head of the girl's kindred, saying, 'A thing that contains oil and salt is a preventive against quarrelling.' The head of the girl's kindred does likewise.

The father of the boy now hands £10, or brass rods valued at the price of two cows, to the father of the girl. The head of the girl's kindred is given brass rods valued at £3, for distribution among the various households of his kindred. The girl's mother receives rods valued at £3. The father's sister receives seven rods, the mother's father twenty rods, the girl's maternal uncle seven, and her father's maternal uncle ten. When these payments have been made, the boy's father kills a goat and hands the flesh to the girl's father, together with a pot of palm-wine. The guests then depart, and on reaching home regale themselves on the goat's flesh and wine.

When the girl has reached the age of five or six, she is brought by her mother to the boy's home and left there for a period of eight days. She is accompanied by a girl friend, and at night sleeps in the hut of the boy's mother. At the end of eight days she and her friend are escorted home by the boy's mother, and the parents of the girl's friend are given gifts of food for the latter's services. If the girl's friend is herself betrothed the gifts of food are sent to the parents of

[1] In some communities (e.g. at Awgu, Mbala, &c.) there may be no fixed bride-price and it is considered indecent to haggle about the amount of the bride-price. Some families are able to pay a higher bride-price than others. A youth may even, after a small payment of 10s. or so, obtain the consent of the girl's parents that the girl shall live with him for a period of two months as a form of trial marriage. If they find that they suit each other he may retain the girl as his wife, after making such payments to her father as he is able. If he has no means at all he may be allowed to retain her, provided he assists his parents-in-law in agricultural and other work, and undertakes to make payments as his means permit. It is to be noted that the bride-price is frequently payable to the girl's full-brother.

her fiancé. The girl, having become accustomed to her fiancé's home, visits it regularly. Sexual relations are not permitted before the age of puberty.[1] But after the girl's first menstruation the lad sends to her mother a gift of forty brass rods, four yards of cloth, a lump of camwood, and one leg of meat. Four brass rods, two 'heads' of tobacco, and a lump of natron are sent to her father. After receiving these gifts the girl's mother plants a coco-yam farm for her daughter near her husband's home, and when this is done the boy must pay up any balance of the bride-price which may be due. The girl's mother also purchases the domestic utensils required by the young wife. Her father presents her with a goat and a number of yams. All proceed with these gifts to the girl's new home. On arrival they are heartily thanked for the gifts given. There are no further formalities as a rule, but at Awgu it is sometimes customary to summon a man and woman who are considered to be lucky people to build a hearth in the home of the young people. The man takes a dried fish, splits it, places it on the new hearth and hands a piece of it to the young husband, who gives it to his wife to eat. He hands a piece also to the wife, who gives it to her husband. The woman who is considered lucky follows suit.

In some groups (e.g. Awgu, Ugueme, Ache), it is customary for girls to go into retirement for a period of some weeks or even months before taking up formal residence with their husbands. During this period they abstain from all forms of physical work and are given an abundance of food, with the intention of fattening them. They smear themselves with camwood three times daily and bathe before each anointment. At the end of the period a feast is held, if the parents have sufficient means. The girls appear publicly in the market-place and are greeted by all their friends, amid the firing of guns.[2] This practice is apparently a puberty rite, as it follows immediately on or soon after the first menstruation. With it may be associated the cicatrization of the abdomen, the excision of the clitoris, and the chipping and filing of teeth. Similar customs are followed by the Isu of Owerri Division, among whom brides are given in marriage at a fixed time of the year, soon after the planting of the yams—no doubt with a fertility purpose.

---

[1] But in some localities (e.g. Ache) sexual relations prior to puberty are permissible.

[2] Puberty rites of similar character are practised in the most distant parts of the Northern Provinces, e.g. among the Margi of Adamawa Province. See my *Tribal Studies*, vol. i, p. 230.

It is to be observed, however, that at the present time there is, as a result of the spread of Christian teaching, a growing tendency to abandon these puberty rites, and marriage customs are being modified by the fact that marriage in Church now confers considerable social prestige. In some groups, indeed, it even seemed that the Christian form of marriage in a Church had almost become the equivalent of taking a title. A woman so married is entitled to be addressed as 'Missis' (Mrs.), and the ceremony of being married in Church is described as *chi missis*, just as the ceremony of taking a title is described as *chi ọzọ*. A man whose wife had not been married in Church would not be allowed to speak at a marriage feast, just as a non-titled man would not be allowed to speak at an *ọzọ* feast. It appeared, moreover, that in some Christian centres, such as Onitsha, European frocks were formerly confined to women who had been married in Church, and if a woman donned a European frock without having been married in Church she would have been regarded as assuming a title to which she had no right. The Church in fact has, in many areas, begun to take the place of societies and clubs.

At Owerri the ceremonial for arranging a marriage is something like the following. A girl may be betrothed at an early age, in some cases even at birth. But the usual age is about seven or eight. If she is a mere baby the first step towards betrothal is a gift, by the boy's father or mother, of a ball of white clay to the girl's mother, who rubs the child with it periodically. The boy's father strengthens his claim soon afterwards by a gift of palm-wine to the mother (who shares it with the father), and by frequent visits, on some of which he brings gifts of beads for the girl.

About the age of seven the girl pays a formal visit to the boy's home, staying with the boy's mother for three or four nights. The object of this visit is twofold: (*a*) that the girl may become used to her future husband's home, and (*b*) that she may be seen and approved by the members of the boy's family. At the end of the visit she is escorted home by some of the boy's relatives, and before going asks her suitor when she may expect to see him again. He may reply 'Soon'; and if he fails to appear shortly afterwards it is a sign that he or his parents no longer wish to proceed with the match. It is usual also to present the girl at the end of the visit with a calabash of wine to give to her parents, and the neglect of this courtesy is regarded as an intimation that the engagement is 'off'.[1]

---

[1] At Amakọfia the girl must bring back the calabash personally, after a day or two.

Thereafter, the girl pays occasional visits to the boy's home. When she reaches the age of nine or ten, her parents may express a wish that the question of the bride-price should be discussed. This would indicate their final approval of the match, and the lad's father, accompanied by elders of his family, would come to the girl's home with seven jars of wine, two legs of goat-flesh, cowries to the value of 2s., one 'head' of tobacco, four kola-nuts, a piece of potash, and an additional sum of cowries now valued at 2d. The cowries valued at 2d. are known as 'the fee for the covering and uncovering of the wine'. For, before the wine is served to the guests, among whom are the elders and younger age-grades of the girl's local-group, the senior elder of the girl's extended-family goes out and picks some *ururu* leaves, which he places over one of the calabashes of wine, saying, 'We are drinking this wine to-day in order that our daughter may live in peace with her husband.' For this service he receives half the cowries (i.e. 1d.). He then uncovers the calabash, saying, 'May they live long and have many children', and receives the remaining half of the cowries. The elders of the local group appropriate four of the jars of wine, giving the remaining three to the younger men. They also take the tobacco, potash, kolas, cowries, and one leg of goat's flesh, the remaining leg being given to the young men.

After regaling themselves with wine the elders on both sides proceed to discuss, or rather argue out, the question of the bride-price. This may be a mere formality, for the parents of both parties may have come to a private agreement beforehand. The preliminary figure demanded by the elders of the girl's group is always considerably in excess of the amount expected, and that offered by the elders of the boy's group is always considerably less. The bride-price is, or was in the olden days, fairly well standardized, though it might be modified according to the good looks of the girl and the means of the boy's parents. Among the Isu the amount of the bride-price in former times was generally about 240,000 cowries payable to the girl's father, and 60,000 to her mother;[1] while at the present time it ranges from £16–£23 payable to the father, and £3–£6 payable to the mother. Among the Oratta the rates were, and are still, rather lower.

If the calabash is brought back by one of the girl's relatives, it is a sign that the girl and her parents wish to terminate the engagement.

[1] At Akwakuma it was stated that the mother's share was only 15,600. In 1931 the exchange value of cowries was 1,200 for one shilling.

The bride-price may be fixed there and then, or the matter may be left until a further meeting of elders is held at the home of the boy's parents. After agreement has been reached the girl's father rises and says, 'Let us leave the matter so, and go and take the customary oath'. The boy's father then conducts the girl's father to a shrine, where an elder of the girl's family takes one of the cultus-emblems and waves it round the head of the boy's father or guardian, or of the boy himself, saying, 'You hereby bind yourself to refrain from injuring us or bringing a false charge against us, should we give our daughter to another, because of your failure to pay the bride-price. Furthermore, you undertake to refrain from appropriating either directly or through an agent anything we may bestow upon our daughter.' The boy's father or guardian then takes the cultus-emblem and, waving it round the head of the girl's father, says, 'And you hereby bind yourself to refrain from seeking to injure us and refusing to refund the bride-price in the event of the marriage being dissolved.' A middleman, a friend or relative of both parties, is present at these proceedings, and he must be present when the bride-price is paid (wholly or in part), as he would be the principal witness at any subsequent dispute. In return for his services he receives from the husband (or his father) a commission of 1*s*. in each £1 paid. These proceedings may refer only to the bride-price payable to the girl's father, that payable to her mother being discussed by the mothers of the two parties in the presence of two or three other women (and possibly also of the respective fathers). For in many cases the amount payable to the girl's mother is paid by the boy's mother and not by his father.

After the settlement of the bride-price the girl (who may now be anything from ten to thirteen years of age) spends more time in her fiancé's home than in her own. She sleeps in his hut. But sexual relations should not occur until formal permission is given by the girl's mother; and permission would not be given unless a substantial part of the bride-price had been paid and the girl had begun to menstruate.[1] When permission for sexual relations has been given the fiancé (who is now virtually a husband) is expected to give gifts to the mother and daughter.[2]

---

[1] If menstruation is unduly delayed permission may be given in order to induce menstruation.

[2] The mother is given a cloth, leg of meat, ball of camwood, and some cowries (the whole valued at £1). The daughter receives a leg of meat, a ball of camwood, and 10*s*.

He is also expected to take steps to provide his wife, who may now be about fifteen years old, with a separate hut of her own. This is done with the object of giving her a definite status as a wife and preventing quarrels between her and her mother-in-law, whose hut she had previously shared during the day-time. At this time also the husband, or his mother, pays over to his wife's mother her share of the bride-price, at the same time calling on her to provide her daughter with a supply of seed-yams, which he plants (with his wife's assistance). Before these yams are harvested he again calls on his mother-in-law to provide her daughter with household utensils (pots, mortar, calabash and metal spoons, stools, kitchen-knife, plates, baskets, &c.). These are brought by the mother-in-law, accompanied by some female friends, and all are entertained to a banquet prepared by the young wife, whose parents may add a chicken and goat to the other gifts. The father may provide her with a pot and doors for her house. The girl has now attained the full status of a wife.

Throughout his married life a man is expected to assist his father-in-law in farm or other work when called upon, and also to place his services at the disposal of his mother-in-law, even to the extent of building her a new house. But there is no mother-in-law avoidance such as is found in many other tribes. A man may even eat food in the company of his mother-in-law.[1] Men generally prefer their fathers-in-law to their mothers-in-law, on the ground that the former are less exacting and more anxious to prevent anything which would lead to a dissolution of their daughter's marriage, lest they should be called on to refund the bride-price. Mothers-in-law, it is stated, care less and are inclined to mischief-making, and even in some cases encourage their daughters to lead a loose life, that they may derive profit thereby.

In the Owerri Division cases occur in which a barren wife 'purchases' a second wife for her husband, and if the second wife bears children these are regarded as the children of the first wife, whom they are brought up to address as 'mother', the real mother being addressed merely by her personal name. Even an unmarried woman may marry another woman by paying a bride-price, and having procured a man

---

[1] There is no general taboo among the Ibo against eating food in the company of women or eating food cooked by a menstruous woman. But men who happen to have 'medicines' or magical remedies in their possession would avoid going near a menstruous woman or eating food cooked by her. Titled men and priests may also have to observe this rule.

to live with her 'bride' would claim any children born. This custom, which is found in numerous Nigerian tribes, shows that a main object in the bride-price custom is to obtain the custody of children. In this connexion it may be observed that if a man's wife becomes pregnant before he has paid the final instalment of his bride-price he may postpone payment until his wife has been safely delivered; that is to say, he may avoid the risk of losing his money through the death of his wife in childbirth!

In many groups there was formerly a rule that if a woman, whose bride-price had not been paid in full, became pregnant by another man than her husband or fiancé, the paramour had to pay the remainder of the bride-price, and the husband obtained the custody of the child. In others again, it appears to have been the rule that if a pregnant woman confessed (during illness) that her condition was due to another man than her husband, and if she subsequently died in childbed, then the paramour had to reimburse the husband with all his marriage expenses. The restoration of both these rules is being demanded in some quarters; and one of the advantages of the new system of village-group courts will be that each village-group will now be able, if it wishes, to enforce its own traditional customs.

Finally, there is in the Owerri Division a legitimate form of paramour relationship known as *Iko-mbara*. By this a husband allows a friend or acquaintance to sleep with his wife regularly on one night of the eight-day week. The paramour is required to give the husband a gift of two jars of wine, one leg of meat, a chicken, and some cash. He is also expected to assist the husband in farm work, when called upon. The practice is particularly common in cases of elderly men married to young women.

Matrimonial Disputes.

The institution of District Native Courts, which is now being replaced, is popularly believed to have led to an enormous increase in divorce. For whereas in the olden days wives were restrained by a variety of local influences, they could under the Native Court system seek and obtain divorces in distant courts for trivial causes, from judges who had no knowledge of the circumstances and no interest in promoting reconciliation. In the past, if a woman considered that she was being badly treated by her husband, she might appeal to a tribunal composed of the 'sisters' and wives of her husband's family, who, after investigating the case, might advise the husband to rectify his conduct and direct him to give a gift to his injured wife. Or they might find that the wife was to blame and warn her to mend her ways or else return to her own home. Or the tribunal might be composed of elders known to be impartial, who would open the proceedings by some such petition as, 'Ala and Ndichie (ancestors), help us to settle this marriage dispute. If this husband and wife are willing to live together as man and wife do you assist to bring this about. But if not, then help the woman to obtain another husband, who will be able to repay the bride-price. If any of us who have been summoned to settle this case sees the truth but ignores it, then do you, Ala and Ndichie, take away his life.'

Serious disputes between husband and wife are sometimes settled by means of a ritual act. Thus, at Onitsha, if a husband, in a fit of rage, were to smash his wife's hearth[1] it would be a grievous insult, and unless he wished to dissolve his marriage he would have to buy a pullet and ask the senior 'sister' or *Ada* of his family to sacrifice it on his behalf. Before doing so the *Ada* would make some such petition as follows: 'This man and his wife quarrelled, and in the heat of the moment he smashed his wife's hearth. He now desires to make atonement, and I, therefore, offer this chicken, according to our custom. Grant that they may live together in peace, and may the husband be free to eat the food cooked by his wife, without fear of evil consequences.' After the sacrifice the *Ada* would rebuild the broken hearth. At Owerri there is a similar rite. The husband takes a chicken, places it against his wife's throat and then against his own, presses it on the rebuilt hearth, and says: 'May no harm come to either of us when we eat again together.' The chicken is thrown away alive into the grove of Iyafọ.[2]

At Onitsha, if a husband were to take the stick symbolizing his *chi* (*nkpulu-chi*) and hand it to his wife, this would be tantamount to a declaration of divorce. If he repented of his conduct he would have to buy a goat that very day, or else on the twenty-eighth day afterwards, and sacrifice it to his *chi*, speaking as follows: 'My *chi* and ancestors, my wife vexed me and I handed to her my *nkpulu-chi*. But now I repent, and wish to live in peace with her. I bring, therefore, this goat to you. Accept this gift, and let my angry words disappear into the air.' Similar rites are performed if a woman hands her *nkpulu-chi* to her husband, but in this case the atoning sacrifice is performed by the head of the husband's family.

[1] The clay pedestal on which she does her cooking.   [2] See p. 36.

A husband may, during a quarrel, tell his wife to leave his home. She may say, 'If you really mean that, you had better throw my cooking utensils outside my house.' If he does so, his wife may pack up her belongings and go. But a female relative of the husband may intervene, replace the cooking utensils, and make the husband apologize to his wife and present her with a gift.

A more formal mode of dissolving a marriage at Onitsha is for the husband to hang his cloth over his wife's shoulder. But he can nullify the consequences of this act by sacrificing a pullet to his ancestors. If he were to continue living with his wife without performing this sacrifice, he might expect to be punished by his ancestors for having made a solemn asseveration (divorce) and failed to carry it out.

The deliberate smashing of cooking utensils is an act which is classed among 'abominable' offences, presumably because this rite is associated with death. If, therefore, a wife were to smash her pots in a fit of vexation, it would cause serious alarm among all the members of her husband's family, and when her anger had subsided she would be invited by the senior *Ada* to provide a pullet for a rite of purification, to be performed by the local priest of Ala.

The wives of titled men or senior elders must treat their husbands with special respect, avoiding in moments of anger the use of imprecatory, threatening, or foul language. Thus if the wife of a titled person were to say to him, '*Lie udene*' ('Go and eat a vulture') or '*Gbulǫba ǫnu*' ('Ugly mug'), she would be required to make amends by bringing him a chicken, with which he would touch various parts of his body, saying, '*Ashia, ashia*,[1] my wife has cursed me, but has repented. Grant that if I eat food with her, or have dealings with her, no evil may befall us.' He would then circle the chicken round his head, kill it, sprinkle some of its blood on his body and throw the corpse away.

Again, if a wife were to say to her husband: 'You would not have treated me in this way if my brother, who was of your age-grade, had been alive'—it would be a serious matter, being tantamount to an expressed wish that her husband might be numbered among the dead. When her anger had subsided she would usually express regret and bring to the *okpara* of the husband's family a pullet for sacrifice (or a goat if her husband were a man of title). Otherwise the husband would refuse to eat food cooked by her, or to speak to her, or even acknowledge her salutations.

Husbands are not penalized to the same extent for using abusive

---

[1] Ritual words of purification.

language to their wives. There is little doubt that many Ibo husbands do, in fact, regard their wives as, to some extent, a form of property which they can treat as they please. This is exemplified in the taboo at Onitsha against a wife using the expression *'Ejili mi ọfọ'* ('I hold *ọfọ* against you', i.e. 'I have authority for my words'). A wife is not supposed to have any authority. On the other hand, it was stated that husbands are not prone to use abusive epithets to their wives, as they are usually owners of 'medicines', and their 'medicines' might give automatic effect to hasty words. In this connexion it may be observed that if, in the olden days of warfare, an Ibo wife were to say to her husband, in a fit of anger, 'May your enemies kill you!' he would, if he were an owner of 'medicine', take speedy steps to induce her to recall her words. He would sacrifice a chicken, pour a little of the blood on his shoulders, and leave the chicken's corpse to rot beside his 'medicine'. But in these days of 'enlightenment' many of the taboos described are losing their force, and at Onitsha and in numerous other centres of Christian effort one may visit dozens of compounds without seeing a sign of any 'medicine' or other symbol of 'paganism'. Nevertheless, the majority of Ibo households still retain the old 'medicines', and many who call themselves Christians are just as unwilling as their pagan brethren to incur the risks involved by breaking a taboo, or failing to take the traditional precautions when a taboo has been broken.

Dissolution of Marriage.

A marriage contracted under native law can be summarily dissolved by either party,[1] provided the bride-price is repaid in the manner prescribed by local custom. Incompatibility is a sufficient cause; but the commonest causes are adultery, loose character, laziness, sterility, or (in olden days) witchcraft on the part of a wife, and cruelty, desertion, failure to support, failure to complete the bride-price or impotence on the part of a husband. A wife is considered justified in abandoning a husband who is known to be a thief, and in former times no woman would continue to be the wife of a man who had committed an offence which had necessitated his flying for refuge to the house of a priest or becoming one of the cult-slaves known as *osu*.

Generally speaking, the rules governing the dissolution of marriage

---

[1] But marriages contracted (by Christians) under the Government Marriage Ordinance can only be dissolved by legal proceedings in the British Courts—an expensive method which may involve severe hardship or make divorce impossible.

among the Ibo favour the husband unduly, for if a husband wishes to get rid of his wife he has merely to tell her to be gone, and he can then reclaim his bride-price, though he may have little or no ground for complaint. The situation of an Ibo wife, indeed, is never easy, for even if she gets on well enough with her husband she may find it difficult to live amicably in the same compound with some of his relatives, or with her co-wives, or the wives of her husband's relatives. Many a marriage has been dissolved, not by the wish of the husband or wife, but through pressure brought on the husband by members of his family or their wives.

On the other hand, there are many influences which operate against arbitrary conduct on the part of a husband or of his relatives. The elders and matrons of the Ibo extended-family have a highly developed sense of impartiality and of the necessity of living together in peace. A husband, therefore, who is inconsiderate to his wife, has usually to face the disfavour of his own relatives as well as of all the married women of the group. The wife's group find numerous ways of expressing their disapproval, and after a case of gross injustice may refuse henceforth to give any of their women in marriage to the husband's group. Then again, where there are children, the bonds of parenthood tend to keep husband and wife together, and in some localities the fact that the birth of children diminishes or cancels the bride-price is also a factor in preventing a husband from getting rid of his wife for some slight provocation. Polygyny is often charged with having an adverse effect on the status of women. But in some ways its effects are beneficial: for a wife who is not being treated fairly can easily find another husband (if she is not too old). It is a serious matter, moreover, for a husband to be left wifeless, for he has no one then to cook his food; and though relatives offer hospitality under such circumstances, they are not usually prepared to keep it up for any length of time. Husbands, therefore, are slow to dismiss their wives for trivial causes, and at the present time the majority of suits for the dissolution of marriages are brought at the instance of wives and not of husbands.

Among the Oratta the formal mode of dissolving a marriage is for the husband to tell his wife to bring him a basket. He then takes her broom, and places it in the basket, saying, 'Take it and go'. The wife may delay her departure in the hope that he will change his mind, and then ask him to place the basket on her head. If he accedes she sets out for her own home, taking with her the whole of her personal property. She is not entitled to take away the yams presented to her by her husband's local-group when she gave birth, as these are regarded as the property of her child, who, if sufficiently old to do without his mother, remains in the father's group. She may not even take away the 'male' yams (or resultant crops) presented to her by her parents when she married, if she has a male child; these yams are claimed for the child, on the ground that the father of the child had helped in their cultivation. This is the present-day rule, but formerly the divorced wife could do as she pleased with the yams. Similarly, if a husband had given his wife a present of a goat in return for looking after his goats, his wife, if divorced, was entitled in former times to take away this goat and its offspring; but nowadays these would be claimed on behalf of her children. The new disability is designed to induce mothers to remain with their families.

The rules governing the return of the bride-price vary in different localities, but it may be said generally that in all cases where it is evident that a wife has abandoned her husband without just cause he is regarded as entitled to a full refund of his bride-price, irrespective of whether the wife had borne children or not. It was even stated in some parts of the Owerri Division that in former times if a wife abandoned her husband, and a meeting of the elders of her group and of her husband's agreed that there was no just ground for her conduct, then the husband became entitled to *twice* the amount of his bride-price, if the wife persisted in refusing to live with him. In these communities it had been customary, on the contraction of a marriage, for the members of the wife's family to swear that, if she left her husband without reason, twice the amount of the bride-price would be repaid. This practice, it was maintained, had the effect of giving marriage a stability which it no longer possesses, for it prevented a wife's parents from encouraging her to change her husband. It is doubtful, however, if the rule quoted was as effective as is claimed, for a wife's family would be seldom likely to admit that she was solely to blame. And the communities in which the custom was practised did not seem over-anxious for its restoration, though it was stated that in their new village-councils the elders sometimes directed that a small sum additional to the bride-price should be paid to a husband whose wife had been clearly at fault.

In many localities the amount of bride-price repayable was in former times reduced if the divorced wife had borne children; and this rule might be observed even if the divorced wife had been considered guilty of flagrant bad conduct. Thus at Mmako and Ugueme only half the amount of the bride-price was recoverable if two children had been born of the marriage. At Mbala, if one male child had been born, the amount of the bride-price which had been paid to the wife's mother was repayable in full, but the amount repayable by the father was reduced by half. If the child born were a female, the father's share was repayable in full, but the mother's share was not repayable. The same rule applied if both children were females. If one of the children were a male and the other a female, the mother's share of the bride-price was not repayable and the father's share was reduced by one-half. If one female child and two males had been born, the mother's share was not repayable, and the father's was reduced by two-thirds.

At Ache the share of the bride-price received by the wife's mother was never reclaimed if a child of either sex had been born of the marriage. The father's share was only reduced by five currency bars and any pigs which he had received, irrespective of the number of children born. At Inyi, also, the mother's share was not repayable. The father's share was reduced by five goats in the case of a male child and seven goats in the case of a female. At Amuda (Isu-Ochi) the husband could not include in his reckoning any gifts given to his wife's mother. He had also to deduct any goats killed by his father-in-law in connexion with the marriage feasts. At Okpanko, Abọ, Mpu, and Eha-Amufu, it was not customary for a husband to reclaim any bride-price on account of an ex-wife who had borne him children. At Lengwenta a reduction, now reckoned at £1, was made in the case of a male child, and of 10s. in the case of a female. These rules were in many districts abrogated under the late Native Court system with a view to simplifying procedure and promoting uniformity. But under the new system of village-group tribunals they are being widely readopted.

In former times a husband who had dissolved his marriage made an immediate request to the wife's parents to refund his bride-price or such proportion as was due, and if they failed to comply within a reasonable time he took the first opportunity of capturing a member of their family and selling him (or her) as a slave. If the wife remained unmarried he might hold his hand and claim any children born to her by promiscuous intercourse.[1] Such children would remain with their

---

[1] If the bride-price had been repaid by the wife's family they would be entitled to the custody of children subsequently born by promiscuous intercourse. The father would have no claim.

mother until weaned, and would then be handed over to the legal husband, who would pay the mother a weaning fee. If she remained childless, or if her family refused to hand over children, he and his relatives would resort to kidnapping. Inter-village fighting frequently resulted, and on this account the group of a runaway wife might threaten to sell her into slavery unless she returned to her husband or found a new husband who would refund the first husband's bride-price.

At the present time the courts do not usually insist on a refund of the bride-price until the divorced woman remarries, thereby enabling the parents to meet their liability from the moneys paid by the new husband. But this rule may work unjustly on the former husband, as he may have to remain wifeless for a long period, especially as many divorced women now prefer a life of promiscuous intercourse or harlotry to remarriage. In some localities, therefore, a qualifying rule has been introduced that the bride-price must be refunded within a stipulated period. And failure to obey this rule may lead to imprisonment of the wife (if she refuses to return to her husband) or of the wife's father or brother. In cases where the new husband refunds the bride-price to the former husband he sometimes, of his own accord, adds a gift (of a goat, usually) to allay ill feeling.

Many husbands who are entitled to reclaim their bride-price may, from feelings of generosity, formally renounce their right. In such cases the procedure observed in the Nsukka Division is as follows: The husband takes his wife to the head of the family and declares his intention. The head of the family produces the ancestral staff or *ofo*, breaks a kola-nut and places one piece of the nut on the staff, giving another piece to the husband and a third to the wife. The husband then declares that he has released his wife for ever, and calls on his ancestors to kill him if he should ever seek one penny from any one on her account. The husband and wife then eat their fragments of kola, and their marriage is thus formally dissolved.

Husbands who forgo their right to a refund of bride-price are not always actuated by feelings of generosity. They may do so from feelings of pique, or because they wish to avoid any further dealings with the woman or her lover. And until recently they might also have done so with the deliberate purpose of preventing the wife from remarrying and thus of giving him a claim over any child born to her by a lover. This vindictive attitude had become so common in certain localities of the Nsukka Division that a by-law was introduced a few years ago, disabling a husband who had refused to accept a refund of his bride-price from having any further authority over his former wife or her subsequent offspring.

Remarriage of Widows.

If a man's wife dies prematurely, his wife's parents may give him another daughter in marriage in consideration of a reduced bride-price. Similarly a widow may be allowed in some groups to remarry outside her late husband's family on advantageous terms, e.g. the husband's heritors may only demand from the new husband one-half of the original bride-price.[1] In some groups (e.g. Okpanko) no bride-price is claimed at all by the husband's heritors, if the woman had borne children. But in others (e.g. Owele), if a widow remarries outside her late husband's family, a full bride-price is demanded. The reason assigned for this was that it encouraged widows to remain with their children. It is for this reason also that, at Owele, a full bride-price is demanded for a runaway wife, whether she had borne children or not, and that widows are not allowed to take away any property from the husband's group—even property acquired by their own efforts. It is held that if a woman abandons her children she deserves to lose her property.

If a widow remarries within her late husband's family there is no formal bride-price, but it is customary for the person who marries her to give her parents a gift of 10s. together with some palm-wine and other gifts on festal occasions. There may also be a formal ceremony. The head of the family takes a chicken and waves it round the head of the woman saying, 'So-and-so, you have now become the wife of so-and-so.' The chicken is killed, cooked, and eaten by all the members of the family. Such a marriage cannot take place before the end of the mourning period.[2] Some widows remain in their late husband's family without remarrying any one. Such may have sexual relations with members of their late husband's kindred or with any one else, and if children are born they are regarded as the children of the deceased husband or of his heir.

It may be said generally that widows nowadays are, to a very much greater extent than formerly, exercising their option of marrying into other families; and in this they are encouraged by the Christian Missions, which look with disfavour on the polygamous custom of a man inheriting a widow when he already has a wife.

---

[1] At Oduma the bride-price for a widow is fixed at £2 5s. It was asserted that most of this money finds its way into the pockets of the Native Court judges!

[2] See pp. 310 et seq.

XII

BIRTH AND THE TRAINING OF CHILDREN

Pregnancy.

IN the village-group of Mboo a woman who conceives for the first
time must don a special cloth known as *Agbale* and wear it for a
period of one month. This cloth is regarded as a mark of affiliation
with Ala, the Earth-deity, and formerly if it were not worn the
woman's child would be destroyed at birth. Before she dons the cloth
her husband summons an old woman, the wife of a member of his
kindred, and hands to her a pup. The old woman, holding the pup,
says: 'To-day this young wife is about to don the *Agbale* cloth, in
order that evil spirits may be driven away. For we have no desire
that evil spirits should become incarnate amongst us. From to-day
the Earth-deity of Mboo is adopting this woman as one of the wives
of the men of Mboo.' Having said this she lays the pup on the ground.
The husband's brother then cuts the pup in two with his matchet.
He also cuts a basket in two and deposits one half of the pup in one
half of the basket, and the other half of the pup in the other half of
the basket. A piece of camwood and a piece of the yellow dye known
as *odo* are also cut in two, and the halves are deposited in the pieces
of basket. The woman takes the two pieces of basket and proceeds to
the 'bush of evil', accompanied by the old woman and her husband's
brother. Here she leaves the baskets. She then goes to a stream and
bathes, and on emerging is given the *Agbale* cloth. Her old cloth is
appropriated by the old woman. It was said that the pup, camwood,
and yellow dye are left in 'the bush of evil' as a bribe to the evil spirits
to refrain from interfering with the woman's unborn babe. But no explanation was offered for the practice of cutting the pup in two. In some
groups (e.g. at Ache), when a woman becomes pregnant, her husband
goes to his wife's village and presents a chicken to the senior priest of
Ala. The priest, standing before the shrine of Ala, speaks as follows:
'Ala, this man has married our daughter and has paid the marriage
fee to her parents. He has brought this chicken to you as your share
of the marriage gifts. His wife has become pregnant and we beg you
to protect her and to bring forth the child without difficulty.' The
chicken is not killed, but is appropriated by the priest.

A month later, the rites known as *Ajanketa* or 'the dog sacrifice' are performed. The husband obtains a branch of an *ogirisi* tree and some gravel from a river-bed. The senior member of the woman's extended-family comes to the husband's home and plants the *ogirisi* branch beside the husband's barn. The gravel is laid at the base of the *ogirisi* tree. He then directs the woman to kneel beside these life symbols, and holding a dog (provided by the husband), speaks as follows: 'We have come here to perform the rites of *Ajanketa*. We have planted an *ogirisi* tree, in order that the child born to this woman may flourish like the *ogirisi* tree. We have set gravel from the river-bed beside the tree in order that, as gravel remains when the river dries up, so may this woman's child remain alive after the waters of childbirth have broken.' A young man then catches the dog by the head, and an old man and old woman grip it by the body. Together they lift it and wave it round the woman's head. As they do so the old man says: 'May the child you deliver, whether male or female, be born alive and remain alive.' This is said four times, and at each time the old man's words are repeated by the woman. Finally the old man says: 'Bear children, male and female, but let the males exceed the females in numbers.' The dog is now slain and the blood allowed to pour over the stones. The flesh is cooked, and pieces are deposited on the stones. The liver is cut in two, and one half is given to the husband and the other to the wife. The old man then addresses the wife, saying, 'You and your husband must agree to be "sweet-mouthed" to one another.' The wife says: 'We do agree, even as we are about to eat a sweet thing together.' She then places a piece of the liver in her husband's mouth, and he places a piece in hers. Having eaten the liver they kiss one another. It may be noted that, among the Ibo, sexual relations between husband and wife are not discontinued during the wife's pregnancy.

In the village-group of Ubomiri (Owerri Division) it is customary for a woman in the fifth month of her first pregnancy to pay a formal visit to her parents' home, accompanied by her husband and some of his relatives. The husband presents his father-in-law with twelve calabashes of wine, and his mother-in-law receives a special gift of £2. The visitors remain for a period of eight days, and are well entertained. At the end of this time the young wife is given, by her parents and other male relatives, gifts of one or two goats, some fowls, water-pots, a mortar, and a stone for pounding camwood. The wife is escorted home by women of her own compound, followed by the men, all of whom are given a return feast in the husband's home. Four days later string anklets are ceremonially tied on her legs, and she proceeds to rub herself with camwood, and dot her body with chalk. At the end of the four days she is escorted by girl friends to the market and is publicly greeted. Another banquet follows in the evening.

The visit to the parents' home is not a normal proceeding in all groups, unless specially ordered by a diviner, for it is thought that if the unborn babe is a reincarnation of a member of the husband's group it may resent being taken from its own group, even for a few days, and the woman may, therefore, abort. The normal procedure in the Owerri Division is as follows: In the fifth month of his wife's pregnancy the husband consults a diviner in order to ascertain the name of the person who should be invited to perform the rite of 'Locking the legs' (*Egbachi okwu*), or affixing the cotton-thread anklets to the legs of the pregnant wife. The diviner usually directs the husband to take his wife and one or two friends to the priest of a certain cult. Before setting out the wife rubs her body with camwood and provides herself with a ball of chalk and a small calabash of wine, which must be drawn fresh from the tree and not allowed to touch the ground until it has been placed before the emblems of the cult. The priest of the cult takes the cord anklets and extends them three times towards the woman's ankles. At the fourth time he fixes them on the ankles. He now crushes the chalk and mixes it with water and palm-wine. Taking some of the mixture in his mouth, he spits it over her body, and invites an elderly matron to continue the process until the woman's body is covered with chalk. The priest is rewarded with a fee of 240 cowries and any of the palm-wine that may have been left over. The diviner may give further orders that when the woman bears her child she must bring a fowl to the priest, as a thank offering to the deity which had protected her during the period of gestation. It is said that the anklets ensure the continuous development of the foetus, but the original intention was, perhaps, to symbolize the binding of the woman to the deity.

The woman continues to smear her body with chalk every fourth day for a period of four weeks. On the final day she goes to the market with a calabash containing a coco-nut, a piece of meat, and sixteen cowries. She is met there by small boys of her family-group who take the coco-nut, break it, and give back the fragments to the woman, together with the meat. The woman gives the sixteen cowries to the boys. This rite is said to initiate the unborn child into the art of trading. The boys are presumed to be offering the coco-nut and meat

for sale, and the woman to be purchasing them with the cowries. On
the road home the woman gives pieces of coco-nut and meat to any
one she meets, and on reaching her house distributes the remainder
among the children of her extended-family, i.e. she gives gifts to the
future companions of her unborn babe.

During the seventh month of pregnancy, medicine-women are
summoned to provide concoctions which will ensure the good health
of the mother and her child. A month or so later a member of the
woman's family brings a fowl for sacrifice to Amadi-Qha, a deity who
is specially associated with human fertility. The sacrifice is performed
at the family shrine of Amadi-Qha, if there is a shrine; otherwise
before a sprig of palm-leaf which is used to represent the deity. After
the sacrifice the woman's brothers and sisters present her with gifts
(and this entitles the givers to return-gifts from the husband's family
when the child is born). The woman hands on some of the gifts to
the senior female member of her husband's family, and gives some
also to her husband's male relatives. Her father presents her with a
leg of meat, a share of which she gives to the head of her husband's
family. Her mother also gives her a leg of meat, some of which she
gives to her husband's mother and the latter's relatives (as they also
are expected to give gifts to the wife's relatives after the birth of the
child). The rest of the meat is shared among the wife's friends; for
if she retained it for her own use she would be sneered at as a friendless
person.

In some groups (e.g. among the Umu-Chi-Eze) when a woman
reaches the quickening period the following rite is performed. A
medicine-man, accompanied by a boy, goes to a stream and drops a
piece of yam into the water. At the same time he holds a fowl close
to the edge of the water. As soon as a fish rises to seize the yam the
medicine-man draws the fowl suddenly backwards, with the intention
of drawing the soul of the fish into the fowl. (For every person has a
fish-counterpart, which is also regarded as a child of the river spirit
and associated with an ancestor seeking re-incarnation.) At the same
moment he shouts: 'Come hither.' He then hands the fowl to the
small boy, who runs home with it at full speed and hangs it up over
the bed of the pregnant woman. The chicken is left there to die, and
the captured soul is believed to enter the woman's womb.

Throughout pregnancy both the woman and her husband may be
subject to various taboos. Thus, in the Nsukka Division, many expec-
tant mothers avoid eating the flesh of the slow-moving animal known

as *nchi*, lest her baby should be slow in learning to walk. At Ubomiri a pregnant woman should refrain from eating the flesh of any animal which had died a natural death; otherwise her child will be born dead. She should also avoid eating the neck of any animal; otherwise her child will have boils on its neck. Both she and her husband must avoid eating the meat of any animal which had been killed in honour of a deity and subsequently exposed for sale in the market; otherwise the pregnant woman will abort, or give birth to an abnormal child which will have to be destroyed. In the Awgu Division pregnant women are said to avoid eating the flesh of monkeys, lest their children should have a monkey-like appearance. They should avoid eating the flesh of leopards lest their children should become thieves. The flesh of the animal known as *agalama* must be avoided, as this animal is paralysed by light at night, and the child when born would be unable to run away from danger. The flesh of the animal known as *awo* must also be avoided, as this animal is believed to be dumb. Husbands must refrain from killing any kind of snake, as snakes are believed to embody the soul-counterparts of men. They must not refuse food cooked by wives, or the babes when born will refuse food and die. They must not shoot hares, lest the babe should be born with a skin like a hare's. And they must not attend any burial, or even help in carrying a dead animal, lest the babe should die in the womb. None of these taboos are absolute laws, but their breach may entail censure if things subsequently go wrong.

Birth.

When labour begins an old man of the husband's family takes a seed-yam with which he draws a straight line down the woman's forehead and abdomen, saying: 'Obasi-Idinenu (Supreme Being) and Ala, help this woman to deliver freely.' He then goes to the threshold of the compound, and, repeating his prayer, cuts the yam in two and lays the pieces on the ground, saying, 'Anyanu (the sun) take this yam to Obasi-Idinenu.' It was stated that the reason for cutting the yam in two was that one-half of the yam was intended for Obasi and the other for Ala. Sometimes the yam is cut into four pieces with the intention of giving one piece to Obasi, one to Anyanu, one to Ala, and one to the ancestors. The intention in drawing the straight line is that the birth may be 'straight', i.e. without complications. In some localities (e.g. at Owele) the husband himself makes the yam offering, with some such prayer as 'Chuku (Supreme Being), come, I pray you, and help my wife to deliver safely. Let not the child die in the woman. You it was that made the child and placed it in the womb. Come and undo the wrapper which you tied. Ancestors, my father, and Ala, come and help my wife to deliver her child freely.'

Any old woman who has had experience may be summoned to act as midwife. She keeps the patient standing, rubs oil on her abdomen, and makes her eat large quantities of chalk.[1] When the midwife perceives that delivery is close at hand she makes the patient sit on a stone, resting her back against one or two women who sit behind her. In some communities (e.g. at Ache) the labouring woman may be invited to make a confession of any act of unfaithfulness to her husband, with the warning that failure to confess may cause her death.[2] She may then mention the name of a lover, or say: 'If I have ever had sexual relations with any other man than my husband may I die in giving birth.' At Ache the lover mentioned has to pay a fine of two fowls to the husband's family.

If the delivery is delayed, the patient's throat may be tickled in order to cause a contraction of the abdominal muscles; and if the midwife is a woman of some skill she may attempt to hasten events by inserting her hand into the uterus, having first washed her hand and smeared it with some concoction. In some cases the midwife may find it necessary to slit the perineum.[3] The baby must be received in the hands of the midwife, and it would be a pollution of Ala if it fell directly on to the ground. It may be noted also that the child must be born outside and not inside the dwelling-hut. No reason was assigned for this, except that it would cause pollution if a child entered a house before it had cried. A child which does not cry soon after its birth is, or was, thrown away into the 'bush of evil'. Children born feet first or with teeth or any deformity were

---

[1] Many women eat quantities of chalk when they reckon that their time is near. The chalk is believed to facilitate birth, but some European doctors state that it has the reverse effect, and causes a drying-up of the waters.

[2] Among the Thonga of South Africa a protracted and difficult birth is considered to prove that the child is not legitimate, and the midwife will invite the woman to confess her guilt and the name of her lover. See Junod, *The Life of a South African Tribe*, p. 40 (revised edition).

[3] Many deaths are caused by the unskilled and unhygienic methods of midwives, as well as by the foul and dangerous drugs of native 'doctors'. If a woman dies in childbed it is a rule in some communities that the unborn babe must be removed from the womb by a foreigner; for if a fellow villager performed this operation he would be polluted, just as he would be polluted if he took part in the execution of a member of his own community.

also destroyed, on the ground that they were incarnations of evil spirits. And twins were allowed to die or were deliberately killed by being enclosed in a pot or ant-hill.[1] For the Ibo hold the common belief that the birth of twins is an indication of the disfavour of the spirits, and a punishment, possibly of adultery. Twin-births are regarded as non-human, and it is a common belief that the *chi* or accompanying soul of a twin is the *chi* of an animal. After the birth of twins a diviner is consulted to ascertain which spirit or ancestor had been offended, and sacrifice is offered to appease his wrath. The mother's breasts are tattooed to save her from milk-fever. If the father thinks that the fact of the twin-birth will not become known he may decide to keep one of the twins—the second-born, as a rule. But generally both parents are glad to be rid of both twins, as twins are believed to be a source of danger to the parents as well as to every one else in the community.

In the Owerri Division, if a woman gives birth to twins, it is believed that the husband or wife, or both, or some relative, had offended the occult powers. The twins must, therefore, be destroyed.[2] All pregnant women in the family-group must immediately leave the group and remain away until the twins have been removed. The twins are taken by a cult-slave attached to the family, or by any male member of the group, and placed in a pot. The cult-slave or an aged woman, escorted by men of the family, then carry the pot to the 'evil bush', and leave it there. On returning home they all purify themselves by the sacrifice of a chicken to Afọ, the spirit of 'the year'. The mother is segregated in a hut specially erected behind the compound and remains there for twenty-four days. She is then led by an old woman to the shrine of Afọ, and is purified by the sacrifice of another chicken. The husband obtains a bunch of unripe palm-nuts, some pumpkins, chalk, and leaves of the *ajoro* and *obogo* trees, and these are cut-up on the ground by a diviner and mixed with water. The diviner and husband sprinkle some of the mixture round the

[1] Animals which give birth to an abnormal number of offspring are also destroyed, together with their young; e.g. a cow that bears two calves, a bitch that bears a single pup, or a hen that hatches a single chicken.

[2] The use of the present tense must not be construed as though the Government has been neglectful in the matter of suppressing twin-murders. The campaign against the practice has been vigorous and perhaps at times even unjust in the severity of its measures. But the killing of twins undoubtedly continues to some extent, because the people still believe that twins are an 'abomination' and because it is difficult to detect cases in which they have been murdered by mere neglect.

compound, saying: 'Evil, begone, and let the land be cool.' A fowl is also dragged round the compound and killed by the diviner.

The umbilical cord of a new-born babe is severed with a razor, and the babe is washed with warm water and smeared with camwood oil. The head is gently moulded and is then shaven to remove the hair of the underworld (*uwǫzǫ*). The afterbirth is buried in a special place by women of the compound, but no further notice is (as in some tribes) paid to it. The mother is then escorted to her hut, which she must enter backwards. Her milk is tested. Some of it is expressed into a piece of coco-nut shell. A black ant is placed in the milk, and, if it dies, a medicine-man is summoned. He bathes the woman's shoulders and breasts with a concoction of leaves, and keeps expressing milk until it becomes (in his opinion) fit for the child's consumption. Meanwhile the child is fed with sips of water or handed to a foster-mother.

The birth of a healthy child is greeted by the attendant women with shouts of joy, and the husband eagerly inquires if the child is of 'our society or yours', i.e. male or female. If the former, the husband shouts out joyfully: 'It is a male.' But if the latter he remains silent. For male children are more welcome than females.[1] All members of the household immediately salute the mother by saying: 'Chuku (God) has done well to you. Take good care of your child.' Male members of the household congratulate the husband by embracing him. The midwife is given a fee of one rod and a few yams or some firewood. In some communities (e.g. at Mboo), if the child is a boy, the midwife is presented with a cock a few days after the birth. This she presses against the mother and child saying: 'I remove from you all evil spirits.' She then sacrifices the cock at the threshold of the compound, and is permitted to take the dead fowl home for her own use.

Circumcision.

Four to eight or twelve days after birth, the child, whether male or female,[2] is circumcised. But if a diviner so directs, or if the child is weakly, the operation may be postponed. The operation is per-

[1] The assumption among many Europeans that female children are preferred by patrilineal Negroes, because a bride-price will be received on their marriage, is fallacious.

[2] Female circumcision is not practised in a number of village-groups of the Nsukka Division, where Igala or Okpoto influence is strong.

formed with a native razor, by any man or woman who is practised in the art. There are no special formalities, but no one who has had sexual relations during the previous night must go near the child while the wound is still unhealed. Bleeding is arrested by spitting water on the wound and by rubbing in palm-oil. It is said that the wound usually heals in a few days and that sepsis seldom occurs. In females the clitoris only may be removed, and in one or two localities (e.g. at Ichi) it was stated that the clitoris is only removed if it is prominent. In such cases the reason assigned for the custom of clitoridectomy is that it prevents excessive sexuality. But the usual explanation is that it facilitates conception. In some areas (e.g. at Eha-Amufu) girls are not circumcised until after their first or second menstruation, and it is an offence punishable by a heavy fine, payable by the male paramour and the girl's parents, for any girl to conceive before she has been circumcised. Circumcision is, therefore, in these areas, an introduction to the adult status.

In a number of localities the labia minora are excised, and there may be mutilation also of the labia majora. This custom is believed to facilitate childbirth, but would seem to have the opposite effect. The Protestant Missions have long opposed female circumcision, no doubt because it is not a European custom. There would seem to be no reason for interfering with the practice of clitoridectomy, but good ground for discouraging mutilation of the labia.

The Purification.

At the end of one lunar month there are, in the Awgu Division, formal rites of purification. The husband invites all the women of his kindred to a feast. The midwife attends, and waves a yam over the head of the mother and child, saying, 'May everything that comes into this compound be pleasant, like this feast. No evil spirit shall assail the mother or her child, for I am now removing all evil spirits from this household.' She then throws the yam on the ground. Taking a gourd of palm-wine, she waves it round the heads of all the women present, saying, 'May you conceive the very next time you sleep with your husbands, so that we may all enjoy many similar feasts.' She tilts the palm-wine on to the ground. If there is a pregnant woman present the midwife touches her abdomen with a cooked yam, which she hands to the woman to eat.

The husband also provides a feast for all the young children of his kindred. Each child brings a potsherd, which the husband fills with soup. Each is also given a cooked yam. The children take their yams and soup outside the compound and eat their meal there. When they have finished they break the potsherds to pieces by stamping on them. It was said that the intention of this rite was to induce ancestral spirits to be reborn. Unless the feast described is given, the mother cannot bring the child outside the compound.

After the feast all the children go to a stream and bathe, and on their return they smear themselves with camwood. Then one of the boys (or one of the girls if the new-born child is a female) takes some palm-wine in his mouth and spits it over the fire in the mother's hut. This he does until the fire is extinguished. The mother then sweeps out her hut, while the boy goes and obtains fresh fire from a neighbouring compound.[1]

After this rite the boy rubs some chalk on the child's forehead, saying, 'If your father or mother sends you on a message do not refuse to go. But if a spirit (*ndi mmuọ*) sends you, say that you have no feet. Let not anything that your parents eat cause any harm to you.'[2] On the following day the boy (or girl) who had quenched the fire returns to the mother's compound, where an old woman takes some camwood in her mouth and spits it over him. The boy then escorts the mother to her husband's farm, where she lays her hands on one of the growing yams, saying, 'To-day the taboo against my touching yams has been removed.' When the yams are dug up, the particular yam which the woman had touched is given to her to eat in the company of her boy-escort. A few days later the husband presents his wife with an ivory bracelet and a necklace of elephant-hair or beads. The mother then paints her body and goes to the market with a pot of wine. There she is greeted and embraced by all her friends, to whom she gives some wine, and from whom she receives numerous small gifts.

There are many variations of the procedure described above. Thus, at Owele, at the end of one month from the day of delivery the husband gives two yams to the small children of the kindred, who clean the yams, cut them into eight pieces, and place them in a pot to boil. The mother meantime is escorted by a little girl to a stream,

---

[1] In some communities the rite of obtaining new fire is carried out four days after the child's birth.

[2] The parents of a newly born child, before helping themselves to food, touch the child's lips with a piece of the food, as a similitude of feeding the child. For babies are regarded as reimbodied ancestors, who must be kept satisfied. If the parents fail to offer food to the child, evil spirits will do so, and the child will follow the evil spirits.

and there bathes herself to wipe away the pollution of childbirth (i.e. of the lochial discharge). On their return they are given two pieces of yam by the children, who eat the remainder.

The mother then brings her child from the hut and is given a yam by her husband. She places the child's hands on the yam and covers them with her own, saying: 'To-day we are reconciled with Njǫku (the yam spirit).' She then roasts the yam, cuts it into small pieces, mixes the pieces with oil, and hands them to the various members of her kindred. Later she places a basket in an open space, and into this gifts of cash are thrown by the female members of her husband's kindred.

The Naming Ceremony.

A few days later (generally on the twenty-fourth day after delivery) the naming ceremony is performed. The brothers and sisters of the mother come to the husband's house, the former bringing calabashes of palm-wine and the latter a supply of yams. The wine and yams are laid on the ground and are offered for sale to the husband's relatives, at a figure considerably over the market-price. They are bought after some argument. A feast follows and the wife's relatives are given gifts.[1] All then go outside to the yard, and the head of the family takes the child in his arms, and raises it in the air four times, saying: 'My son, grow up strong and ever give ear to the behests of your father and mother.' He then asks the father by what name the child is to be known. The father may reply 'Chuku'. The old man looks at the child and says, 'Chuku, the Creator of mankind. That is the name by which you shall answer our call. May long life be yours.' The father now takes the child in his arms, saying: 'Obasi-Idinenu (Lord God), we thank you, we thank you.'[2]

Some time later the father consults a diviner in order to ascertain

---

[1] The wife's father receives a gift of 5s. in cowries from the head of the husband's family, and her mother a similar sum from the husband's mother and her relatives. Her eldest brother receives 4s. from her husband's eldest brother, and her eldest sister (or the *Ada* of her family) also receives 4s. from the corresponding relative, and so on.

[2] Among the Umu-Chi-Eze, when the head of the kindred confers the name, he chews a piece of kola and spits the fragments over the child's mouth, saying, 'Let no evil spirit cause you to die an unexpected death.' With this we may compare the ritual followed at the christening of the son of the Duke of Brabant. The officiating cardinal blew three times on the child's mouth, poured salt on its lips, and recited an exorcising prayer (see *Illustrated London News*, 18 Oct. 1930).

the name of the ancestor whose reincarnation the child is, and he gives the child this name in addition to the one (or several others) already conferred. He takes the mother and child to the grave of the ancestor indicated. The mother squats over the grave holding the child. Her husband then takes a goat and waves it round the child's head, saying, 'So-and-so, I have come to thank you for being reborn by me. May you remain long in life and prosper.' He then kills the goat and pours the blood over the grave. The meat is cooked and eaten, offerings of the heart and liver having first been deposited on the grave.

Sometimes a diviner may direct that the child shall be called after some deity or spirit—a spirit, perhaps, which had been invoked prior to the child's birth. Children are also called after the name of the day of the week on which they were born, or after some event that had marked the day of their birth, or after some friend who had come to see the parents on the day of the birth, and had, with some small gift, requested that the child should be his namesake and become his lifelong friend. A first-born male child is commonly called *Okpara* and a first-born female *Ada*. Many names may be bestowed by different relatives, and it is thought that by giving a child a plurality of names of ancestors additional protection is secured.[1]

At Awgu, if the head of a family or kindred is the holder of an *aro* (or ritual staff of title or public authority), every child born into the kindred must be presented to the staff. The parents take the child to the house of the head of the kindred, to whom they present an egg, a piece of meat, a fish, some yams, and oil. The head of the kindred roasts the yam and cuts off a slice, which he lays on one side. He and the parents eat the remainder. Then taking the egg, meat, fish, and yam, he touches the staff with them, places them on the ground, pours oil and water over them, and squeezes them up all together, saying, '*Aro*, you have seen this child which has been presented to you to-day; let no sickness of any sort assail him, and avert evil spirits, so that he may grow up strong before the eyes of his parents.' He then rubs some of the mixture on the child's body and gives the remainder to the mother, so that she may use it, in conjunction with camwood, as a protective ointment for the child.

Some six months after birth the child is, in many communities,

---

[1] In many communities a child is given a temporary name by his mother or an elderly woman of the husband's household, as a form of security until he is given his proper name.

formally introduced to Ala, the Earth-deity. It is taken by its parents
to the priest of Ala, who circles a chicken (provided by the father)
round its head, saying, 'Ala, this your child has been brought before
you by its parents, in order that you may protect it and that it may
be permitted to share in foods offered sacrificially to you, without
incurring your anger.' If this rite were not performed it is believed
that, should the child partake of any food, part of which had been
offered to the deity, it would die.

When the child has cut his lower teeth, he is taken by his mother
to the head of the kindred, in order that he may be presented to the
ancestors. The head of the kindred deposits a kola at the shrine of
the founder of the kindred and calls on all the ancestors to protect the
child, who is verily one of themselves, as he has cut his teeth in the
proper way. But if a child cuts his upper before his lower teeth this
rite is not observed, as he is not considered to be a bona fide member
of the kindred. He is regarded as having the *chi* of an animal. Such
a child was in former days sold into slavery, the proceeds of the sale
being divided among the elders and titled officials of the town. In
some groups (e.g. at Enugu-Ezeke) the child was allowed to remain
in the community, provided the parents paid a fine of 700 rods to the
principal authorities of the group. At Ukehe a child who cut the
upper before the lower teeth was sent to the home of the mother's
parents and could not return to his father's home until after the
death of his father. He was interdicted from offering sacrifice to Ala,
being regarded as a defiler of the land.

The period of lactation lasts about two years, but some children
are not weaned until three or even three-and-a-half years after birth.
Some indulgent mothers allow their child to remain at their breasts
long beyond the necessary period, and such children become objects
of derision among other children; they may be jeered at as 'breast-
suckers' for many years afterwards. When the child is weaned, the
wife receives gifts from her husband and her friends, and the event
may also be celebrated by a feast. Until recently it was not customary
for husbands to resume cohabitation with wives who had given birth
until the lapse of three years after the birth, i.e. until the child had
been fully weaned. This rule, which is still observed among the less
sophisticated groups, was based no doubt on the observation that
conception interferes with lactation. The rule also served a useful
purpose by safeguarding women from the strain of continuous child-
bearing. But it drove many husbands who had only one wife to form

adulterous unions, or to resort to harlots and run the risk of contracting venereal disease. It is becoming customary, therefore, particularly among young Christians who observe the new rule of monogamy,
for marital relations to be resumed at the end of one year, though
many couples remain continent for a longer period.

The training of children, whether male or female, is almost entirely
the mother's business up to the age of five. Before the child is two
years old the mother begins to teach it obedience, e.g. by giving it
some food and then immediately demanding its return. About the
age of two, the child is taught to eat without assistance, and as it
grows older is told to refrain from talking while eating, and so avoid
growing thin! It is made accustomed to the use of knives by being
given a wooden knife, but is strictly warned of the danger of injuring
itself and others. It is taught also to clean dishes, put them in their
proper place, and sweep the mother's hut. Male children are made
to rake the ground round the compound (the rake having a bamboo
head and stick handle). Girls must not perform this duty, lest later
they should become clumsy in handling plates and pots. At this stage
also children are taught to fetch water in small calabashes, to roast
and peel yams for themselves, to run errands, to collect firewood, and
to use a 'chewing-stick' for cleansing their teeth. They are taught
dance-steps almost as soon as they can walk, and at dances one may
even see children of two or three years of age beating the dance time
with their hands and heads.

At the age of five they receive their first lessons in hoeing, and two
years later they begin to accompany their father and mother to the
farm. Boys are taught to clear the 'bush', to make mats for roofing,
and to carry baskets of yams or calabashes of water. Instruction is
given in planting yams, fixing yam-sticks, training the tendrils, planting corn, and weeding the farm. They are shown the farm boundaries,
and taught how to demarcate the boundaries after the clearing of the
farm.

All through their early years they receive spasmodic moral instruction, to refrain from taking what does not belong to them (e.g. not to
eat food given into their charge for another's use), to avoid using bad
language or being familiar with seniors, to be punctilious in the use
of the recognized places for relieving nature, and to be truthful.
Knowledge of sexual matters is acquired informally, but a mother
warns her daughter not to let boys or men meddle with her, and to
report to her when she has her first menstruation (which in many

groups is an event of ritual importance). A father will warn his son to be careful about his manner of 'playing' with girls, lest he should contract a venereal disease.[1] Boys sleep in their mothers' huts until about the age of eight, and then sleep together in a special hut of their own or in that of a young unmarried man. Or they may sleep with other children in a neighbouring household. Girls sleep in their mothers' huts, or in that of a female relative. But in a few groups they are permitted to sleep with their fiancés when they have reached the age of eleven or twelve. It was stated that at the present time there is great sexual laxity among the boys and girls, and that it is exceptional for girls to retain their virginity until marriage. But in some groups (e.g. of the Nsukka Division) pre-nuptial sexual intercourse did not appear to be against native custom, and is not therefore immoral from the native point of view.

Lore is picked up from parents and grandparents, maternal as well as paternal, as children are sent periodically on visits to their mothers' home. Many are the stories they learn while pulling out the grey hairs of their grandfathers, a task frequently imposed to keep them quiet. Boys acquire a wealth of knowledge also at meetings of elders, which they attend as carriers of the seats and ọfọ bags of their fathers, uncles, and grandparents. As among ourselves, boys follow the behaviour pattern of their elder brothers and father and uncles, and girls that of their elder sisters, mother, and aunts. Respect for elders is strongly reinforced by witnessing at an early age religious rites in which the principle of seniority is markedly prominent. In particular the cult of ancestors is a potent means of enforcing filial obedience. Another means of engendering and maintaining respect for seniority is the system of relationship terms, in the correct use of which children are punctiliously trained from the moment that they have begun to understand the use of words. It will be convenient to give here a list of the principal terms used.

The term *nna* (possessive *nnam*) = father in the classificatory sense. But normally the term, when used by itself (i.e. without the addition of an epithet or personal name), indicates the biological father. It is not permissible to use the personal name of a father unless the speaker is calling him when he is at a distance. A father's or mother's younger brother, if he is not much older than the speaker, may be addressed

---

[1] In some groups girl-prostitutes are not unknown, and some mothers encourage their daughters to live a life of harlotry in order to derive financial advantage for themselves.

by his personal name. If he is fairly elderly he is addressed as *nna*, plus his personal name. A father's or mother's elder brother is always addressed as *nna* plus his personal name. A father's brother may also be addressed as *dada*. If a person has been brought up in the home of his mother's relatives he may learn to call his mother's brothers *dada*, using the term employed by the children of his mother's brothers. The term *nna uku* (big father), plus the personal name, is applied to any elder, i.e. to one older than the speaker's father, or of the same age-grade as the speaker's father, or who has a son of the same age as the speaker. The term *nne* (possessive *nnem*) = mother is used in the same way as *nna* = father. In conjunction with the personal name it is applied to a father's or mother's sister, who may also be called *dada* or *ogbom* (i.e. my beloved, or namesake). *Nna ọche* is applied to either grandfather, or to any male considerably older than the speaker's father. It is also used by a woman in addressing or referring to her husband's father. *Nne ọche* is applied to grand-mothers, and is also used by a woman in addressing or referring to her husband's mother. *Nwa* = son, daughter, or any person of a junior generation including grandchildren and children-in-law. A brother's or sister's child may be addressed as *nwa* if the speaker belongs to a senior generation. Otherwise the personal name, or the term *nwa nne* (child of mother, i.e. brother or sister), is used. *Nwa nne* is also applied to cousins, provided the cousins are not excessively senior.

There is a special term *ọche* or *ọdie* used in addressing a sister's child, a mother's brother's child, or a father's sister's child. If such children are males they may be called *okenne* (*oke* = male). These classes of relatives may be referred to as *nwa nwa* (lit. = child of child), a term which is also used in referring to grandchildren. Brothers and sisters are addressed by their personal names, but elder brothers or sisters may be addressed as *dada*, a term which is also applied to a father's brother or sister.

The general term for brother or sister is *nwa nne* (child of mother) or *nwa nna* (child of father), and these terms may be applied to any member of one's group or to children of women of the group who are married in other groups. *Umunne* (possessive *umunnem*) is also a general term for relatives, and applicable therefore to all cousins and all members of one's group.

Ọgọ is a reciprocal term used between a man and all his wife's rela-tives. A wife addresses her husband's father as *nna dim* (i.e. father of my husband) or as *nna ǫche*, and she calls her husband's mother *nne dim*. Her husband's brothers and sisters are called *nwa nne dim*. The word for husband is *di* (possessive = *dim*), and a woman may apply this word also to her husband's brothers or male cousins if she is on affectionate terms with them. The word for wife is *nyie*, and a man may apply this term to his brothers' wives, if he is on friendly terms with them. But husbands and wives commonly address each other by their personal names or by the term *enyi* = friend. A co-wife is called *nyiedi*.

For misbehaviour young children are generally threatened by their mother with a flogging from the father, or the father's elder brother or sister. Or the mother may punish the child herself by pulling its ear, slapping it, or beating it with a small whip. In exceptional cases the child's food may be withheld. In the small family the father is the principal authority. With him rest all the most important decisions, and as he protects all so he must be obeyed. If a son persistently refuses to obey him, the father may have to produce his *ofǫ* and say to his son: 'You are a most disobedient son; may your children treat you as you have treated me; when you call on them to go on a message may they refuse.' He would then strike the ground with his *ofǫ*, and, if the son did not there and then express remorse, he would probably do so within a day or two, overcome by fear of the vengeance of the family ancestors. In cases of continued refusal to obey a father, a son might be haled before the head of the extended-family, who, backed up by the other elders, would threaten to drive him out of their community. In those groups in which secret societies were active, young initiates who were known to have a headstrong character were subjected to specially rigorous treatment, at the instance of their kinsmen, and the whole system of discipline imposed by the societies on their members tended to encourage in young impressionable men the virtues of endurance, self-restraint, and respect for authority, as well as truthfulness and honesty in their dealings with one another. On the other hand, the merits of the training given by the societies were counterbalanced to some extent by certain obvious defects such as the fostering of a system of secrecy and fraud towards non-initiates, and the prevention of complete frankness between the sexes.

Such is a brief sketch of the manner in which Ibo children, through the early restraints of family life, gradually acquire that state of discipline which the Ibo would describe as their 'custom' and we as the moral code of the community. The Ibo family is not a small group like ours; it entails on each member continual obligations towards a wide circle of relatives; and it teaches, therefore, many virtues which we have to seek outside the family—in the training given to our children at school. In Iboland the family is the preparatory school, and family discipline is the foundation of the law.

XIII

DEATH AND INHERITANCE

Burial Rites.

WHEN a person of social importance becomes a permanent invalid, or so ill that he is likely to die, he may call the family-group together and designate his successor, pointing out that the person so chosen had proved himself to be trustworthy, impartial, and discreet. He may also indicate the names of debtors and creditors, and disclose where any treasure had been hidden. Finally, he may intimate the name of the person who should perform his burial rites. He may select his eldest son or some other member of the family-group. Or he may choose a friend who may be no relative at all, and may not even belong to his own village-group, some one whom he would like to resemble when he returns once more to the world. Or he may choose one person to perform one rite, and another to perform another.

Immediately on his death the following rite is performed. His son or daughter places four large yams on the roof of the hut in which his dead body lies. Soon afterwards a person, specially chosen by the deceased or a diviner, takes the yams inside the hut, and places them on the ground, two at the feet of the deceased, and one close to his right and left side, so that his hands touch the yams. The person selected then says: 'These yams are for you. When you return to the world may your yams be as fine as these. And may I, during my life-time, be a successful grower of yams. I place these yams in your hands by your own direction; see to it that I suffer no harm in consequence.' This rite is known as *Ekpama-ji-aka*, or 'The placing of the yams in the hand'.

The next rite is known as *Ekû-ihu-ọcha*, a phrase which seems to mean 'Making the face (of the dead man) white (i.e. radiant)'. Women of the deceased's family bring a cock fastened to a string of cowries (240), and one of the women who is considered especially lucky (e.g. whose children are all alive), or some person previously indicated by the deceased, holds or hangs the cock over the dead man's head. When the cock shakes its wings (a sign of acceptance by the deceased), it is taken out and hung at the door of the hut or on a branch of an *oterre* tree in the compound. After a while it is taken down and its neck is drawn, the blood being allowed to drip on to the ground at

the threshold. The fowl is then cooked and eaten by the female relatives. The intention in leaving the fowl hung up is, apparently, to
give the deceased time to see and receive the offering.

This is the initial procedure followed at Owerri, but each locality
has customs of its own. Thus at Amo-Imo, when a woman or young
unmarried man dies, the death is immediately announced by crying
and wailing. But, if the deceased had been an elderly man or a person
of family and property, the announcement of his death is postponed,
in order to give the family time to make the necessary elaborate
arrangements for the funeral.[1] The next of kin summons the elders
of the family-group, provides them with wine, and breaks the news.
One or two men are then sent to a diviner to ascertain the cause of
death and the manner of burial. The deceased may have expressed a
wish that his body should not be placed in a coffin or grave, lest by
being covered up he should be unable to see in the next life. The
diviner may confirm this by saying that the body must be left out
in the 'bush of evil' to rot; or he may declare that if it is placed in a
coffin or grave the dead man's spirit will rest peacefully.

After consulting the diviner, a goat is killed and the blood sprinkled
on the symbol of the cult known as *ukwu-n'ije*, the cult which ensures
safety on a journey, i.e. the dead man is given protection during his
journey to the underworld. A dog is sacrificed, and some drops of
the blood poured into the dead man's eyes.[2] A ram and cock may also
be killed and the blood poured over the thumb (*aka-ikenga*) of the
deceased's left hand. A gun is then fired, and formal lamentation,
followed by singing and war dances, is begun. The meat of the sacrificial animals is eaten up on the following day by members of the
deceased's family.

The body (at Owerri) is washed by female relatives of the deceased
or by members of his age-grade or their delegates. It is laid on a
bed of plantain leaves, and in some groups the water used for washing
must be carried from the stream on the shoulders and not (as is usual)
on the head. The body is then freely smeared with camwood, but in
some communities the bodies of titled men are only slightly dabbed
with camwood. The bodies of commoners may be painted with

---

[1] In many groups, if the deceased had been a member of a titled society, wailing
is not permitted (under pain of a fine) until all the titled men of the village-group
have assembled to salute their dead comrade.

[2] This rite at Ama-Imo corresponds to the Owerri rite described on the following page.

indigo, but those of titled men must not be marked in this plebeian way. The rite known as *Ewa-nkita-anya* ('the killing of the dog for the eye') may then be performed, if the deceased had expressed a wish that this should be done immediately after death instead of at the usual time, viz. four days after death. A dog provided by the members of the deceased's age-grade[1] is brought to the compound, with a rope of palm-leaves tied round its neck. Drums[2] are beaten and guns fired. During the drumming a man, specially appointed and renowned for his bravery, carries the dog to the dead man's hut, accompanied by members of his age-grade, and extends the dog towards the corpse, saying, 'I am doing this, not by my own wish but by yours. And I do it in order that you may be a man of bravery in your next life—but of bravery merged with discretion.' Having said this he and the others run out at full speed[3] towards the drummers, who immediately cease drumming when the dog is held up in the air. This is done three times, but at the fourth time the man appointed to perform the rite stabs the dog in the throat at the door of the dead man's hut. In former times it was customary to pour some drops of the dog's blood into the dead man's eyes, but nowadays the blood is poured on four leaves of an *abosse* tree, the leaves being placed beside the corpse.[4]

The dead body of the dog is carried back at a run to the drummers, who stop their drumming but soon recommence. Dancing is begun, guns are fired, and songs are sung, the first song being 'Oh, where is the dog and where are they?' The body of the dog is then handed over to the senior member of the deceased's family-group, who orders it to be cooked, and distributes the meat next morning among the members of the deceased's age-grade. One leg is given to the man who performed the rite and another to the deceased's eldest son.

[1] If the deceased had one wife. But if he had two wives the dog is provided by the second wife.

[2] Special drums are used, viz. those known as *ogudu* or *nkwa-ike*.

[3] The running was said to symbolize the dash to attack in war.

[4] It was said at Owerri that the old custom had been abandoned through fear that the flesh of the dog (which was subsequently eaten) might become polluted by having been brought into close contact with the corpse. At Amanyi it is still the custom, when an Atama dies, for a man to climb up to the roof in which the body lies, make an opening in the thatch, cut the throat of a fowl, and let the blood drip through the opening into the eyes of the corpse, the eyes being held wide open by another man standing beside the corpse. It was said that the object of this rite was to open the eyes of the dead Atama. With this we may compare the Jukun rite of 'opening the mouth'. (See my *A Sudanese Kingdom*, p. 252.)

The corpse is now (at Owerri) laid unclothed and without ornaments in an *ǫjǫ*, or receptacle made of strips of bamboo bound together with fibre and lined with a mat or cloth. The custom, however, of using modern coffins is now spreading rapidly. In some parts of Nsukka Division (e.g. at Enugu-Ezeke) the body is laid on a grass mat and covered with a cloth, which is folded over the body. The ends of the mat are then drawn together and sewn up. The brother or son of the deceased kills a chicken and pours the blood on the ground at the feet of the dead man. The old war gong is then beaten, as a reminder to the deceased that when he is reborn he must prove himself a man of prowess. Two men lift the corpse and place the feet against the gong. They then carry it out to a palm-tree and place the feet against the trunk, to make the dead man a good climber of palms in his next incarnation.[1] The corpse is then taken back to the hut, and there the deceased's brother places a loaded gun in the dead man's hands, which are made to pull the trigger and discharge the shot at an antelope's head stuck on the wall. Simultaneously the hunting-song is sung, and the dead man's hunting-dog is slain to accompany him to the next world.

Grave-burial is now general for all, but formerly was accorded only to the aged or those of social importance, the bodies of young people being thrown into the 'bush of evil'. Even at the present time, in some localities, the bodies of persons who are believed to have died as a result of having sworn a false oath, or having committed some other abomination, are left in the 'bush of evil' without burial. Those who dispose of the bodies carry, attached to their girdle, a palm-leaf, and after depositing the body they touch themselves with the leaf, saying, 'Let all the evil of this man, which might infect me, follow him.' They then throw the leaf away and purify themselves further by bathing in a stream. Those who have died of a disease which had caused their bodies to swell were denied burial, it being said that Ala had given them a belly like a pregnant woman because of their defilement.[2] Women dying in childbirth were also cast away, the body of the child being first removed.[3] Twins and children born feet

---

[1] This is not done at Nsukka, but it is customary to place a knotted palm-leaf on the palm-trees of the deceased, in order to prevent him from taking away the sap to the underworld.

[2] The swelling of the body either before or after death is commonly, in Nigeria, associated with witchcraft. (See, e.g., my *Tribal Studies in Northern Nigeria*, vol. i, p. 435.)   [3] See p. 290, footnote 3.

first were accorded similar treatment. Burial was not denied to those who had died of small-pox, but the bodies had to be buried outside the confines of the village by persons who had had small-pox. The object of refusing burial to these classes of persons was to cut them off from their living descendants and to deter them from seeking to be reborn. But the denial of burial was not always considered a sure preventive of reincarnation, for those who throw the body into the 'bush' sometimes use the formula: 'If you are born again may you not behave in a manner that will bring about a similar fate.'

Graves are dug by sons of sisters of the deceased or by members of his age-grade, inside one of the dead man's huts, or his barn, or behind his compound or on the former site of his compound. If there is no available space in the compound the dead man may be buried in the 'bush', and young people are generally so buried. The grave is rectangular and about four and a half feet deep, but in some communities shaft- and tunnel-graves are used for those who had enjoyed the title of 'Atama' or had belonged to the Ọzọ society. The tunnel or side-chamber is lined with planks of African mahogany, and the dead man is placed in a sitting position on a stool.

The body is now deposited in the grave and is carefully straightened, for if it is buried in a bent position the dead man will be bent in his next life.[1] A strip of the burial cloth is placed over the waist and each arm and knee, but the face remains uncovered. The relatives take up a position at the sides and foot of the grave. They must avoid standing at the head of the grave, as, when the earth is thrown in, the dead man's soul (*nkporo-obi*, i.e. heart-seed) is thought to take its departure from the head of the grave. For this reason also the man who throws in the first earth shouts out, 'Avoid the earth', i.e. 'Begone before the earth touches you.' When the grave has been filled up a gun is fired and all go home, the women weeping. The grave-diggers purify themselves with water which had been poured into a hole in the ground lined with leaves of coco-yam. They may also rub their bodies with various concoctions.

At Mboo (Awgu Division), before the body is placed in the grave, a female member of the kindred may make a few strokes on the body with a mixture composed of camwood, water, an egg, and the leaf of an *ogirisi* tree, saying as she does so: 'So-and-so, when you are re-incarnated you must be a wealthy and prosperous man and live to a good old age.' Loose earth is then thrown in on the body, together

---

[1] In some groups it is laid flat on the back, in others it faces the rising sun.

with the mat and cloth. Even very young sons must throw in a little
earth, as evidence that they had taken a share in their father's burial
rites.[1] The last handfuls are thrown in with the back turned to the
grave, as a sign that they had finished with the dead man. When the
grave has been filled up, branches of palm are laid over the soil,
which is then trampled down hard, to prevent the occurrence of
cracks. For if a crack appears in the grave a diviner must be consulted,
and if the diviner declares that the crack is due to the anger of Ala
on account of some offence committed by the deceased, the grave is
opened and the body thrown away into the 'bush of evil'.

After the inhumation all who had taken part enter a stream and
bathe. Then, facing in the direction from which the stream comes,
they throw some water over the right shoulder. They next face in the
direction in which the stream goes, and do likewise. The intention is
that the stream shall carry away the pollution of death. In some groups
each of the bathers rubs his body with an egg, with the intention that
their pollution shall enter the egg and leave their bodies 'smooth' as
an egg. They may also draw a thorn across their bodies, with the
intention of removing the noxiousness of death, just as a thorn is used
for removing things that have penetrated into the body. The egg and
thorn are subsequently thrown away into the 'bush of evil'.

At Igga, when the body has been placed in the grave, the brother
of the deceased addresses the dead man, saying, 'When you go to the
spirit-world declare to God who it was that killed you, and if it was
one of us do you return and take that man.' The grave-digger then
takes a hoe and puts a little loose earth in the grave. Having done
this he passes the hoe through his legs and catches it behind with his
right hand. He does this a second time, catching the hoe with his
left hand. The grave is then filled in, a small mound of mud plaster
being left at the top. This may be decorated with cowries. Some
days later a goat is killed over the grave. The carcass is taken away
and cooked, and pieces of the cooked flesh are deposited in the grave
by the deceased's brother, who also pours a libation of palm-wine and
begs the dead man to give him prosperity. In many groups it was
customary for the son of the deceased to kill a slave at the burial-rites
of his father or mother.[2] At Eha-Amufu the body of the slave was

---

[1] But a son must not take part in a burial if his wife is pregnant.

[2] Frequently two slaves were killed, one being deposited on each side of their master.
The dead man's feet might rest on the body of a young girl and his head on the lap of
a young boy, who had been placed alive in the grave with his legs and arms broken.

placed in the grave first. This custom has been replaced by that of distributing in the father's or mother's kindred money equal to the purchase price of a slave. At Enugu-Ezeke, when the grave has been filled in, all present take a few grains of loose soil and, addressing the dead man, say: 'We have done our duty by you. So do not come back to trouble us.' They raise the loose earth to their lips and then throw it on the grave. The intention of this is to convey the message to the dead man. At Nsukka the rites are concluded by every one circling his hand round his head, as an intimation that he has severed connexion with the dead man. Guns may be fired if the deceased had been a person of importance.

At Owerri, some days after burial, a rite known as *Eto-ewu-ikpu* or 'The casting of the goat on its back' is commonly performed, provided the deceased man had children. The members of the deceased's age-grade and other elders assemble. A person (chosen by the deceased or a diviner) takes a goat (provided by the deceased's senior wife) and pushes it backwards and forwards towards the dead man's hut four times. He then kills it, saying, 'I do this for you, that in your next life you will beget children who will remain alive, and that you may have a long life.' The last drops of the goat's blood are sprinkled on two *ogirisi* leaves which are placed on the dead man's hut. The goat is cooked and divided, one leg being given to the performer of the rite, one to the senior wife (and her relatives), and one to the son. The son also takes the jaw and heart; some of the ribs are given to the son's wife, and the neck is given to the daughter's sons. The rest is eaten by members of the deceased's age-grade and the other elders. If a wife fails to provide a goat for this rite the heir must do so, and he is entitled to call upon the wife to pay him compensation.

When a man dies at a distance from his home his body is always taken back, when possible, to his home, wrapped up in mats covered by a cloth and placed on a bier or cradle, which is carried on the shoulders of his relatives. The reason assigned for this is that the dead must not be severed from the company of other ancestors—they should be buried close to their living descendants on whom they are dependent for nourishment. Moreover, it is important that the ritual traditional to the kindred should be carried out accurately. This cannot be done by strangers.

When a married woman dies, her relatives are immediately sent for, and after crying and chanting they call on the husband to provide the burial articles, namely, a cloth, tobacco, and a goat,[1] which is known as the *ewu chi* or 'goat of the guardian-angel'. These are handed over through a friend of the husband. Members of the husband's family then proceed to make a wicker basket in which the corpse is tied up and handed over to a band of young men of the woman's group, who take it home at a trot, chanting as they go along '*E, e, olala!*' ('Ah! she is gone!'). At intervals they stop on the road and dance a war dance, waving their matchets and sticks, the war dance indicating that their blood is roused by what has occurred, or that Death must be deterred from pursuing them.

If the woman's relatives had considered that she had been ill-treated by her husband, they might send some female relatives to look after the corpse, and refrain for several days from sending young men to take the corpse away. This would be a severe punishment for the husband, as a husband must fast until his deceased wife has been buried. He cannot feed himself, his hands being regarded as defiled by death, and is only given a few mouthfuls of roasted yam or corn. After the burial he purifies himself and is then free to eat. If a woman expresses a strong desire in her lifetime to be buried in her husband's home her wishes may be respected. But it is unusual, and her relatives may disregard her wishes by addressing a request to the corpse to be allowed to take her home for burial, and then assuming that the answer is in the affirmative!

Mourning Regulations.

For male members of the community there are few mourning regulations beyond the shaving of the head eight days after the burial of a relative. But for widows there is an elaborate ritual. In the Awgu Division, on the day of a man's death, a senior female relative washes the widow's hands with water and rubs them with an unbroken egg, which is then given to a strong young man, who rushes off at full speed and throws the egg into the 'bush of evil'. The widow goes into seclusion for one month (i.e. seven native weeks) and during this time she must abstain from washing. She shaves her head on the first market-day after her husband's death. She keeps a fire burning, and no one may take an ember from this fire, as it is regarded as the property of the dead man. For the first eight days of her mourning she must sleep on the ground and not on her bed.

---

[1] Two goats would be provided in the case of a woman of importance. No goat is demanded if the deceased wife had died young and childless.

(No reason was given for this rule.) Throughout the month she is considered to be unclean, and at the end of the month her room is swept out by a daughter of the deceased, and the sweepings, together with the widow's mat and dishes, are cast into the 'bush of evil'. This must be done at night, presumably in order to avoid infecting any one else. The woman then goes to a stream (before sunrise) and there washes her body thoroughly, using for this purpose leaves of the *opoto* tree and pieces of the creeper known as *akoro*. On concluding her ablutions she says: 'I have washed away all the evil of the death which killed my husband.' She now dons a new garment, which must be made of fibre and not of cotton, and shaves her head. At the end of a year she discards this garment (throwing it into the 'bush of evil'), and is then free to remarry.

At Owerri, when a woman's husband dies, she is made to sit down that day in her hut on a small piece of wood and must refrain from touching any part of her body, as her hands are defiled. After her husband's burial her hands are ceremonially washed by a female of the family, who rubs them with palm-fibre and a snail and chicken. Then the widow's hair is unloosed, and for four days she cries for her husband regularly every morning, praising him and upbraiding him for leaving her.[1] On the eighth day her hair is shaven (by a female of the husband's group). She is permitted to come outside her hut, but remains in a state of taboo and must sit in a corner by herself. At the end of twenty-four days she is escorted to a main market-road by one of her husband's female relatives, who blocks the road by laying a stick and young palm-leaf across it. All passers-by, recognizing by her shaven head and black cloth that she is a widow, present her with cowries, thus enabling her to purchase the necessary articles for mourning. On returning home she prepares food for the females of her husband's group, and is then free to move about as she likes. But for the ensuing twenty-four days she must be accompanied by a female of the husband's group and must carry a knife—a symbol of defence against evil spirits. On the conclusion of this period she may move about alone, but is expected to abstain from sexual intercourse for a year—a rule which is not always observed at the present time.[2]

---

[1] If the deceased had more than one wife each addresses him by a special honorific title. Thus one may address him as a great hunter, another as a great traveller, a third as the husband of fine-looking women, and a fourth as a great warrior.

[2] On the last day of the year she is asked by the female members of her husband's

Widows are regarded as being still the wives of the deceased until a year after death, and it may be noted that a man's property cannot be divided until a year after death.[1] At the end of the year the widow is required to purchase pots, wooden bowls, wooden and calabash spoons, to a total number of twenty. She must also buy and cook some fish and corn, which are eaten at an assembly of relatives on the following day. On that day she removes her black mourning-cloth, rubs her body with camwood oil, and dons a new cloth provided by her husband's heir. She dresses her hair (for the first time since her husband's death), and then joins in the women's dance. The articles mentioned above are handed over to the women of her husband's group, but two of the pots are left at the corner of the compound as a gift to her late husband. There the pots remain for twenty-four days, when, if they are still unbroken, they are appropriated by the senior woman of the group. That night the widow sleeps with her husband's heir, if it had been agreed that she was to become his wife.

At Amo-Imo for the first eight days after the husband's death the widow must remain in a fixed position in her hut. She must not touch her body and is given a stick with which to scratch herself.[2] She does not feed herself, but is given food by a female member of her husband's family.[3] She must not wash, and sleeps on plantain leaves. She bewails her husband between cockcrow and daybreak each day. Four days after her husband's death her hair is shaven by female members of her husband's family, a tuft of hair being left, which is shaven off at the end of twenty-eight days. On the eighth day also hair on the pubes and armpits is removed and burnt, and the widow washes her hands in a solution of ashes, *ukpa* leaves, and kola leaves. The water used must have been obtained from a hollow in a

group to swear that she has had no sexual relations, and if she refuses to swear is required to pay a fine of 4s. If she is pregnant she becomes an object of abuse and is called on to pay a large fine. But no fine is demanded if she had become pregnant by her husband's heir. Among the Isu the rules are not so strict.

[1] In the case of a poor man his property is automatically appropriated by his heirs at the end of a year (after the final funeral rites), but in the case of a rich man the division of the property is settled at a formal meeting of his relatives.

[2] In the totemic rites of Cape York an initiate is not allowed to touch his body and is given a stick with which to scratch himself. See D. F. Thomson in *J.R.A.I.*, vol. lxiii (1933).

[3] This rule is being relaxed, and among the Oratta the widow is given the first few mouthfuls of food by another and then helps herself.

tree, and the solution is poured over her hands by a female member of her husband's family. The widow is then led forth from her hut by the *Ada*,[1] armed with her husband's knife, and holding his bag. She dons his hat and hangs his gown over her shoulder.[2] Arrayed thus she goes out to the bush, alternately crying and singing her husband's praises.

At the end of twenty-eight days the widow is allowed to resume cooking, after presenting a goat to the female members of her deceased husband's family.[3] But though she may cook for herself and other females with safety, no male (not even her own son) may eat food cooked by her until the lapse of a further period of sixteen days, when she washes herself and rubs her body with chalk, camwood, and charcoal. She is then escorted to the market by old unmarried widows, carrying a basket covered with palm-leaves, and, after throwing away a few cowries in the market-place, is given money by her friends and relatives, and makes a few purchases, returning home unescorted. She now washes off the chalk, charcoal, and camwood from her body, and in the evening sets out for her parents' home.

On the following morning her heritor arrives, and after presenting palm-wine, salt, and 240 cowries to her relatives, and being entertained by them, escorts her back as his wife to his home. If none of her late husband's relatives claims her in marriage, she is paid a formal visit by a female relative of her husband.[4]

If a widow does not remarry, but has children by promiscuous intercourse, these children are regarded as the children of the husband's heir, even if the heir were a young son by another wife. If

[1] i.e. senior female of the family-group.

[2] The intention apparently is to divorce herself from her husband, for when a husband divorces his wife he hangs his cloth or gown on her shoulders.

[3] If there are several widows the senior widow presents a goat and the others a fowl. But in some groups a goat is not demanded if the widow had been childless.

[4] My notes do not indicate whether she returns with the female relative to her late husband's home. Among the Oratta she cannot, at this stage, remain more than four days in her parents' home. Otherwise her husband's spirit would come back and take her off to the next world. It will have been observed that in the Ama-Imo group it is not necessary for a widow to remain unmarried until the conclusion of the final funeral rites. She may begin to live a married life with her late husband's son or next of kin on the conclusion of the rites described above. Even among the Oratta the old rule that a widow must remain unmarried for a full year after her husband's death is breaking down. And at Ubomiri (Isu) it was stated that, if a woman had had scant regard for her late husband, she might take up residence with a new husband within ten days of her late husband's death, provided she had carried out certain formalities.

the only heir were a young son of the widow the children would be regarded as having been begotten by the deceased husband.

The Final Funeral Rites.

The spirit of a dead Ibo is considered to hover round his home, or wander aimlessly in the underworld, until the final funeral rites have been performed. These are known as *Ekwa-Ozu* (or *Okukwa-Ozu*) a phrase which means 'The Lamentation (or crying) for the Dead'. Why they should be so described is not clear, for there is little manifestation of grief. But it was stated that the rites are a remembrance of the sorrow felt and expressed at the time of the person's death. The *Ekwa-Ozu* rites are commonly referred to in English as 'The Second Burial', though there is no apparent reason for the use of this expression.

Ekwa-Ozu rites are not performed for young men who had died before they had married and become fathers, nor for women who had had no issue. For the spirits of such are unworthy of attention, being impotent to aid or injure their living relatives. But the rites are essential for all persons (male or female) who had been considered wealthy or socially important, and for any senior elder or matron, whether rich or poor. If an extended-family fails to perform the rites for such, the *Oha* or senior elders of the community will draw attention to the neglect, and may even seize a goat belonging to the family—an instance of what might appear to be a mere social convention having something of the force of law.

The responsibility for performing the rites falls mainly on the principal heir, who should endeavour to carry them out within a year of the dead man's death. But the period may be extended, if the deceased's family had been unable to find the necessary means, and cases have occurred of the final funeral rites being postponed for as much as ten or twenty years. On the other hand, some heirs postpone the rites unduly, with a view to making an unnecessarily lavish display of wealth—a practice which does not always meet with approval. Though the heir bears the major part of the expenses he is assisted by other relatives, some of whom provide strips of cloth, some a goat, some a dog, and some a keg of powder. Each grown-up male member of the family must borrow a gun, if he has none of his own, and would be fined a fowl if he failed to do so.

On the appointed day drums are beaten early in the morning, and the gunmen line up in pairs and fire off their guns one after the other.[1] Soon afterwards musicians, hired for the occasion, begin to arrive, together with the guests, including the deceased's relatives by marriage. At midday the *Oha* assemble, and are presented by the heir with two goats, which they kill. The first goat is known as the *ofo* goat, the deceased having been an *ofo* holder, while the second is called 'the goat of the heart' (*ewu-obi*), i.e. the goat which will strengthen the dead man's heart, which had become weakened by the troubles of the world. Sometimes the goat is called *ewu-inye-aho* or 'the goat of endurance', i.e. which will confer endurance in the next life. The *Oha* give some of the goat's flesh to the heir, that he may entertain his guests from other villages. The strips of cloth are hung on a pole between the dead man's night and day huts. A live cock and live ram (with an iron bell on its neck) are tied to the pole. Throughout the day there is a great deal of feasting, accompanied by drumming and singing. In the evening, after most of the guests have been dismissed, a person appointed by a diviner takes a gun and fires at the ram.[2] No shot is used and the person who fires must do so at close range. It would be an ill affair if he missed the target, for the object of the rite is to ensure that the dead man shall be a good marksman in his future life. The ram and fowl are then taken down and divided among the *Oha* and heir; but a share may also be given to sons of the deceased's daughters. Feasting is kept up for a period of from four to eight days, and on the final day a visit is paid to the market, where songs are sung and guns discharged. On the following morning a cow, goat, or dog is killed, and some of the blood is poured over the deceased's cultus-emblems, which are then piled together and scattered by gun-fire. This concludes the final funeral rites, as practised in the Owerri Division.

In the Nsukka Division the ritual is much the same. The proceedings are opened by the firing of guns, and on the following day a feast is provided, at which the dead man is believed to be present and to partake. Songs are sung, and verses introduced in his honour: 'That generous man who knew when children were hungry, who was wont to assist the poor; that generous man who loved us all, has gone

---

[1] One bottle of powder is distributed to each pair of gunmen and must be wholly used up in the rites. It is said that unscrupulous persons sometimes attempt to purloin some of the powder for their own use later.

[2] At Ubomiri the ram's head must be severed with a matchet at a single blow. At Amo-Imo a piece of white cloth and a fowl are hung up on the symbol of Anyañu (the sun) and are blown to pieces by the gunmen.

away. Verily, it is hard to find any one like him. Amosi[1] has gone; Ajode[2] has gone; Ogbute[3] has gone; he who did something to another's son (i.e. killed a man) has gone; he who killed a slave for his dead father[4] has gone.' Gongs are beaten and guns fired during the singing, and large quantities of palm-wine are consumed, small libations being first poured on the ground for the dead man's consumption. The deceased's daughter parades about, carrying a horse-tail, to show that her father had had the 'horse-title', and that a horse will soon be killed in his honour.

On the following market-day men of the deceased's village parade round the market with a horse provided by the deceased's son, and then take up a position in the corner of the market, where they spend the day singing and receiving gifts from friends of neighbouring villages. The horse is killed a few days later in the centre of the deceased's village, and the meat is cooked and eaten by all members of the village. The head, skin, and tail of the horse are appropriated by the eldest son, who hangs the skull up in the roof of his house.

In the Awgu Division the final funeral rites are sometimes begun by the destruction of the *chi*[5] symbols of the deceased. The eldest son or heir goes to the symbols and lays beside them two yams, saying, 'My father, I am giving these yams to you. When you are reborn may you be a farmer of many yams.' He then takes a goat and, standing before the symbols, says, 'My father, I am going to kill this goat on your account. When you are reborn may it be as my own son, and may everything that you do turn to your advantage. As you are now in the spirit-world be pleased to avert evil from me.' He slays the goat and pours the blood over the symbol. He may also sacrifice a cow, if his means allow. The *chi* symbols of the deceased are then cut down and thrown away. The guests now give themselves up to dancing and feasting, guns being fired off at frequent intervals. Friends from other villages may supply the powder, and receive in return the gift of a cow. In this case the liver and head of the cow must be given to the dead man's son, that they may be placed on the grave.

Next day those members of the kindred who had themselves killed cattle in honour of their dead fathers, come to the house of the

---

[1] *Amosi* is a title borne by one who has killed a horse.
[2] *Ajode* is a hunting title.   [3] *Ogbute* is a title given to warriors.
[4] Such a one bears the title of *Ogbunogbodo*.   [5] See p. 55.

deceased's son, to receive a share of the cow killed on this occasion; and eight days later a banquet is provided for the entire kindred and their relatives by marriage. Songs are sung by the women in honour of the deceased, and of his son, who is now hailed as an *Ogbu-Nyiwa* ('Killer of many animals'), and as *Omechara-nnaya* ('Completer of his father'), or *Ome-ihe-ako* ('Doer of something with property'). In former times, if the son were a member of the guild of head-hunters, he would be hailed by a further title of *Ogbu-ka-Obasi-nnaya*, i.e. destroyer of the *Obasi* or head-hunting symbol of his father.

As many members of the old head-hunting guilds are still alive it may be of interest to describe the special ritual formerly (and I believe still occasionally) followed on the death of one of these. The rites were carried out by the son, provided he himself belonged to the guild; otherwise by the head of the guild. The officiant (son, or principal head-getter) stood before the symbol (an *abosse* tree) and spoke as follows: 'My father, I have brought to you this day a dog and chicken in order that I may be permitted to cut down your *Obasi*. When you are reborn slay not your own children, and may they not slay you. May you kill none by accident, but may you kill your enemies with the intent to do so. Whatever good you desire may it be accomplished.' The dog and fowl were then killed, and the blood was allowed to flow on to the ground in front of the symbol. The symbol was then cut down and thrown into the 'bush of evil'. The flesh of the dog and fowl was cooked and eaten by the warriors, young and old. During the feast old war-songs were sung, such as: 'I am a kite which kills and carries off', 'I am an evil spirit (*Ekweesu*) for an unfortunate man', 'I am the killer of a woman's husband, and the woman mourned her loss in the compound'. In some communities the head-getter's emblem was an *obo* tree and was known as his *ikenga* (i.e. upper arm). Before it was cut down the prayer was: 'When you are reborn may your *ikenga* stand straight. May you be a killer of enemies, and not of fellow clansmen. May your son, who is succeeding you, look after his family as you did.' The officiant then took a matchet, and with a single blow struck off the head of the sacrificial ram. The symbol was now cut down and a feast held, the meat being dipped in a sauce of oil and pepper which had first been deposited in a human skull.

In the Awgu Division the final funeral rites are concluded by offerings at the dead man's grave. The eldest son or heir cuts up pieces of the livers of the various animals which had been sacrificed during the rites, and, accompanied by some of the elders, goes to the grave and speaks as follows: 'My father, we have observed all the customs of our forefathers. Help me, therefore, to look after my people as you did when you were with us. Avert evil and permit no bad thing to overtake any of our kindred. In whatever household you are reborn may you have a happy life and not die a sudden death.' He then deposits pieces of kola and liver on the grave, the remainder being eaten by all present. Finally, he beats a wooden gong four times, as a public announcement that he has finished the rites. All the old men then shake hands with the deceased's eldest son and return home.

Immediately after the final funeral rites the deceased's property is formally divided. It would be an affront to the dead man, and dangerous to all concerned, if this were done sooner. But it frequently happens that a dead man's property is urgently required, and yet the heir is unable, through poverty, to carry out the final rites within a reasonable period. To meet this difficulty a simulacrum of the rites may be permitted as a temporary measure, consisting mainly in the firing of guns, with a view, apparently, to deceiving the deceased that the whole ritual had been duly carried out. His property may then be divided with comparative safety. But before giving an account of the rules of inheritance a few remarks may be offered on the meaning attached to the final funeral rites.

It is said that the first funeral rites start the dead man on his journey 'home'. They provide him with the preliminary dues, and it is for this reason that money is frequently placed in the grave, or (in the form of cowries) is attached to the sacrificial fowl. But the first funeral rites are insufficient to enable him to reach the abode of the dead, and without the assistance of the final rites his spirit would wander aimlessly around, or continue to haunt his former home. Moreover, his social status in the spirit world depends on the funeral rites. For the funeral feast is attended not merely by himself but by the whole company of his fellow spirits, and if the fare provided is poor they will form a poor opinion of their new companion. For the same reason it is necessary to continue to offer sacrifice (or food) to the dead. For ghosts or spirits entertain one another, and a ghost who is always receiving hospitality and giving none becomes an object of contempt, and will take vengeance on his living descendants for having placed him in this position. The final funeral rites are, therefore, designed to send the dead man away fully satisfied, and qualified to attend the feasts provided by the living relatives of other ghosts. Relatives who fail to perform the rites are said to 'have roasted their father'.

Such is the popular interpretation of the final funeral rites. But if we look a little deeper it is clear that the rites serve other useful purposes. They comfort the living by giving them the assurance that they will one day be reunited with their dead relatives and friends. And they free them from the fear of being haunted by the ghosts of persons whom they may once have injured. Moreover, by postponing, as it were, the departure of the dead for several months, or even for a year, they enable his relatives to adjust their lives gradually to the new conditions, and save them from an unseemly, not to say dangerous, haste in appropriating his property. The institution of the final funeral feast also operates as a kind of dinner-club, the members of which entertain each other in turn. It is almost actionable at law to withhold an invitation from one who had previously entertained another in this way. Finally, the custom of 'crying for the dead' is a means not only of honouring the dead, but also of exalting the living, in the person of the descendant who bears the expenses. So much is this so, that the custom is used as a recognized method of obtaining a title. In the Nsukka Division, for example, a man who carries out the final funeral rites on a lavish scale is ever afterwards entitled to be called *Omezuru* or 'The Complete Doer'.

Inheritance.

The rules governing inheritance are consistent with the general character of the social organization, and at the same time are so elastic and based on such equitable principles that they can be easily modified to meet changing conditions, such as the progressive tendency towards individualization.

Property held by virtue of an office passes to the successor. Thus, lands or palms[1] held in trust by the head of a family for the family's benefit, cannot be alienated without the family's consent and must be handed on intact, together with his official *ofo*, and other insignia of office, to the next senior elder or other person chosen as his successor. It may be remarked that in the Nsukka Division special plots of land

---

[1] Palms growing wild in the forest are not heritable, as they are owned by the entire group or by nobody. But palms on farm or home lands are owned by individuals or by families. Waterside palms used for matting are sometimes owned by families and sometimes by individuals.

are sometimes attached to the offices of Atama, Onyisi, or Eze. A priest's cultus-apparatus passes to his successor.

As regards private property, i.e. property obtained by gift or inheritance from a father or some one else, or by purchase or individual effort, the governing principle is primogeniture or inheritance by the eldest son. But, though the eldest son inherits the major share of all property, he is bound to look after the interests of his younger brothers and half-brothers, of whom he becomes the social father. The manner, therefore, in which the inheritance is used depends largely on circumstances. Thus, if a father had died leaving two sons, and had during his lifetime provided the elder but not the younger with farming land and a supply of seed-yams,[1] then the younger son would on his father's death have an automatic claim to any seed-yams left in his father's store. Again, if the elder son were unmarried at his father's death, he would immediately set aside a sum sufficient to obtain a bride for himself, and would then (at Awgu) appropriate two-thirds of the remainder of the estate, leaving one-third to his younger brother. But if he were already married, and his younger brother were not, then he would first assign to his younger brother a sum sufficient for a bride-price, and appropriate two-thirds of the remainder, leaving one-third to his younger brother.

Where there are sisters, the eldest son is entitled (on his father's death) to receive the bride-price obtained for the eldest sister, even if she is only a half-sister. A second son can only take the bride-price of a full sister. But if the second son had no full sister, and the third son had more than one full sister, then the bride-price obtained for one full sister of the third son would be allotted to the second son (provided he was still unmarried).

If the eldest son is sufficiently grown-up to carry out the burial rites of his father, an expensive duty, he is entitled to recoup himself from his father's estate. Indeed, one of the principal reasons for giving the eldest son a larger share of the inheritance than his brothers is to enable him to perform this primary duty. Incidentally, it was stated at Awgu that if a brother or son of the deceased were unable or refused to perform the burial rites of his brother or father, any other member of the deceased's extended-family might undertake this duty, and if he did so he became entitled to a major share of the deceased's property. But he would thereby make himself responsible

---

[1] A father usually supplies his sons with seed-yams when they marry, and also with a house, farming land, a matchet, and possibly a gun.

for the upkeep and marriage of the deceased's children. Such cases are of rare occurrence, as a man's foremost duty in life is to see that his father or brother is buried with as much ceremony as his means permit. This is not merely a pious act. It is done in order to avoid pursuit by the dead man's ghost. It also confers a social status on the person performing it—the more elaborate the burial rites the more important the performer becomes in the eyes of the people. No more abusive remark can be made to a man than 'You never even killed a rat for your father's funeral!'

Widows are heritable, and may become wives of brothers or (in some localities) of sons of the deceased. An eldest son may give one of his father's widows (with her consent) to his father's younger brother, without demanding any bride-price. If the widows marry outside their husband's family, the heritor is entitled to demand a bride-price, and may include in the demand moneys given to the widow to enable her to offer sacrifice at the conclusion of her mourning period. The bride-price received may be divided among the sons in proportion to their marriage requirements, unmarried sons taking precedence over married sons, and allowance being made for any sums already paid for a prospective bride. It is *infra dignitatem*, however, for a son to receive a bride-price (or any part of it) on the remarriage of his widowed mother. In towns where levirate marriage is practised, the brother who marries the widow must provide a wife for his deceased brother's son, if the son has no wife of his own. If the deceased brother had left two widows, one brother, and one grown-up unmarried son, the son would inherit the widow who was not his own mother, while the brother would inherit and marry the other. In this case it would not be incumbent on the brother to pay any compensation to the son. It may be noted that, where levirate marriage is practised, widows are not compelled to marry their deceased husband's brother should they be disinclined.[1] Also that they are not allowed to remarry until one year after their late husband's death. In some groups[2] a widow may remain unmarried in her late husband's home and have promiscuous sexual intercourse. Resultant children are regarded as children of the husband's heir, even if the

---

[1] Inheritance of widows is regarded with disfavour by Christian Missions. It should be remembered, however, that one of the objects of levirate marriage is to enable a widow to live a married life in close association with her children by the former husband.

[2] e.g. among the Oratta and some groups at least in the Awgu Division.

heir were a young lad, the son of one of her late husband's other wives. If the only heir happened to be the widow's own son the children would be regarded as having been begotten by the deceased husband. In some groups (e.g. Ngbwidi) sons may inherit, but may not marry, their fathers' widows, while in other groups (e.g. Okpanko and Mpu) sons neither inherit nor marry their fathers' widows, nor do brothers inherit the widows of brothers or half-brothers.

If the eldest son is too young to inherit, the deceased's brother takes charge of all property, including widows, farm-land, crops, palms, live-stock, implements, and cash. But he is bound to provide for the keep and marriage of his deceased brother's sons. For the latter purpose he may use a bride-price received for his deceased brother's daughter. In due course, when the children have grown up, they take possession of their father's lands and palms and any balance of property that their uncle may have in hand. If the uncle has squandered the property, or failed to act equitably towards his nephews, he is liable to an action for damages.[1]

A man's compound may be inherited by the deceased's brother, if the latter had been living with him at the time of his death. But, as most married men own compounds of their own, it frequently happens that the father's compound is inherited by some junior unmarried son. The hut of the dead father is sometimes broken down, the eldest son taking away to his own house the skulls of horses which had adorned the roof. Private cults are not usually inherited, and the symbols are destroyed when the owner dies. But the family *ọfọ* is taken over by the senior surviving brother, or by the eldest son, as the case may be. Cult-*ọfọ* are also heritable. Sometimes the heirs to cults are chosen by divination or by reference to one of the well-known oracles.

A man who feels that his end is near may divide out his property among the various members of his family, so as to avoid disputes after his death. He does this particularly if he distrusts his eldest son, or observes that his sons are prone to quarrelling among themselves. He may also make final gifts to his daughters, and may bequeath small articles of property to his sister's son. If he is rich he may bequeath a cow. A case came to my notice of a rich important man over-riding local custom by bequeathing the family *ọfọ* to his eldest son when normally it should have passed to his younger brother. But the old man first secured the consent of all the members of his family, including

[1] See pp. 124 and 230.

the brother, who agreed to forgo his claim to the *ọfọ* on condition of receiving certain gifts. Having made these arrangements the old man summoned all the elders of the village and addressed his eldest son as follows: 'To you, my eldest son, I bequeath my *ọfọ*. You are to-day appointed to be my successor as head of the family. To this your uncle and brothers have agreed. They are to respect you in all things, and this *ọfọ* must remain with you and your descendants.' He then struck the ground with his left hand and breathed on the *ọfọ* with the intention of conveying his words to the ancestors immanent therein. These proceedings were considered irregular, but as they were carried out by general consent they were not considered illegal.

Sons of slave-women have the same rights of inheritance as the sons of free-women, and the property of sons is heritable by fathers, though brothers and not fathers are responsible for the burial rites. The property of a man who dies after having taken an oath is forfeit to the spirit or deity that killed him and is handed over, therefore, to the priest. But it may be thrown away into the taboo 'bush', if the divining-apparatus so directs.

A woman's property is heritable by her children, but the children may allow their father a share. Thus, at Awgu, a woman's land,[1] palms, and cash are divided up amongst her sons, the eldest son taking the largest share, but using it, if necessary, in the interests of his younger brothers. Her goats, fowls, crops, and cooking utensils are divided amongst her daughters, the eldest taking the largest share but being expected to use it for the wedding outfit of her young unmarried sisters. Sisters do not inherit from brothers (except articles of trifling value such as grindstones for snuff). In the absence of children, a woman's property is claimed by her husband. But purely feminine property would be handed to her sisters. The rule permitting a husband to claim his wife's property, in the absence of children, is justified on the ground that in this way he receives compensation for an unproductive bride-price. It was stated at Owerri that in former times if a wife died childless her relatives consulted a diviner in order to ascertain whether her death was due to wrong conduct on the part of her husband. If the husband were pronounced blameworthy the wife's relatives demanded the return of any property she had acquired. But otherwise they provided the widower with a new

---

[1] A woman cannot inherit land, but she may lease it or even (in some localities) buy it.

wife for a nominal consideration, and the new wife inherited the former wife's property.

In some localities it seemed that the husband was permitted to appropriate any property left by his wife, whether she had left children or not, and this custom (which appears to have grown up recently) was justified by the assertion that a woman, on marriage, brings no form of wealth to her husband's home. It is presumed, therefore, that any wealth she acquires after marriage is acquired through the agency of her husband.

It may be noted finally that a man's property is always divided up in presence of the elders of the kindred, in order to prevent disputes between half-brothers. But a woman's property is divided out by her husband or by her sons, since full brothers seldom quarrel with one another on matters of inheritance.

XIV

PRACTICAL CONCLUSIONS

AS this book purports not merely to give an account of the system
of law and authority in a Nigerian tribe, but also to be a study
in 'Indirect Rule', I propose in this final chapter to attempt to justify
the latter claim and to show the practical bearing of our investigations
on present-day problems of Ibo administration. But first let us
understand what is meant by 'Indirect Rule'. The name suggests
that it is the opposite of direct rule, and direct rule presumably implies the centralization of the functions of government in a suzerain
power which controls its subjects by means of its own staff of civil
servants. But direct rule on these lines would usually be impractic-
able in any dependent territory of large dimensions, particularly if
the dependent peoples were culturally distinct from those on whom
they depend; and even in the ancient world most great imperial
powers were compelled to resort to some measure of indirect rule,
that is to say, to utilize to some extent the political machinery of the
dependent peoples. 'Indirect Rule', therefore, as a general principle,
is not the special invention of the British, but has been an everyday
instrument of government almost from the beginning of history. But
the manner in which it has been applied is another matter; and it
can be claimed for British Administration that it has carried the
principle of 'Indirect Rule' to the pinnacle point of its development.
The most striking advance in recent times was made by Sir Frederick
(now Lord) Lugard in Northern Nigeria. When the British Government assumed control of this vast territory at the beginning of the
present century, it found in existence a highly developed system of
Muslim government, including a Fulah sultanate composed of numerous provinces, each administered by a feudal governor with his own
council and executive, army, police, treasury, and judiciary. Here was
a ready-made machine, and Sir Frederick was not slow to use it, more
especially as the Imperial Government was unable or unwilling at
that time to bear the expense of supporting a large staff of British
officials in Nigeria.

Yet the task to which Sir Frederick set himself was no easy one.
Slavery had been the basis of the social organization, and the country
had been devastated by raids for slaves and drained of its resources by

the insatiable demands of its despotic rulers and their armies of satellites. Nevertheless, the bold policy was adopted of retaining these rulers and the entire machinery of government, while abolishing only the status of slavery and a number of other institutions which were inconsistent with modern civilized ideas. The venture proved to be an unparalleled success. Within a few years Northern Nigeria had been transformed into a highly prosperous protectorate, with the full co-operation not merely of the mass of the people but also of their former rulers, who had now become the heads of highly efficient Native Administrations. Sir Frederick, moreover, did not rest content with a striking practical success, but 'proceeded to rationalize his achievement', as Miss Margery Perham has so admirably said;[1] and by formulating the rules of the administrative technique which had gradually been evolved, with the help of a remarkably able and enthusiastic staff, he provided (in 'The Dual Mandate') a standard exposition of the principles of 'Indirect Rule', and a text-book of administration for all Colonial Governments.[2]

But is 'Indirect Rule', then, nothing better than an opportunist policy, a mere administrative convenience to fit particularly favourable circumstances, such as those which existed in Northern Nigeria in the first years of the present century? It is certainly not so to-day, and it is true to say that in Northern Nigeria, from its very inception in 1900, the policy of 'Indirect Rule' was deliberately pursued not with a view to present necessity but to future development. It was framed indeed on the belief that if a backward people is suddenly confronted by a powerful modern state, and is not given the time and assistance necessary to enable it to face the new situation, it is liable to lose its stability, and indeed its soul. Its political and social organization is likely to break up, and what was before a well-ordered community, in which all the members had a definite series of obligations to one another, may become nothing but a disorganized rabble of self-seeking individualists.

[1] In a lecture on 'Indirect Rule' delivered at the Society of Arts in 1934. In the writing of this chapter I have been conscious of saying many things which have been said, and better said, by Miss Perham, both in the lecture referred to and in two chapters of her recent book which I had the privilege of seeing before publication.

[2] 'The Dual Mandate' will of course require revision from time to time to meet the demands of changing conditions and wider experience, particularly as regards the administration of pagan tribes. In this connexion readers are referred to Sir Donald Cameron's brochure on *The Principles of Native Administration and their Application*, published by the Nigerian Government in 1934. (Price 1s.)

But, if the policy of 'Indirect Rule' is to be founded on indigenous institutions, it is clearly open to the very grave danger of degenerating into a policy of stagnation and segregation, preventing the spread of education and new ideas, and seeking to stereotype institutions which might soon cease to have any functional validity. In this way it would defeat the very object for which it was framed, namely the provision of a bridge by which the people might pass safely from the old culture to the new. It would prevent them from making that gradual but necessary adaptation which would save them from being swept away by the torrent of new religious, economic, social, and political forces. If 'Indirect Rule' is to avoid this danger, and it is a danger which has caused the policy to be viewed with grave suspicion by many Europeans and also by progressive Africans, then it cannot afford to be static, but must be essentially evolutionary and constructive. The native institutions must be given full scope to adapt themselves to changing conditions.

Having cleared the ground in this way, we may define 'Indirect Rule' as a system of government by which the controlling power encourages among its dependent peoples the fullest possible use of their own dynamic institutions as instruments of local self-government on lines consistent with modern requirements. This may not be a watertight definition, as varying views may be held as to what would constitute the fullest possible use of any institution, or what things would be consistent or inconsistent with modern requirements, but the definition will serve well enough to show the broad basis on which the policy of 'Indirect Rule' is now interpreted by the Nigerian and some other British Colonial Governments. By the system of 'Indirect Rule' native societies are enabled to continue their corporate life, to retain and develop their own political experience, and to speak and to be consulted through their own familiar institutions. The system confers freedom of expression conjoined with responsibility; it provides training in the art of self-government through an unbroken chain of responsibility extending from the individual to the central authority; it is a means, therefore, for reforming administration from within rather than from without; and it fosters the great principle of governing from the standpoint of the governed. Under it the function of the controlling power becomes that of a teacher and trustee rather than of a master and dictator.

From our definition it is clear that the principle of 'Indirect Rule' is, in theory at least, applicable to politically undeveloped communities no less than those possessed of consolidated constitutions. Indeed, it is true to say that the least developed communities are precisely those that require the indirect policy most, as their very want of unity and absence of any form of central control make them proportionately more vulnerable to the forces of disintegration. But the practical difficulties of applying 'Indirect Rule' to backward communities are also proportionately greater, because not merely is there no form of central government but even in the local groups authority may be so widely distributed that, in the absence of close study, it may scarcely seem to exist.

In South-Eastern Nigeria, therefore, it had seemed out of place even to speak of 'Indirect Rule', as there were no rulers; and it was assumed that the only possible form of government was government on direct lines, the British District Officer (or District Commissioner as he was then called) taking the place of the missing chief. Thus, prior to 1914, the sole instruments of native administration in the South-Eastern Provinces were 'Native Courts' in which the British District Officers sat as presidents.[1] Each court had jurisdiction over a wide area, including within its ambit a multitude of unrelated social groupings. The native membership of the bench was formed by choosing from each village a representative who was given a 'warrant' as a formal appointment. These representatives sat in turn with the District Officer, but as assessors rather than judges. The courts were not, therefore, 'native' in any real sense. The judges or 'court members', moreover, were required to see that the orders of the District Officer were carried out in their own villages, and so, as the sole recognized executive authorities, assumed the title and functions of chiefs—and of highly despotic chiefs at that. The traditional authorities were ignored, and many of them ceased to function.

On the amalgamation of Northern and Southern Nigeria in 1914[2] Sir Frederick Lugard, who had (in 1912) returned to Nigeria as Governor-General, proceeded to institute in the Southern Provinces some of the principles of 'Indirect Rule' which had borne such magnificent fruit in Northern Nigeria. The South-Western Provinces, with the framework provided by the ancient kingdoms of the Yoruba, presented suitable conditions for building up Native Administrations

---

[1] The courts were modelled on the old Consular Courts of Equity, in which the British Consul sat with native assessors.

[2] Northern Nigeria now became known as 'The Northern Provinces' and Southern Nigeria as 'The Southern Provinces'.

on Northern Nigerian lines, and steps were, therefore, taken to restore the ancient tribal machinery before the disintegration, which had already set in, had become complete.[1] At first the Northern Nigerian model was closely copied, with the result that artificial districts were created, and the powers of chiefs exaggerated at the expense of the councils and societies which had exercised so much authority in former times.[2] Local self-government was also insufficiently extended to the village communities, where the system of administration by means of district Native Courts was allowed to continue. The co-operation of the 'intelligentsia' was enlisted by means of advisory boards or the selection of individuals to central and district councils, but the results were not always satisfactory, as the administration tended to be top-heavy and unrepresentative. Yet by gradual adjustments the Native Administrations of the South-Western Provinces have become flourishing and up-to-date institutions, loyally supported by all classes of the community, including the educated 'intelligentsia'.

Sir Frederick next turned his attention to the South-Eastern Provinces; but here the administrative problem appeared to be insoluble. An attempt was made to strengthen native authority by removing the British District Officers from their posts as presidents of the Native Courts; but this step alone, unattended by administrative reconstruction, was insufficient to effect any substantial reform. Indeed, it merely served to strengthen the false position of the 'Warrant Chiefs' and give them additional opportunities for corrupt conduct. When, therefore, the Secretary for Native Affairs (Mr. S. M. Grier[3]) toured the South-Eastern Provinces in 1922, he reported to the new Governor, Sir Hugh Clifford, that the Native Courts had become one of the principal disintegrating forces in the country, and were believed by the majority of the British Administrative Officers to be thoroughly corrupt. They were the sole connecting link between the District Officer and the people, their members had usually no hereditary title to authority in their own villages, and they were controlled by semi-educated court-clerks, who issued summonses without reference to any chief, gave orders for arrest, took custody of prisoners, and were the recognized means for transmitting orders from the District Officer to the 'Warrant Chiefs'. Mr. Grier recommended that the District

[1] See Sessional Paper No. 28, 1930, para. 4.
[2] Disturbances occurred in Oyo Province in 1916, and in 1918 there was a serious revolt in Egbaland.
[3] Now Sir S. M. Grier, K.C.M.G

Officers should be reinstated as presidents of the courts, that the hereditary chiefs of all towns and villages should be the only chiefs recognized by the Government,[1] and that where possible the old clan councils under the clan chiefs should be revived.[2] These recommendations seemed to envisage a system of 'chieftainship' which existed only in a few localities.

In the following year Mr. G. J. F. Tomlinson,[3] who had also been asked to visit and report on the administration of the South-Eastern Provinces, recommended a thorough reorganization. 'The first and most elementary requirement', he said, 'is that the Native Court areas should coincide with the distribution of the clans.' He also drew attention to the importance of the village councils and of the part played in administration by the system of titles. He deprecated the proposal to reinstate the District Officers as presidents of the Native Courts, as this would be a retrograde step which would tend to prevent the recognition of the proper native authority and rob the court of any claim to be a native tribunal.[4] Subsequent events proved the soundness of Mr. Tomlinson's conclusions. But the thorough reorganization recommended by him was never seriously begun,[5] and thus a golden opportunity was lost; for after the introduction of taxation the difficulty of obtaining reliable information was immeasurably increased.

Soon after the appointment of Sir Graeme Thomson as Governor, in 1925, it was decided that no substantial progress could be made in the Government's policy of educating the peoples of the South-Eastern Provinces in the art of self-government unless funds to establish Native Administrations were made available by means of direct taxation. Moreover, it appeared to be a matter of equity that, when the rest of Nigeria was paying direct taxes, the South-Eastern Provinces should not be exempt. The Native Revenue Ordinance should, therefore, be applied to the untaxed provinces in April 1927, and half the proceeds of the direct-tax should be devoted to the establishment of local Native Administrations.

The formal announcement of the Government's intention to institute taxation and set up Native Administrations was received with

[1] Many of the Native Court judges or 'Warrant Chiefs' had been given their appointments as a reward for their services to the Government.

[2] See Sessional Paper No. 28, Annexure I, para. 146.

[3] Now Sir George Tomlinson, K.C.M.G., C.B.E.

[4] See Sessional Paper No. 28, Annexure I, para. 156.   [5] See ibid., para. 160.

sullen acquiescence in most localities, and in some districts there was considerable passive resistance to the assessment that followed. At Warri, on September 30th, 1927, the Officer administering the Government of Nigeria (Sir Frank Baddeley) was given an unfriendly reception, and on his departure to Lagos a riot occurred during which the police had to use their fire-arms. For some weeks Warri Province remained in a disturbed condition. The disturbances were said to be part and parcel of a premeditated plan of resistance to taxation, of which the main features were that no one should attend the Native Courts nor trade with European firms. No arrests by police or Native Court messengers were to be permitted and if any one were arrested he was to be rescued. The indigenous organization, long neglected, was to some extent revived, and functioned for the time being in opposition to the established order. The Native Court members or 'Warrant Chiefs', almost without exception, were brushed aside as Government agents who had agreed to the tax, and for that offence a large number of them were heavily fined by self-constituted tribunals, while in several instances they were assaulted and their property looted. Other persons also were fined for infringements of the laws laid down by the leaders.[1] A large force of police had to be concentrated in Warri Province, and it was not until the end of the year (1927) that peace was fully restored. The disturbances, if they bore no other fruit, revealed the fact that native organizations existed which could be (and have since been) utilized as an integral part of the system of government.[2]

The actual collection of the first year's tax (1928–9) was effected with less trouble than was expected, and half of the revenue was paid into the newly established treasuries which, at this stage, and for some years afterwards, were native only in name, as the funds remained in the custody of the local District Officers and were administered by them. Nor, indeed, had any real framework of native administration been as yet devised; for in spite of genuine attempts made on the eve of taxation to arrive at a clearer understanding of the social organization of the people, the Government had still no adequate information on which it could lay even the modest foundations of a system of native administration. The necessary information could only have been provided by a programme of long and patient research conducted

[1] Sessional Paper No. 28, 1930, para. 18.
[2] Warri, from being one of the most rebellious communities, has become (1936) one of the most contented and progressive, showing remarkable initiative and keenness.

scientifically over a wide area. The Commission appointed to examine into the causes of the women's riots in 1929 gave it as their
considered opinion that 'much greater progress in the policy of the
resuscitation and political education of the natural rulers of the people
should have taken place before any attempt was made to introduce
direct-taxation; for the Administrative Officers concerned would then
have come more closely into touch with the people by virtue of the
very process of inquiry which is now taking place after, instead of
before, the introduction of taxation'.[1] This opinion was subsequently
endorsed by the Secretary of State for the Colonies.

The women's riots broke out suddenly in November of 1929. It
is unnecessary to describe them in detail—how mobs of frenzied
Amazons, sometimes numbering 10,000, with their heads decorated
with palm-leaves and wild fern (a symbol of war), their faces smeared
with charcoal, and carrying cudgels of bamboo or cassava, marched
from village to village assaulting the 'Warrant Chiefs' and compelling
them to deliver up their caps of office—a mode of degradation practised by the Ọzọ and other titled societies—how they pulled to pieces
or burnt down the Native Court buildings, destroyed bridges, looted
European trading stores, released prisoners, and in many cases offered
active opposition to armed bodies of Government police or troops.

The riots continued for several weeks, but before the end of the
year order had been restored in most areas by means of military
patrols. Two Commissions of Inquiry followed, the second of which
toured the disturbed areas and examined close on five hundred witnesses. In the opinion of this Commission, which included two African
members, the main cause of the riots was the widespread belief that
women were to be taxed. But the whole question of taxation, whether
of men or women, was intimately connected with the general system
of native administration, and that this system was thoroughly detested
had been amply proved by the methods pursued by the rioters, as
well as by the subsequent evidence. It was an artificial system which
had no basis in native institutions. In his dispatch, therefore, dealing
with the findings of the Commission, the Secretary of State for the
Colonies expressed the opinion that the disturbances had clearly
demonstrated the necessity for a campaign of anthropological research.

By this time, however (i.e. 1930), the Nigerian Government had
already embarked on an extensive campaign of this kind (in the
provinces east of the Niger). The guiding principles of this were

[1] Sessional Paper, No. 28, 1930, para. 300.

that the indigenous social and political organization of each group
studied was to be described in detail, and recommendations made for
utilizing such native institutions as appeared to be capable of functioning at the present time, due regard being paid to the changes
being produced by the spread of education, Christianity, new economic conceptions, and other factors of acculturation. Moreover, the
administrative proposals made were to be such as would be likely to
receive the approval of the people as a whole.

This was the theoretical scheme; but, as all who have had any experience of administration know, there is a world of difference between
theory and practice. Moreover, the thoroughness of the research was
very much limited by the need for some speedy form of reorganization, and also by the fact that the administrative staff, instead of
having been enlarged to meet the difficulty, had been reduced in
consequence of the financial slump. Nevertheless, reports on over
two hundred groups have been submitted in the course of the last
four years (1930–4), and reorganization has proceeded apace on lines
which will be indicated presently.

With this historical background we may now ask what lessons of
practical administrative value can be learned from the data presented
in this book. A number of indications have already been given, but
the main points may be summarized as follows. The first point is the
immense importance of the kinship grouping, i.e. of the organization
which we have described as an extended-family or kindred. Here we
have the fundamental unit of law and authority, a group of consanguineous relatives which usually yields ready obedience to a well-recognized head or heads, and is so closely knit together by common
interests and common obligations that the conduct of one of its
members is the close concern of all. The kinship or family-group
functions as a unit for many everyday matters, and in the past
managed its own affairs without external interference, unless the
interests of other groups were also involved. The village or village-
group is nothing more than a collection of kindreds, and the village
council a collection of heads of kindreds or their representatives. Indeed, the law of the village-group is merely an extension to itself of
the means used by the kindred to regulate the conduct of its members.
The kinship or family organization is, therefore, the cradle of morality,
the basis of the political structure, and the mainstay of the good-
ordering of the entire community.

It is not contended, of course, that the individual is of small account. On the contrary it is clear from our studies that every individual was held responsible for his own behaviour, and that ample scope was given in Ibo society for a fairly full development of the individual personality. One might go further and say that the Ibo are individualistic to an unusual degree, as is evident at public meetings where any person is entitled to give expression to his views.[1] But the fact remains that the family organization is still the strongest force of cohesion in Ibo society, and that, in spite of the changing conditions which are making for increased individualism, the stability of that organization has not in most areas been seriously impaired. It is incumbent, therefore, on the Government to recognize and utilize fully this basic institution and to avoid the mistake of regarding any Ibo community as a mere collection of individuals. The kin should be allowed to settle their own disputes in the traditional fashion, as far as possible, and the authority of the kindred heads should be upheld by dealing through them instead of directly with individuals. They should be made the channel by which taxes are assessed and collected, and the kin should be held responsible, as in former times, for the arrest of a criminal or his appearance at a public trial. This should be the general policy, but pursued in an elastic and not a rigid manner, and with the full concurrence of the people. No family-group should be forced to show a loyalty or unity which it does not feel, for kinship groupings are not static but, like all living organisms, are in a constant state of change.

The next point of importance is that if government and law began in the kinship-group it ended in the village-group or commune. A number of village-groups, it is true, might be conscious of a sense of relationship and act as a unit in the face of some common danger; and membership of the Ozọ society also created bonds wider than those of the village-group. But for all practical purposes the village-group was the highest unit of government. Here was an association of people bound together by the closest bonds of common interest, sharing the same lands, markets, and water-supplies, the same cults and traditions, and with its own parliament and judiciary. The village-group in fact was a small independent republic.

It follows, therefore, that if native administration is to have any real basis in native institutions it can only be based on those of the

---

[1] The conditions described here closely resemble those of the Maori communities so excellently described by Dr. Raymond Firth in his *Primitive Economics of the New Zealand Maori* (e.g., pp. 121 ff.).

village-group. To attempt to base it directly on a purely artificial creation like a District Native Court, which had no relation to any form of social life, was an experiment which was doomed to failure. Granting the necessity for creating a wider sense of solidarity than the village-group, and the impossibility of adequate supervision by the District Officer of large numbers of village-groups, it still remains essential that native administration must grow naturally out of its own roots and not be imposed artificially from above. The first step, therefore, in any system of reorganization must be the restoration to the village-group of an adequate share of the management of its own affairs. That is to say, that each village-group should have its own council, and its own executive and judicial authority to dispose summarily of all minor cases and to serve as a clearing-house for the more serious cases which would be beyond its competence. In this way social institutions of value can be maintained, social cohesion encouraged, and an outlet provided for an expression of public opinion on administrative affairs. At the same time the wider outlook should be promoted, and this can best be accomplished by the voluntary federation of a number of village-groups who, like the Isu-Ochi,[1] may already have some sense of unity based on common customs and interests and possibly also on a common dialect. Thus district councils and tribunals will spring into being which have a real foundation in native life, unlike the former artificial creations which not merely failed to command the allegiance of the people, but sapped the foundations of authority within the village-groups. Let us not forget that it was through our English village institutions that we ourselves developed the art of self-government.

The third point of outstanding importance is the wide distribution of authority in the Ibo social group. Kings or priest-chiefs may have functioned in a few communities like Onitsha, Aguku, Oreri,[2] or Bonny; and an individual of exceptional wealth and personality may occasionally in his own village have wielded autocratic powers; but normally a village was governed by the whole body of the people, the heads of families and rich or titled or able men forming a kind of senate in this miniature republic. In such an organization, composed

[1] See pp. 90 ff.

[2] I have given no account of the priest-chiefs of Aguku and Oreri, having no personal knowledge of the Awka Division of Onitsha Province; but an interesting description by my colleague Dr. M. D. W. Jeffreys will be found in *Africa*, vol. viii, No. 3, under the title 'The Divine Umundri King'.

of kindreds each jealous of its own rights, there was normally no room
for an individual claiming executive authority outside the limits of
his own family-group. It was totally against the whole conception of
native rule, therefore, to invest the local member of the District
Native Court with an authority which not merely covered the whole
of his own village but frequently extended to neighbouring villages
as well. Moreover, even if the Ibo were to be saddled with chiefs,
they should have been chiefs of the African type, not mere machines
for keeping order, but fathers of their people, whose despotic powers
were kept in check by means of councils, societies, taboos, and other
political and social machinery.

The next step in reorganization would, therefore, be the restoration
of authority within the village-group to those classes of persons who
were accustomed and best able to exercise it, namely, the heads of
families, priests, holders of important titles, and rich or able men.
In this connexion stress has been laid (in the chapters dealing with
the social and political structure) on the fact that, although the Ibo
have a great respect for seniority, they do not allow this respect to
endanger the welfare of the group. When practical qualities of wisdom and decision of character are lacking in the senior member of
the group the leadership is given to another. Moreover, in the past,
young men frequently took a prominent part in public affairs either
as holders of Ozọ titles, or as proxies for aged relatives, or merely
because of their own outstanding ability. The whole system was
elastic and allowed full scope for the emergence of individual talent.
There is room, therefore, in the indigenous system for educated
young Christians of to-day to take a part, and perhaps a leading part,
in the government of their village-group. On this subject there will
be more to be said at a later stage.

Finally, in our attempt to derive lessons of practical utility for
administrative purposes, it will be necessary to make some evaluation
of native law in terms of present-day requirements. It is quite clear
from our studies that even in days long antecedent to the spread of
European influence the Ibo-speaking peoples were, in the widest sense
of the term, a law-abiding people. They had well-established norms
of conduct maintained by numerous institutions framed for the express purpose of preserving order and harmony within their own
immediate group, as well as a measure of equilibrium with neighbouring groups. Thus, violence was restrained by a whole series of
regulations in which the principles of retaliation and compensation

were prominent; honesty was imposed in a variety of ways such as severe penalties for theft and the insistence on truth-speaking by means of oaths; adultery was kept in check by penal measures in some circumstances, retaliation in others, or by the mere disapproval of one's social group, which feared the possible consequences of adultery in the form of inter-village fighting, the closing of its markets, or the violation of its own women; respect for elders was maintained by various regulations including the use of fixed terms of relationship; and in short there were innumerable ways and means of preserving a general sense of decorum and respect for the rights and feelings of one's fellows.

But as the law of any society is an expression of its own culture, and as Ibo culture is totally different from ours, it follows that in spite of many points of contact with our legal system, that of the Ibo presents marked divergences. Their sense of values does not coincide with ours. Thus, to accuse an unsophisticated Ibo of practising witchcraft would be a much more serious matter than charging him with having embezzled a large sum of money, whereas to an Englishman the former charge would mean nothing at all. Again, in English law adultery is never anything more than a private injury, whereas in Ibo law it may be treated as a private injury if committed in a house, but if committed on a farm it is a public abomination. Similarly, to steal from a farm a yam valued at 1s. would be a very different matter from stealing 1s. in cash.[1] Then again there is the native attitude towards homicide which differs from ours in a variety of ways. Thus to the Ibo vendetta was a duty, and so was the killing of witches and twins. And death or enslavement was imposed for numerous offences which to us would appear to be comparatively trivial. And yet it is not so long ago that in England persons convicted of witchcraft were judicially executed, and during the early part of the nineteenth century English law awarded death to any one who stole five shillings' worth of goods from a dwelling-house, or broke a window and tried to lift a latch, or forged a will, or made the counterfeit of the smallest coin. And in the eyes of the Ibo we appear brutal and unjust even at the present day in awarding death to those courageous and public-

---

[1] It is not possible to say why adultery and thefts committed on farms are regarded as specially heinous. It may be due to magico-religious beliefs connected with fertility; or the magico-religious attitude may have been evolved as the best method of preventing offences which are particularly easy to commit without detection.

spirited persons who rid the community of witches and of twins. Moreover, in judging of the severity of Ibo laws we must not forget that, in the absence of prisons, the community had no other means than death or selling into slavery by which it could rid itself of a habitual criminal. Indeed, to-day it is a frequent cause of complaint that prisons only give temporary relief, and that habitual criminals keep returning to the community after terms of imprisonment, fortified by good food to continue their depredations! Prison conditions, it is said, are too pleasant to act as a sufficient deterrent, and imprisonment has not yet come to be regarded as a social disgrace.

Another important factor differentiating Ibo from English legal conceptions is that in Ibo society a man's conduct is largely conditioned by his status. Everybody has a fixed place in society with definite duties assigned to his grade. Persons of the same status form a class of their own, as it were, and are responsible for each other, and observe certain patterns of behaviour towards classes above or below them. The Ọzọ society is a close corporation of privileged bureaucrats. Age-grades impose certain standards of conduct on their members and punish any dereliction. A senior wife can lord it over a junior, an elder brother over a younger, and so on. Now one effect of this system, and it is an important effect which may be misunderstood by European administrative or judicial officers, is that a person of junior status should not sue a person of senior status directly—he should do so through the mediumship of a person of similar status.[1] And thus it is that in judicial proceedings a prosecution or defence may be conducted by some one who, to a European observer, has no connexion with the case at all. Serious offence can be given by ignoring native etiquette in such matters, in deference to the English principle of complete personal responsibility.

This brings us to another important aspect of native law, namely, collective responsibility. This is the direct outcome of the form of the social organization, and is based primarily on the kinship unit which we have called the extended-family or kindred, the members of which are so closely bound together that the conduct of one may affect them all. But the sense of collective responsibility, being founded ultimately on the principle that union is strength, extends also to the local group composed of many kindreds. It is a powerful

---

[1] Mr. Driberg has drawn attention to this aspect of African law in a suggestive article published in *The Journal of Comparative Legislation and International Law* of November 1934.

factor, therefore, in promoting social cohesion, and when it is allowed full play in matters of law and authority is of immense value as a means of imposing a high standard of conduct on the members of the group. Numerous instances have been given to show how the heads of kindreds and local groups constantly warned the younger men to exercise self-restraint, lest the ill-advised conduct of one of their number should implicate them all. Not that the principle of collective responsibility was applied indiscriminately, for the group did not hesitate to repudiate blatant ill behaviour on the part of any of its members.

The principle of collective responsibility still operates in various ways at the present time. Thus, it may induce the group of a person charged with an offence to protect him from arrest, or, if he is arrested and fined, to pay his fine. And the Nigerian Government recognizes the principle to some extent, for one of its laws[1] provides that punishment may be imposed on an entire group in certain (unusual) circumstances for an offence committed by a member or members of that group. In this connexion it may be of interest to observe that in Transjordan a recently established British Board of Control has been granted powers to arrest and detain the relatives up to the fifth degree of the aggressors in tribal raids and robberies, until the aggressors have been delivered and the stolen property restored. It is stated that this system has already had excellent results, and the degree of security in Transjordan has been very much increased.[2] Nor, indeed, was the principle of collective responsibility unknown to English law in bygone days. For in the feudal period the institution of the 'frank-pledge' made every member of a tithing responsible for the conduct of the rest. Collective responsibility, however, tends to obscure individual responsibility, and in Iboland to-day the English conception of complete individual responsibility is now being recognized in all Native Courts—an inevitable change for the better, but one which, unfortunately, goes hand in hand with the general loosening of the bonds of brotherhood.

Then again there is a vast difference between the sanctions of English laws and those of the Ibo. For the most part regulations are obeyed in all communities because they are recognized as necessary

---

[1] The Collective Punishments Ordinance. But this Ordinance is now virtually a dead letter.

[2] See the article entitled 'Beyond the Jordan. British Law for the Beduin', in *The Times* of 13 July, 1935.

for the proper functioning of society. But to give these regulations the force of law, sanctions are required, i.e. rewards or penalties for their observance or non-observance. The nature of the sanctions in any community depends on its cultural complex, and as the cultural complex of the Ibo is totally different from that of the English, their sanctions must also be different. Thus, to take an example, Ibo society includes the dead no less than the living; and hence, as has been repeatedly shown, the ancestors were in the past (and still are) a governing factor in the maintenance of law and order. The law was in fact what the ancestors had considered good or bad in the past, and in every case of importance they were believed to be present to see that there was no deviation from traditional practice, and that the proceedings were conducted in a spirit of equity and truth. The *ọfọ* of the elders were a symbol and indeed the medium of their presence, and a means of securing truthful evidence, as any witness might be called on to swear on his *ọfọ*.

Then, too, there was Ala the Earth-deity, a disciplinary force of great authority acting in conjunction with, but wholly distinct from, the ancestors. Just as Jupiter, the ancient deity of the sky, by whom men were wont to swear, became among the Romans the embodiment of justice, so did Ala, the Earth-deity, come to be regarded by the Ibo as the guardian and indeed the source of morality. Most of the offences classed as 'abominable' were considered to be offences against Ala, and, even when the offence had been expiated by punishment, the community had still to be cleansed by sacrifice. The whole system of magic and taboo served as a solid buttress of the law, a means of conferring a feeling of security, of protecting property, and constraining people to perform their innumerable obligations. Incest was kept in check by magical means, and it was magic that gave their efficacy to oaths. Among other religious sanctions one might mention the use of sacrifice as a means of allaying feelings of hostility and of modifying laws,[1] and the custom of giving sanctuary[2] which operated as a check on hasty revenge and its frequent consequence—inter-village fighting.

But what, it may be asked, will happen to the indigenous system of law when the people begin to abandon their old beliefs, as they are now doing, and the religious sanctions gradually lose their validity? If, for example, the belief in magic becomes impaired, then it must follow that some of the best methods of protecting property will be

[1] See, e.g., pp. 210, 212, 262.   [2] See, e.g., p. 131.

rendered null and void. And the oath, which depends for its efficacy on a general belief in its magical effects, will no longer serve as one of the chief guarantees of honesty and good conduct.

The answer to this question is that there will be a gradual and easy adjustment, so long as the Native Courts are allowed to function as genuine native institutions and are not forced to conform to standards of English law, of which many of the sanctions are meaningless in terms of Ibo culture. Even if the old gods are not replaced by new, we may be sure that new sanctions will be found for such social regulations as continue to be serviceable—sanctions based on traits of their own culture or on those taken over from ours. Faith in the power of the ancestors to influence human conduct may wane, but faith in the value of precedent or standards which have stood the test of time will, in some guise or other, continue to live. Some of the old ethics will disappear with the old gods, but new gods will create new ethical values, and new ethical values in turn will create new conceptions of deity. It has become almost an anthropological commonplace to say that magic on the whole worked well. It served a useful purpose, no doubt, but we cannot lightly discount the fact that diviners, witch-doctors, and ministers of ordeals were frequently bribed to give a favourable or unfavourable decision, and that if they happened to be honest men it was an even chance whether an innocent man was punished or a guilty one escaped. Magic, moreover, becomes less necessary as knowledge increases. Already magical methods are giving place to a surer method of sifting evidence on English lines, and to the evolution of a new standard of truth. But magic still continues to play a part in giving validity to oaths. In this connexion it might help to purify the courts if, in areas where the Native Court judges still adhere to the old religion, the proceedings were opened, as they sometimes were in the olden days, by a petition to Ala and the ancestors to be present at the trial and punish any of the judges who showed favour on account of a bribe or for any other reason. It might be a good thing also if the practice became general of requiring candidates for membership of the Native Courts to swear an oath that they would abstain from accepting bribes.

Retaliation is another principle which has had to be discarded with the better ordering of society. It is still resorted to occasionally in the villages, but has long ceased to be regarded as a legitimate means of settling disputes. The decision recorded on p. 229 is a good instance of the new attitude of mind. The custom also of seizing a person's property as a guarantee of his appearance at a trial, a form of bail, is also now discontinued, on the ground that, like retaliation, it is liable to lead to brawls. The same may be said of the former system of distraint for debt. Pledging of the person and of land for debt, and the charging of excessive interest on loans, are pernicious customs which are gradually being eradicated without ill effects in other directions.

On the other side of the account we have seen that, among numerous features of value, the Ibo attached more importance to equity than what we should call the strict letter of the law, and recognized the principle that circumstances alter cases. The judges had close local knowledge of the points at issue and of the personal characters of the parties concerned.[1] And they were concerned not merely with giving equitable decisions but with putting an end to disputes which would upset the harmony of the community. Thus native tribunals were commonly courts of arbitration rather than courts of law, and the judges were not so much magistrates as chairmen voicing the opinion of a public assembly. 'Trials', therefore, were often nothing more than an organized expression of public opinion, and served the purpose of allowing grievances to be aired, a litigant's object being, frequently, to vindicate his character publicly, rather than mulct his opponent in damages.

It is clearly desirable that all valuable features of native law should, wherever possible, be retained, and for this purpose there can be no better instrument than village and village-group councils, and the assignment to them of a definite measure of judicial authority. These local councils cannot obviously be given unlimited powers, but they can at least be given summary jurisdiction for settling minor disputes, and serve also as a clearing-house or court of preliminary investigation for the more serious cases. The closuring of these councils in the past, as judicial tribunals, was a serious mistake, since it not merely weakened the foundations of local authority, but robbed the people of an effective means of giving expression to their opinions and grievances.

Before leaving the question of native law there are one or two further points that call for remark. Firstly, there is the universal complaint that owing to our insistence on leniency towards adultery this offence has increased to an outrageous extent. In olden days an adulterer was liable to heavy penalties, including assault, in which the members of his group and their womenfolk might also become

[1] See, e.g., p. 232.

involved. In many cases also adultery was considered as an outrage on Ala, and the whole community would take action against the persons who had thus imperilled its safety. But nowadays, as adultery is merely a civil offence, an adulterer escapes with a money payment, and the rich are placed at an advantage. There is a good deal of truth in these assertions, and it would appear just that the Native Courts should be empowered to impose heavier penalties than are at present permissible. But at the same time it must be remembered that the increase in adultery cannot be ascribed solely to the relaxation of the law. It is largely, if not chiefly, due to the new safety of communications which enables men and women to travel about at will far away from the home influences which would normally act as a restraint. Then, again, there is the question of incest in the form of marriage with close consanguineous relatives. How is the breach of this taboo to be punished at the present time? Can it be made a penal offence at all? Perhaps it can best be kept in check by mere social ostracism. But this is one of the matters which a village-council should decide for itself. Native opinion is not always rigid even in matters such as this, and the rules of exogamy are frequently circumvented in a legitimate manner by means of a sacrificial rite. On the other hand two closely related Christians may marry in defiance of the rule of exogamy, and so cause feelings not merely of outrage but of intense fear among the other members of the kin.[1] In such circumstances the kin can hardly be blamed for driving the offenders out of their community.

Then, again, there is the question of native systems of land tenure —a matter of overwhelming importance. Throughout Nigeria great care has been taken by the Government to safeguard native rights in land. In the Northern Provinces all land is, by Ordinance, held in trust for the people by the Governor, and no land can be alienated to non-natives without his permission. No grants of freehold are made, but building and agricultural 'Rights of Occupancy' are given, with conditions as to improvements and revision of rent at stated intervals. In the Southern Provinces lands are not at the disposal of the Governor in the same way, but they may not be leased to a non-native without the consent of the Governor. In some cases ownership by non-natives has in the past been recognized by the Government, but generally speaking the only title that is recognized in a non-native is a leasehold limited to a period of 99 years. Mortgages by natives of

---

[1] But cases of this kind now seldom occur. See p. 264.

leasehold property are only permissible in a number of important trading centres, such as Onitsha.[1]

In spite of these safeguards the situation regarding land can hardly be viewed with complacency, as the Government is still without adequate information on the various native systems of land tenure. This can only be obtained by scientific investigations conducted over a wide area, the history of specific plots of land being meticulously traced. Generalities are useless, and information supplied by Chiefs or other Native Authorities in answer to questionnaires may be completely misleading. Much of the mass of information supplied in the past is worthless.[2] Moreover, the native systems of land tenure are not uniform or static. They vary in different localities and modify themselves to meet changing conditions. And they will soon be profoundly affected by the growing corpus of case law. The situation, therefore, calls for close scrutiny and the acquisition of much additional data.[3] Continued ignorance and a policy of drift are likely to lead to serious complications at no distant date.

Finally there is the problem of witchcraft.[4] From the administrative point of view there are, or should be, two sides to this difficult question. On the one hand there is the obvious duty of the tutelary power to protect innocent people from the consequences of being charged with a purely imaginary crime, and to discourage a form of belief which has a terrorizing and paralysing influence and is also a fruitful source of numerous forms of fraud. And on the other hand there is the equal duty of avoiding as far as possible measures which, by their harshness and indiscriminate application, would tend to alienate the mass of the people.

Most African negroes are firm believers in the power of witchcraft, and as this belief is closely bound up with magic, and therefore with

---

[1] See the *Nigeria Handbook* (1933), p. 194.

[2] The official handbook of the Nigerian Government endorses the opinion of the 1908 Committee on Land Tenure in Northern Nigeria that 'all land was the property of the community', and of the 1912 Committee that in Southern Nigeria land was held or inherited 'always subject to the approval of the original grantors'. (*Nigeria Handbook*, 1933, p. 194.) Both these statements are misleading.

[3] An instructive report on land tenure among the Yoruba has recently been submitted by Mr. Ward-Price. Many more reports of this character are required. Some of the facts presented by Mr. Ward-Price seem to have surprised the Government, though they should have been common knowledge.

[4] For a summary of witchcraft beliefs and the native methods of dealing with charges of witchcraft see pp. 79–84 and 325 ff.

the entire social and moral system, it is not one which can be eliminated by a mere alteration in the law. The believer in witchcraft feels he has a right to protect himself by every means in his power, and chief among these is the employment of a witch-doctor or a practitioner of counter-magic. A witch-doctor is therefore considered just as essential in most negro communities as a medical practitioner is amongst ourselves, and, though some witch-doctors may abuse their powers for selfish ends, as a class they are regarded as champions of morality. And yet British Colonial Governments impose the severest possible punishments on any one proved to be a witch-doctor. Thus, in Uganda, the mere profession of being a witch-doctor or witch-finder entails a penalty of imprisonment up to five years,[1] while in Tanganyika the 1928 Ordinance authorizes a penalty up to seven years and a fine of £200 on any one who declares another to be a witch, acting with intent to cause injury.[2] In all Colonies those who take part in the killing of the supposed witch are liable to the death penalty, and this penalty is frequently exacted. And yet the persons who take action against supposed witches do so in the belief that they are avenging the murder of a relative or friend, and protecting the community from future murders. They are frequently the most public-spirited members of the community and therefore the very men whose co-operation in administration would be of the greatest benefit. Moreover, chiefs who were formerly the protagonists of anti-witchcraft measures are now required by the Government to play the opposite part, and in Nigeria are even liable to three years' imprisonment if they fail to report cases in which action has been taken against supposed witches.

Thus our laws relating to witchcraft appear to be unnecessarily severe, and to fail to show that understanding of native mentality which we show in so many other directions, and which is the keystone of successful native administration. We deal with the whole complex of witchcraft beliefs from the twentieth-century standpoint, forgetting our own immediate past, and endeavouring to hurry the African along at breakneck speed. We, who are now beginning to realize the importance of psychology in the treatment of the sick, deny to the African his own mode of treating disease by psychological methods. We stop all outlet for his fears and leave him with a sense of insecurity, since witches are now, in his view, free not merely to

---

[1] Laws, chapter 130.

[2] In Nigeria the penalty for accusing another of being a witch or having the power of witchcraft is limited to six months.

carry on their nefarious work, but also to propagate their species. Our laws also appear to the native to be illogical, as they deny the reality of witchcraft and yet punish those who profess to be or charge others with being witches. And do not white men themselves practise witchcraft in numerous ways and devour one another from motives of greed, vengeance, or jealousy?

But what are the remedies for this impasse? It is contended by many that Christianity is the only cure, and it is true that Christianity has already brought relief to thousands of Ibo who were formerly firm believers in the power of witchcraft. But Christianity does not necessarily rid a community of this belief, as the history of witchcraft in European societies clearly proves; and among the Ibo to-day there are thousands of professing Christians, including persons of the highest intelligence, who still retain their belief in witchcraft. Indeed, to many converts their new-found faith is itself a superior form of magic which leaves the belief in witchcraft wholly unimpaired. They will assert that just as there is a Devil (in Christian doctrine) so there are witches, and that Christ Himself played the part of a supreme witch-doctor by detecting and casting out devils of the grossest kind.

There is another obvious remedy for witchcraft beliefs, namely the teaching of science in schools. In particular, instruction in the causation of disease tends to free the mind from the idea that disease and death are due to the action of witches. The pupil learns the story of malarial infection, why small-pox can be prevented by vaccination, or yaws cured by one or two injections, and so on. Instruction on these lines is already being given in numerous schools throughout Nigeria, but more might be done there and in other Colonies with the direct purpose of freeing the mind from the bondage of witchcraft and the baser forms of magic. Meanwhile, there would appear to be a clear case for reframing some of our laws so as to make a more generous allowance for native attitudes of mind. British magistrates and judges, also, can help adjustment by adopting an attitude of sympathetic understanding, and they should be given wide discretion in passing sentence. In this connexion it is obviously of great importance that those responsible for framing and administering the British law should be thoroughly acquainted with the principles of native law. This is all the more necessary now that the British judiciary and executive have been divorced.[1] A purely juristic attitude, disso-

---

[1] Up to 1934 Administrative Officers were the 'Commissioners' or judges in the British Provincial Courts, and this system worked remarkably well.

ciated from the sociology and psychology of the people, the attitude which asserts that the function of judges is to administer the law and not justice—is contrary to the spirit of 'Indirect Rule'. We cannot profess to apply native law and yet interpret it solely by our own rules or ways of thinking. Nor is it sufficient for a British judge to summon to his aid one or two individual natives to prove the native law. Native law cannot be determined satisfactorily in this manner. In all important native cases which have to be decided by British judges the Native Courts should be encouraged to hold preliminary investigations. But the British judges themselves should be well versed in native law, native institutions, and native psychology.

Turning now to the measures of reform which have been actually carried out as a result of the investigations pursued, it may be said generally that the old artificial district courts have been gradually abandoned as a basis of native administration, their place having been taken by clan and village-group councils, which are a direct expression of native life and organization. Nor are these councils purely judicial bodies. They have been endowed with executive functions, and as such have been gazetted as 'Native Authorities', and made directly responsible for the good administration of their own areas. The councils of the constituent groups of the clan or village-group are also now encouraged to function informally as subordinate 'Native Authorities', without being formally gazetted by the Government. As part of their executive duties these councils are made responsible for the collection of taxes, and although only the larger groups have so far been entrusted with their own Native Treasuries all are being encouraged to take an active interest in finance.[1] Estimates of revenue and expenditure are being kept in each group, and the people are in this way being made to understand the relation between taxation and the cost of public services, and to take an interest in economic matters as well as administrative and judicial. An active local interest is also being aroused in education, public health, and public works. In many localities as much as 60 per cent. of the Native Administration revenue is being devoted to the purely local requirements of the village-group or clan.

On the judicial side the councils have been armed with powers which enable them to deal with all minor offences in their own areas, such as those which can adequately be punished by fines up to £2 or

[1] In the Southern Provinces as a whole there are now (1936) seventy-five Native Treasuries.

£3 or imprisonment up to a month or two. In civil matters the councils may try cases involving claims up to £10, or in some cases of £20, or even more in matrimonial suits. The powers vary according to local circumstances. The subordinate councils are allowed to act informally as judicial tribunals, and thus play the part of a clearing-house for the clan courts, which become in effect courts of appeal. But neither these tribunals nor the clan courts are empowered to dispose of serious cases or matters outside the range of native custom. For these newly made courts have still to prove their competence, and in any case the graded system of administering justice is just as essential to an Ibo under modern conditions as it is to a European. In this connexion Sir Donald Cameron, the late Governor of Nigeria, has laid it down that

'it is a mistake to believe that all possible cases should be taken in the Native Courts, if the "prestige" of those Courts is to be assured. There are cases which they ought not to take and some which many of them are not competent to take; and to try the Native Administrations which, after all, are but instruments in the administration of Nigeria, beyond their powers and their capacity, must, surely, be unsound policy.'[1]

In the matter of procedure, too, every effort has been made to make these Native Courts really native, instead of crude imitations of English tribunals. Proceedings are conducted as far as possible on traditional lines, and the semi-educated clerks who formerly controlled the courts have now been relegated to a minor position. In the subordinate courts clerks are dispensed with altogether, some literate member of the village being called on to make out the summonses, and enter in the record-book the names of the litigants, the amounts of the fees, and brief notes of the judgements. The fees are small sums ranging from traditional gifts in kind in the minor courts to a few shillings in the clan courts, half of the amount being appropriated by the judges. In some clan courts the judges are paid fixed salaries from Native Administration funds. The duties of court messengers, who were formerly henchmen of the court clerk and had every opportunity for being despotic and corrupt, are now carried out by one of the junior age-grades, or any of the local villagers whom the judges may see fit to employ.

But the most far-reaching change is in the personnel of the councils (or courts). No longer do one or two individuals exercise autocratic control over dozens of village-groups; for the new clan and

[1] *The Principles of Native Administration and their Application*, p. 9.

village-group councils are now composed of the heads or official representatives of all the kindreds in the group. Thus the kinship organization, which is the basis of Ibo society, has been given formal recognition, and the chain of responsibility which binds the individual to his immediate relatives, his village, and his village-group or clan has been preserved in every link. And as a corollary those native institutions which were formerly of use for the maintenance of law and order can once more function, within the limits imposed by present-day conditions.

As regards the presidency in these councils, it occasionally happens that there is a headman who commands the loyalty of all and can therefore be appointed president of the council. But normally authority is so little concentrated that, if the council has a president at all, he is merely a ceremonial head, the holder of the senior *ọfọ*, or the official spokesman (as in former days). The question of the presidency, therefore, is one which depends wholly on local circumstances, and is left entirely to the council itself. Most councils arrange for a number of their ablest men to hold the office in turn—a rule which will hinder the recrudescence of despots like the old 'Warrant Chiefs'.

It may appear that the institution of councils composed mainly of heads of kindreds is open to the objection that such councils are likely to pursue a purely reactionary policy, obstructing the spread of education and Christianity, and hindering measures of administrative progress generally. Moreover, in addition to the danger of stereotyping institutions there is also that of stereotyping mediocrity, by preventing young men of ability from taking their proper share in the conduct of public affairs. It must be in the interest of every society to make the fullest use of its most intelligent members, and it must be one of the primary functions of 'Indirect Rule' to produce capable rulers.

All this is very true. But the terms of appointment generally allow very considerable latitude to the kindreds in the choice of their representatives on the councils. For, if the holder of the senior *ọfọ* or of the senior title is a person of inferior ability, the kindred chooses, as it did in the past, some other man of personality and ability. He may be comparatively young, and possibly a Christian with a considerable degree of education. Moreover, the council representatives may usually be accompanied at meetings by junior members of their families, who may speak on behalf of aged relatives less skilful in debate than themselves. In this way, as in former times, the young can be trained in public affairs and continuity maintained. On behalf of the elders it may be said that they are the traditional authorities and have a great sense of public duty, and have also, in the control of their own families, learned to move with the times. Nevertheless, the working of the councils will have to be closely watched, in order to secure that they are acceptable to the people as a whole, and take cognizance of the needs of all classes of the community. It is possible and indeed probable that, with the progress of time, considerable modifications will have to be made. The councils may be found to be too unwieldy for the conduct of everyday affairs, and the rewards of attendance too few when distributed over so many members. An ineffective executive may be worse than a bureaucracy. It is possible, therefore, that most of the work will come to be delegated to small executive committees. But, whatever the nature of the development, the people should be able to protect themselves from the old forms of despotism, and to have adequate control over their own local affairs.

Before leaving the subject of the clan councils and courts there are two final observations. Firstly, it is to be noted that prior to 1934 there was no right of appeal from Native Courts in Nigeria. But the courts were subject to control by the British Resident (i.e. Provincial Commissioner) who could suspend or modify any sentence, order a rehearing, or transfer the case to a British Provincial Court. But by a new law the right of appeal is now established, and in the case of these primitive courts of the Ibo the appeal lies to the District Officer or the Courts of British Magistrates. The second point concerns the relations of the District Officer with the clan councils (and courts). As these councils are a new departure the District Officer will require to become thoroughly acquainted with their technique, and to learn to work with the council as a whole. In this connexion Dr. Audrey Richards has very aptly remarked,[1] as regards another part of Africa, that a District Officer is often disheartened when, after calling up one or two councillors, he fails to get any useful advice or response. The reason is that the elders are not accustomed to work in this way, and are afraid that private conferences with the District Officer will merely involve them in trouble afterwards.

The Future and Wider Outlook.

But, having got back to the basic unit of administration among the Ibo, it must not be supposed that the whole problem of native

---

[1] See *The Journal of the Royal African Society* for October 1935.

administration in Iboland is thereby solved. On the contrary this is merely the first step. There are and will be numerous other problems. Foremost among these is the necessity for creating the wider solidarity. For it is obvious that the Nigerian Government cannot rest content with a form of polity which imposes on a small band of Administrative Officers the immense task of supervising directly hundreds of village-group councils, without the assistance of any intermediary form of Native Authority. Moreover, it is not merely the creation of large numbers of new Native Authorities that adds to the difficulties of supervision, but the fact that the personnel of the councils is so large. By increasing the number of those who are made responsible it has become increasingly difficult to bring home responsibility to any one.

Every evolving community must advance from small to large, and the Ibo must advance from what Durkheim would call the 'socio-centric' outlook of the village-group or clan to the more cosmopolitan outlook of a larger world. And this process should be accompanied by the growth of a healthy individualism, while preserving at the same time, as far as may be possible, the sanctions of the old home life. The best method of attaining this end would seem to be the promotion of the federal idea, a number of contiguous clans or village-groups uniting voluntarily to form district Native Administrations of considerable size, on the same model as the clan administrations already described. As district administrations on these lines have already in some areas been formed, it will be of interest to quote Sir Donald Cameron's directions in this respect:

'The most elementary form [of district council] is', he says, 'a council of authorities[1] which may be no more than a deliberative body; or the authorities may pool their funds and co-operate only to the extent of occasional meetings, at which as a rule the District Officer should preside for the administration of their common resources. The greatest practical difficulty in the case of these councils arises from the absence of an appropriate central executive, especially when the council consists of a considerable number of authorities, for though normally each member of the council retains its executive authority in its own area it is unavoidable that certain executive functions must be discharged by the council as such, especially in connexion with the Native Treasury. In these circumstances, if a native with previous administrative experience is employed as Court and Treasury clerk at the Council Headquarters, he is naturally apt to concentrate all real power in his own hands, especially as the members of the council may all be illiterate. In

[1] This term is used for the sake of brevity; it includes petty chiefs, headmen and clan, sub-clan and village-group councils.

some cases it has been found possible for the president of the council (if there is a president, either permanent or in rotation) to act in this sense as its executive officer in between meetings, and in some cases an executive committee has been appointed. Where either course is impossible, the next best arrangement is for these duties to be carried out in the District Office under the personal supervision of the District Officer, the council paying the necessary clerical staff. As the present Councillors come to be replaced by educated men and the council system becomes firmly established, this arrangement can be modified in whatever way circumstances may suggest.'[1]

With the evolution of large-scale methods of administration, which look beyond the needs of the village communities, we may expect to see a progressive modification of native law. With the break-down in the magico-religious system, law will become more and more secularized; and with the growth of individualism, consequent on the social inequality caused by increased specialization, education, and other factors, there will be a gradual divorce between law and the present form of social organization. New laws will be required to meet new conditions, and it cannot but be that British forms of procedure will tend to be taken as models. Yet there is no reason why Ibo law should blindly follow the British system. In particular it will be necessary to avoid the danger of allowing the Native Courts to fall under the control of sophisticated natives who can read and write, or be dominated by lawyers who can exploit their knowledge of the mysteries of the law to their own advantage and the detriment of the people. Not that the Native Courts should be considered merely as a means of obtaining a crude form of justice: there must be steady progress and improvement. But they should be courts of equity rather than courts of law, and suited to the needs and the culture of the Ibo. Where the British system appeals to the Ibo, and accords with their cultural requirements, it should not be withheld but actively encouraged.

Education also, with its new concepts, if not carefully controlled, may prove a dangerous gift. In the past the curriculum has been framed too much to meet the demands of the Government and European commercial firms, and the country has been swamped with half-educated persons who had hoped to obtain clerical appointments. But the primary object of all education should be to qualify men and women to take the fullest possible part in the life of their own community; and this can only be done through the medium of their own

---

[1] *The Principles of Native Administration and their Application*, para. 60.

culture, which, be it noted, is never static but is always undergoing change. While giving full play to the growth of a healthy individualism, education must not be allowed to destroy the loyalties which hold the community together. It must preserve and foster the deep sense of social service which is characteristic of Ibo life, and it must raise the standard of knowledge, not of a few individuals, but of the whole community. New knowledge must be grafted on to the old. It is essential, therefore, that the Education Department should work in close association with the Administrative Department, and that Education officers should make themselves thoroughly acquainted with all phases of the indigenous systems of law and discipline. And it is also desirable that Mission education should be co-ordinated with the general administrative policy of training the people to manage their own affairs and of inculcating ideas of leadership and responsibility.

Moreover, if education is to be designed to meet the needs of the community, it cannot be confined to members of the male sex. Women wield enormous influence and should be educated to use it for the good of the whole community. They should be educated not simply for specific vocations such as medicine, nursing, or teaching, but for all the affairs of everyday life—domestic duties, hygiene, mothercraft, and agriculture. As Miss Margaret Wrong has recently remarked,[1] a form of education which does not help but positively hinders women from becoming better wives and better mothers can be of little advantage to the community, and is not likely to enlist the sympathy of the other sex.

But, if the object of education should be to fit men and women to cope with their environment, it does not follow that obstacles should be placed in the way of those Ibo who seek the higher forms of English education. For these are the men and women who can do most for the advancement of their fellow countrymen. Provided that they do not form an aristocracy cut off from their own people, they are the class best suited for leadership in the future, and for promoting, as many of them are doing, the synthesis between the old culture and the new. Though few in numbers they can exercise a commanding influence.

It would be idle to suppose that administrative difficulties will cease with the creation of clan and district councils, or that the granting of a fuller measure of responsibility must necessarily be

[1] In an issue of *West Africa.*

followed by the proper use of it, or by increased efficiency, as we view efficiency. But long ago Mill pointed out (as Dr. Marett reminds us) that the educative value of representative government out-weighed any deficiency on the administrative side, and the same applies to the policy of 'Indirect Rule'. Under this policy, which is a constructive policy, the Ibo will be free to work out the forms of government most suited to their needs, with such assistance and guidance as we are able to give. That guidance must be active, continuous, intelligent, and, above all, sympathetic and patient. The policy of 'Indirect Rule' itself begets sympathy. For it forces the British Administrator to study and work through native institutions and so gives him the knowledge which breeds respect and understanding. It is almost true to say that a great measure of the success which has attended the policy of 'Indirect Rule' is due to this sympathetic understanding of native institutions and native psychology, and has led some observers to form the opinion that the success of the policy has been due less to the policy itself than the high character, temper, and sympathy of the British officials who have been entrusted with its working. In speaking of the necessity of continuous and sympathetic guidance Sir Donald Cameron observes that

'we should endeavour to give the Native Authorities an interest and an object beyond the routine performance of their duties, to interest them in the scheme of government; to show them common interests, to engage their sympathies and active co-operation in our efforts to promote the welfare and progress of their people: for their primary duty is to their people, and by the manner in which they fulfil it they will be judged.'[1]

And elsewhere Sir Donald remarks that

'no attempt should be made to stereotype the various administrations and force them into one pattern or another. It suffices if, in each case, the Native Administration is in accordance with the wishes and traditions of the people and adequately fulfils the object of its existence, that is the discharge by the local native authorities of the functions of local government in native affairs, to such extent as circumstances may permit in each case and with due regard to expansion in the future.'[2]

Thus, while the Ibo advances along the path of political progress, and from the smaller solidarity to the larger, we must not expect that his difficulties will become simpler, but rather that they will become more complex. And this, indeed, seems to be the law of nature. The

[1] Op. cit., para. 47. Sir Donald is here quoting the earlier words of Sir Frederick Lugard (Instructions 1906, p. 202).   [2] Op. cit., para. 22.

large and highly evolved organisms attain greater efficiency, but their very complexity exposes them to greater dangers. We must be on the look-out, therefore, for new kinds of difficulties, as well as for reactions arising from contra-acculturative movements. Yet the vigour and intelligence of the Ibo people, which have made them one of the largest and most progressive tribes in Africa, would seem to indicate that they will be able to adapt and to enlarge their institutions so that, on a foundation of clan and district Native Administrations, these institutions will grow up into a solid edifice of constructive nationalism.

INDEX

Aba, 10.
Ababua, 1 fn. 1.
Abadja [*sic*], 3.
Abaja, 3.
Abaja-Ozu, 3.
Abakaliki, 16.
Abam, 3.
Abaw, 4.
— Afaw, 4.
— Kwale, 4.
Abeokuta, x.
Abiriba, 3.
Abnormality, 25, 30, 290, 291.
Abọ, 56, 217, 256 fn.
Aboh, 11, 13.
'Abominations', 28, 30, 31, 115, 120, 130, 131, 132, 199, 210, 213, 218, 219, 223, 225, 240, 262, 278, 290, 291, 306.
Abongpa, 12.
Abo-Ogugu, 254.
Abortion, 84, 289.
Abosse tree, 85, 175, 176.
Abstinence, 50.
Abuse, 75. *See also* Behaviour, insulting.
Accusations, false, 224, 227, 242.
Ache, 37, 38, 44, 102, 136, 170, 211, 225, 237, 238, 258, 261, 271, 282, 290.
Achihi, 38, 136, 237.
Ada (married or senior sister), 190, 201, 210, 220, 277, 278, 295, 296, 313.
Adams, 7.
Adâyi, 101, 150, 151, 168.
Adjournments, 157.
Administration, British, 332, 338, 346 fn., 351, 353, 354. *See also* Government; District Officers; Courts, British; Rule, Indirect.
—Native, v, vi, ix–xii, xv, xvi, 195, 196, 326 fn., 328, 351, 354, 355. *See also* Authorities, Native; Courts, Native; Rule, Indirect.
Adoption, 106 fn., 135, 140, 142 fn.
Adugu, 161.
Adultery, 48, 70, 119, 146, 147, 181, 189, 190, 201, 218–23, 268, 279, 298, 337, 342, 343.
Affrays, 135, 181, 233, 247. *See also* Brawling; Warfare.
Afikpo, 3.

Afọ (day of week or the year), 36, 291.
'*Africa*', 1 fn., 4, 155 fn., 335 fn.
'*African Society, Journal of the Royal*', 350 fn.
Agamega, 158.
Agbala (or Agbara), 18, 44, 74, 130, 155.
Agbale cloth, 285.
Agboala, 12.
Agbor, 4, 12.
Age-grades, 15, 40, 106, 112, 113, 114, 137, 156, 157, 166, 191, 192, 197–205, 206, 214, 229, 233, 249, 273, 278, 305, 309, 338.
Agricultural Department, 18.
Agriculture, 15, 16, 17, 18, 19, 31, 49, 98, 105, 112, 202, 204, 215, 270. *See also* Cassava; Yams, &c.
Agu, 39, 42, 237 fn. *See also* Agu-Nsi.
Aguku, 335.
Agunese, 238 ff.
Agu-Nsi, 63, 85.
Agwagu, 188.
Aho (body), 53.
Ahọ (the year or day of week). *See* Afọ.
Aiagare (species of fowl), 64, 84, 211.
Ajana (= Ala, q.v.), 174.
Ajanketa, 285.
Aja ọfia, 101. *See also* 'Bush of evil'.
Aje (title), 189, 193.
Ajode (title), 316.
Ajọku (or Ajọkuji or Njọku or Ifijiọku), 32, 33, 34, 156, 166, 215, 238 ff., 295.
Ajọ-Omumu, 42.
Aka snake, 31, 256, 257.
Akabo, 103, 181 fn.
Akazue, 189, 193 fn.
Ake-Eze, 3.
Akọro, 39, 173, 179.
Akpa creeper, 143.
Akwakuma, 273.
Ala (or Ale or Ana or Ane or Ani), 20, 24–33, 40, 48, 59, 61, 83, 89, 101, 116, 124, 125, 126, 127, 130, 131, 133, 134, 135, 167, 171, 172, 208, 209–13, 215, 217, 218, 219, 221, 224, 225, 231, 235, 236, 239, 240, 241, 242, 247, 248, 253, 254, 255, 256, 257, 258, 264, 277, 278, 285, 289, 290, 297, 306, 340, 341, 343.

372 INDEX

Underworld, 25, 61, 69, 71, 75, 77, 292.
Unemployment, 16.
United African Company, 14.
Unwana, 3.
Ure symbol, 162.
Ururu tree, 21, 24, 32, 63, 175, 176, 177.
Ututu, 4.
Uwọzọ (underworld), 292.
Uzaba (or Uzu-Aba), 21, 258 fn.

Values, sense of, 337.
Vendetta, 337. See Homicide.
Venue, 231, and Chapter X passim.
Village, definition of, 89.
Village-group, definition of, 89.
— organization, 89, 92, 127, 333, 334.
Violation (of women). See Rape.
Voice-disguisers, 67, 71.

Waddell, Rev. Hope, 8.
Ward-Price, H. L., 344 fn.
Warfare, 7, 9, 10, 11, 14, 25, 30, 38, 42, 44, 47, 91, 111, 113, 128, 135, 142 (outposts), 156, 185 fn. (civil war), 197, 207, 209, 233, 242–7, 255, 257 fn.
War-god, 244.
Warrant Chiefs. See Chiefs.
Warri, Province, i.
— town, 331.
Water, holy, 41, 45.
— life-giving, 37.
— spirits of, 36, 44.
Wealth, power of, 113, 135, 136.
— spirit of, 42, 205.

Weaning, 169, 283, 297.
Week, the Ibo, 36 fn.
'West Africa', 353 fn.
West African Company, 14.
Westermarck, Prof. E., 131, 244.
Widowers, 59.
Widows, 30, 59, 60, 70, 126 fn., 169, 181, 284, 310–14, 321.
Witchcraft, 44, 45, 70, 73, 79–84, 226–8, 279, 306, 337, 344–6.
Witnesses, 232, 240, &c.
Wizards, 83, 84. See Sorcery; Witchcraft.
Women (status of), vi, ix, x, 17, 19, 33, 35, 36, 49, 52, 57, 59, 62, 70, 71, 72, 74–80, 98, 100, 117 ff., 125 ff., 140, 142, 146, 148, 158, 161, 169, 171, 179, 190 fn., 192, 197, 198, 200, 201–3, 214, 217 ff., 221, 225, 226, 249, 256, 265, 267, 279, 280, 309, 310, 324.
Women's riots. See Riots.
Wounding, 213.
Wrestling, 26, 197, 199, 230.
Wrong, Dr. Margaret, 353.

Yam (cultivation and rites), 16, 17, 22, 24, 31, 32–5, 49, 57, 76, 151, 156, 167, 168, 170, 188, 202, 204, 205, 215, 217, 229, 238 ff., 249, 275, 281, 293, 298, 303, 320. See also Ajọku.
Yanibo, 9.
Yaws, 346.
Year (agricultural and solar), 26, 36.
Yoruba tribe, 5, 11, 14, 68, 159, 189, 190, 328, 344.